NEOLI꜉ ꜉AL
CULTURE

NEOLIBERAL CULTURE

Jeremy Gilbert (Editor)

London
Lawrence & Wishart 2016

Published in association with *new formations*

The essays in this book were first published as *new formations 80-81
Neoliberal Culture*.

British Library Cataloguing in Publication Data.
A catalogue record for this book is available from the British Library

ISBN 9781 910448 571
e-ISBN 9781 910448 694

Lawrence and Wishart Limited
Central Books Building,
Freshwater Road,
Chadwell Heath, RM8 1RX

Contents

INTRODUCTION

Jeremy Gilbert

This collection of essays takes as its subject the genesis, persistence and poly-valency of neoliberalism across a range of cultural sites and discursive genres. The volume opens with a long introductory essay by the editor, situating the contributions to the collection and its topics historically, and in terms of the existing scholarship on neoliberalism, linking together all the contributions while addressing the question of what kind of object 'neoliberalism' actually is.

Amongst the contributors, Paul Patton examines the relationships between neoliberal ideas and those of John Rawls, while Paul Gilroy considers the appeal of discourses of entrepreneurial self-help for members of black and migrant communities in contemporary neoliberal cultures. Jo Littler, like Gilroy, demonstrates in her contribution that neoliberal government has increasingly legitimated its practices and the form of society that they produce in terms of an ideal of meritocracy, which valorises a hierarchical and highly unequal set of social relations while claiming to offer individuals from all backgrounds an equal chance to compete for elite status.

Jodi Dean's essay identifies the ways in which the complexification of social and economic life is both actively produced by neoliberalism and becomes an alibi for the inefficacy of political challenges to it. Neal Curtis similarly investigates the persistence of neoliberal assumptions and practices in government and popular journalistic discourse following the disastrous financial crash of 2008. His argument draws on Heidegger's understanding of the nature of *Dasein*, the coherence of the subject's lifeworld, and the importance to the subject of maintaining the coherence of their 'world', even in the face of events which seem wholly to disprove their earlier assumptions about it. Exploring a more detailed instance of neoliberal ideology, Lucy Potter and Clare Westall chart the ways in which ideas and practices around the production, preparation and consumption of food have been mobilised in order to invite continued affective investment in consumption and consumerism while simultaneously legitimating the austerity programme which has formed the core of the UK government's resolutely neoliberal response to the post-2008 crisis.

Nicky Marsh's essay discusses the highly circumscribed rhetoric of neoliberal 'failure' which emerged from that moment, moving on to consider the conceptualisation of failure in the writing and teaching of American experimental novelist William Gaddis. Specifically Marsh addresses Gaddis' 1975 novel *JR* – which satirises the emergent world of asset-stripping and financialised capitalism – and in particular its relation to the writings of Norbert Wiener, widely regarded as the founder of cybernetics, and a sometime colleague and collaborator of Milton Friedman's. In a complementary fashion, Mark Hayward focuses on one highly specific history of technological innovation, charting the progress of twentieth-century developments in electronic technologies which contributed to the development of the teleprompter, the ATM machine and the self-service photo booth, and the participation of this history in the development of a techno-social regime of 'neoliberal optics'.

Stephen Maddison's contribution considers the pornography industry and its apparent promotion of modes of sexuality which might be regarded as wholly consistent with neoliberal culture – treating sex itself as a consumptive rather than a relational act, and participating in the general commodification of sex which is one of the most striking characteristics of neoliberal culture today – while Angela McRobbie looks at the precise forms of accommodation which current forms of neoliberalism make with the historic demands of feminism and the women's movement. McRobbie's key object of analysis is the emergent figure of the working mother, now fully valorised by the types of mainstream media outlet that until recently vilified any deviation from the mid-twentieth century family model. McRobbie points out that for all of her difference from the 'traditional' housewife, the ideal neoliberal mother is now expected to engage in forms of costly and highly restrictive self-management in order to demonstrate that working motherhood is no obstacle either to glamorous and highly sexualised modes of self-presentation – a continuation of the 'post-feminist masquerade' in which young working women are expected to participate – or to efficient and responsible household-management.

One of the most widely-read recent critiques of neoliberal culture, Mark Fisher's very widely-cited *Capitalist Realism*, analyses the persistence across a range of sites of an attitude which assumes neoliberal capitalist norms to be unchallengeable at the level of actual social or political practice. We finally present, as a contribution to this collection and to wider political and theoretical debate, a dialogue between the issue editor and Fisher reflecting upon some of the political implications of his analysis, and of the possibilities for democratic challenge to neoliberal culture in the immediate future.

WHAT KIND OF THING IS 'NEOLIBERALISM'?

Jeremy Gilbert

The term 'neoliberalism' is believed to have originated in the 1930s with the work of Arthur Rüstow and the *Colloque Walter Lippmann*, an international meeting of liberal theorists including Friedrich Hayek and Ludwig von Mises. This is the origin attributed by Foucault in his now famous lectures at the *Collége de France*.[1] Broadly speaking, most critical scholarship on neoliberalism either follows the career of the set of theses developed by these thinkers and their followers – as they emerged from obscurity to become the ruling dogma of advanced capitalism at the end of the twentieth century – or else stresses the history of neoliberalism as an actual enacted programme of government, beginning with Pinochet's coup in Chile in 1971. The pivotal point of relay between these two histories was, of course, the 'Chicago School' of economics centred on Milton Friedman, students of whom devised Pinochet's programme of privatisation and union repression.[2]

The approaches taken by the contributors to this volume encompass the best of both of these traditions while also innovating beyond and between them, in the process exploring a number of different interpretations of the meaning and significance of 'neoliberalism'. Within the broad family of ideas normally designated 'neoliberal' there are obviously a range of positions on and approaches to the core issues of economic policy, public sector governance and market management; each of these in turn is potentially compatible with a range of opinions and approaches to social policy, cultural practice and public administration, while nonetheless retaining a high degree of internal consistency and expressing a strong set of connecting themes. This fact has confused some commentators, leading in some cases to the claim that 'neoliberalism' as such is an incoherent concept with no objective referent.[3] The denial of the very existence of neoliberalism as a potential object of analysis tends to go along with the rejection of related concepts like ideology, capitalism and hegemony. Such positions arguably tend to be predicated on a rather simplistic understanding of the concepts being rejected: assuming, for example, that 'neoliberalism' could only be a meaningful term if it referred to a wholly uniform and explicit doctrine, manifested in a homogenous and discrete policy programme.

This volume is clearly predicated on the assumption that there is such a thing as neoliberalism, but the challenge, which the 'neoliberal deniers' present to any such body of work, remains a serious one. It is clearly the case that there have been marked practical and conceptual differences between many of the ideas, programmes and policies to have been labelled 'neoliberal' by commentators, while the very notion of 'neoliberal culture' assumes a set of connections between these and many other elements of contemporary social life which must be demonstrated rather than assumed. The basic question which this problem raises is: what *kind* of a thing is 'neoliberalism'? In this introductory essay I will consider a range of possible answers to the question, considering the status of neoliberalism as an aggregation of ideas, a discursive formation, an over-arching ideology, a governmental programme, the manifestation of a set of interests, a hegemonic project, an assemblage of techniques and technologies, and what Deleuze and Guattari call an 'abstract machine'.

NEOLIBERAL IDEAS AND THEIR DISCURSIVE REGULARITIES

There will not be space here for an exhaustive account of the ideas of the founders of 'neoliberalism' and 'ordoliberalism' – Hayek, von Mises, et al. – or for one which departs in any significant way from that offered by Foucault. Instead we begin with a consideration of Foucault's approach to this subject and his key conclusions about it. By the time of Foucault's lectures on neoliberalism and biopolitics, his main methodology had moved on from the 'archaeology' of his early work towards the more dynamic investigation of changes in relations of power and knowledge which he sometimes called, after Nietzsche's *Genealogy of Morals*, 'genealogy'. Nonetheless, some remarks from his famous summary of his method in *The Archaeology of Knowledge* are certainly germane here. Proposing the 'discursive formation' as the proper object of study in the history of ideas, Foucault writes that it should be considered as 'a unity of distribution that opens a field of possible options, and enables various mutually exclusive architectures to appear side by side or in turn.[4] 'The discursive formation is not therefore a developing totality, with its own dynamism or inertia, carrying with it, in an unformulated discourse, what it does not say, what it has not yet said, or what contradicts it at that moment; it is not a rich, difficult germination, it is a distribution of gaps, voids, absences, limits, divisions'.[5] The explicit point here is that simply because a set of statements, ideas and practices does not have the absolute uniformity of a pure doctrine, it can nonetheless be identified and analysed as a coherent object.

In his lectures, Foucault offers a careful and not unsympathetic exposition of neoliberalism's intellectual evolution and its main tenets, although it is implicitly left to his audience to determine whether this aggregation of ideas possesses even the unity of a 'discursive formation'. He takes a particular interest in the relative novelty of neoliberal approaches to the role of government in managing populations and facilitating the development of individuals' capacities, pointing to a crucial difference between neoliberalism and 'classical' liberalism, in particular as manifested in the tradition of *laissez faire* associated with thinkers such as Adam Smith and the classic liberal orthodoxy of Victorian economics. This tradition has tended to view government intervention into social and economic scenes, other than for the purpose of inhibiting monopoly-formation and protecting property rights, as generally unnecessary and deleterious to the cultivation of the kind of entrepreneurial culture and market economy to which is aspires. Neoliberalism takes a quite different view, inspired by similar ideals and aspirations, but heavily influenced both by the example of social liberalism and social democracy in according a more positive role to state institutions, and by the political success of various forms of collectivism – fascist, socialist and communist – in the early and mid-twentieth centuries.

Put simply, neoliberalism, from the moment of its inception, advocates a programme of deliberate intervention by government in order to encourage particular types of entrepreneurial, competitive and commercial behaviour in its citizens, ultimately arguing for the management of populations with the aim of cultivating the type of individualistic, competitive, acquisitive and entrepreneurial behaviour which the liberal tradition has historically assumed to be the natural condition of civilised humanity, undistorted by government intervention. This is the key difference between classical liberalism and neoliberalism: the former presumes that, left to their own devices, humans will naturally tend to behave in the desired fashion. By contrast the latter assumes that they must be compelled to do so by a benign but frequently directive state. This, according to neoliberals, is partly because a certain habitual tendency towards collectivism, if left unchecked, will lead commercial producers, workers, service-providers, managers and government officials to act only in their selfish corporate interests. It is also, they believe, because such corporate selfishness is itself only an expression of an even more basic tendency towards competitive, acquisitive and uniquely self-interested behaviour which is the central fact of human social life. Whereas Smith seems to expect the division of labour in a market society to lead to a relatively egalitarian and co-operative distribution of roles and resources, neoliberalism understands individual interests to be largely mutually exclusive, self-interest to be the only motive force in human life and competition to be the most efficient and socially beneficial way for that force to express itself.

NEOLIBERAL EQUALITIES

Andrew Gamble points out, with good grounds, that neoliberal rhetoric and policy prescriptions have always been split between the radically anti-state, aggressively *laissez-faire* rhetoric of the Anglo-American libertarian Right and the 'social market' tradition more closely associated with German 'ordoliberalism'.[6] We could include in the former category the work of the Austrian 'anarcho-capitalists' such as von Mises and the hugely influential writings of Hayek. However, it is highly debatable what influence the libertarian tendency has ever had on significant public policy programmes: even in the case of governments such as Margaret Thatcher's, claiming explicit inspiration from Hayek, *laissez faire* neoliberalism only ever provided a part of the rhetorical justification for the broad programme of privatisation while the actual reductions in public spending effected were far from impressive. Actually existing neoliberalism seems to have been characterised by a consistently interventionist approach.

Of course, the same could be said of actually existing liberalism in the nineteenth century, which was never short of programmes promoting particular modes of civility and subjectivity, and whose entrepreneurial ideal of self-help has bequeathed a crucial legacy to contemporary neoliberal culture, as Paul Gilroy demonstrates in his contribution to this volume. Gilroy's timely intervention examines the appeal of discourses of entrepreneurial self-help for members of black and migrant communities in contemporary neoliberal cultures: finally observing that, as regrettable as the prevalence of such ideas may be from a leftist perspective, the fact that neoliberalism is adaptable and adoptable by them may also be an indication of the relative integration of such communities into societies such as that of the UK. From this perspective, perhaps what is most strikingly novel about neoliberal theory is its commitment to certain kinds of highly individualistic egalitarianism, promoting programs aimed at widening property ownership and distribution and securing equality of access to the competitive labour market for members of disadvantaged social groups, irrespective of their class or ethnic background.

This issue is explored from differing perspectives by several of the contributors. Paul Patton examines the fascinating relationships between neoliberal ideas and those of John Rawls, arguably the most influential thinker on the Anglophone 'centre-left' of the past four decades, particularly in the light of Rawls' advocacy of 'property-owning democracy' as an *alternative* to capitalism.

Patton argues very persuasively that Foucault's interest in neoliberalism may in part have been sympathetic, motivated partly by his famous observation that there had never yet existed a socialist art of government[7] (a remark generally interpreted as implying that it would be good if there were such a thing), whereas the early neoliberal thinkers were of interest precisely for their close attention to possible new techniques for the management of populations: to the art of government, as it were. Patton suggests that Foucault's interest in these thinkers may also have been partly inspired by that hostility to concentrations of arbitrary power (political or economic) which the early neoliberals seem to share with Rawls, which itself resonates with various conceptual and practical traditions of radical democracy.

Against that tradition which reads Foucault's concern with power and its usage as informed by an essentially anarchist politics, Patton points to Foucault's explicit criticism of Leftist 'state phobia'. Conversely, while Foucauldian scholarship from the 'governmentality' school has for some time promoted the idea of Foucault as a reformist – even, implicitly, a resource for technocrats[8] – Patton's argument implies that it is a mistake to divorce those aspects of his intellectual project which seem only concerned with the detached analysis of governmental mechanisms from a broader normative – and even, arguably, utopian – dimension. At the same time Patton implicitly reminds us of one of the most under-examined but potentially significant conceptual innovations made by Foucault in this lecture series: his suggestion that there is no such thing as 'the State', but only varying projects for, processes of and degrees of 'statification'[9] on the part of competing tendencies, groups and institutions. Intriguingly, this is an assertion which is surely consistent with Marx's own critique of alienation and reification,[10] according to which it is crucial to recognise 'the state' as a malleable product of human interactions.

Neoliberal egalitarianism is not the egalitarianism of Marx and the wider traditional Left, however: 'from each according to their abilities, to each according to their needs' and 'the free development of each shall be the condition for the free development of all' could hardly be further from the conception of the good society, which informs either the writings of early neoliberal theorists or the policy agendas of neoliberal governments. Both of these phrases – central tenets not just of communism but of socialism, social democracy, and even, arguably, of the 'social liberalism' of L.T. Hobhouse and his tradition – imply a level of reciprocity and an aspiration to lived equality which is entirely at odds with neoliberal assumptions. As Jo Littler demonstrates in her contribution to this volume, and as Gilroy also mentions in his, neoliberal government has increasingly legitimated its practices and the form of society that they produce in terms of an ideal of meritocracy, which valorises a hierarchical and highly unequal set of social relations while claiming to offer individuals from all backgrounds an equal chance to compete for elite status. Rawls, on Patton's reading, also seems at least partially to endorse such a model.

In the light of these complementary observations, we could argue that what defines the regularity of neoliberalism as a discursive formation is precisely the persistence of an individualistic conception of human selfhood and of the idea of the individual both as the ideal locus of sovereignty and the site of governmental intervention. In fact this observation may help us to explain the peculiar persistence and success of neoliberalism in recent decades. While it can clearly be understood as a modernising project in the tradition of liberalism and its forebears in radical Protestantism, neoliberalism's attention to the specificity of discrete governmental tactics and to the management of individuals *qua* individuals is arguably what has enabled it to flourish so impressively under postmodern conditions. If the fragmentation of the social world has presented major challenges to competing programmes and philosophies of government requiring a greater level of social cohesion and public consensus for their successful legitimation – from communism to traditional conservatism – neoliberalism has been able to take full advantage of the same situation in order to promote a vision of individualised competition in the marketplace as the only effective or legitimate mechanism for the distribution of rewards or the adjudication of opinions.

NEOLIBERAL IDEOLOGY

Neoliberals themselves tend not to welcome the label 'neoliberal'. While some deny significant differences between their own perspectives and those informing classical liberalism,[11] others tend to refute any notion that their assumptions and policy prescriptions are informed by a consistent philosophical approach at all, instead characterising themselves as addressing discrete, largely technical problems of government from a point of view unencumbered by ideology or grand designs.[12] One of the most characteristic tropes of such discourse – exemplified by the rhetoric of Tony Blair and his government – is the repeated use of the term 'modernisation' to describe a specific programme of labour-market deregulation, tax-cutting, privatisation and union repression which any objective view must recognise as in fact only one possible way of reforming and updating social and economic institutions in the twenty-first century. From this perspective, the gesture of positing a 'neoliberalism' which is much wider in scope than the texts discussed by Foucault or his followers, and is active across a far more diverse set of fields, even if its constituent elements do not necessarily recognise themselves as belonging to a specific or consistent formation at all, is a contentious one in itself. Such a move belongs to the tradition of ideology critique which has been problematised by generations of critics at lease since the 1960s – not least Foucault himself – for its tendency to identify uniformities of interest and intention where none may actually exist. However, in the case of a formation such as neoliberalism, the onus of proof is surely on those who wish to deny that neoliberalism functions as a full-blown ideology as classically understood.

The gesture of identifying neoliberalism as a broad ideology even where its constituent elements may not recognise themselves as adhering to it, is surely justified in this instance by at least two key factors. One is the sheer regularity and similarity of the basic elements of 'neoliberal' policy the world over: privatisation of public assets, contraction and centralisation of democratic institutions, deregulation of labour markets, reductions in progressive taxation, restrictions on labour organisation, labour market deregulation, active encouragement of competitive and entrepreneurial modes of relation across the public and commercial sectors. The other is the extent to which a range of significant cultural phenomena seems clearly to share and work to reproduce the basic presuppositions of neoliberal thought and the long-term social objectives of neoliberal policy.

In the former case, perhaps the extreme case for consideration is the development of economic policy in China since the early 1980s. David Harvey's widely-read *A Brief History of Neoliberalism* devotes a well-researched chapter to this history. Harvey clearly assumes that a policy regime explicitly oriented to the maximisation of private and corporate profit through the deregulation of labour markets, the political repression of organised labour, and the privatisation of state and communal assets, is specific enough and similar enough to its European and American counterparts to be described without hesitation as 'neoliberal'. Harvey and comparable Marxist commentators[13] have rarely if ever even alluded to the problem of whether or not Chinese policy has ever been directly influenced by the classic neoliberal literature; but on their terms this is a question which can justifiably be regarded as secondary to an analysis of the mechanics of actually existing neoliberalism.

In the latter case, it is the widespread dissemination of highly competitive, individualistic, meritocratic norms at sites as diverse as self-help literature, popular fiction, mainstream television, consumer publishing, music culture and food journalism which attracts notice. Here again, the explicit and implicit assumption of the objects under discussion seem so overwhelmingly consistent with the norms and objectives of classical neoliberalism that the onus of proof must be on those who might wish to refute the assumption that they belong to a singular discursive formation, and that they are in fact expressions of a coherent ideology. From this perspective, to which the majority of contributions to this issue are clearly sympathetic, it is perfectly legitimate to describe as 'neoliberal' policies, texts, concepts and programmes which share neoliberalism's core assumptions and objectives whether or not they make any explicit reference to European and American economic theory of the mid twentieth century: in fact understanding these non-explicit connections, and the interests and power relations which they serve, is a crucial objective of much of the political and cultural analysis presented here.

To understand how the phenomena under consideration function ideologically, it is worth recalling Althusser's classic account of the working of ideology and 'Ideological State Apparatuses'.[14] The first point to make here is that ideology almost by definition works to refute its own specificity and historicity: it is only fully effective, arguably, to the extent that it can pass itself off as promoting trans-historical 'common sense'.[15]

At the same time, Althusser argues, this common-sense is not primarily a matter of clearly-held beliefs to which the subject consciously accedes, but of the materially instantiated, institutionalised, 'ritual' forms of behaviour in which they are obliged or persuaded to engage. This is an approach which clearly prefigured and arguably influenced both Foucault's studies of discipline and government and Deleuze and Guattari's analyses of the 'machinic' dimensions of power, despite the fact that all would at some point try – if only rhetorically – to refute the very category of 'ideology'.[16] It also influenced Butler's sophisticated theorisation of the performative and iterative nature of gender discourse.[17] Neal Curtis' essay in the collection makes a novel and intriguing contribution to this tradition, while drawing on a wholly different intellectual lineage. Curtis examines the persistence of neoliberal assumptions and practices in government and popular journalistic discourse following the disastrous financial crash of 2008. His argument draws on Heidegger's understanding of the nature of *Dasein*, the coherence of the subject's lifeworld, and the importance to the subject of maintaining the coherence of their 'world', even in the face of events which seem wholly to disprove their earlier assumptions about it. Curtis offers thereby a compelling account of the sheer inertia which seems to have characterised public imaginative responses to that crisis and to have inhibited the emergence of radical responses to it, even at those sites where critical reflection ought to be most vigorously promoted: universities.

A related similar argument, drawing on more conventional conceptual resources, is made by Mark Fisher's very widely-cited *Capitalist Realism*,[18] which analyses the persistence across a range of sites of an attitude which assumes neoliberal capitalist norms to be unchallengeable at the level of actual social or political practice. We present as a contribution to this collection a dialogue between myself and Fisher reflecting upon some of the political implications of his analysis. Drawing in part on Žižek and Lacan, one of the most intriguing elements of Fisher's account of 'capitalist realism' is his emphasis on its ideological efficacy even in the face of explicit rejection by the very subjects whose behaviour it organises. Put crudely, perhaps the most commonplace relation to capitalist realism – or neoliberal ideology – in the contemporary world is an explicit rejection of its norms and claims accompanied by a resigned compliance with its demands. We know that we don't like neoliberalism, didn't vote for it, and object in principle to its exigencies: but we recognise also that unless we comply with it, primarily in our workplaces and in our labour-market behaviour, then we will be punished (primarily by being denied the main consolation for participation in neoliberal culture: access to a wide range of consumer goods), and will be likely to find ourselves inhabiting a radically different social terrain. This paradox is made bearable by a crucial feature of neoliberal ideology itself: the insistent belief that it is our private, personal beliefs and behaviours which define our 'true' selves, whereas our public behaviour can be tolerated precisely to the extent that it is not invested with any emotional significance.

The very complex relationships between the personal and the public, and the ways in which those relationships are managed by neoliberalism, are central topics of concern for two contributions to this collection which address in very different ways issues of gender and sexuality. Stephen Maddison's paper considers the pornography industry and its apparent promotion of modes of sexuality which might be regarded as wholly consistent with neoliberal culture, treating sex itself as a consumptive rather than a relational act, and participating in the general commodification of sex which is one of the most striking characteristics of neoliberal culture today. At the same time Maddison looks to innovations such as the experimental film *Made in Secret* – which purports to document the activities of a radical Canadian collective's attempt to produce a non-sexist, non-individualist, pro-queer porn movie – for their potential to challenge such attitudes and practices. Drawing on Lazzarato's concept of 'immaterial labour' (more recently developed by Hardt and Negri with their notion of 'biopolitical labour'), Maddison posits 'immaterial sex' – sexuality expressed in virtual forms, and at the level of communication and affect – as a site of increasingly intensified exploitation for sex workers but also a source of potential efficacy and agency, specifically where it can be mobilised in resolutely non-individualist and non-commodified forms.

Although its topic is very different, Angela McRobbie's essay points to a similar fault line between neoliberalism and its political opponents, the central issue being the conflict between individualism and collectivism. Bringing together many of the themes of the volume, McRobbie builds on her important recent work and that of other commentators to look at the precise forms of accommodation which current modes of neoliberalism make with the historic demands of feminism and the women's movement. McRobbie's key object of analysis is the emergent figure of the working mother, now fully valorised by the types of mainstream media outlet that until recently vilified any deviation from the mid-twentieth century family model. McRobbie points out that for all of her difference from the 'traditional' housewife, the ideal neoliberal mother is now expected to engage in forms of costly and highly restrictive self-management in order to demonstrate that working motherhood is no obstacle either to glamorous and highly sexualised modes of self-presentation – a continuation of the 'post-feminist masquerade' in which young working women are expected to participate – or to efficient and responsible household-management. Crucially, McRobbie identifies the ideological and practical rejection of all forms of collectivist and state-supported childcare – which she understands as key demands of socialist and social democratic feminism in the twentieth century – as a fundamental feature of the neoliberal programme and its wider ideological manifestations.

Almost all of the contributions to this collection can be drawn on to support an account according to which neoliberalism is understood in terms of its persistent promotion and reproduction of an ideology of competitive individualism, itself a contemporary manifestation of what C.B. Macpherson famously called 'possessive individualism': a model of human nature and human society according to which acquisitive individualism is both an inherent feature of the human personality and the only logical basis for human civilisation.[19] However, in encountering arguments such as Curtis', Fisher's, Gilroy's, Littler's and even McRobbie's, it is always useful to recall Abercrombie Hill and Turner's classic problematisation of 'the dominant ideology thesis',[20] according to which it is dangerous to overstate the efficacy of ideological rather than practical and material obstacles to radical political mobilisation. Put very simply (and this is my own formulation/simplification rather than anyone else's), it is perfectly possible to recognise the exploitative and iniquitous nature of capitalism, and the social and personal costs of neoliberalism, without being motivated to oppose them. Put even more crudely, as long as feeding one's children (still the principal preoccupation of most adult humans, as it has been throughout history and before) remains an achievable but difficult task, then energies are likely to be devoted to the accomplishment of that goal: energies which cannot then be channelled into political activity of any kind. Where this objective becomes unachievable, populations are likely to resort to desperate, perhaps revolutionary, measures. Where it becomes too easily realised – as it did for the generation which came to maturity in the post-war years of social-democratic ascendancy – then capitalism is also likely to find itself subject to challenge by constituencies no longer intimidated by the immediate threat of destitution. Much of the neoliberal programme can be understood in terms of the efficacy and precision with which it engineers precisely the outcome of an economy and a society within which feeding their children and keeping them out of relative poverty remains an achievable but highly demanding task for most actors: actively producing insecurity and 'precarity' across the working population, without allowing the level of widespread desperation to pass critical thresholds.[21] As such, it could be argued that the genius of the neoliberal programme is that it really requires no ideological component at all.

This argument is worth bearing in mind as a corrective to the naive tendency to imagine that it is mere ignorance of the social facts which keeps populations acquiescent with neoliberalism (a tendency typical of popular North American commentators such as Naomi Klein and Noam Chomsky), but it would not do to take it too far. Apart from anything else it would leave unanswered the question of just why there is so much evident ideological work – as all of these studies show that there is – put into the normalisation of neoliberal assumptions at sites as diverse as schools, tv programmes and supermarkets. In fact what all of these analyses point to from their different positions is a key function of ideology within neoliberal culture: to secure consent and generate political inertia precisely by enabling the experience of precarity and individualised impotence to be experienced as normal and inevitable. The distinction with a simplistic understanding of ideology is crucial here however: what is normalised by contemporary ideological mechanisms is not an explicit set of beliefs – only a tiny minority of the public in any neoliberal society has actually wanted or willingly voted for much of the neoliberal programme – but a set of negative affects whose normalisation prevents them becoming the basis for a sustained popular critique of neoliberalism. Put crudely, the point of neoliberal ideology is not to convince us that Hayek was right; it is to console us that the sense of insecurity, of perpetual competition and individual isolation produced by neoliberal government is natural, because 'that's what life is really like': this, for example, is the message and intended affective consequence of almost all 'reality television'. What emerges from all of these accounts – as well as from Foucault's and Patton's – is a picture within which we can see the inseparability of neoliberalism the ideology from neoliberalism conceived as a concrete programme for the government of individuals and populations. They each legitimate each other while materially producing conditions which are conducive to each other's propagation, in a politico-cultural feedback loop which can easily be experienced as simply unbreakable.

Jodi Dean's essay takes this analysis still further, identifying the ways in which the complexification of social life and economic life is both actively produced by neoliberalism and becomes an alibi for the inefficacy of political challenges to it. Dean deploys the psychoanalytic concept of drive – that compelling force which is manifest in the compulsion to repeat and goes beyond any mere desire for an object – to understand the affective feedback loop driving both the behaviour of financial markets leading up to the 2008 crash and, arguably, the inability of current mainstream politics to think itself out of a repetition of the events and behaviours which produced it. Crucially, Dean points to the tendency for the hypercomplex opacity of scenes such as the derivatives market, to become the excuse for a failure of governments to make any significant attempts to intervene in them, thereby perpetuating the power and unaccountable authority of a self-sustaining plutocratic elite. Here, Dean's analysis of the psychic mechanisms of finance capitalism converges with Littler's account of meritocracy as an ideology which serves to legitimate the status of a self-serving elite based around the main global centres of financial trading.

ACTUALLY EXISTING NEOLIBERALISM: POWER, GOVERNMENT AND INTERESTS

This raises a crucial issue about the consistency of neoliberalism as both an ideology and a governmental programme, as distinct from the aggregation of ideas and texts discussed by Foucault and compared by Patton with the philosophy of Rawls. The great historic value of Patton's analysis arguably only becomes apparent when we consider that what he has demonstrated is the *non-inevitability* of the recruitment of that family of ideas to the wider ideological project which Dean calls 'real existing neoliberalism'; this is an account to which Gilroy's discussion of black articulations of neoliberalism also lends great richness and credibility. In order to explore this issue further, however, it is clearly necessary to consider the question of what the apparent objective of existing neoliberalism has actually been, given that, on all available measures, it has not led to a wider distribution of wealth and resources, a more egalitarian income spread or, crucially, an increase in social mobility relative to the 1950s and 1960s,[22] which are exactly the outcomes that a programme informed by classic neoliberal ideals ought to have tried to produce. While access to the property market and to certain kinds of consumption (foreign travel, for example) has increased, the key measure of 'equality of opportunity' accepted by most social scientists is social mobility, and social mobility has not increased at all under neoliberal governments in any instance. In fact the combined decreases in social equality and social mobility generated by neoliberal government in practice lend very serious weight to David Harvey's claim that the fundamental aim of actually existing neoliberalism has been the 'restoration of class power' on the part of the capitalist class, following a major erosion of that power in the middle decades of the twentieth century.

Dean, echoing the work of political economists such as Andrew Glyn,[23] points to the expansive role of the financial sector in contemporary capitalism. This suggests that neoliberalism should be understood as bound up not merely with a restoration of capitalist class power, but with a re-balancing of the relative power of industrial and financial capital within that class, and to some extent a re-composition of capital itself and its constitutive practices. It is important to sound a note of caution here as to how far this represents a radical break within the history of capitalism. Speculative finance has exercised considerable power at previous moments in that history (during the period, roughly, 1870-1929, for example). The great historian of capitalism, Fernand Braudel, believed that long-range, international speculative finance – trading in risks and virtual goods while gambling on future commodity prices – was the basic constitutive activity of capitalism as such from the moment of its inception in the Italian mercantile cities of the fifteenth century.[24] As such the moment of neoliberalism may represent an assertion of capitalist class power of unprecedented magnitude and abstract purity, but not a moment of absolute novelty.

At the same time it is important to note that various constituencies outside of the financial elites (although never very distant from them socially, culturally, politically or geographically) have benefitted from the major social and economic changes with which neoliberalism has been associated. A new social elite, quite different culturally (if not socially, functionally or genealogically) from the historic 'establishment' has arguably crystallised from the interconnections between the worlds of finance, commercial media, information and communications and technologies, and some branches of government, in recent decades. Less powerful social groups – most notably managers of both commercial and public-sector organisations – have been able to acquire power and obtain privileges to the extent that they have been willing and able to reproduce the culture of that elite while serving its interests. Typically, this culture tends to endorse a highly individualistic worldview which is explicitly hostile to all forms of collective organisation or public provision while remaining highly defensive of privileges which its members – as Littler shows in her essay – must believe themselves to have won fairly in the open competition of the labour market. By the same token this elite culture is genuinely hostile to visible forms of prejudice and discrimination, especially on grounds of gender, sexuality or race, which seem to go against its individualist ethos. It will even make common cause in defence of this position with forces from the Left, against perceived threats from conservative constituencies, when necessary (hence the heavy financial support for Barak Obama's election campaign coming from major Wall Street investment banks in 2008). As such, professional women (at least those sufficiently affluent or motivated not to require state or community support to raise children), gay professionals and entrepreneurs and non-white professionals and entrepreneurs have all benefitted considerably from the cultural ascendancy of this neoliberal elite and its values, as McRobbie, Maddison and Gilroy all explain in their contributions.

However, it is clear enough that such gains – both socially and materially – have been enjoyed almost precisely to the extent that the groups and individuals in question have been able to participate in and facilitate the wider project of neoliberalisation, and that the hard economic benefits of that process have accrued to them only and exactly to the extent that they have been able to draw close to and access the real concentrations of wealth in the financial institutions: be it via salaries, pensions, bonuses, options or royalties. As such, the successes of these groups do nothing to problematise the claim that what defines the consistency of actually existing neoliberalism as a governmental programme is simply its promotion of the interests of finance capital and the processes of financialisation above and – if necessary – to the exclusion of all other interests. Littler's description of this elite as a 'plutocracy' – which may at first strike the reader as somewhat archaic – seems therefore, on reflection, both apposite and precise. Indeed, Dean offers concrete examples of major financial institutions using very similar language to describe themselves and their practices.

THE HEGEMONIC PROJECT OF NEOLIBERALISM

Dean, like Curtis, gives considerable attention to the political, epistemological and ontological conditions of possibility both for the 2008 crash and for the subsequent persistence of neoliberalism as the animating ideology of most governments worldwide. Lucy Potter and Clare Westall focus more closely on the contours of neoliberal culture in post-crash Britain. As Dean points out, it is problematic simply to associate neoliberalism with the expansion of consumer culture, partly because the great historic moment of such expansion was certainly that of Keynesian demand-management and welfare capitalism, partly because the neoliberal assault on global wage levels arguably runs contrary to any long-term goal of expanding popular consumption levels. Despite the veracity of such observations, there can be little question that the neoliberal epoch has in fact been characterised by an expansion of consumption levels in the richer countries – enabled through an enormous inflation of household debt and by the export of production to parts of Asia with extremely low labour costs – and, more significantly, by the influence of discourses such as Public Choice Theory, a key component of neoliberal government since the 1980s, which have attempted to re-model a vast range of social relationships (most notably between public sector professionals and service users) as retail transactions, promoting a consumer mentality as the only mode of active and empowered subjectivity available in any public or private situation. Clearly the expansion of (indebted, exploitative) consumption has been the major compensation for the decline of real wages and relative economic position, as well as the decline in opportunities for meaningful democratic input to political decision-making, suffered by most citizens of such countries since the 1970s. As such the precipitous deterioration of living standards, and wage/price ratios in the UK since 2008, might have been expected to provoke a major crisis of consent for neoliberalism.

The fact that this crisis of consent has so far clearly not materialised – despite the occasional riot – forms the backdrop to Potter and Westall's detailed analysis of the 'foodscape' of contemporary Britain. Potter and Westall chart the ways in which ideas and practices around the production, preparation and consumption of food have been mobilised in order to invite continued affective investment in consumption and consumerism while simultaneously legitimating the austerity programme which has formed the core of the UK government's resolutely neoliberal response to the post-2008 crisis, in keeping with the broader policy agenda accepted by and across the European Union (and distinct from the Obama administration's quasi-Keynesian stimulus strategy). The challenge of perpetuating an ideology which is organised primarily around the interpellation of subjects as consumers, while simultaneously legitimating a political programme which actively undermines the capacity of citizens to consume, is one which requires the mobilisation of very specific ideas of self-sufficiency and the creativity of domestic labour, as Potter and Westall demonstrate in persuasive detail. Of course, such an analysis only fully makes sense in the context of an understanding of neoliberalism as the ongoing attempt to mobilise a particular set of ideas and governmental practices, and to some extent an entire ideology, in the pursuit of a particular set of interests, neutralising and forestalling the emergence of political threats to this endeavour: in other words, as a hegemonic project.

Rather like 'neoliberalism', 'hegemony' is a concept which a number of commentators have recently suggested no longer usefully describes the functioning of contemporary power relations. Most such accounts tend to argue from a position which assumes 'hegemony' to describe a situation in which active and explicit consent to the social authority of a hegemonic group or ideology is consciously expressed by subaltern groups. From this perspective, the situation already described in this essay, in which it is hard to identify much clear enthusiasm amongst populations for the political philosophy of neoliberalism or even for its general norms, is not describable as one of neoliberal hegemony. However, this account of 'hegemony' is really not one which is compatible with Gramsci's or any post-Gramscian account, because it simply does not take into account two issues which are crucial to any such theory of hegemony. Firstly, it ignores the possibility that, as Gramsci points out, subaltern groups may at times consent only 'passively'.[25] Secondly, it ignores the variety of ways in which different groups can be mobilised, recruited, pacified, neutralised or marginalised by a hegemonic project: for example, in the case of neoliberalism, it is clear from the foregoing analysis that only the core neoliberal elite and key strategic sectors of its periphery (notably corporate management) have to be recruited to any kind of active belief in neoliberal norms, as long as no singular alternative wins widespread popular support, in order for the rest of a population to remain convinced of the unviability of any political challenge to those norms. The result may well be a broadly shared culture of 'disaffected consent', wherein a general dissatisfaction with neoliberalism and its social consequences is very widespread, but no popular alternative is able to crystallise or cohere with sufficient potency to develop the necessary critical mass to challenge neoliberal hegemony. By 'hegemony' I mean specifically *not* a condition of generalised domination, but rather, in Gramsci's sense, a position of social, cultural and political 'leadership' enjoyed by a particular set of interests and the norms which give ideological expression to them. The power enjoyed by the elite which shares these interests is not the power to order every aspect of daily life, but rather to determine the general direction of travel in which social processes tend. This seems very well to describe the position of neoliberalism today in many national contexts and indeed at the global level.

This is not to say, however, that what we might call – following Scott Lash – the 'epistemological' dimension of power has simply become unimportant.[26] Curtis shows very clearly how the inability to imagine an alternative to neoliberalism has contributed to a situation in which the very failure of neoliberal economics has been redefined as an excuse for more and intensified neoliberalism in the form of the European Union's austerity agenda. Clearly, the meanings which groups and individuals give to events, phenomena and identities remains a crucial issue, and the heavy symbolic work done by key media actors in order publicly to define various social and cultural changes in neoliberal terms is clearly demonstrated here by contributors to this issue such as McRobbie, Gilroy, Littler, Potter and Westall.

One way of understanding this issue is in terms of the necessity for neoliberal propagandists to construct plausible narratives explaining the meaning of key social changes of recent decades. As Hall et al showed 25 years ago,[27] neoliberal advocates achieved a high level of political success in the 1970s by constructing a public narrative which both responded to a set of political demands – from militant labour, black people, women, youth and the counterculture – and offered an explanation and solution for the social crisis which those demands precipitated. The narrative of the New Right defined those demands as largely unreasonable and proposed to respond to the crisis by repressing them with a combination of neoliberal economics and social authoritarianism. In the long term, as I have suggested elsewhere,[28] the social conservatism of the New Right was not politically sustainable in the cultural context produced by both neoliberalisation – with its tendency to erode social norms in favour of competitive individualism – and the relative success of the new social movements in challenging entrenched forms of sexism, racism and homophobia. Today, therefore, it is necessary for neoliberal hegemony that the experience of changing gender relations in the labour market be defined very carefully in terms which do not accord any authority to the historically collectivist dimension of organised feminism; that the right to sexual self-expression be acknowledged in terms which nonetheless marginalise the historic demands of gay liberation and the counterculture for an authentic sexual utopianism; that the legatees of colonialism and slavery be offered inclusion in the cultural mainstream on terms which resonate with their own history while reinforcing neoliberal norms. The processes by which each of these operations is conducted are precisely the topics of McRobbie's, Madison's and Gilroy's respective contributions to this collection.

At the same time as representing a historic political response to the challenge posed by oppositional constituencies, neoliberalism also represents a response by capital and its agents to the changing technological milieu of the late twentieth century. It may yet be too early to say whether the cybernetic and digital revolution is as significant an event of world history as the industrial revolution. What is clear is that the threats posed and opportunities offered to the interests of finance capital by that enormous shift constitute a key context for the emergence and success of actually existing neoliberalism, and the mobilisation of neoliberal ideas by finance capital in the service of its hegemonic project. On the one hand, as I, like others, have commented elsewhere, the emergence of post-Fordist techniques of production, distribution and management can be understood in part as a response to the challenges posed to capital at the end of the 1960s;[29] on the other hand it can be seen as itself presenting a set of opportunities to capital, of which the adoption of the neoliberal strategy was the ultimate realisation. Actually existing neoliberalism would not have been implementable without the mobilisation of a set of techniques and devices which made possible a vast automation and depersonalisation of both industrial processes and financial transactions. Without robotics, container shipping, and above all electronic command and control systems, it would not have been possible to undermine the bargaining power of organised industrial workers, on which the political viability of the social democratic state had always depended. Without the development of a complex and mutually supportive array of techniques in mathematics, information processing and the creation of credit, the expansion of both the financial markets and the consumer economy could not have taken place as it did.

TECHNICAL ASSEMBLAGE AND ABSTRACT MACHINE

This construction and mobilisation of what we might call the 'neoliberal technical assemblage' is a key concern of both Nicky Marsh's and Mark Hayward's contributions to this volume. Marsh's essay echoes strongly both Patton's engagement with proto-neoliberal political ideas and Curtis' and Dean's attention to the political response to neoliberal government's demonstrable breakdown in 2008. Discussing the highly circumscribed rhetoric of neoliberal 'failure', which emerged from that moment, Marsh moves on to consider the conceptualisation of failure in the writing and teaching of American experimental novelist William Gaddis. Specifically Marsh addresses Gaddis' 1975 novel *JR* – which satirises the emergent world of asset-stripping and financialised capitalism – and in particular its relation to the writings of Norbert Wiener, widely regarded as the founder of cybernetics, and a sometime colleague and collaborator of Milton Friedman's. Marsh explores Wiener's proximity to and distance from the neoliberal 'rational choice' theorists who would make use of some his ideas, and in particular draws attention to his positing of a model of the human subject defined by its exterior relations and its actions rather than its interior motivations or self-interested rationality. Wiener's and Gaddis' scepticism as to the simple predictability of systemic outcomes and their attendant risks prefigures uncannily the situation described by Dean, wherein the existence of a financial market so complex as to be genuinely unknowable becomes the alibi for a neoliberal refusal to exercise democratic control over the economy and the interests in which it is organised.[30] And ultimately what Marsh, like Patton, partly shows us is the extent to which the neoliberal assemblage has depended upon a very specific manipulation of tools and techniques that could have been put to quite other uses.

Hayward focuses on one highly specific history of technological innovation, charting the progress of twentieth-century developments in electronic technologies which contributed to the development of the teleprompter, the ATM machine and the self-service photo booth, and the participation of this history in the development of a techno-social regime of 'neoliberal optics'. As Hayward himself remarks, and convincingly demonstrates, 'neoliberalism is a complex social formation that involves many different elements; it is more than simply a body of conceptual and theoretical arguments about the economy which has subsequently been implemented within various contexts, a process by which "neoliberalism proper" fans out across society. The technologies discussed here and their analysis in light of neoliberal optics, draw our attention to the way that a number of pre-existing technologies and cultural practices have been enlisted in the service of the process of neoliberalisation'. Hayward makes innovative use of the thought of Gilbert Simondon to investigate the contribution of these technologies to the emergence of a neoliberal regime of individuation, for example relating how the invention of the photobooth was motivated by a specific desire to allow students graduating from Yale university to take their own yearbook pictures in order to avoid the homogenising conformity characteristic of professional portraiture. Here, even as early as 1929, several years before the *Colloque Walter Lippmann*, we encounter the idea that *individuality* should be seen as the ultimate privilege of a particular kind of elite: an elite which, unlike its antecedents, is constitutively unwilling to recognise its own corporate character, its members' status having been hypothetically earned – meritocratically – at an elite educational institution. We might say that here, in the moment of the photobooth's conception and implementation, we can see already operable the 'abstract machine' of neoliberalism.

I have used this latter term elsewhere, borrowed from Guattari and Deleuze, to suggest something of the virtual and dynamic consistency of neoliberalism.[31] For Deleuze and Guattari, 'abstract machine' is a name for the immanent dynamics of an assemblage or formation,[32] emphasising that the consistency of any such object is to be understood at a certain level of abstraction, rather than in the homogeneity of its concrete instantiations, while also stressing the extent to which such consistency is a function of productive and transformatory processes rather than merely the static 'distribution' of Foucault's 'discursive formation'. The abstract machine is constituted by a set of vectors, emergent tendencies and potentialities with greater or lesser chances of expression and actualisation. We might put this very crudely by saying that the abstract machine works to make certain outcomes probable while others less so. In the case of neoliberalism, then, what is it that defines the specificity of this 'abstract machine'?

I would suggest that if any function defines the machinic specificity of neoliberalism, it is the tendency to potentiate individuals *qua* individuals while simultaneously inhibiting the emergence of all forms of potent collectivity. Whether we are referring to self-photographing Yale graduates, self-helping black entrepreneurs, self-reliant working mothers, lone porn users, rational-choosing economic subjects, austerity-age 'foodies' or self-motivating meritocrats: it is entirely, but genuinely, as *individuals* that the neoliberal machine contributes to a real expansion of powers and freedoms. What is achieved by the obfuscatory insistence on the political unknowability of capitalism, the 'idiotic' (to use a term explored by Curtis) insistence on sustaining the neoliberal project in the face of its own failure, and the reduction of all egalitarian ideals to the pursuit of equality of opportunity, is precisely the inhibition of any possible emergence of collective and democratic solutions to social problems. There is little point in denying that for most of our contributors and for this author, neoliberalism therefore presents itself as a problem to be overcome. In the dialogue between myself and Mark Fisher, there is some tentative exploration of what such overcoming might involve. What we hope is that this collection will at least contribute to a wider understanding of neoliberal culture in all its complexity, its possibility, and its limits.

NOTES

1. Michel Foucault, *The Birth of Biopolitics: Lectures at the Collège de France 1978-9*, Baskingstoke, Palgrave, 2008, p132.
2. David Harvey, *A Brief History of Neoliberalism*, London, Verso, 2005.
3. For example, Clive Barnett, 'Publics and Markets: What's wrong with Neoliberalism?' in Susan Smith, Sallie Marston, Rachel Pain, and John Paul Jones III (eds), *The Handbook of Social Geography*, London and New York, Sage, 2010.
4. Michel Foucault, *The Archaeology of Knowledge*, London, Tavistock, 1972, pp73-4.
5. Ibid., p134.
6. Andrew Gamble, 'Two Faces of Neoliberalism' in Richard Robinson (ed), *The Neo-Liberal Revolution: Forging the Market State*, Basingstoke, Palgrave, 2006.
7. Foucault, *The Archaeology of Knowledge*, op. cit., p94.
8. For example, Tony Bennett, *Culture: A Reformer's Science*, London, Sage, 1998.
9. Foucault, op. cit., p112.
10. Karl Marx and Friedrich Engels, *The German Ideology*, London, Lawrence and Wishart, 1970.
11. Gamble, op. cit.
12. For example, Geoff Mulgan, *Life After Politics*, London, Demos, 1997.
13. For example, Shaun Breslin, 'Serving the Market or Serving the Party? Neo-Liberalism in China' in Richard Robinson, op. cit.
14. Louis Althusser, 'Ideology and Ideological State Apparatuses: Notes towards an Investigation' in *Lenin and Philosophy and Other Essays*, London, Monthly Review Press, 1971.
15. Antonio Gramsci, *Selections from the Prison Notebooks*, London, Lawrence and Wishart, 1971.
16. Gilles Deleuze and Félix Guattari, *A Thousand Plateaus*, London, Athlone, 1988, pp3-4.
17. Judith Butler, *Bodies that Matter*, London, Routledge, 1993.
18. Mark Fisher, *Capitalist Realism*, London, Zero Books, 2009.
19. C. B. Macpherson, *The Origins of Possessive Individualism. From Hobbes to Locke*, Oxford, Clarendon Press, 1962.
20. Nicholas Abercrombie, Stephen Hill, Bryan S. Turner, *The Dominant Ideology Thesis*, London, Allen & Unwin, 1980.
21. C.f. Maurizio Lazzarato, *Expérimenations Politiques*, Paris, Éditions Amsterdam, 2009.

22. Daniel Dorling, *Injustice: Why Social Inequality Persists*, London, Policy Press, 2011.

23. Andrew Glyn, *Capitalism Unleashed: Finance, Globalization and Welfare*, Oxford, Oxford University Press, 2006.

24. Fernand Braudel, *The Perspective of the World*, London, Harper & Row, 1979.

25. Gramsci, *Selections from the Prison Notebooks*, op. cit., p12.

26. Scott Lash, *Intensive Culture: Social Theory, Religion and Contemporary Capitalism*, London, Sage, 2010.

27. Stuart Hall, Chas Critcher, Tony Jefferson, John N. Clarke and Brian Roberts, *Policing The Crisis: Mugging, the State and Law and Order*, London, Macmillan, 1978.

28. Jeremy Gilbert, 'The Second Wave: the specificity of New Labour neo-liberalism' in *Soundings*, 26, (2004), London, Lawrence & Wishart, 2004.

29. Jeremy Gilbert, *Common Ground: Democracy and Collectivity in an Age of Individualism*, London, Pluto, 2013.

30. C.f. Nigel Thrift, *Knowing Capitalism*, London, Sage, 2005.

31. Jeremy Gilbert, *Anticapitalism and Culture: Popular Politics and Radical Theory*, Oxford, Berg, 2008.

32. Deleuze and Guattari, op. cit.

'... We Got to Get Over Before We Go Under ...' Fragments for a History of Black Vernacular Neoliberalism

Paul Gilroy

In a culture where neo-liberal ideas represent a widely-circulating current, the free, ubiquitous and all-encompassing character of 'wealth' is a dominant theme. This is increasingly money in its naked, materialistic 'Americanised' form – shorn of the old, deferential, aristocratic, upper-class connotations and moral liberal reservations which have accompanied – and inflected – it in the British context.

Stuart Hall

The cultural revolution wrought by neoliberalism is altering the symbolic currency of racial difference. In 2005, Tim Campbell, a young British man of Caribbean heritage, won the first series of the UK version of the US business reality TV show, *The Apprentice*. The series celebrates business and management by dramatising the intense competition between contending wannabe executives. Predictably, the winner takes all and is rewarded with a chance to operate at a high level in the corporate world under the patronage of the business leader who runs the show. The losers are consigned back to the groaning pit of insecurity. It is not too crude to describe this television franchise as a weekly parable supporting the liturgy of neoliberalism: marketisation and privatisation secured by the liberation of individual entrepreneurial freedoms and skills.

After his historic triumph, Campbell rapidly became the poster-boy for what was then spoken of as a rising tide of interest in entrepreneurship among Britain's 'minority ethnic' communities – a possibility which dovetailed readily with the ideology of New Labour as well as the broader, timely architecture of what Anthony Barnett has dubbed their 'corporate populism'.[1] It was no surprise that Campbell was taken up widely as a wholesome, 'role model' whose winning smile and evident graciousness could, for example, be projected vividly into the imaginations of disoriented young people who were being invited, through innovative, business-friendly, secondary-school curricula, to follow in his footsteps towards the distant, glittering citadel of personal and financial success. It was not so much that wealth would descend upon anyone following that primrose path towards a classless society – though it surely would – but rather that their journey to that elusive, golden goal would be properly organised and overseen along neoliberal lines. Newly-fluent in what Alistair Beaton has described as 'management bollocks',[2] Britain's emergent legion of project managers would metaphorically don their hi-viz jackets and steward these excursions, ensuring that they would be done the right way: by harnessing individual self-realisation to the imperatives of a business culture that culminated in the revelatory manifestation of a revised hierarchy. A freshly diversified synod of generic, MBA-ed business-leaders, no longer just a gaggle of old white men, would stand proudly at the summit of achievement and invest the results of this neoliberal revolution with all the force of inevitable nature.

That well-tailored image of avowedly meritocratic, corporate diversity corresponds closely to the chapter of neoliberal transformation that has been entitled 'The Age of Obama'. It endows the project of globalisation, conceived as a process of 'Americanisation', with polychromatic, heterocultural vitality. Proof that US business culture is somehow ahead of Britain's local version can be discovered in the former's apparent preparedness to divest itself of white supremacism. Even if racism remains intractable elsewhere, it seems that neoliberal capitalism is ready to free itself from the fetters placed upon it by the historic commitment to pigmentocracy. Multiculturalism may have been pronounced dead by mere politicians but its sovereign authority has been usurped by the expanding cohorts of diversity management.

As well as running his own charity ('The Bright Ideas Trust' tasked with the empowerment of ethnic minority entrepreneurs), Tim Campbell became a stalwart of the Department of Work and Pensions Ethnic Minority Advisory group. He was a Cabinet Office Social Enterprise Ambassador and a Child Ambassador for London. In the 2012 New Year Honours List, he was finally rewarded with an MBE for his 'services to Enterprise Culture'. These serial triumphs provide a useful historical marker because they convey the evolving significance of racial difference in the core of a corporate operation that is disposed to invest strongly in the trappings of diversity and plurality. This has been done not only in order to secure access to new markets, clients and capital but also to communicate something potent and novel about the great managerial revolution that had begun to touch and to change all of Britain's institutions, reforming their language and altering their grasp of their own mission as well as their understanding of the contending forms of value that were bound up in their practice before cuts and austerity specified new general rules.

It is not possible to disassociate these historic developments from the entrenchment of the neoliberal habits and styles of thought that operate spontaneously as a kind of common sense and institutionally as a mode of governmentality. Several issues are knotted here. A problem of periodisation is introduced into the genealogies of liberalism and neoliberalism. It raises difficult questions about exactly when specifically neoliberal themes entered into a dispersed but nonetheless popular enthusiasm for capitalist commerce, business and privatisation. Answering them is no simple matter and Mark Fisher has been insightful in seeing the idea that there is no alternative to capitalism as a key to the functioning of this contemporary assemblage[3] which is too volatile to be described straightforwardly as the consolidation of neoliberal hegemony. Indeed, the idea of hegemony might itself need to be revised to take a number of recent developments into account. Overdeveloped capitalism's market state promotes cultural and technological matrices that represent a qualitative change in the relationship between information and power. Agno-political formations result from the saturation of civil society with public relations messages. Manufactured – groomed – ignorance is complemented by the expanding bio-political dynamics of 'psychopharmacological societies' which are shaping novel varieties of selfhood. Attention deficit becomes a social phenomenon when headsets disrupt listening, eyes are focused more easily on phone screens than on faces, and the prospect of controlling one's own technocultural bubble defines the limits of freedom for a society that is being drained of imagination. On one side, a revised history of the information order that characterised twentieth-century fascism and authoritarian populism[4] and, on the other, a torrent of prescriptions for anti-depressant and anti-anxiety medication, can help to explain how fluctuating demotic support for neoliberal perspectives has been reproduced. It is evident even among the lowest strata of Britain's evolving racial order. Among those working and non-working non-classes,[5] populist politics has repeatedly been articulated as misoxeny, racism and anti-immigrant sentiment. Mediated by the power of News International and the scrupulously balanced commentaries supplied by overpaid BBC info-warriors, that structure of feeling has often been voiced by precarious and vulnerable people who might be thought to have little to gain from the hyper-individuation, marketisation and business-centred view of social life that the neoliberal mentality requires and generates.

An additional difficulty can be identified as the result of the successful processes of assimilation and integration that were built upon the seemingly organic political conservatism of many settler migrants and their locally-born descendants. This taboo subject is less significant electorally than it is in the wider political culture where it has helped to cement the idea that racism no longer presents a significant obstacle to individual success. Without that anachronistic distortion, we become masters and mistresses of our own fate. The lives of B-list celebrity figures such as Thatcherite footballer turned TV personality Ian Wright, and bipolar former heavy-weight boxer Frank Bruno, yield paradigmatic instances. Thinking about the ominous political trajectory of those sporting icons, perhaps to the accompaniment of John Lennon's 'Imagine' in the somewhat amended form in which it was sung at the 1983 Conservative Party election rally by the Jamaican-born Hot Chocolate front-man, Errol Brown MBE, raises still more disquieting possibilities. It is not just that the atypical heroism associated with sporting triumph or, in Bruno's case, with failure and mental illness, functions as a symbol for success in other more mundane fields of everyday life and commerce. The particular forms of postcolonial celebrity that become visible under the existential glare of the military-entertainment complex[6] are also imagined to represent and even to embody the valour, tenacity and intelligence that characterise the exercise of 'leadership' skills. The same 'skill-set' builds character and communicates positively on the sports-field, in the boxing-ring and in the boardroom alike. How that motivational magic can be shared is a mystery known only to an elite cast of after-dinner speechmakers but its contemporary potency is scarcely in doubt.[7] Sport, like the military experiences upon which it so regularly signifies, is thought to provide a means to instil uniquely desirable qualities.[8] However, it has also been used to generate a large mirror in which the division of the neoliberal world into a new configuration – the two great tribes of winners and losers – can be glimpsed and made legitimate.

The spectacular, multicultural triumph of 'Team GB' at the London Olympic games of 2012 provides further support for this heuristic judgement. Signifiers of diversity were instrumental in securing that golden panoply of merited success. The value of multiculture to Britain's geopolitical 'branding' aside, the elated worship of winners as the redemption of a recently riot-torn country augmented the neoliberal fantasy that anything can be achieved if the correct disposition has been adopted. It need not be repeated that these days, if individuals fail to take advantage of opportunities to free or improve themselves, then the fault is all their own. After his second triumph, no less of an authority than double gold-medal winner Mohammed 'Mo' Farrah CBE, confirmed the timely message that 'it is all about grafting'.[9] This cruel proposition chimes loudly with the buried histories of working class and immigrant Conservatism. It sanctions the ideology of hustling, and getting by – by any means necessary – and summons up the disquieting prospect of today's black and multi-culti Britons not exactly as ideal, neoliberal subjects but as people whose testing life experiences can increase their vulnerability to the seductions of a vernacular neoliberalism. The dreams of uplift, security and possibility, the prospect of hope in a better future secured through consistently hard yet always ennobling labour, are gathered into the familiar neoliberal concept of 'aspiration'.[10]

The idea that anyone can be helped by government to change themselves and thereby to alter their life chances by the sheer, dedicated force of their own will, is now fundamental to the legitimacy of neoliberal reform and the notions of merit that it still seems to need. My unpopular point is that this poetics operates very powerfully, and often unrecognised, when it appears in blackface. As with previous varieties of popular racial drama, the principal audience for these performances is often located some distance away from the vital, unruly multicultural communities in which black and other minority Britons dwell and sometimes even thrive.

THE NEW VICTORIANS?

In a world where History is disaggregated into specific, fragmented 'backstories' it is essential to approach the confluence of autopoietic desire and managerial rhetoric historically. It is therefore necessary to acknowledge the alignment that can be established between the archive of Victorian self-improvement literature[11] and the theories of individual, social and national uplift propagated in the period after slavery by some leaders of former slaves. This connection has been noted before as a distinctive stage upon which the drama of freedom's acquisition was enacted.[12] Samuel Smiles, Benjamin Disraeli and the other thinkers whose theories of race and family, self and nationality, education and ignorance found an eager audience among that new reading public, were not politically homogenous. Though *Self-help* was first published in 1859, it is easy to imagine what resonance its positive view of anti-slavery, Granville Sharp and Thomas Clarkson might have acquired in the context of post-bellum reconstruction or of state-making in nineteenth-century Liberia:

> ... it is nevertheless equally clear that men must be the active agents in their own well-being and well-doing; and that, however much the wise and the good must owe to others, they themselves must in the very nature of things be their own best helpers.[13]

The technologies of the free black self that were deduced from various Victorian writings by nineteenth-century polymaths of colour and melded into the political theory and liberation theologies of the black Atlantic, require an extended treatment. It will stretch back through the political imaginations of figures like Martin Delany and Lewis Woodson. That genealogy cannot be provided here.[14] What is more important than the general category into which the resulting body of work might be placed, is its implausibly tidy articulation of individual, social and national goals which are linked together as if they were homologically related and could be nourished by the same sterling qualities of fortitude, discipline, resilience and stamina in which they were sourced. The legacy of that idea has also provided important resources upon which today's black vernacular neoliberalism can draw. The story of striving – today's 'aspiration' – seems more plausible and becomes more generally appealing when it is presented as the vindication or redemption of racialised forms of both natural difference and social suffering. Any individual's successful battle to overcome the effects of racism can supply conclusive evidence that racism is no longer something to be concerned about.

The idea that each person is essentially responsible for their own fate is controversial within Christianity but it seems to have been experienced by many slave descendants as a liberatory promise – a dimension of freedom that could foster a transformation of people into agents, releasing them into dimensions of transcendent ipseity that were denied by racial discourse and its institutional vectors even in the post-slavery period. As

Booker T. Washington would make clear, not least in his bitter conflict with DuBois over education, any well-executed task, no matter how menial or exploited, could be considered a source of self-restoring pride, manly discipline and racial opportunity if only its redemptive possibilities could be properly engaged. The inscription of a particular, post-slavery work ethic was combined with a sharply gendered mode of racial self-government involving distinctive vocabularies of self-description and self-mastery that were alloyed with favoured forms of conduct and even bodily technique. Lessons in the comportment of the respectable racial self were involved not only in Washington's commitment to 'the gospel of the toothbrush' but in his well-publicised narration of the yogic sweeping of Mrs Ruffner's recitation room,[15] an event that provided the unanticipated mechanism for his personal elevation.[16] That template was influential, at least until the mythology of Madame C.J. Walker's minority entrepreneurship took wing some years later.

Brevity again demands that I pass over a long and complex sequence that should not be compressed. We should not, for example, overlook the great resonance of Marcus Garvey's 'African Fundamentalist' notions of individual, national and racial uplift which were transmitted widely and had considerable impact upon the outlook of African nationalism in the early twentieth century, particularly among the elite US-educated leadership caste who studied at historically-black institutions like Fisk, Wilberforce, Howard and Virginia Theological Seminary.[17] Even at that early stage, the view of racial self-reliance as the blissful outcome of independent business and commercial activity combined readily with the occult, esoteric wing of black nationalist and Pan-African philosophy as well as the vindicationist approach to nation-building it created.

Though aspects of the anti-lynching campaign against racial terror suggest otherwise,[18] the acquisition of private, individual wealth seems to have been easily reconciled with more social understanding of enrichment as a collective enterprise conducted comfortably within the boundaries of a segregated world. The tension between these two approaches – one individual, the other communal – would increase as unevenly developed US capitalism moved beyond its Fordist phase and the country's racial nomos was altered by economic crises on one side and the award of substantive citizenship to Negroes on the other.[19] The resulting confusion is audible in James Brown's much sampled 'Funky President' (1974) and other spritely, Nixon-era hymns to the ideal of black capitalism.

MONEY, THAT'S WHAT I WANT

The enduring significance of African American culture as both a conduit and a source of these enduringly powerful examples of progress and uplift thanks to business acumen and financial gain is undeniable. Complexities in the multicultural marketing of difference mean that its appeal is not limited to black or minority ethnic audiences. The unique seductions and pleasures of the US black vernacular are not only part of that nation's cultural and military diplomacy,[20] they get dispersed through the elaborate social and cultural networks that derive from unpredictable, private sources like the energetic advocacy of Oprah Winfrey. Contemporary heirs to the project of self-enrichment as collective vindication have pursued their activities even while the terms upon which individual and communal destinies can be connected have been recast by the historical and demographic changes mapped by William Julius Wilson and others.[21] One of the best contemporary illustrations of this development at work is provided by the popularity of the neoliberal, self-help books penned by the Hawaiian motivational speaker, entrepreneur and financial educator Robert T. Kiyosaki whose work has acquired an enormous readership partly as a result of his repeated appearances on Winfrey's Show.[22] Kiyosaki's career as an investor, economic adviser and proponent of financial learning through game-playing (Monopoly is a favourite) cannot be easily summed up. Since they first appeared in 1997, the many multi-million-selling volumes in his Time-Warner published 'Rich Dad, Poor Dad' series have been eagerly received among the would-be self-improvers and wealth-accumulators in north American ghettoes and beyond.[23] The latest book, *Midas Touch: Why Some Entrepreneurs Get Rich And Why Most Don't*, is one of several that have been co-written with Donald Trump and the Hollywood icon Will Smith has been another great publicist for Kiyosaki's approach to wealth and finance.[24] The books are published in the genre of self-help literature but overlap into the imaginative territory marked out in the tradition of fiction that descends from Horatio Alger.[25] Kiyosaki trades upon the idea that his readers are being provided with secret, arcane knowledge about wealth and income which has hitherto been the exclusive preserve of the rich. His original format staged the transfer of this precious information in the odd, autobiographical form of a family romance distinguished by two contending paternal influences. The first was Kiyosaki's own 'poor' biological father, an over-educated, salaried professor with a high income but no wealth who made the grave mistake of imagining that the family dwelling was an asset rather than a liability. The second was the entrepreneurial dynamo whose life-lessons supplied the strategic, pedagogical core of the first book: the father of one of Kiyosaki's childhood friends. This was a book about the proper modes of masculinity as much as the correct technique for accumulating wealth. Written long before the sub-prime mortgage scandal, much of it was devoted to the time-worn strategy of buying multiple properties and then renting them out. More insidious is the work that the newly-enlightened, wealth-bound man is expected to perform on himself in order to ensure that he has properly adopted a rich person's view of the world and its manifold opportunities which derive in no small measure from successful prosecution of colonial warfare.

Rich dad used to tell Mike and me stories about his trips to Texas. 'If you really want to learn the attitude of how to handle risk, losing and failure, go to San Antonio and visit the Alamo. The Alamo is a great story of brave people who chose to fight, knowing there was no hope of success against overwhelming odds. They chose to die instead of surrendering. It's an inspiring story worthy of study: nonetheless, it's still a tragic military defeat. They got their butts kicked. A failure if you will. They lost. So how do Texans handle failure? They still shout, "Remember The Alamo"'.[26]

AN AMERICAN IDEOLOGY

Far from the Lone Star State, many of these themes have been taken up in the writing and proselytising of Britain's black nationalists. Work done by one of the most interesting of them, Pascoe Sawyers, becomes an index of how that political tendency has been transformed during the last two decades. His goals are rather more grand than merely individual wealth acquisition. A self-published primer *MePLC: Your Life Is Your Business* was inspired by the work of a number of north America's conservative apostles of self-help: Brian Tracy, Earl Nightingale, Jim Rohn. Conveniently, it also boasts a preface by the ubiquitous Tim Campbell and provides a wealth of useful opportunities to consider the theoretical counterpointing of vernacular neoliberalism among black communities in Britain.[27]

Though he had an extensive track record in the field of local government, Sawyers' personal website announces that he is now an influential 'leadership development' consultant and author of a 'ground-breaking personal development book ... in which, among other things, he identifies being Fearless, Optimistic, Creative, Unique and a Storyteller as the five key traits shown by individuals who are effective "leaders of self"'.[28] That coinage bears the imprint of the Afrocentric psychology of Na'im Akbar, another Winfrey guest.[29] It is a telling phrase which might also be read profitably as an update of Marcus Garvey's near-mystical commitment to the racial ideal of 'self-first'.[30]

Logically, one cannot be anything other than a leader of others but this confusing concept of self-leadership neatly distils some of the tensions in a poetic and autopoietic idiom which requires the multiplication of the unitary self as part of a retreat from the world. Cultivation of the will necessitates a privatisation of resistance. The same jarring concept neatly captures this inward turn as well as the scalar disruption involved in the implosion and disaggregation of the social under the pressures of neoliberalism's impact. We are reminded that there is no such thing as society. The slick substitution of identity for political solidarity fixes the transformation consequent upon the privatisation and individualisation of anti-racist endeavour that generous readers might detect in Sawyers' poetic blending of self-help pieties and management-speak with well-worn orientalist and black nationalist themes: 'Me, myself and I are the only people I have total control over, which is why, in the final analysis, my life is unashamedly about me, me, me'.[31] The link between this perspective and racial solidarity remains obscure.

During the 1990s, Sawyers had been editor of *The Alarm*, a lively, independent black nationalist publication based in northwest London that combined cultural and political content in supposed service of panAfrican solidarity and collective community development. Its occult, Afrocentric disposition aside, *The Alarm* was friendly to the then rising agency of the Nation of Islam and drew inspiration from their continuing commitment to the collective racial gains that could be won through small business activity. This has remained a strategic priority for the organisation during the intervening years. Reporting recently on the seventeenth (2012) annual Black Enterprise Entrepreneurs Conference and Expo, the Nation of Islam newspaper, *The Final Call* commented that

> The number of Black-owned businesses in the US had 'increased by 60.5 percent between 2002 and 2007, raking in receipts of $137.5 billion. Yet despite this growth, Black-owned businesses still make up only seven percent of all US businesses and 87 percent of Black businesses had

sales of less than $50,000 ... 54.5 percent have only between one and four employees'.

A torrent of statistics framed the news that this year's conference included a special presentation by Tavis Smiley, the media celebrity, business partner and best friend of radical, prophetic socialist Professor Cornel West. In his address to the NOI gathering, Smiley 'shared some of the successes and challenges of building his brand, which includes a publishing company, speakers' bureau and media entities'.[32]

Neither the demographics nor the spatialisation of Britain's minority communities correspond with the approaches to wealth, class and community that emerged from the US racial nomos and are commonplace in its particular traditions of black capitalism. So, Sawyers moves further into an explicitly neoliberal idiom by developing the timely suggestion that 'we are all chief executives in our own Personal Leadership Company and [showing] why accepting that your life is a business is the first and most important step along the road to fulfilling your aspirations, whatever they are'.[33] This dubious proposition is probably the obverse of debates about the legal personhood of corporate bodies and their ability to benefit from the juridical order of individual rights. It highlights where the ebbing traditions of Ethiopianism and vindicationism have yielded to generalised neoliberal dogma and a managerialist ideology.

Sawyers is open about the origins of his approach in US history and culture. In an interesting section of the book on the fundamental importance of optimism, a positive mental attitude and adding positive emotions to your 'MePLC emotional bank account' he suggests connections between his philosophical approach and that of a range of north American worthies from William James to Peter Drucker via Henry Ford.

There is a risk of taking this narcissistic rhetoric too seriously and misinterpreting its metaphorical power. However, a significant threshold has been crossed when we move on from saying that our life is like a business to saying that it is, in fact, a business like any, or all, others. There is a vast deal of difference between approaching one's life as a business and relating to it as if it were, for example, either a gift from God or a work of art. In Sawyers' approach, business seems to have taken over the space previously inhabited by those alternatives: the first sacred and the second profane. Of course, the supplanting of the 'Afro-baptist' tradition by forms of evangelical Christianity as concerned with the accumulation of wealth and power as with gaining access to heaven is another recent change which supports the generalisation of neoliberal ideas.[34] One African evangelical church based in London attracts its multicultural congregation with promotional material that does not mention God or Heaven specifically but lays emphasis instead upon technical 'tools' such as wealth creation and personal development seminars. Their recruitment website sets out what prospective visitors to their holy events can expect to find:

> An interactive 90-minute seminar of [sic] the power of realisation will be delivered, complete with prayers, real-life stories and much more! Please note that this event does not promise to change your life but is guaranteed to provide tools that have been tested by many, that can motivate and empower you to achieve the change you desire. You are advised to arrive early to avoid disappointment as seating at the various locations is limited.[35]

HIPHOP: MARTIALITY, MASCULINITY, MACHIAVELLI

Enthusiasm for the selfish pursuit of riches has been disseminated through the medium of hiphop culture where it has been combined with ruthlessness and an explicit appetite for domination and manipulation that is also apparently a business asset. An excellent contemporary example of this confluence is provided by the activities of rapper, producer and entrepreneur Curtis Jackson aka 50 Cent. Jackson is a complex figure whose Republican political affiliation and broad business interests illustrate the realignment I am exploring. He is something like a popular avatar of the demotic neoliberalism that is both steeped in and warranted by several generations of uplift and self-reliance narratives that supplied ideational ballast to earlier versions of the proposition that liberation from racial hierarchy could be achieved through the medium of black capitalism. Once again, it would be entirely wrong to imagine that the allure of this kind of example is limited by its exclusive appeal to African Americans or other black people.

Late in 2009, 50 Cent published a book about how to conduct oneself morally in social life and in business. It was called *The 50th Law* and was co-written with Robert Greene, a successful author who had come to 50's attention as a result of earlier volumes on ruthless business strategy and psychology. One of these, *The 48 laws of power* – an avowedly Machiavellian self-help handbook – had proved highly appealing to a young African American readership weaned on the politer fare churned out by mainstream music biz entrepreneurs like Russell Simmons who had co-written a bestseller in 2007 – with a foreword by Donald Trump – that promised access to a mere twelve laws which could orient readers to both success and happiness.[36] They had turned in that direction seeking guidance and discovered a contemporary successor to those Victorian publications that specified how to take charge of one's own destiny in the most difficult circumstances. The importance of Greene's book can be gauged from the fact that it has proved to be extremely popular in US prison libraries where it has edged Malcolm X's autobiography into second place as the most requested volume.[37] Its success resulted in Greene becoming a consultant to a range of corporate actors. His trademark writing technique employs aphoristic fragments drawn from an unlikely pantheon – Bismarck, Catherine the Great, Mao Tse Tung, Haile Selassie and various others – in order to illustrate real-world application of his 48 rules which are designed to guide the acquisition and exercise of power. He employs what he announces loudly is a self-consciously amoral approach, mimicking Machiavellian and Nietzschean language and leaving the informed reader to weigh the ethical implications of his laws they may opt to implement.[38] This way of proceeding provides a tepid, mainstream endorsement of the thug-life gangsterdom affirmed in the uplift-legend of 50 Cent's well-remunerated journey from the streets, via the operating table, to the recording studio and, eventually, the boardroom. Greene's books became influential among hiphop's organic intellectuals many of whom are reported to have had his homiletic aphorisms tattooed onto their buffed-up bodies. Predictably, Greene's work is name-checked in numerous hiphop tunes while his connection to 50 Cent has rewarded the latter a welcome measure of respectability with which to lard his affected contempt for others judged weaker than himself.[39] Unlike 50, Greene has proclaimed himself to be a supporter of the Democratic party. He restated his liberal politics in a 2012 interview with *The Guardian*. He says:

I'm a huge Obama supporter, Romney is satan to me. The great thing about America is that you can come from the worst circumstances and become something remarkable. It's Jay-Z and 50 Cent and Obama and my Jewish ancestors – that's the America we want to celebrate. Not the vulture capitalist. These morons like Mitt Romney, they produce nothing. Republicans are feeding off fairytales and that's what did them in this year and hopefully will keep doing them in forever, because they're a lot of scoundrels.[40]

In this context, it is important to mention that the jointly written volume was produced to resemble a Bible. The edges of its pages were gilded and the cover was embellished with an ominous gothic script in Latin: 'Nihil timendum est' (fear nothing). With that choice, the authors and the publisher's marketing department tried to make a selling point out of the fact that the book is addressed to the crisis of meaning generated by the disassociation of Ethiopianism, PanAfricanism and their Christian underpinnings.

Rising to that challenge, Green and 50 Cent attempt a comprehensive reformulation of African American history and its modern cultural canon. Miles Davis, Charlie Parker, Malcolm X, Dostoyevsky, Nietzsche, Henri Bergson and a host of other notables were ventriloquised to facilitate the reconfiguration of African American culture as a paean to the psychological and moral attributes of the hyper-individuated, neo-liberal self, cast in the ideal form of the merciless and fearless business leader unencumbered by doubt of any kind. The orientalism of this idiom is brought home not only by the frequent citations to Sun Tzu but also in a pseudo-Buddhist stream of ascetic commentary that affords a sequence of alibis for absolute selfishness. Perhaps unexpectedly, this strand of thought culminates in the suggestion that life is best lived against the horizon of death.

The final chapter in this ghettofied journey from *Amour propre* back to *Amour de soi* is entitled 'Confront Your Mortality: the sublime' and takes its epigraph from Frederick Douglass' famous combat with the brutal overseer Edward Covey.[41] The book concludes contradictorily with an invocation of oceanic connection to everything that resolves into 50 Cent's final pearl of wisdom:

> When I nearly died, it made me think – this can happen again at any second. I better hurry and do what I want. I started to live like I never lived before. When the fear of death is gone, then nothing can bother you and nobody can stop you.[42]

The place of death in what is now an identifiably New Age script, suggests that this variety of self-governance is based in business ethics but extends into a solipsistic, determinedly anti-social approach to life. Its patented individualism conforms proudly to military specifications but is purged of either duty or lateral obligation to others. This is a world without reciprocity that connects with the rigors of incarceration as well as to the non-negotiable rules of a natural hierarchy in which aristocrats of the will can dominate others without the unwelcome intrusion of conscience.

Something of the same masculinist voice guides a whole apparatus of mentoring, role-modeling and the other reparative schemes premised upon the notion that the destiny of black communities resides essentially in the integrity of their beleaguered manhood which can be transformed by a series of technical initiatives. In Britain, boys and young men provided the initial target for governmental intervention. They were judged to have been presented negatively in the media but rather than address the media habits implicated in that outcome, government agencies would rather try to re-engineer the outlook and conduct of the boys themselves.

> ... research has highlighted the largely negative image of black boys and young black men in the media. The outcome has been a recognised need to improve the visibility of positive black male role models at a national level.[43]

This approach is symptomatic of neoliberalism's preferences for post- and virtual sociality over the slow labour of building solidarity in real time. It is drawn from a scheme to re-make black identity through the reconfiguration of gender relations that was initially elevated into government planning by New Labour's 2008 REACH project.[44]

Since then, war in Afghanistan and elsewhere has become much more important in marking out the boundaries of the UK's imagined community. The result is a novel, diverse configuration of authoritarian political culture in which burgeoning militarisation is addressed, among other things, to the projection of the United Kingdom as a nation that is increasingly integrated and only residually multicultural.

Any stubbornly persistent cultural variations are made visible through the conduct of gender relations which require proper management if aspiration, opportunity and the conditions for assimilation are to be maximised. Only that holy labour can really restore the nation's departed greatness and conserve its ebbing cultural distinctiveness assailed less by encounters with alterity than by the corrosive impact of neoliberal capitalism.

The distinctly biopolitical dynamic at work in the embedding of a neoliberal outlook has been treated at length by others.[45] Here, I want to point out only that, in line with the new role of sporting endeavour as a technology that divides the world tidily into elite winners and a mass of precarious losers, it also reveals the changing axiology of racial difference and the new currency of an unruly multiculture far too easily captured and harnessed to serve corporate ends. Small wonder that after being central to the festive Olympic celebration of Britain's NHS, Jessica Ennis, the poster-girl for a post-imperial country's dynamic futurity, ended up leasing her own image to become a 'partner' in the corrosive business of selling private health care. Jessica Ennis took on the role of 'vitality ambassador' for the insurance company Pruehealth.

> I think the Vitality programme is absolutely brilliant – we all love to be rewarded for hard work and Vitality has so many ways to incentivise its members. Everything I stand for is echoed in the values of Vitality and I hope I can make people see that achieving your personal health goals is really a matter of planning the journey and sticking with it.[46]

WHAT THIS ARGUMENT IS NOT

In some earlier work, I tried to turn attention towards the revolutionary conservatism of sections of the trans-national black movement in the twentieth century.[47] At that time, a central seam of black nationalist theory had encompassed occultist and corporatist tendencies which, in different ways, carried the technocultural and hierarchical stamps of a generic fascist culture. Since then, those tendencies have not only moved closer to the mainstream but also proved compatible with the ruthless 'Machiavellian' inclinations of much managerialist ideology and the selfish individualism of the thug turned CEO – the same, determined, upwardly-mobile figure re-affirmed in the writing of Robert Greene and 50 Cent. There are multiple contradictions in that formation. The hustler ethic espoused reflexively at an ironic distance by Jay Z in his autobiographical volume *Jay Z Decoded* is not, for example, readily amenable to the strict, penal discipline that contextualises the pretentious, pseudo-philosophical speculations of Greene and 50. However, they are both part of the same substantial political shift in which selfishness and privatisation have displaced racial structures onto an interpersonal scale and facilitated the replacement of imperfect democracy by what we are told is the non-negotiable force of a natural hierarchy.

This limited intervention can only scratch the surface of a deep and complex cultural history. Like the relationship between individual success and the possibility of collective uplift, the strategy, which suggests that the routine damage wrought by racial orders can be privately overcome through the acquisition of personal wealth, remains an enormous issue. Their histories must be reconstructed with great care. They open eventually into larger problems bearing upon the ways in which successive forms of capitalism have been able to solicit the co-operation of their primary victims into their own exploitation and destruction.

I would like to be able to take for granted that these modes of domination always involve conflict but it is probably better to be more explicit and acknowledge that even sporadic and reactive resistance against them matters greatly. Those immediate reactions can carry the possibility of alternative ways of organising life and work even in environments where such speculation has been forbidden. Yet that precious, necessary resistance can sometimes be difficult to distinguish from accommodation. Its ambiguities mean that it should not be banalised but nor should we pretend that it is always likely to triumph in attractive, dialectical or teleological patterns. The elemental struggles for justice and human dignity can have no end point, so there is no final triumph to be won. Rather than focus on endless resistance supported by tireless criticism, this short piece asks not only how particular groups of people have become resigned to neoliberal capitalism but also how they have been induced to enter into its hall of distorting mirrors seeking the hope that by buying in rather than selling out, their lives and the world will become better.

I want to emphasise that the contradictory motivations of neoliberalism's dupes and footsoldiers are not being ridiculed here. This should be read as a plea that their reactions should be taken seriously – certainly more seriously than the pedlars and celebrants of neoliberal theology are inclined to take the false hopes they disseminate with such cruel cynicism. I also feel obliged to state that I am not wholly against the idea that accountable management of institutions might, on occasion, improve their functioning. However, I do not think that the uniform or ritual application of vacuous self-help and managerial theories is essentially positive or that their sometimes bizarre poetics are likely to defend or enhance democracy in the workplace.

Neoliberal techniques of power, management and communication have repeatedly been allied with technological change to generate conflict, compound inequality and increase unhappiness. They are deployed as part of a battle to control work processes and fatally to diminish the autonomy of working people.[48] This position cuts against the achievements of a whole political generation of black community activists who have, with varying degrees of enthusiasm, accepted the privatisation of the struggle against racial inequality and hierarchy and begun to sell their expertise and insight in the form of consultancy services. As the dreams of collective uplift have been replaced by the practical gravitas of evidence-based expert guidance, this group has moved in to contest the heavily fortified spaces of corporate and governmental power, armed with all the tools and techniques of the neoliberal revolution which are disposed to refine and enhance capitalist control of social and cultural life rather than to feed the possibility of any alternative to it. If they have not become resigned to the unjust condition of the world, they must imagine it can be tinkered with and that the lot of minorities will be improved as a result. To put it mildly, I retain grave doubts about what can be achieved by implementing the credo of 'diversity management' in the private sector and I have looked in vain for reflexive, critical commentaries on the impact of these supposed reforms on the fading life of Britain's dwindling public sector institutions. There, the expertise of diversity management in policy development and in institutional administration has usually been an aid to the privatisation process.

Given past responses to my work, it is necessary for me to conclude by saying that I do not regard black people as uniquely gullible or think that they are any more vulnerable than anybody else to being tricked by the operations of totalising, neoliberal ideology. It bears emphasis that minority audiences or readerships are by no means always the primary market for racial stories of authoritarian (self)discipline and eventual redemption. Contemporary racism will delight in narratives of this type which terminate in the idea that if one is prepared to graft, even deeply entrenched racial hierarchy and inequality can be overcome. Instead of that verdict, struggles against racism, to protect community, pursue justice and enhance democracy both locally and remotely must be remembered and celebrated. However, just like the rest of the left with whose fate the struggles of racialised minorities have long been entwined, dissenting forces have not proved capable of applying a brake to neoliberalism's regressive reforms. The continuing effects of systematic racism on black life cannot be dismissed and there are instances where that very impact seems – perhaps even where racism is to be sacrificed in capital's interests – to have inclined people towards the solutions proffered by neoliberal styles of thought which can be taken over, possessed and made one's own. In other words, the history of being denied recognition as an individual has actually enhanced the appeal of particular varieties of extreme individualism. It is absurd to imagine that the trans-national formation of black Atlantic culture is somehow permanently sanctified by its historic roots in the suffering of slaves. That noble history offers no prophylaxis against the selfish ecstasy of neoliberal norms.

In spite of racism, Britain's black communities are more present in the country's evolving cultural mainstream than we sometimes appreciate. Neoliberal culture and economic habits unearthed the value in previously abjected black life. There is now a distinctive local version of the mainstream themes of the neoliberal revolution which has been shaped by a restless, global capitalism that needs to be able to operate in as many different accents as it can. Where the demotic masquerades as the democratic and populism distorts politics, there is good reason to ask whether an authentic liberatory moment might not reside in postcolonial peoples and minority ethnic groups being just as selfish, ignorant, right-wing and conservative as everybody else? I am not proposing that depressing threshold as the measure of redemption from racial hierarchy. But we must ask whether it is only a vestigial sentimentality that prevents us from being able to accede to it as a new index of Britain's integration.

NOTES

1. Anthony Barnett *Prospect,* February 1999 and 'Corporate Populism', *New Left Review* 3, (May-June 2000). See also Campbell in action: http://www.youtube.com/watch?v=8lC2SYfcDME

2. Alistair Beaton, *The Little Book of Management Bollocks,* Pocket Books, 2001; see also Robert Protherough and John Pick, *Managing Britannia,* Imprint Academic, 2002; and Harry G. Frankfurt, *On Bullshit,* Princeton University Press, 2005.

3. Mark Fisher, *Capitalist Realism,* London, Zero Books, 2009.

4. Robert O. Paxton, *The Anatomy of Fascism,* Knopf, New York, 2004; Ernest K. Bramsted, *Goebbels & the National Socialist Propaganda 1925-45,* Michigan, Cresset Press, 1965.

5. André Gorz, *Farewell To The Working Class,* London, Pluto Press, 1984.

6. Tim Lenoir, 'All but War Is Simulation: The Military-Entertainment Complex' *Configurations,* 8, 3, (Fall 2000): 289-335.

7. http://www.primeperformers.co.uk/sports-speakers, last accessed 3.01.2012.

8. These elements combine most notably in the extraordinary figure of the maimed, black, heroic, ex-marine turned property entrepreneur, Ben McBean. http://www.thesun.co.uk/sol/homepage/features/4824679/Ben-McBean-now-successful-businessman.html.

9. BBC news interview 12.08.12.

10. See for example *Unleashing Aspiration: The Government Response to the Final Report*

of the Panel on Fair Access to the Professions, http://www.ukipg.org.uk/meetings/ further_and_higher_education_working_party/Unleashing-Aspiration_Govt_ Response.pdf, last accessed 2.01.2013. 'The Government recognises that a culture of aspiration, as well as the provision of opportunity, is a central part of a socially mobile society. The aspirations people have to better themselves drive social progress. We will work to ensure young people aim high and aspire to make the most of the opportunities available to them, through an aspiration raising campaign, improved careers guidance and a network of inspirational mentors' (p10). See also Tessa Jowell's 2005 essay 'Tackling the "poverty of aspiration" through rebuilding the Public Realm', http://www.demos.co.uk/files/ tessajowellpublicrealmessay.pdf.

11. http://www.affirmyourlife.co.uk/pdfs/Samuel%20Smiles%20-%20Self-Help%20 -%20National%20and%20Individual.pdf, last accessed 3.01.2012.

12. Eric Foner, *Nothing but Freedom: Emancipation and Its Legacy,* Baton Rouge, Louisiana State University Press, 1983; Wilson J. Moses, *The Golden Age of Black Nationalism,* 1850-1920, Oxford University Press, 1984.

13. Samuel Smiles, *Self Help,* Oxford University Press, 2002, p36.

14. Much of this story has been told by Juliet E.K. Walker, *The History of Black Business in America: Capitalism, Race, Entrepreneurship: Volume 1, To 1865,* UNC Press, 2009.

15. See chapter 3 of Washington's *Up From Slavery,* Dover, Thrift Editions, 2012.

16. Robert J. Norrell, *Up from History: The Life of Booker T. Washington,* Harvard University Press 2009.

17. George Shepperson, 'Notes on Negro American Influences on the Emergence of African Nationalism', *The Journal of African History,* 1, 2, (1960): 299-312.

18. Ida B. Wells and A.M. Duster, *Crusade For Justice,* University of Chicago Press, 1970.

19. Jason Chambers, *Madison Avenue and The Color Line,* Penn University Press, 2008.

20. Hishaam Aidi, 'The Grand (Hip-Hop) Chessboard: Race, Rap and Raison d'État', *Middle East Report* 260, Fall, 2011 pp25-39.

21. William Julius Wilson, *The Truly Disadvantaged,* Chicago University Press, 1989.

22. http://www.richdad.com/.

23. In 2006, the Wall Street Journal estimated that worldwide sales of the original book had topped 26 million, http://online.wsj.com/article/ SB116052181216688592.html?mod=money_page_left_hs.

24. http://www.youtube.com/watch?v=qfKahKFCC-c.

25. See Allen Trachtenberg's introduction to Horatio Alger's novel *Ragged Dick Or, Street Life in New York with the Boot-Blacks,* Signet Classics, 1990.

26. Robert Kiyosaki with Sharon Lechter, *Rich Dad, Poor Dad: what the rich teach their kids that you can learn too,* Time Warner, 2002, p176.

27. The book is also endorsed by Joan Blaney CBE, http://www.joanblaney.org/, last accessed 3.01.2013.

28. http://www.mylifeismybusiness.co.uk/#/about-pascoe/4529937807.

29. See his *The Community of Self,* Mind Productions & Associates; Revised edition, 1985.

30. Marcus Garvey, *Life And Lessons,* Robert A. Hill and Barbara Bair (eds), University of California Press, p5, 1987.

31. Sawyers, op. cit., p6.

32. http://www.finalcall.com/artman/publish/Business_amp_Money_12/article_8926.shtml, last accessed 3.01.2013; http://www.blackenterprise.com/events/entrepreneurs-conference/ last accessed 3.02.2013.

33. This text is taken from the cover of *MePLC: Your Life Is Your Business*, My Life Is My Business Publications, 2007.

34. Hermione Harris, *Yoruba in Diaspora: An African Church in London*, Palgrave, 2006, http://doi.org/b4ncj9.

35. http://realiseevent.com/index.php/the-event/, last accessed 2.01.2013.

36. Russell Simmons with Chris Morrow *Do You!* Gotham Books, New York, 2007; see also Russell Simmons with Chris Morrow, *Super Rich: A Guide To Having It All*, Gotham Books, New York, 2011.

37. Dwight Garner, 'The Readers Behind Bars Put Books to Many Uses', *New York Times*, 19.10.2010, http://www.nytimes.com/2010/10/20/books/20book.html?_r=1, last accessed 3.01.2013.

38. Greene's blog can be found at: http://www.powerseductionandwar.com/, last accessed 3.01.2013.

39. http://www.newyorker.com/archive/2006/11/06/061106fa_fact_paumgarten#ixzz0ewY9nDQZ, last accessed 3.01.2013.

40. Robert Greene interviewed by Dorian Lynskey in *The Guardian*, 3.12.2012. http://www.guardian.co.uk/books/2012/dec/03/robert-greene-48-laws-of-power?INTCMP=SRCH, last accessed 2.01.2013.

41. See my discussion of this episode in *Black Atlantic* Harvard University Press, 1993.

42. 50 Cent and Robert Greene, *The 50th Law*, Profile Books, p288.

43. Dear Mr Gilroy,

I am sending you this email by way of introduction, I work for ******** & ******* and we have been asked to assist Hazel Blears (Sec State, DCLG) on a new initiative called REACH. This has come out of the Stephen Lawrence Steering Group and the Race Equality Advisory Panel – research has highlighted the largely negative image of black boys and young black men in the media. The outcome has been a recognised need to improve the visibility of positive black male role models at a national level.

That's where we come in. We've been asked to help find the government's first national black male role models. We are approaching people who might have an interest in taking part who could be an inspiration to young black men. The time commitment will be one day per month for a period of one year and the role will be to act as representatives on TV, radio, give talks, go into schools etc. We are looking for 20 role models but everyone who expresses an interest will be asked to play a role in some capacity. We are letting people know about the initiative and encouraging applications. I have enclosed the details for your information and would be extremely interested in your thoughts and ideas.

(For your information the closing date has been extended to 15th September)

With kind regards

44. http://webarchive.nationalarchives.gov.uk/20081106035133/; http://campaigns.direct.gov.uk/reach/; http://webarchive.nationalarchives.gov.uk/20081106035133/; http://www.direct.gov.uk/en/campaigns/Reach/dg_170589, last accessed 3.01.2013.

45. Nikolas Rose, *The Politics of Life Itself*, Princeton University Press, 2006.
46. http://pruhealth.pruhealth.co.uk/individuals/vitalityjessica, last accessed 6.02.2013.
47. Paul Gilroy, *Between Camps* [second edition], Routledge, 2005.
48. See for example Richard Preston's 'Smiley culture: Pret A Manger's secret ingredients', *Daily Telegraph*, 9.03.2012, http://www.telegraph.co.uk/foodanddrink/9129410/Smiley-culture-Pret-A-Mangers-secret-ingredients.html, last accessed 3.01.2013.

Foucault's 'Critique' of Neoliberalism: Rawls and the Genealogy of Public Reason

Paul Patton

Foucault devoted seven out of the twelve lectures he delivered at the Collège de France in 1979 to German and American neoliberalism.[1] Readers often assume that the purpose of these lectures was to 'critique' neoliberalism, where the nature of this critique is to be understood in the terms of one or other of the programmatic formulations he proposed around this time. For example, in his 'What is Critique?' lecture to the *Société Française de Philosophie* the previous year, he suggested that the critical question he sought to pursue was not why we are governed but how: 'how not to be governed like that, by that, in the name of those principles, with such and such an objective in mind and by means of such procedures, not like that, not for that, not by them'.[2] John Protevi follows this formula in suggesting that the purpose of the 1979 lectures on neoliberal governmentality was 'to provide tools by which the governed can understand the rationality that informs the way that they are governed and thereby better resist intolerable governance'.[3] In 'What is Enlightenment?' Foucault suggested that his genealogical practice of criticism should be understood as an historical investigation of the events and processes that have made us what we are so that we can find ways to escape our present social identities. In this sense, the aim of critique is to 'separate out, from the contingency that has made us what we are, the possibility of no longer being, doing, or thinking what we are, do or think'.[4] I drew upon this formulation in a 2010 essay in suggesting that, to the extent that Foucault's brief genealogy of neoliberal governmentality was also a critical history of the present, its aim was 'to find points of exit from or transformation in present social reality'.[5]

Comments such as these, I now think, are evidence of widespread confusion about the object and aims of Foucault's lectures on neoliberalism.

This confusion involves, firstly, what is meant by neoliberalism in these lectures. They focus on the forms of rationalisation, objectives and modes of exercise of a particular kind of governmental power, rather than the policies and procedures of actually existing neoliberal governments. These lectures help us to understand the rationality, objectives and methods of this kind of power. They do not pursue the strategy outlined in the first part of 'The Subject and Power' that consists in taking forms of resistance against particular modalities of power as the 'starting point' or the 'catalyst' for their analysis.[6] They do not address the strategies by which neoliberal techniques of government were introduced or the struggles they may have provoked, nor do they address the different political dynamics that allowed what David Harvey calls the construction of consent in favour of neoliberal government policies, much less the kinds and degree of economic restructuring and social differentiation that followed.[7] None of this should be surprising when we consider that these lectures were delivered shortly before the election of Margaret Thatcher's government in Britain in May 1979 and over a year before the election of Ronald Reagan as US president in 1980.

There is also considerable confusion about the nature of the critical project that is undertaken in these lectures. I think it is more modest and open-ended than the kinds of critique referred to above. In the third lecture on German neoliberalism, Foucault suggests that his aim is simply to grasp neoliberal government 'in its singularity' (*Birth of Biopolitics*, p30). Certainly his reconstruction of the program of government outlined by the German ordoliberals serves further polemical aims such as challenging what he called the 'state phobia' that was common among the French left at the time. Foucault's lectures explicitly sought to disqualify the kind of political analysis that simply applies pre-existing historical moulds in order to suggest, for example, that neoliberalism is just Adam Smith revived, or the final achievement of the market society described by Marx, or the further extension of state power. But these are side-effects of the principle objective of these lectures, which was the same as that pursued in all his historical studies, namely 'to let knowledge of the past work on the experience of the present' (*Birth of Biopolitics*, p30). Because knowledge of the past can work on our experience of the present in many ways, this is a more open-ended objective than those suggested by the attempts to characterise the lectures as critique.

In the spirit of this kind of historical reflection on the present, I want to suggest another reading of those lectures that connects them with the kind of critique of liberal political reason that we find in the work of John Rawls. Rawls' aim was to spell out the normative principles of a just and democratic government, along with at least the outlines of an institutional and policy framework within which such political power should be exercised. In exploring this connection, I follow Colin Gordon's lead in his 1991 introduction to *The Foucault Effect*, when he suggested that it would be helpful to 'establish lines of communication with twentieth-century enquiries into allied areas of political philosophy and the history of political ideas'.[8] An obvious obstacle to this enterprise is the apparent gulf between Foucault's predominantly descriptive enterprise and Rawls's overtly normative approach. I will show that Foucault is more normative than is often realised and that Rawls is not simply normative but also descriptive of the institutions and policies of just and fair liberal government. In effect, Rawls's long- overlooked conception of a property-owning democratic society suggests an egalitarian alternative to the forms of neoliberal governmentality described by Foucault, and even more so to the forms of neoliberalism actually implemented in the decades since Foucault's lectures.

NORMATIVITY IN RAWLS AND FOUCAULT

Rawls is unashamedly utopian in setting out the normative principles that should inform the government of a just and democratic society. He seeks to describe 'how things might be, taking people as a just and well-ordered society would encourage them to be'.[9] A just and well-ordered society is one in which three conditions are met: first, all citizens, or at least 'an enduring majority' of citizens, accept and know that others accept one or other of a family of reasonable liberal conceptions of justice; second, the basic structure of the society is known to be effectively regulated by one or more of this family of reasonable liberal conceptions; third, citizens have an effective sense of justice and so comply with the basic institutions which they regard as reasonable (*Political Liberalism*, ppxlvii,35). These conditions are intended to spell out the kind of political unity available to citizens of a modern liberal democracy. This is the unity of citizens who, while they do not share the same moral commitments, beliefs and ways of life, collectively exercise coercive political power over one another. The exercise of such political power is legitimate, according to Rawls, when it takes place in accordance with a constitution the essentials of which all citizens as free and equal may reasonably be expected to endorse in the light of principles and ideals acceptable to their common human reason (*Political Liberalism*, p137).

By contrast, Foucault consistently avoids questions of legitimation in favour of a focus on the question of how power is exercised. As he says in 'The Subject and Power': '"How" not in the sense of "How does it manifest itself?" but "How is it exercised?" and "What happens when individuals exert power over others?"'[10] At the beginning of the 1979 lectures he is explicit about his intention to apply this approach, which he had previously developed in connection with a 'micro-physics' of the forms of power exercised on bodies and small groups of individuals, to the ways in which the practice of large-scale government of entire societies has been theorised. He proposes to study different kinds of governmentality in a similarly descriptive manner and to avoid reliance upon universals such as 'the sovereign, sovereignty, the people, subjects, the state and civil society' (*Birth of Biopolitics*, p2) He suggests that part of the reason for his interest in neoliberal government was to show that this normatively neutral focus on the ways in which power is exercised was not confined to the infra-state domain of micropowers but should be considered simply as 'a point of view, a method of decipherment which may be valid for the whole scale, whatever its size' (*Birth of Biopolitics*, p186).

Foucault's avoidance of questions of legitimation and justification in favour of a focus on the question of how power is exercised does not mean that normative concerns play no role in his analyses. Another justification that he gives for studying neoliberal governmentality is what he calls 'a reason of critical morality' that relates to the intellectual and political context in which these lectures were written (*Birth of Biopolitics*, p186). The lectures included an explicit challenge to the 'state phobia' that regarded state power as a phenomenon with its own essential characteristics and dynamics. At the heart of this state phobia is an essentialist conception of the state that enables administrative, welfare, bureaucratic, fascist and totalitarian forms of state all to be regarded as expressions of the same underlying form, such that 'there is a kinship, a sort of genetic continuity or evolutionary implication between different forms of state' (*Birth of Biopolitics*, p187).

Foucault objects, firstly, that this essentialist conception of the state allows its protagonists to deduce a political analysis from first principles and to avoid altogether the need for empirical and historical knowledge of contemporary political reality. Secondly, he points out that state phobia is not confined to the left and that the versions current in his intellectual milieu overlook the long tradition of suspicion of the state from within twentieth century liberalism. His analysis of the origins and emergence of German neoliberalism seeks to show how this kind of critique of the state and its 'intrinsic and irrepressible dynamism' was already formulated during the period from 1930 to 1945 in the context of efforts to criticise the whole range of interventionist policies from Keynesianism to National Socialism and Soviet state planning (*Birth of Biopolitics*, p189). He argues that the influence of anti-state liberalism in the post-war period meant that all those on the left who participate in this state phobia are 'following the direction of the wind and that in fact, for years and years, an effective reduction of the state has been on the way' (*Birth of Biopolitics*, p191).

Foucault's efforts in the course of these lectures to distance himself from state phobia imply that he had no fundamental objection to government or to the institutions and policies that this entails. He was not an anarchist. On the contrary, during the period in which these lectures were written, Foucault was at the very least a willing observer of efforts to rethink the political orientation and strategies of the French left. Recent commentators have made much of his association with elements of the so-called 'Second Left', a minority current within the Socialist Party with links to the CFDT.[11] The anti-statist 'self-management' approach of the latter shared some of the concerns of neoliberals. It may or may not be true, as Behrent claims, that 'Foucault's interest in neoliberalism appears to owe much to his attraction to the Second Left'.[12] However, it is against the background of such debates, and electoral failure of the Left in 1978, that he raised a question about the nature of socialist governmentality at the end of the fourth lecture: 'What would really be the governmentality appropriate to socialism? Is there a governmentality appropriate to socialism?' (*Birth of Biopolitics*, p94) His answer was that if there is such a thing as socialist governmentality, it remained to be invented.

It is worth dwelling for a moment on this question 'what would be the governmentality *appropriate* to socialism?' since it points to the issues addressed by normative political theorists such as Rawls. Socialism here can only refer to an ideal conception of society. How could this question be answered without reference to the normative principles that would characterise a socialist society? These might include the absence or at least the diminution of class divisions in relation to wealth, opportunity, or the value of civil and political liberties. More positively, they might include principles that seek to give effect to the equality of all citizens, such as a right to basic subsistence or equality of opportunity for those similarly endowed and motivated. They might include the kind of presumption of equality that underlies Rawls's difference principle whereby departures from equal access to primary social goods are allowed only on the condition that they benefit the least well off. Foucault does not address these questions, either on his own behalf or in relation to the policy prescriptions of neoliberal government. Egalitarian political philosophers, liberals and socialists alike, do address these questions. Moreover, it is interesting to note that some egalitarian normative theorists, including Rawls, have also been receptive to elements of neoliberal thought.

RAWLS AND LIBERAL GOVERNMENTALITY

In view of his focus on the principles of just, legitimate and stable government, it would be easy to suppose that Rawls does not pay much attention to the ways in which political power can be exercised over and above certain minimal constraints imposed by his theory of justice. In Foucault's terms, this would amount to saying that he does not concern himself with the 'how' of governmental power.[13] This is a mistake. The two principles of justice that Rawls argues would be chosen by rational and reasonable parties behind a veil of ignorance both have substantial implications for economic institutions and policies. Even though they are proposed as consequences of an ideal theory that addresses a simplified model of society, the institutional and policy requirements of Rawls's justice as fairness amount to elements of governmentality in Foucault's terms.

The first principle requires that any legitimate government will have to maintain a secure and stable system of basic civil and political liberties. Importantly, in Rawls's later formulations of this principle, governments also have to ensure a 'fair value' of those liberties for all citizens, which means approximate equality in the resources available to citizens to make use of the formally equal civil and political liberties: 'Each person has an equal claim to a fully adequate scheme of equal basic rights and liberties, which scheme is compatible with the same scheme for all; and in this scheme the equal political liberties, and only those liberties, are to be guaranteed their fair value' (*Political Liberalism*, p5). The second principle of justice as fairness requires that governments will have to ensure fair equality of opportunity and that inequalities in the distribution of primary social goods will work to the advantage of the least well off: 'Social and economic inequalities are to satisfy two conditions: first, they are to be attached to positions and offices open to all under conditions of fair equality of opportunity; and second, they are to be to the greatest benefit of the least advantaged members of society' (*Political Liberalism*, p6). Fair equality of opportunity requires, in addition to the absence of overt discrimination against any particular caste, class, sex or religious affiliation, genuinely equal prospect of achievement for everyone endowed with similar abilities and motivation. This implies a need for policies to counteract negative effects on opportunity produced by socio-economic inequalities or the legacies of historical injustice: for example, public education and other 'opportunity- improving early childhood interventions'.[14]

The principle of fair equality of opportunity also requires the provision of healthcare services for all citizens. One of the ways in which Rawls simplified the model of society to which his justice principles applied in *A Theory of Justice* (1971) was by assuming the absence of disease or disability, such that citizens were supposed to be fully functional over their normal life span. Others have argued that we can bring the theory closer to real world conditions by dropping this assumption and supposing that fair equality of opportunity requires the provision of healthcare broadly defined to include public health policies, environmental protection as well as access to personal medical services.[15]

Public education and health care may well go some way towards achieving fair equality of opportunity. However, complete equality will not be achieved so long as the family remains the primary institution for childcare. For this reason, Rawls takes the second principle of justice to require measures to reduce if not to eliminate underlying social and economic inequality between families. Similarly, in relation to the fair value of political liberties required by the first principle, measures such as the public financing of elections and free public discussion on matters of basic justice might go some way towards insulating the political process from the corrosive effects of large concentrations of wealth and capital. However, it is unlikely that such policies alone would be sufficient to preserve fair value of basic liberties. For this reason, Rawls always preferred an economic system known as 'property owning democracy' that he adopted from the British economist James Meade.[16] Meade and other so-called revisionist Labour politicians and advisors during the 1940s and 1950s sought to dramatically reduce social and economic inequality by directly addressing 'the underlying *ex ante* distribution of property and marketable skills rather than simply accepting these as given and undertaking only *ex post* income redistribution through the welfare system'.[17] As an alternative to nationalisation, they proposed measures to ensure the dispersal of property ownership, such as inheritance laws, progressive taxes and incentives or other measures to encourage saving among the less well off.

Rawls's two principles of justice as fairness have been widely but wrongly supposed to provide some form of apologia for social democratic capitalism.[18] In fact, both laissez-faire and welfare state capitalism are ruled out as inconsistent with the requirements of a just economic regime since both allow inequalities of wealth that would undermine the fair value of political liberties and fair equality of opportunity. In the revised version of his lectures published shortly before his death as *Justice as Fairness: A Restatement*, he made it clear that welfare-state capitalism would not preserve fair value of political liberties since it allows large inequalities in the ownership of productive property 'so that the control of the economy and much of political life rests in few hands' (*Justice as Fairness*, p138). The same is true for laissez faire capitalism, but this system is also ruled out on the additional grounds that it would allow differential incomes on the basis of economic efficiency alone, thereby violating the difference principle.

In *Justice as Fairness: A Restatement* Rawls acknowledged that the distinction between property-owning democracy and welfare-state capitalism was not made sufficiently clear in *A Theory of Justice*. He clarified the differences between them and insisted that he always regarded property-owning democracy 'as an alternative to capitalism' (*Justice as Fairness*, pp135-136). The major difference is that, unlike welfare-state capitalism, the institutions of property owning democracy will be designed to disperse wealth and the ownership of capital, thereby preventing the control of economic and political life by a small part of the population. Second, whereas welfare-state capitalism redistributes income to those at the lower end of the scale, property-owning democracy seeks to ensure widespread ownership of productive assets along with access to the education and training that equips individuals with human capital, thereby enabling them to 'manage their own affairs on a footing of a suitable degree of social and economic equality' (*Justice as Fairness*, p139).[19]

Rawls's opposition to unrestrained and welfare-state capitalism does not imply opposition to all forms of market economy. On the contrary, he takes the principles of equal liberties and fair equality of opportunity to require a market-based system in which citizens have a free choice of careers and occupations and in which there is no central direction of labour.[20] On this point, he agrees with Hayek who also defended the importance of free choice of occupation and its association with a market economy. This should not be surprising given that, as the historian Ben Jackson comments with reference to Meade, many of the points made by authors such as Hayek about respecting consumer sovereignty and freedom of occupational choice 'found a sympathetic audience at the time among elements of the social democratic left'.[21] However, in contrast to Hayek and other proponents of minimal government, Rawls distinguished between the allocative and distributive functions of markets. While he insists on their role in the efficient allocation of resources, he denies that the distribution of wealth and other primary social goods should be left to markets alone.[22] State socialism and laissez-faire capitalism are thus eliminated as potential means of achieving just economic government. This leaves two regimes of political economic institutions and policies potentially compatible with the requirements of justice as fairness, namely liberal or market socialism and property-owning democracy. The choice between them is not determined by the principles of justice alone but must be made in the light of the political traditions, social forces and particular historical circumstances within a given country (*Theory of Justice*, p242, 248).

NEOLIBERALISM AND EGALITARIANISM

The emphasis on individual autonomy in Rawls's conception of property-owning democracy provides one indication of the impact of neoliberal ideas on his political economic thought. In fact, the influence of neoliberal ideas on his conception of the nature and functions of government is pervasive. In *A Theory of Justice* he characterised the role of government in terms of providing for public goods that could not otherwise be provided for by market mechanisms, correcting failures and imperfections in market processes such as those resulting from the emergence of monopolies, lack of information or external diseconomies, and generally ensuring that a market economy will function in accordance with the requirements of justice.

I assume that the basic structure is regulated by a just constitution that secures the liberties of equal citizenship (as described in the preceding chapter). Liberty of conscience and freedom of thought are taken for granted, and the fair value of political liberty is maintained. The political process is conducted, as far as circumstances permit, as a just procedure for choosing between governments and for enacting just legislation. I assume also that there is fair (as opposed to formal) equality of opportunity. This means that in addition to maintaining the usual kinds of social overhead capital, the government tries to ensure equal chances of education and culture for persons similarly endowed and motivated either by subsidizing private schools or by establishing a public school system. It also enforces and underwrites equality of opportunity in economic activities and in the free choice of occupation. This is achieved by policing the conduct of firms and private associations and by preventing the establishment of monopolistic restrictions and barriers to the more desirable positions. Finally, the government guarantees a social minimum either by family allowances and special payments for sickness and employment, or more systematically by such devices as a graded income supplement (a so-called negative income tax) (*Theory of Justice*, p243).

The idea of a negative income tax endorsed by Rawls had a long history in post-war neoliberal thought. Milton Friedman put forward an early version of the proposal at the first meeting of the Mont Pélerin Society in 1947 (Origins of Neoliberalism, p146). He later popularised the idea in his *Capitalism and Freedom* (1962).[23] It was explored as a policy option in the US under the Nixon administration (1969-1974). Although it was not adopted at the time, and has never been implemented in its pure form, variants of the proposal have been adopted in the US and elsewhere in the form of earned income tax credits for low income earners. Negative income tax is one of the policies discussed by Foucault in a lecture devoted to the early stages of the adoption of neoliberal ideas in France during the 1970s. He recounts how French economic ministers and advisers during the 1970s considered the abandonment of post-war social security policies based on principles of national solidarity and full employment in favour of a neoliberal social security system that would avoid imposing additional costs and constraints on the operation of a market economy. The introduction of a negative tax that would replace various forms of welfare assistance with monetary payments to those whose income fell below the taxable threshold was one of the policies considered (*Birth of Biopolitics*, pp203-207) This policy offered a way of ensuring a basic level of access to health and other goods and services on the part of those unable to pay for them that would be neutral with regard to the labour market and the economic imperative of maintaining price stability. Foucault suggests that negative taxation amounted to an implementation of the 'rule' that no one be excluded from the economic game. This rule is a consequence of the neoliberal idea that assistance should be provided to those unable to participate in the economic game only in order to ensure the maintenance of an enterprise society (*Birth of Biopolitics*, pp206-207).

The appearance of policy proposals such as negative taxation in the context of Rawls's proposed alternative to capitalism suggests that a market-oriented social order is not necessarily opposed to ideas of equality of opportunity, social justice and economic security. Hayek and Popper discussed the possibility that the Mont Pélerin Society should be open to liberal socialists as well as neoliberals and Hayek made it clear in his opening paper in 1947 that efforts to promote greater economic security and equality were compatible with his conception of a free society (Origins of Neoliberalism, pp136-137). Ben Jackson argues that, at this early stage, neoliberal criticism was not directed at leftist political ideals but rather at the methods advocated to achieve those goals (Origins of Neoliberalism, p136). He provides evidence to show that the primary target of neoliberalism during the 1930s and 1940s was fascist and communist state planning rather than Keynesian macroeconomic policies or the emerging welfare state. Some members of the group, such as Rüstow and Röpke, even argued that a genuinely free and competitive economic order would require intervention to ensure a wider diffusion of private property, along the lines suggested by Meade and the revisionist British socialists: 'their "ordo-liberalism" envisaged the creation of a decentralized economy composed of smaller population centres and enterprises and characterized by a more equal spread of individual property holdings' (Origins of Neoliberalism, p143). Others accepted that taxes on capital, especially inheritance tax, could be legitimate means to promote equal opportunity. While there were some such as von Mises who rejected all forms of state intervention beyond those implied by the minimal role accorded to the 'night watchman' state (i.e. doing little more than guaranteeing the rule of law), others were prepared to support particular forms of state regulation, such as legislation to break up monopolies and large corporations, and even redistribution in the interests of a social minimum wage and equality of opportunity. Jackson suggests that during the early phase of neoliberal policy discussion there was 'a broad acceptance of the need for a state-sponsored minimum income, and of a legitimate role for fiscal policy in narrowing inequalities of opportunity. The early neoliberals were not advocates of a completely unpatterned distribution of income and wealth, nor of constructing a market economy without a safety net' (Origins of Neoliberalism, p145).

***

Reading Foucault's lectures alongside Rawls's political liberalism opens up several lines of communication between his predominantly descriptive approach to political thought and overtly normative approaches. First, from a Rawlsian perspective, we can say that Foucault's sketches toward a history of neoliberal governmentality illuminate the historical character of public reason. A concept of public reason lies at the heart of Rawls's conception of legitimate democratic government. By 'public reason' he means the reasoning of citizens about constitutional essentials and matters of basic justice, including the basic structure of society and its public policies (*Political Liberalism*, p224). In their public deliberation, citizens in a well-ordered and pluralist society must respect a duty of civility and offer reasons to one another in terms that all can reasonably be expected to endorse. The publicly acceptable conceptions of justice that can be objects of overlapping consensus provide a discursive framework within which citizens and public officials can argue in ways that are not beholden to their particular moral, philosophical or religious views. Because this idea of public reason implies that citizens should appeal only to 'beliefs, grounds and political values it is reasonable for others to also acknowledge', it implies relatively stringent restrictions on the kinds of argument that citizens can put forward in relation to constitutional essentials and matters of basic justice (*Justice as Fairness*, p27).

These restrictions do not apply in the realm of what Rawls refers to as background culture, which encompasses 'our personal deliberations and reflections about political questions, or to the reasoning about them by members of associations such as churches and universities' (*Political Liberalism*, p215). Within the sphere of background culture, citizens may argue about all kinds of things related to the political and the public good, including theories of justice and the nature and business of government. This is the sphere of non-public reasoning in which citizens are free to argue from the perspective of their respective comprehensive beliefs and commitments. Foucault's own analyses of neoliberal governmentality, along with his critical remarks about the state phobia prevalent in his own intellectual milieu, are offered from the position of citizen within civil or political society. As such, they belong to the background culture of politics in which Rawls situates his own political philosophy and that of other normative theorists such as Habermas.[24]

Although he does not draw attention to it, Rawls is committed to the idea that public reason is an historical phenomena, subject to change as the family of reasonable political conceptions of justice changes, along with the norms of reasoning, argument and evidence that govern democratic deliberation. It follows that public reason is historical in a way not dissimilar to the 'discursive formations' that Foucault described in his earlier work: these were more or less systematic bodies of statements or things that could be said in a given empirical domain at a given time. So too, in a given society at a given time, what can be said within the sphere of public reason will change as the elements and conditions of public reason themselves change over time.

As well as distinguishing between background culture and public reason, Rawls occasionally refers to the 'public political culture' of democratic societies, where this includes their political institutions and the public traditions of their interpretation (*Political Liberalism*, pp13, 223, 227). It is clear that he means this public political culture to include the range of fundamental ideas that inform the family of liberal conceptions of justice, such as the idea of citizens as free and equal and the idea of society as a fair system of cooperation. Public reason proper lies at the heart of this public political culture. At the same time, the normative ideas that inform liberal conceptions of justice must be supplemented by a range of economic, sociological and psychological ideas in order to be fully developed into a conception of the basic structure and institutions of a just society. These too, we may suppose, form part of the public political culture that informs the various conceptions of justice. Ideas about the proper functions of government, such as reducing inequality or ensuring fair value of political liberties for all, along with the policies by which they might be achieved, clearly fall within the domain of public political culture. So too do the views about the appropriate purposes, functions and techniques of government that Foucault considers under the rubric of governmentality.

While the texts of neoliberal governmentality analysed by Foucault do not fall within the sphere of public reason proper, they do have consequences for the kinds of policies put forward and the forms of reasoning offered in support of those policies. The political and economic theories of the ordoliberals have emerged from the pages of academic journals such as *Ordo* and private forums such as the Mont Pelérin Society to become guiding principles of government throughout the capitalist world. In doing so, they have have filtered into public policies that affect the basic structure of many Western capitalist countries, thereby progressing from background culture to public reason proper. Negative tax provides one concrete example of the manner in which neoliberal thought has generated public policy proposals. Foucault's discussion of American neoliberalism provides further examples of the way in which rational choice approaches to 'human capital' and criminality can lead to policies grounded in economic rationality alone (*Birth of Biopolitics*, pp248-260). At the point where they are put forward as appropriate mechanisms of government, these policies fall within the sphere of public reason as Rawls defines it. In Rawlsian terms, examples such as these show how the elements of background political culture can impact directly on the content of public reason. Neoliberal thought has been a significant vector of change in the nature and content of public reason in liberal democracies over the course of the twentieth century. Foucault's analyses draw attention to some of the sources of the revolutionary changes that have taken place since 1979 in the implicit rules governing what can and cannot be said in the sphere of liberal public reason.

A second line of communication between Foucault's genealogical approach and normative political theory concerns the anticapitalist import of Rawls's egalitarianism. His view of the appropriate institutions and policies of government shows that neoliberal political culture is much broader than the texts covered in Foucault's lectures. It is apparent not only that Rawls has a theory of governmentality in Foucault's sense of the term, but also that this is a theory in which the influence of neoliberal ideas is pervasive. His conception of the appropriate institutions and policies of government conforms to the neoliberal model as Foucault describes it: no longer a separation between the market and the sphere of government but a superimposition of the two, a form of government that accompanies the market economy 'from start to finish' (*Birth of Biopolitics*, p121). That is, a form of government that does not intervene directly in market processes, but one that regulates in order to maintain the conditions for effective competition, to prevent the formation of monopolies, and to ensure that the social conditions are conducive to the effective operation of markets and the effective agency of individuals and groups within those markets. Human

capital theory is a key element of American neoliberalism to which Foucault
devotes several lectures. Its impact is reflected in one of the reasons that
Rawls gives for preferring property-owning democracy over welfare-state
capitalism, namely that while the latter simply redistributes income, the
former aims to ensure widespread ownership of productive assets along with
access to the education and training that equips individuals with human
capital, thereby enabling them to 'manage their own affairs' on the basis
of relative social and economic equality (*Justice as Fairness*, p139).

At the same time, it is clear that Rawls's conception of government
is entirely set within a conception of society as a just and fair system of
cooperation between its members, which in turn leads to the idea that an
economic system in which the ownership of wealth and capital is widely
dispersed is necessary in order to comply with liberal principles of justice.
David Harvey suggests in his discussion of the means by which political
consensus in favour of neoliberal policies was achieved by democratic means
in the US and Britain, in contrast to the ways in which it was achieved by
imperial power in other parts of the world such as Chile or Iraq, that

> Neoliberal rhetoric, with its foundational emphasis upon individual
> freedoms, has the power to split off libertarianism, identity politics,
> multiculturalism, and eventually narcissistic consumerism from the
> social forces ranged in pursuit of social justice through the conquest
> of state power.[25]

This is, he argues, more or less what occurred in the aftermath of the social
and political upheavals of the late 1960s in which campaigns for greater
personal freedoms cohabited with concerns for social justice. Whatever the
merits of this analysis as political sociology of the 1970s and 1980s, it does
imply, as he also notes, that there is no necessary incompatibility between
the values of individual freedom and social justice.

Rawls's political liberalism is one of many attempts to develop a
conception of the nature and function of government that ensures the
freedom of individuals to manage their own lives on a basis of relative
equality.[26] From the perspective of a more comprehensive genealogy of
twentieth century neoliberal economic and political thought, the examples
of Meade, Rawls and other proponents of property-owning democracy
show that there is an egalitarian family of market-oriented approaches to
government that would need to be considered alongside the German and
American varieties of neoliberalism. This egalitarian strand of neoliberal

thought represents a potential source of answers to Foucault's question about the nature of socialist governmentality. As we noted above, answering that question would require consideration of the normative principles that socialist institutions and government policies are intended to serve. The anti-capitalist conception of property-owning democracy is one of many unrealized possibilities that might emerge from the combination of egalitarian political norms and neoliberal techniques of government. Retracing the history of this particular combination might point to further ways in which, to use Foucault's words, knowledge of the past could 'work on our experience of the present'.

Earlier versions of this essay were presented at The Foucault Effect 1991-2011, *Birkbeck College, 3-4 June 2011 and at* New Foucault: A Symposium, *University of Western Sydney, 9 November, 2012. It draws upon a longer chapter, 'Foucault and Rawls: Government and Public Reason,' in Vanessa Lemm and Miguel Vatter (eds),* The Government of Life: Michel Foucault and Neoliberalism, *New York, Fordham University Press, 2014. I am grateful for the suggestions of many people in discussion at these forums, and to John Protevi for his comments on an earlier draft.*

NOTES

1. Michel Foucault, *The Birth of Biopolitics: Lectures at the Collège de France 1978-1979*, Michel Senellart (ed), Graham Burchell (trans), Houndmills, Basingstoke and New York, Palgrave Macmillan, 2008, hereafter *Birth of Biopolitics*.

2. Foucault, 'What is Critique?' in J. Schmidt (ed), *What is Enlightenment?* Berkeley and Los Angeles, University of California Press, 1996, p384.

3. John Protevi, 'What Does Foucault Think is New About Neoliberalism?', *Pli, The Warwick Journal of Philosophy*, 21, (2010): 1.

4. *Essential Works of Foucault 1954–1984*, vol. 1: *Ethics*, Paul Rabinow (ed), Robert Hurley et al. (trans), New York, New Press, pp315-316.

5. Paul Patton, 'Foucault and Normative Political Philosophy' in Timothy O'Leary and Christopher Falzon (eds), *Foucault and Philosophy*, Chichester, Wiley-Blackwell, 2010, p212.

6. *Essential Works of Foucault 1954–1984*, vol. 3: *Power*, James D. Faubion (ed), Robert Hurley et al. (trans), New York, New Press, 2000, p329

7. David Harvey, *A Brief History of Neoliberalism*, Oxford, Oxford University Press, 2005, pp39-63.

8. Colin Gordon, 'Governmental Rationality: An Introduction', in Graham Burchell, Colin Gordon and Peter Miller (eds), *The Foucault Effect: Studies in Governmentality*, Hemel Hempstead, Hertfordshire, 1991, p2.

9. John Rawls, *Political Liberalism: Expanded Edition*, New York, Columbia University Press, 2005, p213, hereafter *Political Liberalism*.

10. Foucault, *Essential Works*, 3, *Power*, op. cit., p337.
11. Michael C. Behrent, 'Liberalism Without Humanism: Michel Foucault and the Free-Market Creed, 1976-1979,' *Modern Intellectual History*, 6, 3, (2009): 552-555; 'A Seventies Thing: On the Limits of Foucault's Neoliberalism Course for Understanding the Present', in Sam Binkley and Jorge Capetillo (eds), *A Foucault for the 21st Century: Governmentality, Biopolitics and Discipline in the New Millenium*, Newcastle upon Tyne, Cambridge Scholars Publishing, 2009, pp19-20. See also Michel Senellart, 'Course Context' in Foucault, *Security, Territory, Population: Lectures at the Collège de France 1977-1978*, Michel Senellart (ed), Graham Burchell (trans), Houndmills, Basingstoke and New York, Palgrave Macmillan, 2007, p371.
12. Behrent, 'Liberalism Without Humanism', op. cit., p553.
13. Patton, 'Foucault and Normative Political Philosophy', op. cit., p207.
14. Norman Daniels, 'Justice, Health and Healthcare', *The American Journal of Bioethics* 1, 2, (2001): 3.
15. Ibid., pp2-3
16. Rawls acknowledges his debt to James E. Meade's *Efficiency, Equality and the Ownership of Property*, London, Allen and Unwin, 1964. See Rawls, *A Theory of Justice: Revised Edition*, Cambridge, Mass., Harvard University Press, 1999, p242 fn.13, hereafter *Theory of Justice*; also Rawls, *Justice as Fairness: A Restatement*, Cambridge, Mass., Harvard University Press, p135, hereafter *Justice as Fairness*. For an overview of the 'tangled conceptual history' of the concept, see Ben Jackson, 'Property-Owning Democracy: A Short History' in Martin O'Neill and Thad Williamson (eds), *Property Owning Democracy: Rawls and Beyond*, Chichester, Wiley-Blackwell, 2012, pp33-52.
17. Ben Jackson, 'Revisionism Reconsidered: "Property-Owning Democracy" and Egalitarian Strategy in Post-War Britain', *Twentieth Century British History*, 16, 4, (2005): 418.
18. Richard Krouse and Michael McPherson, 'Capitalism, "Property Owning Democracy", and the Welfare State' in Amy Gutmann (ed), *Democracy and the Welfare State*, Princeton, Princeton University Press, 1988, p79.
19. For discussion of Rawls's criticisms of welfare state capitalism and the arguments for property-owning democracy derived from his principles of justice see Martin O'Neill, 'Free (and Fair) Markets Without Capitalism: Political Values, Principles of Justice and Property-Owning Democracy', in O'Neill and Williamson (eds), *Property Owning Democracy: Rawls and Beyond*, 75-100.
20. Rawls, *A Theory of Justice: Revised Edition*, op. cit., p241.
21. Jackson, 'At The Origins of Neoliberalism: The Free Economy and the Strong State, 1930-1947', *The Historical Journal*, 53, 1, (2010): 150, hereafter Origins of Neoliberalism.
22. Arthur DiQuattro, 'Rawls versus Hayek', *Political Theory*, 14, 2, (1986): 308.
23. Milton Friedman, *Capitalism and Freedom*, Chicago, University of Chicago Press, 1962.
24. Patton, 'Foucault and Normative Political Philosophy', op. cit., p210.
25. Harvey, *A Brief History of Neoliberalism*, op. cit., p41
26. See for example Rodney G. Peffer, *Marxism, Morality and Social Justice*, Princeton, N.J., Princeton University Press, 1990; John E. Roemer, *A Future for Socialism*,

Cambridge, Mass., Harvard University Press, 1994; Bruce A. Ackerman and Anne Alstot, *The Stakeholder Society*, New Haven, Yale University Press, 1999; Jeffrey Reiman, *As Free and as Just as Possible: The Theory of Marxian Liberalism*, Wiley-Blackwell, 2012, and the essays in O'Neill and Williamson (eds), *Property Owning Democracy: Rawls and Beyond*, op. cit.

MERITOCRACY AS PLUTOCRACY: THE MARKETISING OF 'EQUALITY' UNDER NEOLIBERALISM

Jo Littler

OF LADDERS AND SNAKES

> We are building an Aspiration Nation. A country where it's not who you know, or where you're from; but who you are and where you're determined to go. My dream for Britain is that opportunity is not an accident of birth, but a birthright.
>
> David Cameron, Conservative Party Spring Conference, March 2013

In the UK Conservative politicians have repeatedly evoked the image of Britain as an 'Aspiration Nation': as a country in which all people, no matter where they're from, have the opportunity to climb the ladder of social mobility.[1] This is the language of meritocracy: the idea that whatever our social position at birth, society ought to offer enough opportunity and mobility for 'talent' to combine with 'effort' in order to 'rise to the top'.

Meritocratic rhetoric is not confined to the UK. In the US, for instance, President Obama's 2013 inaugural address proclaimed that 'we are true to our creed when a little girl born into the bleakest poverty knows that she has the same chance to succeed as anybody else'.[2] Meritocracy has deep and varied historical lineages; in the UK, it can be connected back to the Victorian self-help tradition, and in the US to the emergence of the idea of aspirational consumerism as defining the 'American Dream' in the early twentieth century. Today, in many countries across the global North, the idea that we *should* live in a 'meritocracy' has become integral to contemporary structures of feeling: assumed by both right-wing and left-wing political parties, heavily promoted in educational discourse, and animating popular culture, meritocracy has become an idea as uncontroversial and as homely as 'motherhood and apple pie'.[3] Why should issue be taken with such an apparently innocuous concept, one whose potency lies in its investment in the conception of social mobility, pitted against 'older' forms of inherited privilege?

In this essay I argue that we should pay close attention to meritocracy because it has become a key ideological means by which plutocracy – or government by a wealthy elite – perpetuates itself through neoliberal culture. It is not, in other words, merely a coincidence that the common idea that we live, or should live, in a meritocratic age co-exists with a pronounced lack of social mobility and the continuation of vested hereditary economic interests.[4] Meritocratic discourse, as I show below, is currently being actively mobilised by members of a plutocracy to extend their own interests and power. Contemporary meritocracy operates to *marketise the very idea of equality* and can be understood in the light of Foucault's formulation of neoliberalism as a state in which competitive markets are not conceptualised as the 'natural' order of things (as they were under classical liberalism), but as entities that need to be *produced*.[5] This helps explain some of the tenacity of the power of meritocracy, despite its clear contradictions, and how it works as a mechanism to both perpetuate, and create, social and cultural inequality.

This essay explores this argument by sketching partial but revealing genealogies of meritocratic discourse. Discussions of meritocracy have largely either taken place around education or have been empirical analyses of whether or not the meritocratic nature of existing social institutions can be verified.[6] Reflecting on the cultural politics of its genealogy can add to our understanding of meritocratic ideas and the worlds they have shaped. In this article I pursue this analysis through three sections. The first brief section considers what might be wrong with the notion of meritocracy. The second traces some key points in the travels of the concept within and around academic social theory, moving from Alan Fox and Michael Young's initial, disparaging use of the term in the 1950s, to Daniel Bell's approving adoption of the concept in the 1970s, and on to its take-up by neoconservative think tanks in the 1980s. The third section considers the use of meritocracy as a plank of neoliberal political rhetoric and public discourse. This focuses on the resonance of the term in relatively recent British culture, from a Thatcherite 'anti-establishment' version through to the explicit Blairite adoption of the concept, and on to its contemporary life in coalition discourse as part of David Cameron's putative project to build an 'Aspiration Nation'. For to understand how meritocracy is deployed by neoliberalism we need to comprehend it both in terms of its relationship to broader contexts and in terms of the specific ways in which it is being shaped at the present time.

WHAT'S WRONG WITH MERITOCRACY?

What *is* wrong with meritocracy? Given that the concept of meritocracy is today largely normalised as wholly beneficial, it is worth highlighting some of the problems with the concept as it is generally understood in the present.

To begin with, the logic of meritocracy assumes that 'talent' or 'intelligence' is inborn from birth: it depends, in other words, on an essentialised conception of intellect and aptitude. It primarily assumes an ability which is inborn and either given the chance or not to 'succeed'. This notion of intelligence is singular and linear. It is in opposition to conceptions of intelligence as multiple and various, which can change and grow in numerous directions. Carried to its logical conclusion, such a hermetic conception of intelligence as a sealed and singular entity shares, as Young intimated in *The Rise of the Meritocracy,* the logic of eugenics.[7] This elitist 'myth of inherent difference' accelerated in intensity in affluent nations during the 1950s, and in Britain, as Danny Dorling points out, 'the state enthusiastically sponsored the division of children into types, with the amount spent per head on grammar school children being much higher than on those at the alternative secondary moderns'.[8] What Dorling terms 'apartheid schooling' was challenged in the 1960s and 1970s, but it was this 1950s rising tide of elitist stratification in both schools and society that in part prompted Michael Young's initial use of the term in 1958.

The second key problem with meritocracy is that it endorses a competitive, linear, hierarchical system in which by definition people must be left behind. The top cannot exist without the bottom. Not everyone can 'rise'. Unrealised talent is therefore both the necessary and structural condition of its existence. The forms taken by contemporary celebrity and the reality/talent shows have exemplified this structure,[9] publicly dramatising their assumptions while offering the basis for key forms of public entertainment. Meritocracy offers a 'ladder' system of social mobility, promoting a socially corrosive ethic of competitive self-interest which both legitimises inequality and damages community 'by requiring people to be in a permanent state of competition with each other'.[10] The classic meritocratic trope of the ladder was recently reinvigorated in the UK by David Cameron's 2013 Conservative Party Conference pledge to offer the 'ladder of opportunity for all to climb'. As Raymond Williams argued in 1963, the ladder is a perfect symbol of the bourgeois idea of society, because while it undoubtedly offers the opportunity to climb, it is a device which can only be used individually; you go up the ladder alone'. Such an 'alternative to solidarity', pointed out Williams, has dazzled many working-class leaders, and is objectionable in two respects: it weakens community and the task of common betterment and 'sweetens the poison of hierarchy' by offering growth through merit rather than money or birth, whilst retaining a commitment to the very notion of hierarchy itself.[11]

The third key problem with the ideology of meritocracy is in the hierarchical ranking of professions and status it endorses. Certain professions are positioned at the 'top', but *why* they are there – and whether they *should* be there – tends to be less discussed. Why do a singer or entrepreneur become roles to aspire to above those of a vet or a nurse? Why, as income disparity widens, are celebrity-based professions rising in ascribed status? Whilst one obvious answer is 'income', these questions are not ones that the contemporary neoliberal logic of meritocracy foregrounds. There is also a historical dimension to the answer, which relates to the shifting composition of social mobility. Academic research on social mobility usually differentiates between 'absolute' and 'relative' social mobility.[12] 'Absolute' social mobility refers to the movement in occupational classes from one generation to the next. In the UK there was a high level of movement between 1945 and the mid 1980s due to the growth in professional employment in the public sector (especially in education and health) and in service sector employment, which drew disproportionately on the newly-educated children of manual workers: a phenomenon which has since reduced with the combined effects of public sector spending cuts since the 1980s and shrinkage in the service economy. Measuring 'relative' social mobility involves comparing rates at which those from 'lower down' move up, compared to how many 'higher up' fall down; and as Vikki Boliver and David Byrne argue, not only has there been 'little if any sign of [people] becoming any more equal over time' but with a crumbling middle class, 'upward mobility increasingly necessitates downward mobility'.[13] Such patterns help explain both the mid-century cultural validation of professional occupations and the expanding late twentieth-century focus on entrepreneurialism and celebrity. In a landscape of extreme poverty and wealth, entrepreneurialism and celebrity rags-to-riches tales become highlighted, or rendered 'luminous', to borrow Angela McRobbie's term;[14] they become publicly visible opportunities to 'escape' an otherwise entrenched position of social subordination.

The notion of 'escape', however, introduces the fourth, interconnected, problem: meritocracy's validation of upper-middle class values as norms to aspire to and it's rendering of working-class cultures as abject. The language of meritocracy is about moving 'upwards' in financial and class terms, but whilst this may entail, for example, being better fed, it does not mean existing in a 'better' or 'happier' culture. Middle-class suburbs are not usually better places for socialising or connecting with a range of people than housing estates, for instance.[15] Discourses of meritocracy, however, assume that all movement must happen upwards, and in the process contributes to the positioning of working-class cultures as the 'underclass', as abject zones and lives to flee from. As Imogen Tyler has shown powerfully in her book *Revolting Subjects*, this is a tendency that has exacerbated under neoliberalism.[16]

The fifth key problem with meritocracy, and the problem which moves us into the territory of considering why it has such currency and power, is that it functions as an ideological myth to *obscure* economic and social inequalities and the role it plays in curtailing social equality. Recent social science research mapping social mobility has gestured in this direction; McNamee and Miller for instance have argued that in America meritocracy is a description that is both inaccurate and harmful, and that its use legitimises inequalities of power and privilege through 'claims that are demonstrably false'.[17] As we will see later, one of the key components of this ideological myth is how 'effort' – which in a meritocratic system combines with 'talent' to produce merit – is over-valued, and social and economic location is not considered or ignored. The emphasis on 'effort' is the key element of meritocracy that has been expanded in recent years.

Meritocracy might therefore be broadly characterised as a potent blend of an essentialised and exclusionary notion of 'talent', competitive individualism and the need for social mobility. The following sections analyse this particular cultural cocktail, and consider how the claims of meritocracy have worked and circulated in terms of social theory, political narrative and public discourse.

1. THE GENEALOGY OF A CONCEPT: SOCIALIST ROOTS

In order to trace the way the concept has travelled, we can revisit the moment of its emergence; for although the discourses it mobilised have longer histories, this is one useful and significant starting point. Michael Young is widely regarded as coining the term 'meritocracy' in his 1958 book *The Rise of the Meritocracy*, which is the earliest citation of the word in the OED. Contrary to popular opinion, however, the term was in fact used two years earlier by Alan Fox in his article 'Class and Equality' in the journal *Socialist Commentary*, as the British historian David Kynaston recently notes in his book *Modernity Britain: Opening the Box*, 1957-59.[18] As Kynaston is not especially interested in meritocracy he devotes only a couple of sentences to his discovery, but in terms of the etymology of the word and its cultural currency, this is a significant and quite remarkable finding.

What is striking about Fox's article is that it is more extensively critical and politically radical use of the term than Michael Young's (which I discuss below). Alan Fox was to become an influential industrial sociologist whose radical perspective on industrial relations challenged the liberal orthodoxy of the discipline. In 1956 he was a researcher at Nuffield College Oxford, where he worked on a history of British trade unions and a history of the National Union of Boot and Shoe Operatives (ODNB 2013). The journal the article appeared in, *Socialist Commentary*, was the weekly publication of the Socialist Vanguard Group, a political group on the left of the Labour party. In 1955 Clement Atlee described *Socialist Commentary* as 'a useful corrective to the *New Statesman*' (a more mainstream UK left weekly magazine).[19]

Fox's article is a careful sociological summary of the policies, social apparatuses and ideologies that reproduce and legitimate social stratification. It considers the role of 'the four scales' – income, property, education and occupation – in solidifying inequality of position. It discusses how these factors are interconnected, with, for example, low incomes having made it impossible for workers 'to break out of the vicious circle which cramped their lives' (Class&Equality, p12). Fox tends to focus on industrial work. He suggests that we might understand social inequality by looking at extremes of occupational status and ways of categorising their social standing ('Is it dirty and laborious or the reverse of those things? Is it carried out under discipline and supervision, or under conditions permitting personal independence, initiative and discretion?'). Whilst he raises the hope that mechanisation and worker's demands on the shop floor will make blue collar lives better, he suggests that this is only part of the story. For even if mechanisation improves and unionisation succeeds, social stratification will remain. For Fox, inequality will remain as long as we assume it to be a law of nature that those of higher occupational status must not only enjoy markedly superior education as well but also, by right and of necessity, have a higher income into the bargain. As long as that assumption remains – as long as violations of it are regarded as grotesque paradoxes – then so long will our society be divisible into the blessed and the unblessed – those who get the best and most of everything, and those who get the poorest and the least. This way lies the 'meritocracy'; the society in which the gifted, the smart, the energetic, the ambitious and the ruthless are carefully sifted out and helped towards their destined positions of dominance, where they proceed not only to enjoy the fulfilment of exercising their natural endowments but also to receive a fat bonus thrown in for good measure.

This is not enough. Merely to devise bigger and better 'sieves' (equality of opportunity') to help the clever boys get to the top and then pile rewards on them when they get there is the vision of a certain brand of New Conservatism; it has never been the vision of socialism (Classs&Equality, p13).

I quote this at length because it is both a remarkable and remarkably unquoted passage. It indicates the radical origins of critiques of meritocracy – roots that have been obscured – alongside the extent to which it has travelled as a term. For Fox, 'meritocracy' is a term of abuse. It denotes a society in which 'the gifted, the smart, the energetic, the ambitious and ruthless' not only reap the rewards for their (dubious or admirable) skills but receive *too much*: these 'fat bonus'[es], the rewards piled on them, are excessive and mean that others suffer.

As a result of this analysis, he suggests 'cross-grading' as a route towards greater equality, which is conceptualised not only in financial terms, but also in terms of time, education and leisure. He offers pointers towards policies of redistribution; these

> might mean, perhaps, refusing to accept the idea that to prolong the education of secondary modern pupils beyond the age of fifteen is 'a waste of time'. It might mean that those who perform the dull and repetitive jobs in which our economy abounds receive substantially more leisure than the rest (Class&Equality, p13).

Fox's article, in which the earliest use of 'meritocracy' to be recorded to date appears, is therefore an explicitly socialist argument against the very logic of 'meritocracy'. These origins were forgotten, however, until 2013, in favour of consistent attention to Michael Young's playful, dystopian social satire, *The Rise of the Meritocracy*.

FROM YOUNG TO 'MATURE' MERITOCRACY

The Rise of the Meritocracy was published in 1958 and set in 2034. It is voiced by a pompous narrator who draws on the PhD thesis of the now-deceased social scientist 'Michael Young' – who (we learn at the end) died in a ferocious battle caused by the problems with the new social system of meritocracy. 'Meritocracy' here is understood as produced through the formula I + E = M, or 'Intelligence combined with Effort equals Merit'. The first half of the book depicts early twentieth-century Britain from the vantage point of a science-fiction future. It charts the demise of the old, class-bound, nepotistic order, in which kinship triumphs over skill and the rich bequeath their social worlds to their children, as a world overthrown by movements for greater social equality. The second half relates the ascendancy of the new system of merit, which turns out to lead not to an equal society, but rather to a new caste system in which IQ determines social station. In this world, the lower rungs of both ex-rich and ex-poor are dim-witted and, to borrow contemporary terminology, 'socially excluded'; careers tend to dip after people reach 40 or 50; and there is a roaring black-market trade in brainy babies. The book concludes by gesturing towards the 2034 'Battle of Peterloo' when an alliance of housewives and 'Populists' fight back on May Day against meritocracy. We learn that it was in this battle that 'Michael Young' died.

Rejected by a number of publishers, including one who wanted it refashioned into a novel in the style of Aldous Huxley's *Brave New World* – which Young did, although that particular version, intriguingly, never got published – *The Rise of the Meritocracy* eventually became a UK bestseller. This was in itself indicative of what Mike Savage has described as the unprecedented power of sociology in mid-twentieth century Britain.[20] The book portrays a hidebound, class-bound British society as grossly unfair, and registers the seismic post-war moves towards a more egalitarian society and the redistribution of resources by the welfare state. But it is also, clearly, a book in which meritocracy is not depicted as a problem-free goal that such class-bound societies should strive for. On the contrary, it is presented as an ideology or organising principle that will become a problem by leading to new inequalities of power and forms of social stratification.

Through its satire, *The Rise of the Meritocracy* was both questioning the way the social order was being re-made and connecting to older political-philosophical debates around merit. These debates included, for example, Emile Durkheim's vision of society providing 'free space to all merits'; those of the US structuralist-functionalists of the 1940s and 1950s, who sought to update his ideas; and the scepticism of British social democratic radicals of the interwar period like Tawney, Cole and Hobson, who argued that the production of 'merit' needed to be understood instead as a more egalitarian co-operative process.[21] Young's political-philosophical position was closer to the latter. As a key writer of the 1945 Labour Party manifesto *Let Us Face the Future* and Labour's Director of Research, Young wrote The *Rise of the Meritocracy* in part as a warning shot to his party against newly emergent forms of social division.[22] The book is critical of tendencies toward over-valorising innate ability and of expanding hierarchies in education. As Raymond Williams argued in a review of Young's book, '[w]e think of intelligence as absolute and limited because we have been told to think so, by this kind of society. It seems increasingly obvious, in practice, that our concepts of intelligence are peculiarly unintelligent'.[23]

'Meritocracy' came to shift away from this overtly satirical meaning so that notoriously, by the 1990s New Labour under Tony Blair had adopted a non-satirical idea of 'a meritocratic society' with gusto. Shortly before his death, Young wrote of how the term had been adopted by Blair and widely disseminated in the US, but not in the way he intended. It had been misunderstood, and so New Labour should stop using the term, he argued in an oft-quoted article for the *Guardian*. For Young, the unironic way 'meritocracy' was now deployed, which worked by 'sieving people according to education's narrow band of values [...w]ith an amazing battery of certificates and degrees' meant that social stratifications had hardened, those demoted to the bottom of the social pile were deemed unworthy and demoralised; and that 'no underclass has ever been left as morally naked'.[24]

I will come to the issue of how meritocracy changed in meaning from the 1960s onward below, but it is worth considering how Young's book itself – or rather, the text and its author's paratextual framings of it – may have contributed, despite themselves, to such 'misreadings'.[25] For whilst *The Rise of the Meritocracy* is a text which is known for being disparaging of meritocracy, there is also a fair amount of ambiguity on this issue to both the text and itself and to Michael Young's comments on it. Its author claimed that *Rise* was 'intended to present two sides of the case – the case against as well as the case for a meritocracy' (*Rise of Meritocracy*, pxvii). In the book, whilst 'meritocracy' is valued for its ability to dismantle inherited privilege, it is also damned for its power to create new, unfair social divisions. The fictional 'Chelsea Manifesto' is the clearest expression of an alternative to both, with its often powerful arguments for equality, for valuing 'kindliness and courage, sympathy and generosity' over narrow conceptions of intelligence; and yet this alternative vision is truncated and cut off. Neither was the author's paratextual activity always consistent. For instance, Young stated that he supported the ideal of a classless society, yet when asked in the 2000s whether the book was arguing for resistance to the nascent elitism of the meritocracy by promoting 'the comprehensive idea', replied with an unexpansive but unequivocal 'no'.[26]

Young, who was director of the Institute of Community Studies at the time of writing the book, later became a founder and co-founder of a variety of institutions key to post-war British life and progressive social education, including the Open University, The Consumer's Association and the University of the Third Age. He was deeply committed to formations which enabled innovative forms of participation and engagement with political and social structures. It is for this reason that his legacy is held in such high regard in the UK today. This is a political-conceptual lineage which connects Young's work with that of contemporary advocates of participatory democracy; the tentative conclusion of the book's story, in which the housewives and other populists rise up together, is symptomatic of this tendency.

Yet whilst arguing against 'the big organisation', Young's primary model or template for participation was the nuclear family. As Hilary Land makes clear in her essay about *Rise*, the book, whilst anticipating a feminist critique of 'merit', does not particularly challenge conventionally gendered divisions of labour;[27] nor, we can add, its heteronormativity, nor its singular means of conceptualising 'social closeness'. We can also note that Young's antipathy towards large organisations involved being decidedly ambivalent / hostile towards nationalised industries; at its most left wing, this involved promoting mutual aid and 'neighbourly socialism'; at its least, it involved joining the Social Democratic Party (SDP) and not making any explicit critique of capitalism. The emphasis on economic and cultural redistribution which is foregrounded in Fox's account is downplayed in Young's.

What this means is that whilst *Rise* clearly critiques an essentialised and individualised notion of *merit* and implicitly eugenicist approaches to intelligence, its relationship to comprehensive provision, and indeed to capitalism, is somewhat less clear. And whilst responsibility for what happens to any concept, book or term cannot obviously be laid at the feet, the brain or the typewriting fingers of the author, the persistence of such textual lacunae is a key factor in how the term later became deployed. The paradoxical nature of Young's historical position is also apparent in the tendency of commentators to describe him as the original 'social entrepreneur',[28] a phrase which has now become decidedly ambivalent: reflecting not only innovative brilliance at creating socially beneficial initiatives (at which Young excelled), but also what was to become a wider saturation of the field of social policy by neoliberal entrepreneurialism.

'JUST' MERITOCRACY?

In 1973, in his classic text, *The Coming of Post-Industrial Society*, Daniel Bell – American sociologist and friend of Michael Young – pronounced that 'the post-industrial society, in its logic, is a meritocracy'.[29] The impact of the 1960s movements and struggles by those disenfranchised by the worker hierarchies of the Fordist settlement – women, non-whites, gay people – entailed a hugely significant challenge to and partial rupture of the dominant lines of social stratification. For example, after the 1963 Equal Pay Act in the US, and the 1970 Equal Pay Act in the UK, it was no longer legal to pay men and women differently for doing the same job, even if the struggle over equal pay for work of equal value – and against cultural prejudices against what it is *possible* for a woman or man to do – remains necessary.

These challenges to social mobility were engendered through and alongside the shift to a 'post-industrial', post-Fordist society and culture. Post-Fordist culture and society has involved a range of notable developments, including: the rapid growth in consumer-oriented production, branding and the service sector, the mobilisation of just-in-time ICTs in the service of 'the creative industries', industrial downsizing, manufacturing contracting-overseas, and the neoliberal erosion of worker's rights and the social provisions of the welfare state in favour of privatised solutions and social risk being borne by 'the individual'.[30]

In *The Coming of Post-Industrial Society*, Bell uses 'meritocracy' to refer primarily to the new forms of social mobility which are engendered within allegedly 'post-industrial' society. This is important: as use of the term 'meritocracy' in Bell's text works to neutralise and erase those more problematic (or 'dystopian') aspects of the term present in Young's work and powerfully critiqued in Fox's essay. Bell elaborates upon his ideas about meritocracy in a now more obscure text: a 1972 article 'On meritocracy and equality' in the journal *The Public Interest*. This article is fascinating as it forms a mid-point in the journey of meritocratic ideology from object of satirical scorn (in *Rise*) to central and explicit tenet of neoliberalism (as in the pamphlet which I consider in the next section from the Social Market Foundation). *The Public Interest* was a quarterly American public policy journal aimed at journalists, academics and policy makers founded by Daniel Bell and Irving Kristol in 1965. Irving Kristol, writer, journalist and publisher, was dubbed 'the godfather of neoconservatism' when he featured on the cover of *Esquire* magazine in 1979, a moniker he later adopted and adapted in his books including *Reflections of a Neoconservative, The Neoconservative Persuasion* and *Two Cheers for Capitalism*. Bell dropped his involvement with the journal from the late 1970s, as it lurched further to the right.[31]

Bell's interpretation of meritocracy was therefore a meeting point between Young's social-democratic version – Young explicitly refers to Bell as 'a friend' in the 1994 introduction to *The Rise of the Meritocracy* – and neoconservatism (*Rise of Meritocracy*, pxv). This is palpable in the article. It is a thorough, carefully written piece, in which Bell argues for a distinction between 'equality of opportunity' and 'equality of result'. There has been a conceptual confusion between these positions, the article argues, drawing on the work of John Rawls. Which do we want? Bell claims that 'equality of result' is a socialist ethic, whereas 'equality of opportunity' is a liberal one.[32] In the process, he questions the value of affirmative action programmes and comes, eventually, to argue for 'a just meritocracy' which is 'made up of those who have earned their authority', as opposed to an 'unjust' one which 'makes those distinctions invidious and demeans those below'.[33]

In this text the usage of 'meritocracy' comes to adopt the lineaments of the form we know today. It is an unambiguously positive and valorised term. It is also one which argues in favour of 'opportunity'. This is familiar territory to a contemporary readership. However, what distinguishes it from current usage are two important contextual points. First, the terrain on which meritocracy operates is one of high confidence in economic growth, as evidenced by virtue of Bell being able to debate whether or not 'we have reached the post-scarcity state of full abundance'. This is clearly a moment before either the 1970s recession or the later 'peak oil' crisis hit. Second, and related, the position from which Bell speaks is defined by a political context in which widespread support for the Keyesian consensus has not yet collapsed, a context that has resulted in 'a steady decrease in income disparity between persons'.[34] To put it bluntly: putting a competitive vision of meritocracy into play is not hugely conspicuous or controversial at a time when there is a strong social safety net.

From this position, in which the Fordist welfare settlement offset the worst extremes of capitalist division and its attendant social squalor, and from high confidence in expanding economic growth, meritocracy is, for Bell, to be conceived as a social system in which 'just' rewards and small gradations of privilege and position can be given to differential talent. From here, it might even be used as a motor for greater growth:

> And there is no reason why the principle of meritocracy should not obtain in business and government as well. One wants entrepreneurs and innovators who can expand the amount of productive wealth for society.[35]

And so the ambiguities of *The Rise of the Meritocracy* are resolved in favour of a specific usage which is quite different from Young's. For Bell, IQ is far less problematic than for Young. He is not so interested in the potential of local or participatory power or the extent of social levelling proposed by Fox. He is interested in achieving a social order in which the excesses of capitalism are curbed by the state, and hopes that meritocracy can be recalibrated in such a way as to avoid it solidifying into the new caste system imagined by Young, instead providing an incitement-engine for a dynamic yet just society. Here meritocracy starts to become posited as an engine of 'productive wealth'.

MERITOCRACY IN THE NEOLIBERAL LABORATORY

Bell's vision of meritocracy emerged from a historical situation characterised by the presence of a strong welfare state which could offset the most extreme effects of market-produced social inequality. In this context, meritocracy could be imagined as a dynamic engine both of 'opportunity' for social mobility, shaking up an ossified class system, and for ambiguously imagined 'productive wealth' – a term vague enough to be used by actors across the political spectrum. By the 1990s, however, this ambiguity was being aggressively exploited by the right, as the concept of 'meritocracy' became mobilised in explicit opposition to social democracy.

In Britain, a 1995 pamphlet by Adrian Wooldridge from the Social Market Foundation, *Meritocracy and the classless society*, argued for a vision of meritocracy which was explicitly pitted against comprehensive education, student grants, housing benefit, and any other kind of collective provision. Meritocracy is here opposed to what Wooldridge calls the 'niceness revolution' of the '60s and '70s. As part of this, it is explicitly opposed to 'community'[36] and to the welfare state, which is figured as 'an obstacle' to spreading meritocratic values'.[37] Meritocracy in Woolridge's version then is explicitly bound up with the logic of a capitalist market and with entrepreneurialism, and very much against the collective provision of social democracy and the welfare state. Here meritocracy fully embraces the liberal idea of 'equality of opportunity' and renders it synonymous with economic growth, capitalist competition and marketisation. Meritocracy is marketised and marketisation is good.

We can understand the development of this framework more capaciously by drawing on Michel Foucault's series of distinctions between liberalism and neo-liberalism in his prescient 1978-9 *College de France* lecture series (which forms the backdrop to his account of biopolitics, published in French in 2004 and English in 2008). Foucault is insistent on the need to grasp the distinctions between liberalism and neoliberalism, to grasp their singularity, to 'show you precisely that neoliberalism is really something else' (*Birth of Biopolitics*, p130). For Foucault, the 'something else' neoliberalism became was a situation in which 'the overall exercise of political power can be modeled on the principles of a market economy' (*Birth of Biopolitics*, p131). In other words, it was not just that the market became dominant, but that, since the 1970s it has begun to structure the way political power itself works.

Foucault describes how, to create this regime, classical liberalism had to be subjected to a number of transformations. A key transformation is that whilst classical liberalism accepts monopolies, neo-liberalism doesn't: competition under neoliberalism is not considered natural, but structured (*Birth of Biopolitics*, pp134-137). Moreover, the only 'true' aims of social policy for neoliberalism can be economic growth and privatisation; thus the multiplication of the 'enterprise' form within the social body, Foucault states, is what is at stake in neoliberalism, and it is what comes to constitute the 'formative power of society' (*Birth of Biopolitics*, p148).

In Wooldridge's formulation, meritocracy becomes a means of actively intervening to multiply the enterprise form within the social body. For example, he sees danger both in the hereditary interests of the Lords, and in Thatcher's inability to 'undermine the comprehensive principle in state schools'.[38] The vision, in other words, is of a starkly stratified society, one in which people can travel according to their inborn 'merit'. It finds legitimate vast inequalities of wealth and poverty as long as the potential to travel through them for those savvy enough is maintained. The distaste for the masses, towards the 'all and sundry' model of comprehensive education, combines revulsion toward 'standardisation' and toward the masses who fall out of view when the socially mobile are focused upon. These terms are elided.

Interestingly, Woolridge's pamphlet was produced by the Social Market Foundation (SMF), a cross-political party think tank. The very name 'Social Market Foundation' bears out Foucault's claim that neoliberal rhetoric works to incite marketisation throughout the social body, while strongly echoing Michael Young's language of social entrepreneurialism: neoliberalism, as analysed by Foucault, and Young's own political discourse, here become almost wholly intertwined. In this influential pamphlet, a product of several decades of New Right thinking, 'meritocracy' is unambiguously posited as an engine of competition *against* supposedly debilitating forms of social collaboration.

2. MERITOCRATIC FEELING: THE MOVEMENT OF MERITOCRACY IN BRITISH POLITICAL RHETORIC

The meaning meritocracy was taking at this moment was then clearly being shaped by the public emergence of neoliberalism from the 1970s. What we might call 'meritocratic feeling' – drawing from Raymond Williams' idea of 'structures of feeling' alongside recent emphasis on affect – was shaped through political discourse, emotive appeals and cultural rhetoric.[39] In Britain neoliberal policies and ideas of meritocracy were profoundly shaped, from the late 1970s, by Thatcherism, which made a meritocratic appeal to social mobility whilst dismantling the welfare state's social safety net and initiating the long wave of privatisation with the sale of public utilities like gas, telecommunications and rail.[40] Thatcherism normalised the marketisation of public services as the only possible response to the supposed malaise of the Keynesian industrial economy and articulated it to a very specific and partial idea of social mobility.

It is worth re-visiting the specific terms in which meritocratic aspiration was expressed. This form of meritocratic discourse linked a notion of achievement and merit towards successful consumption and away from intelligence. It habitually expressed distaste for ingrained privilege, particularly if it was in any way supported by the state. At the same time it was typically characterised by social conservatism in its attitudes to sexuality and gender: in particular attaching huge rhetorical importance to the heteronormative nuclear family and by repeatedly invoking imperialist white privilege.[41] Whilst Thatcherism worked in multiple ways to secure consent for its politics, one of the most important was its meritocratic appeal to consumerism as a general mode of participation in public life which invited people to identify with the notion of themselves as consumers rather than as workers or citizens in a range of public settings. The presentation of acquisitive consumerism as *the* route to empowerment in any social context was closely bound up with the implicit assumption that the accumulation of consumer goods was at once a sign of merit and its tangible reward. One of the most significant moments in her first term was precisely designed to re-position a population of public-resource users as private owner/consumers: when she gave municipal tenants the right to buy the housing they lived in for prices that were very far below market rates.[42] Crucially this government-subsidised housing stock wasn't replaced. With the removal of social housing from the market and the dismantling of rent controls and of legal protections for tenants, private landlords were free to raise rents astronomically, fuelling both the long-term housing boom which has had such deleterious effects on those social sectors unable to benefit from it, as well as massively increasing the public cost of subsidising the rents paid by welfare claimants to private landlords.[43]

Consumption became central to Thatcherism's iconography of 'getting ahead'. The new vanguard of conspicuous consumption were the businessmen and women, the stockbrokers and yuppies whose speedily-acquired lavish lifestyles were documented in Sunday supplements and glossy ads. The idea of money pouring through the social body was enshrined in Harry Enfield's comic TV character 'Loadsamoney!' (who had the cash, and flashed it; but he didn't know how to spend it, just waving it around in a wad, embodying the new class distinctions between those who knew how to dispose of their income and those who didn't). At the same time, income equality rose faster than in recorded history, child poverty doubled, unemployment rocketed, and the privatised utilities generated at least as many user complaints as the publicly-owned predecessors which they had been expected to outperform.

This, then, was a moment when people were imagined exclusively as individual consumers, as wholly bounded entities whose only significant sites of sociality were their families. As Thatcher said in an interview for the magazine *Women's Own*, 'there is no such thing as society. There are men and women and children and there are families'. This phenomenally atomised view of society was made to seem familiar and unthreatening by figuring Britain as a household, with Thatcher in charge, balancing the household budget. As Angela McRobbie discusses elsewhere in this issue, drawing on Foucault, such figurations of 'good housekeeping' have been a recurring motif of national neoliberal cultures.[44] While Thatcher was an arch anti-feminist, figuring the nation as a household with a consumer purse created a gendered appeal.[45] Thatcher always had low electoral popularity but she was very successful at winning over women, particularly lower middle-class and upper working class women. These were receptive constituencies both because they had traditionally been denied access to power and because one of the few zones in which traditionally women have had, though in circumscribed fashion, more power than men, is consumption.[46] The use of consumerism as a means and an apparent visual index of greater social mobility was key to securing consent for Thatcherite neoliberalism.

Under Thatcherism, then, what I am calling 'meritocratic feeling' was shaped and encouraged through aspirational femininity in particular and a very bounded, individualised (and/or nuclear family-based) form of consumerism in general. Popular support for Thatcherism was an expression of some of the most significant iniquities and discontents which the Fordist settlement had generated through its reliance on a hierarchical system of class, race and gender. Resentment at ingrained class hierarchies and gendered subordination were – along with gay rights and anti-racism – what fuelled the fractures in this settlement and the rebellions of the late 1960s, those social movements which were rupturing and staking their claim in 1968. Thatcherism's deployment of a meritocratic popular consumerism addressed the gendered and classed components of this disgruntlement in particularly important ways. Its culture and rhetoric persuaded women, and especially lower-middle-class women, the people who voted for her most, that the pursuit of satisfaction as an individualised consumer in the private sphere was the route to empowerment and social mobility. Under Thatcherism meritocracy was thereby presented as a pragmatic and emancipatory social solution to the gendered inequalities and industrial ruptures of the Fordist welfare settlement.

BLAIRISM AND BEYOND

By the late 1990s, this marketised meaning of 'meritocracy' had become a key theme within New Labour policy discourse, which, whilst equally populist, was somewhat less anti-intellectual than Thatcherism. New Labour's use of meritocratic themes had in part been influenced by the work of yet another prominent sociologist, Anthony Giddens, who in *Where now for New Labour?*

argued strongly that 'we should want a society that is more egalitarian than it is today, but which is meritocratic ... a meritocratic approach to inequality is inevitable'.[47] As John Beck argues, when the 'm' word was not always apparent, it was there in its constellation of synonyms: social inclusion, poverty of aspiration, social justice, talent, empowered individuals.[48]

This dual embrace of the idea of retaining forms of social protection (which included, for example, the introduction of the minimum wage and paid paternity leave) alongside the erosion of social protection via neoliberal expansion (through, for example, the extended privatisations of the Private Finance Initiative (PFI) , the introduction of academy schools, and the deregulation of the European labour market) structured and guided New Labour's time in power. This back-and-forth movement was memorably termed 'New Labour's double shuffle' by Stuart Hall.[49] However, as Jeremy Gilbert pointed out in his response to Hall's argument, the forms of protection being promoted were less consistent with social democratic egalitarianism than with neoliberal meritocracy which sought to provide 'equality of opportunity' on marketised and individualised terms.[50]

The idea of movement 'up' the social ladder also raises the question of what exactly is being reached *for*. In *The Rise of the Meritocracy* what is being reached toward is a blend of money and classed prestige. By the late 1990s both were being reconfigured in the wake of the Thatcherite challenge to the social order and New Labour's embrace of the financial sector, financialisation and of London as a centre for financial transactions and as the principle motor of the UK economy.[51] As New Labour's Trade and Industry Secretary Peter Mandelson famously put it in 1998, 'we are intensely relaxed about people becoming filthy rich'.[52] What was being positioned as 'the top' of the ladder was mutating, as CEO pay soared and 'the demotic turn' of reality TV shows popularised tempa-celebrities – or 'celetoids', to borrow Chris Rojek's definition.[53] What merit was, and how it was being ranked, was therefore changing to reflect New Labour's dual imperatives of corporate growth and populist access – a phenomenon Anthony Barnett astutely termed 'corporate populism'.[54] As John Beck caustically put it, in his wonderful analysis of New Labour's use of the term in relation to education, while even a brief dip into the history serves to highlight how meritocracy and measurement are perennially contested matters, this appears 'to have had remarkably little effect on politicians, particularly those of the centre Left or centre Right, in whose discourse and policies, meritocratic ideas remain persistently prominent'.[55]

But as the marketising effects of neoliberalism ripped through the forms of social protection built up in the mid-century, and the gap between rich and poor became increasingly graphic, more empirical and critical work emerged in and around social science in the 2000s on the limitations of 'social mobility' as a descriptive concept and a normative aim. In their 2009 book *The Meritocracy Myth*, for instance, American sociologists Stephen McNamee and Robert Miller examine the prevailing belief that 'people get out of the system what they put into it based on individual merit' through an extensive series of case studies. They conclude that, while US society has reduced some of its prejudicial inequalities structuring the opportunities for women and non-whites, 'the most important factor for determining where people end up economically is where they started in the first place', that 'the race is a relay race'.[56] 'The simple fact', they write, 'is that there is far more talent, intelligence, hard work, and ability in the population than there are people lucky enough to find themselves in a position to exploit them'.[57]

'ASPIRATION NATION' AND THE HYPOCRISY OF THE NEW ELITES

At present in Britain the powerful language of aspiration, social mobility and opportunity for all to rise through the social structure has not become muted, despite a double-dip recession, still-growing inequality, and a historically unprecedented drop in living standards for the working majority. On the contrary: it has escalated under the Conservative-LibDem coalition government, whose use of the idea of meritocracy represents a new stage in its 'development'. In this instance it has been deployed without the introduction of ameliorating initiatives or forms of collective provision (like the minimum wage), and in conjunction with specific policies aimed at cutting the incomes of the poor (like the Bedroom Tax). The coalition government has continued, and sped up, the implementation of neoliberal policies marketising the welfare state (such as the extension of internal markets and corporate involvement in prisons and in the health service) whilst using the alibi of the recession.[58] At the 2012 Conservative Party conference, David Cameron declared that under his leadership Britain is now an 'aspiration nation': 'we are the party of the want-to-be better-off'.

According to Cameron's stated worldview, the ability to 'believe in yourself', and by extension, your child, is primary. This is a discourse which vests not only power but also *moral virtue* in the very act of hope, in the mental and emotional capacity to believe and aspire. Hope and promise become more integral in an unequal society in which hard work alone has less and less chance of reaping the prizes. Through this rhetorical mechanism, instead of addressing social inequality as a solvable problem, the act of addressing inequality becomes 'responsibilised' as an individual's moral meritocratic task. This process devolves onto the individual personal responsibility not just for their success in the meritocratic competition, but for the very will to compete and expectation of victory which are now figured as moral imperatives in themselves. Not investing in aspiration, in *expectation*, is aggressively positioned as an abdication of responsibility which condemns yourself – and even worse, your child – to the social scrapheap. To quote Cameron's 2012 Conservative Party conference speech:

> It's that toxic culture of low expectations – that lack of ambition for every child – which has held this country back.
> the Labour party theorists ... stand in the way of aspirational parents by excusing low expectations and blaming social disadvantage (*Guardian* 2012).

Here aspirational meritocracy works by positioning itself against – increasingly aggressively – any investment in collective provision as both a symptom and a cause of 'low expectation'. In his 2013 party conference speech, Cameron re-iterated the 'aspiration nation' theme, intensifying the rhetoric by describing himself as engaged in a battle against opponents whom he characterised explicitly as non-hard workers – 'smug, self-satisfied socialists'. 'That's who we're fighting against', he asserted; 'And we know who we're fighting for: for all those who work hard and want to get on'.[59]

Here, social disadvantage is only 'real' in that it is an obstacle over which pure mental will and aspiration – if they are expressed correctly by being combined with hard work – can triumph. These tropes and discursive elements generate an affective mode which Lauren Berlant aptly identifies as 'cruel optimism'. This is the affective state produced under neoliberal culture which is cruel because it encourages an optimistic attachment to the idea of a brighter future whilst such attachments are, simultaneously, 'actively impeded' by the harsh precarities and instabilities of neoliberalism.[60] If 'Aspiration Nation' is related to such 'cruel optimism', it also draws on the English trope of 'having a go', which involves a sort of non-competitive competitiveness, of being prepared to compete without any expectation of winning, out of a recognition that sporting competition is a mode of social participation; although the difference is that in the Aspiration Nation you can't just do your best: you have to *want to win*.

Even the psychosocial resources required to engage in aspiration are considerable and easier for some classes to obtain and deploy than others. There is a rich tradition in the cultural studies of education analysing how middle-class children are encouraged to aspire whilst working class children are – to cite the title of Paul Willis's classic book – *Learning to Labour*.[61] Valerie Gilles' recent analysis of aspirational language used – or not – by parents when talking about their child's behaviour at school is particularly instructive here. Her research showed how for working-class parents, the attributes most likely to be proudly described were children's ability to stay out of trouble, get on with others, and work hard, which inculcates the strength to struggle and to defend scant resources; whereas middle-class parents foster 'the right to be bright' and code problematic behaviour in the classroom in terms of intelligence and of needs the classroom should be able to accommodate, which helps reproduce middle-class success. Gilles criticises New Labour's education policy for encoding middle-class behaviour as morally correct and blaming the poor 'with almost missionary zeal' for their own failure.[62]

Such tendencies have been continued and extended in politics and popular culture since 2005. There is now a widespread tendency to 'blame the parents' for any problems at the expense of any other social factor such as economic and social impoverishment. This tendency is conveyed, for instance, through the fixation on parenting styles 'over and above all other factors' in relation to children's behaviour and life chances;[63] foregrounded through framing of parental responsibility by TV programmes such as *Supernanny*[64] and in government and media responses to the London riots.[65] This tendency is tied up with how, as Angela McRobbie argues in this issue, the family is increasingly figured as a bounded entrepreneurial unit.[66]

'Aspiration Nation' as a rhetorical strategy, and as an expression of meritocratic feeling, connects self-belief and aspiration with the trope of hard work. It is striking how, again and again, 'hard work' combined with self-belief is employed by an unprecedentedly privileged cadre of politicians and millionaire elites to justify their position and success and to prescribe this as the route for others. 'Working hard and wanting to get on' is the way to progress. This trope has been repeatedly deployed by Conservative MP and Mayor of London Boris Johnson, who, in the words of the *Daily Mail*, 'hailed the Olympics for embodying the "Conservative lesson of life" that hard work leads to reward'[67] and more recently told Britons that they needed to work harder otherwise jobs would go to economic migrants.[68]

How does this rhetoric of 'hard work', such a feature of the contemporary meritocratic deal, work, given that there is a swathe of research proving that *inheriting opportunity* in the form of finance and social connections is by far more important a factor in the route to riches?[69] It is notable that plenty of millionaires who inherited their wealth, including Boris Johnson and David Cameron, conveniently promote hard work as the most influential factor in social mobility. Such discourse simultaneously helps to erase any image of over-privileged indolence from the speaker's persona whilst interpellating the listener as able to achieve a similar social status; a degree of social mobility which is in practice attainable only for a tiny minority. As MacNamee and Miller put it, 'meritocracy tends to be believed in more by the privileged'.[70] But the rhetoric of 'hard work' is crucial to today's meritocratic feeling. In research recently conducted in St Pauls, an elite North American fee-paying school, Khan and Jerolmack noted that typically these students were conscious of the idea of their privilege, and replaced a frame of entitlement with one based around merit by continually emphasising how hard they'd worked. The researchers argued that 'they generally do not work hard, although they are adept at performing a kind of busyness that looks and feels like hard work.' (Students that did regularly go to the library were conversely positioned as 'freaks'). As they put it, '"hard work" is mostly a form of talk – but important talk nonetheless. It is a rhetorical strategy deployed by students in a world of "new elites"'. These are elites 'saying meritocracy but doing the ease of privilege'.[71]

Similarly, the coalition's investment in 'hard work' is classed: it is coded as 'graft' even when it's being voiced by million/billionaires, celebrities and children at elite private fee-paying schools. This is not completely new: it was a key element in the rhetoric of Thatcherism as well as Blairism. Thatcher notably used a version of this rhetoric which was both structured through the decline of deference and classed through its rhetoric of rising up through the classes. As Peter Clarke and Tom Mills point out, the importance to her success of her husband's considerable wealth was barely acknowledged by Thatcher. She preferred to dwell on her humble roots as a grocer's daughter and to imagine that her achievements were attributable to drudgery and self-discipline'.[72] Cameron and his cabinet, just like Boris Johnson, do not draw on such early moments in their self narrative to calibrate work as classed graft, mainly because they don't have them: their backgrounds are aristocratic or quasi-aristocratic. They do, however, borrow the classed rhetoric of 'hard work' – just like the privileged children interviewed by Khan and Jerolmack; and the very act of saying 'hard work' invites those who do work hard to identify with them and flatters the rest. Then 'hard work' is connected, rather than to a particular lower-class reflexive position, to *the necessity of having aspirations*: you can't have one without the other, in this worldview: to lack either is a moral failure. In this way Cameron and Johnson do what Thatcher did but de-articulate the highly selective, reflexive class biographical detail and replace it with a generalised notion of aspiration. These actions are similar ones to those offered by Blairism, although the crucial difference is the Conservatives' dispensing with the concessions to equality of opportunity that Blair promoted – whilst pushing through neoliberal reforms – in favour of a much more dramatic cutting of the social safety net. This makes the distance aspiration needs to travel that much further and far less likely to be traversed.

STRIVERS V SKIVERS

Meritocracy is a word with a short etymological history – under 60 years – but during this time it has gradually and dramatically shifted in its meaning. It has moved from a disparaging reference to an embryonic system of state organisation creating problematic hierarchies through a dubious notion of 'merit', to a celebratory term connecting competitive individualism and an essentialised notion of 'talent' with a belief in the desirability and possibility of social mobility in a highly unequal society. It emerged as a word at the high point of the British welfare state both as a celebration of the greater degrees of social equality and social mobility that many – though not all – experienced at that time, and simultaneously as a critique of emergent hierarchies based on troublingly essentialised notions of aptitude and an ambiguous anxiety about the forms of inequality such notions were beginning to engender. It was initially mobilised as a term through a radical socialist discourse: an origin which until now has been lost and obscured in favour of Young's left-liberal stance.

As a discourse, meritocracy was mobilised gradually into, through and by neoliberalism, although this has happened in diverse, sometimes erratic ways. It has been and continues to be shaped as a discourse by diverse constituencies, agents and sites including popular culture, social theory and political rhetoric. As this essay has attempted to show, what I have termed 'meritocratic feeling' has taken different forms in neoliberal culture. In Britain, for instance, Thatcherism's elision of collective state welfare with the ingrained privileges of 'the great and the good', and its exploitation of the gendered weaknesses of the Fordist settlement were mobilised into an anti-intellectual acquisitive, consumerist form of meritocracy. The 'meritocratic feeling' promulgated by the Conservative-Liberal Democrat coalition government at present perpetuates – like the Labour government before it – a possessive individualist, consumerist notion of meritocracy; but it is a meritocratic feeling which moves further by vesting moral virtue in the act or affects of aspiration and hope; one which is, when combined with the trope of 'hard work', explicitly pitted against any form of collective provision or mutual forms of social reproduction. 'Aspiration nation' defines itself against mutuality. You are a striver or a skiver: believing in the necessity of any kind of collective form of social reproduction is demarcated as simply a lazy excuse for not striving.

Through neoliberalism meritocracy has become an alibi for plutocracy, or government by a wealthy elite. It has become a key ideological term in the reproduction of neoliberal culture in Britain. It has done so by seizing the idea, practice and discourse of greater social equality which emerged in the first half of the twentieth century and marketising it. Meritocracy, as a potent blend of an essentialised notion of 'talent', competitive individualism and belief in social mobility, is mobilised to both disguise and gain consent for the economic inequalities wrought through neoliberalism. However, at the same time, such discourse is neither inevitable nor consistent. It requires actively reinforcing and reproducing and can be augmented and shaped in a number of different places and spaces. The alternative to plutocracy-as-meritocracy is a more plural understanding of 'merit' – which considers 'merit' on a collective and not a purely individual basis – alongside mutual and co-operative forms of social reproduction which create greater parity in wealth, opportunity, care and provision.

NOTES

1. Patrick Wintour, 'David Cameron presents himself as leader of an 'aspiration nation', *Guardian*, 10.10.2012. Isabel Hardman, 'Budget 2013: It's all about the "Aspiration Nation"', *Spectator*, 20.03.2013, http://blogs.spectator.co.uk/coffeehouse/2013/03/budget-2013-its-all-about-the-aspiration-nation/http://www.guardian.co.uk/politics/2012/oct/10/david-cameron-leader-aspiration-nation.

2. The White House, Inaugural address by President Barack Obama, 2013, accessed at http://www.whitehouse.gov/the-press-office/2013/01/21/inaugural-address-president-barack-obama.

3. Adrian Wooldridge, *Meritocracy and the 'Classless Society'*, London, Social Market Foundation, 1995, p7.

4. Danny Dorling, *Injustice: Why Social Inequality Exists*, Bristol, Policy Press, Kindle edition, 2011; Martin Marmot, *Status Syndrome: How social standing directly affects your health*, Bloombsbury, 2005; Stephen J. McNamee and Robert K. Miller, *The Myth of Meritocracy*, Lanham, Rowman & Littlefield, 2009; Richard Wilkinson and Kate Pickett, *The Spirit Level: Why Equality is Better for Everyone*, London, Penguin, 2010.

5. Michel Foucault, *The Birth of Biopolitics: Lectures at the College de France*, 1978-9, Graham Burchell (trans), Basingstoke, Palgrave MacMillan, 2010, hereafter *Birth of Biopolitics*.

6. Ansgar Allen, 'Michael Young's The Rise of the Meritocracy: a Philosophical Critique', *British Journal of Educational Studies*, 59, 4, (2011): 367-382; Ansgar, 'Life without the 'X' factor – meritocracy past and present', *Power and Education*, 4, 1, (2012)· 4-19; John Beck, *Meritocracy, Citizenship and Education: New Labour's Legacy*, London, Continuum, 2008; Valerie Gilles, 'Raising the meritocracy: parenting and the individualisation of social class', *Sociology*, 39, 5, (2005): 835-852; Shamus Khan and Colin Jerolmack, 'Saying Meritocracy and doing privilege', *The Sociological Quarterly*, 54, 1, (2013): 9-19.

7. Michael Young, *The Rise of the Meritocracy*, 2nd revised edition, London, Transaction Books, 2004, hereafter *Rise of Meritocracy*.

8. Dorling, *Injustice*, op. cit., p870.

9. Jo Littler, 'Celebrity and "meritocracy"', *Soundings: A Journal of Politics and Culture*, 26, (2004): 118-130; Nick Couldry and Jo Littler, 'Work, Power and Performance: Analysing the 'reality' game of The Apprentice', *Cultural Sociology*, 5, 2, (2011): 263-279.

10. Rebecca Hickman, *In Pursuit of Egalitarianism: and why social mobility cannot get us there*, London, Compass, 2009.

11. Raymond Williams, *Culture and Society*, London, Hogarth Press, 1958, p331.

12. Hickman, op. cit., p11; John Goldthorpe with Catriona Llewellyn and Clive Payne, *Social Mobility and Class Structure in Modern Britain*, London, Transaction, 1980.

13. Vikki Boliver and David Byrne, 'Social Mobility: The politics, the reality, the alternative', *Soundings: A Journal of Politics and Culture*, forthcoming.

14. Angela McRobbie, 'Feminism, the family and the new "mediated" maternalism, *New Formations*, this issue, pp119-137.

15. As author Zadie Smith recently pointed out on *Start the Week*, Radio 4, 24.06.2013. Thanks to Doreen Massey for alerting me to this programme and discussing these issues with me.

16. Imogen Tyler, *Revolting Subjects: Social abjection and resistance in neoliberal Britain*, London, Zed Books, 2013; see also Owen Jones, *Chavs; The demonization of the working class*, London, Verso, 2012, and Bev Skeggs, *Class, Self, Culture*, London, Routledge, 2003.

17. McNamee and Miller, *The Myth of Meritocracy*, op. cit., p22.

18. David Kynaston, *Modernity Britain: Opening the Box*, 1957-59, London, Bloomsbury, 2013, Kindle location 3666; Alan Fox, 'Class and Equality', *Socialist Commentary*, May (1956): 11-13.

19. R.M. Douglas, 'No Friend of Democracy: The Socialist Vanguard Group 1941-50', *Contemporary British History*, 16, 4, (2002): 51-86.
20. Mike Savage, *Identities and Social Change in Britain since 1940: The Politics of Method*, Oxford, Oxford University Press, 2010. In this book, Young is simultaneously noted as influential whilst *The Rise of the Meritocracy* is absent from the discussion.
21. Beck, *Meritocracy*, op. cit.
22. Asa Briggs, 'The Labour Party as Crucible' in Geoff Dench (ed), *The Rise and Rise of Meritocracy*, Oxford, Wiley-Blackwell, 2006, 17-26.
23. Raymond Williams, 'Democracy or Meritocracy?', *Manchester Guardian*, 30.10.1958, p10.
24. Michael Young, 'Down with meritocracy', *Guardian*, 29.06.2001, accessed at http://www.guardian.co.uk/politics/2001/jun/29/comment.
25. Young stated in the introduction to the 1994 edition that 'the most influential books are always those which are not read' (Young, *The Rise of the Meritocracy*, Transaction Publishers, 1994, pxv) and later wrote that he didn't think that Blair had actually read his book (Young, 'Down with meritocracy', op. cit.). Claire Donovan has argued, somewhat tenuously, that many academics who have cited it haven't read it either (Donovan, 'The chequered career of a cryptic concept' in Geoff Dench, *The Rise and Rise of Meritocracy*, op. cit.). Various reviewers have also argued that its style is problematic (e.g. Richard Hoggart, 'IQ plus Effort = Merit', *Observer*, 2.11.1958; Paul Barker, 'A tract for the times' in Geoff Dench, *The Rise and Rise of Meritocracy*, op. cit.).
26. Geoff Dench (and Young), *The Rise and Rise of Meritocracy*, op. cit., p74.
27. Hilary Land, 'We sat down at the table of privilege and complained about the food' in Geoff Dench, *The Rise and Rise of Meritocracy*, op. cit., p59.
28. Asa Briggs, *Michael Young: Social Entrepreneur*, London, Palgrave, 2001.
29. Daniel Bell, *The Coming of Post-Industrial Society: A Venture in Social Forecasting*, New York, Basic Books, 1973, p409.
30. Ulrich Beck and Elizabeth Beck-Gernsheim, *Individualization: Institutionalised Individualism and its political consequences*, London, Sage, 2001; Scott Lash and John Urry, *Economies of Signs and Space*, London, Sage, 1993; Zygmunt Bauman, *Individualisation*, Oxford, Polity, 2000; Luc Boltanski and Eve Chiapello, *The New Spirit of Capitalism*, London, Verso, 2007; Colin Crouch, *Post-Democracy*, Oxford, Polity, 2004.
31. Paul Buhle, 'Daniel Bell: Obituary', *Guardian*, 26.01.2011, http://www.guardian.co.uk/education/2011/jan/26/daniel-bell-obituary.
32. Daniel Bell, 'On meritocracy and equality' in *The Public Interest*, 29, (Fall 1972): 48.
33. Bell, 'On meritocracy and equality' op. cit., p66
34. 'Traditionally, the market was the arbiter of differential reward, based on scarcity or on demand. But as economic decisions become politicized, and the market is replaced by social decisions, what us the principle of fair reward and fair difference?' Bell, 'On meritocracy and equality' op. cit., p63.
35. Bell, 'On meritocracy and equality' op. cit., p66
36. Wooldridge, *Meritocracy and the 'Classless Society'*, op. cit., p45.
37. Ibid., p43.
38. Wooldridge, *Meritocracy and the 'Classless Society'*, op. cit., p9.

39. Raymond Williams, *Marxism and Literature*, Oxford, Oxford Paperbacks, 1977; Melissa Gregg and Greg Seigworth (eds), *The Affect Reader*, Durham, Duke, 2012.

40. Stuart Hall, *The Hard Road to Renewal*, London, Verso, 1988.

41. As Adam Curtis's film *The Attic* shows, the iconography of Victorian Britain was central to her imagery, at the same time as she waged war on a traditional 'great and the good'; see http://www.bbc.co.uk/blogs/adamcurtis/posts/MRS-THATCHER-THE-GHOST-IN-THE-HOUSE-OF-WONKS.

42. Thanks to Jeremy Gilbert and Nick Thoburn for conversations on this topic.

43. Jonathan Prynn and Miranda Bryant, 'London rents at all-time high as prices rocket eight times faster than wages', *Evening Standard*, 18.04.2013, http://www.standard.co.uk/news/london/london-rents-at-alltime-high-as-prices-rocket-eight-times-faster-than-wages-8578230.html.

44. McRobbie, this issue, pp119-137; Foucault, *The Birth of Biopolitics*, op. cit.

45. Bea Campbell, *The Iron Ladies. Why do women vote Tory?*, London, Virago Press, 1987. Heather Nunn, 'Running Wild: Fictions of Gender and Childhood in Thatcher's Britain', *EnterText*, 1, 3, (2001), http://arts.brunel.ac.uk/gate/entertext/issue_3.htm; Nunn, *Thatcher, Politics and Fantasy: The Political Culture of Gender and Nation*, London, Lawrence and Wishart, 2002.

46. Rachel Bowlby, *Just Looking: Consumer Culture in Gissing, Dreiser and Zola*, London, Methuen, 1985; Victoria de Grazia and Ellen Furlough (eds), *The Sex of Things: Gender and Consumption in Historical Perspective*, University of California Press, 1996; Jo Littler, 'Gendering anti-consumerism: consumer whores and conservative consumption' in Kate Soper, Martin Ryle and Lyn Thomas (eds), *Counter-Consumerism and its Pleasures: Better than Shopping*, Palgrave, 2009; Mica Nava, *Changing Cultures: Feminism, Youth and Consumerism*, London, Sage, 2002.

47. Anthony Giddens, 'Where Now for New Labour?' London, Polity Press 2002, pp38-9.

48. Beck, *Meritocracy*, op. cit., pp12-17.

49. Stuart Hall, 'New Labour's double shuffle', *Soundings*, 24, (July 2003): 10-24.

50. Jeremy Gilbert, 'The Second Wave: The specificity of New Labour neoliberalism', *Soundings*, 26, (2004): 25-45.

51. Doreen Massey, *World City*, Oxford, Polity, 2007.

52. Victor Keegan, 'Economics Notebook: Raising the Risk Stakes', *Guardian*, 26.10.1998, http://www.guardian.co.uk/Columnists/Column/0,,325036,00.html.

53. Chris Rojek, *Celebrity* (FOCI), London, Reaktion Books, 2001.

54. Anthony Barnett, 'Corporate Populism and Partyless Democracy' in A. Chadwick and R. Heffernan (eds), *The New Labour Reader*, Oxford, Polity, 2003; Jo Littler, 'Creative Accounting: Consumer culture, the "creative economy" and the cultural policies of New Labour' in Tim Bewes and Jeremy Gilbert (eds), *Cultural Capitalism: Politics after New Labour*, London, Lawrence & Wishart, 2000.

55. Beck, *Meritocracy*, op. cit., p11.

56. McNamee and Miller, *The Myth of Meritocracy*, op. cit., p16.

57. Ibid., p19.

58. Stuart Hall, Doreen Massey and Michael Rustin, *The Kilburn Manifesto*, London, Lawrence & Wishart, 2013.

59. Huffington Post, 'Cameron Spring Conference Speech A Rousing Battle Cry Against Labour's 'Self Satisfied Socialists', 16.03.2013, http://www. huffingtonpost.co.uk/2013/03/16/cameron-spring-conference-battle-labour-socialists_n_2890437.html.

60. Lauren Berlant, *Cruel Optimism*, Durham, Duke, 2012.

61. Paul Willis, *Learning to Labour: How working-class kids get working-class jobs*, Farnham, Ashgate, 1977.

62. Gilles, 'Raising the meritocracy', op. cit.

63. Tracey Jensen, 'Tough love in tough times', *MAMSIE: Studies in the Maternal*, 4, 2, (2012), http://www.mamsie.bbk.ac.uk/Jensen_SiM_4_2_2012.html.

64. Mark Fisher, *Capitalist Realism*, London, Zero Books, 2009; Tracy Jensen, 'What kind of mum are you at the moment? Supernanny and the psychologising of classed embodiment', *Subjectivity*, 3, 2, (2010): 170-192.

65. Kim Allen and Yvette Taylor, 'Placed Parenting, locating unrest: failed femininities, troubled mothers and rioting subjects', *MAMSIE: Studies in the Maternal*, 4, 2, (2012), http://www.mamsie.bbk.ac.uk/back_issues/4_2/index. html; Littler, 'Work, Power and Performance', op. cit.

66. McRobbie, this issue, pp119-137.

67. Geri Peev, 'Games embody the Tory ethic of hard work that leads to reward, says Boris', *Daily Mail*, 6.08.2012, http://www.dailymail.co.uk/news/article-2184687/ Boris-Johnson-London-2012-Olympics-embody-Tory-ethic-hard-work-leads-reward. html#ixzz2QG4E5oVC.

68. Boris Johnson, 'Migrants get jobs because we're not prepared to work as hard', *Daily Telegraph*, 7.04.2013, http://www.telegraph.co.uk/news/politics/9977793/ Migrants-get-jobs-because-were-not-prepared-to-work-as-hard.html.

69. Dorling, *Injustice*, op. cit; Chrystia Freeland, *Plutocrats: The rise of the new global super-rich*, London, Allen Lane, 2012.

70. MacNamee and Miller, *The Myth of Meritocracy*, op. cit., p3.

71. Khan and Jerolmack, 'Saying Meritocracy and doing privilege', op. cit.

72. Tom Mills, 'The Death of a Class Warrior: Margaret Thatcher 1925-2013', New Left Project, http://www.newleftproject.org/index.php/site/article_comments/ the_death_of_a_class_warrior_margaret_thatcher_1925_2013

THOUGHT BUBBLE: NEOLIBERALISM AND THE POLITICS OF KNOWLEDGE

Neal Curtis

On 22 July 2009 economists Tim Besley and Peter Hennessy wrote a letter on behalf of the British Academy to the British monarch, Queen Elizabeth II, attempting to answer her question as to why no one saw the 2008 financial crisis coming. Their conclusion that this failure was the result of a systemic lack of oversight 'combined with the psychology of herding and the mantra of financial and policy gurus' is highly revealing, as it counters many of the key tenets of the dogma that brought about the crash. Their conclusions are interesting because the reference to psychology raises the spectre of the 'animal spirits' that Keynes[1] gave as a reason why markets could not be considered rational and ought not be left to regulate themselves. At the time Keynes was writing, because such an understanding of the human condition merited state intervention and a central role for public works, free-marketeers were required to strenuously and vigorously re-state their case by arguing that such spirits were merely the effect of a market that was not yet free enough.

A similar refrain can be heard today. In keeping with all fundamentalisms neoliberals today insist that there was nothing wrong with what free-marketeers believed in; what were perceived to be problems with unregulated markets were in fact caused by the non-believers whose lack of faith prevented the full flowering of freedom and this alone explained the failure. Such advocates are often in thrall to the dystopian stories of Friedrich Hayek or the pseudo-science of Milton Friedman, if not the corporate porn of Ayn Rand, and believe it their duty to reach out to the invisible hand offered them by the prophet Adam Smith. Only this will guarantee the deliverance of humankind to the paradise which Friedman called the 'free private enterprise exchange economy'.[2] Thus when the letter refers to 'gurus' we may infer that Besley and Hennessy were speaking about the financial priesthood that turned the entire global economy into a delusional cult that even in crisis continues to maintain its claims to truth. It should also be noted that the persistence of this particular brand of dogmatic thinking – the infallibility of markets and their extension through deregulation and privatisation – suggests that nothing has been learnt from the revelation that what economists believed they knew about the functioning of markets was entirely spurious. This means that speaking about knowledge in such a context becomes quite difficult.

Empiricism and the practices of modern science have bequeathed us a conception of knowledge as derived from the examination of objective phenomena and sense perceptions via experimentation and repeatable processes of verification. However, the fact that further rounds of deregulation and privatisation are seen to be the solution to a problem for which the most proximate cause was a lack of regulation seems to suggest that this empirical model of knowledge is no longer prevalent. Lack of evidence is no longer a hindrance to the further entrenchment of a belief system. In fact the current conception of knowledge under these conditions seems to be much closer to the medieval meaning of 'knowledge', where the word *cnawlece* referred to the practice of confession through which a person would submit themselves to the claims of a specific authority. This meaning of knowledge is most readily evident in the modern word 'acknowledge', which in certain uses still connotes the recognition of a superior entity, body or office. Ordinarily, empiricism's demands for proof and verification challenges the authority of priests and mystics, but with the establishment a largely unaccountable corporate aristocracy who continue to propagate faith in the self-regulating character of markets despite all evidence to the contrary, it is perhaps appropriate that we should be called on to simply acknowledge the supremacy of the market rather than interrogate the assumptions underpinning its mystery.[3]

While it is not my intention here to examine the knowledge or pseudo-science that supports the neoliberal faith in markets, as there are many good accounts that have already done this,[4] I do wish to address the relationship between knowledge and neoliberal or free market dogma from two distinct yet related perspectives. The first is to seek to understand how such a dogma can persist even when it has been seen to fail. I will argue that this issue is not simply reducible to a question of false consciousness or lack of knowledge. For those in charge of economic policy, the ideology of austerity assumed to be an appropriate response to the crisis is little more than the means by which they might consolidate their wealth, further promote private interests, and eradicate the last vestiges of welfarism; while for those on the receiving end of austerity, it appears more acceptable to blame the most vulnerable than think through the failings of a financial sector used to mask structural limits in the capitalist system.[5] But it is not for a lack of knowledge (in the modern, empirical sense) that people carry on regardless.

The persistence of a way of thinking and acting is hard to reduce to a question of false-consciousness when, even if they may not fully understand the problem of capitalist over-production, so many people appear to know that it was the banks and the failures of the financial sector's watchdogs that got us into this mess. In the UK this argument, if not completely uncontested, is certainly not a position exclusive to left-wing radicals, but has become a fairly popular refrain. What intrigues me, then, is the way in which a dramatic reduction in public spending has been widely accepted as the solution to a crisis in private speculation. I would like to argue that while privatisation, deregulation and free markets have become central components of neoliberal common sense, such an analysis remains too epistemological, and that it is necessary to take a more ontological approach. While sharply discontinuous with the analysis of the reproduction of social relations on the left I will argue that Martin Heidegger's analysis of anxiety as a response to those moments where our world breaks down offers further insight into why people carry on regardless. The brilliance of Gramsci's analysis of common sense is that it ensures the continuation of a system while remaining 'ambiguous, contradictory and multiform',[6] permitting an explanation of how a transnational system claiming universality can maintain itself through periodic expressions of nationalism and racism as is currently evident in the UK, but the argument made here is that an ontological analysis helps us understand why such identifications might be comforting in the first place.

Secondly, this essay will turn to the institution most closely connected to knowledge production, namely the university. It will be argued that as a public institution it is the one remaining unit of social governance outside the neoliberal group-think, or the 'herding' referred to above. With the media now largely entrained as an echo-chamber for corporate discourse[7] it is the university that remains the predominant institutional location for dissent and heterodox knowledge. This is not intended to detract from the important challenge posed by a host of social movements; it is rather to draw attention to the orchestration of diverse social institutions such that harmony is privileged over dissonance just as the hierarchical order of oligarchy is privileged over the dangerous equality of democracy. The quiet war that has taken place within the university as an institution over the last 25 years has been one aimed at overcoming its continued capacity to produce noise as well as productive communication, friction as well as flow. In conclusion it will also be suggested that there is a link between this production of noise and the anxiety felt at times of crisis and that the ability for universities – especially in humanities departments that have traditionally engaged with the loss of and search for meaning – to maintain spaces in which noise and anxiety might be explored is essential for our ability to think beyond the dogmatism of our times.

CARRYING ON REGARDLESS

When news of the 2008 financial crisis first broke, the story was clearly a complex one given the role of the financial sector in the global economy. However, from the first day the accounts of the problem were quite focused and introduced a new Americanism into everyday English: sub-prime loans. Along with this we received brief tutorials on the latest financial tools known as Credit Default Swaps and other forms of securitisation that were supposed to have diluted risk to such an extent that the dreaded word 'bust' ought never to have been heard again. The problem was that this belief in risk-free lending encouraged the traditional banking sector – but perhaps more importantly for reasons of regulation and cash ratios the shadow banking sector – to take on bad debt that turned out to be so toxic no amount of dilution could prevent systemic poisoning and eventual collapse. Although problems leading to crisis are endemic to the capitalist system, the practice of securitisation was the most proximate cause of the 2008 crash. This is known by economists, and in a different way, perhaps understood more generally as the recklessness of casino-style banking, so a large part of the population of many countries know this as well.

However, because we had been taken so far into this speculative frenzy by the financial sector, the banks were deemed 'too big to fail' (i.e. too fundamental to the global economy for governments to decline to underwrite their liabilities, no matter what the cost to the public finances). Consequently the subject of the main news story rapidly moved from being reckless financiers – or 'banksters'[8] – and the perils of deregulation to being the need to bail them out with public money. This in turn led to much talk of the deficits which exchequers would be faced with after the bail outs, which in turn led to widespread commentary to the effect that public services and the welfare state could no longer be supported at current levels, which in turn, and with breath-taking speed, became a discourse pertaining to a bloated and unaffordable public sector that needed cutting back, which served as the ideological justification for new waves of privatisation and the further 'rolling back' of the state.[9] In effect the crisis in private speculation was dealt with by transferring the problem to the public sector and creating a crisis in government spending. The tightening of the public purse-strings, justified as necessary 'austerity', is the chief mechanism for protecting the private wealth that has functioned under these circumstances, while the increased need to involve the private sector in works the state could no longer afford to carry out offers new opportunities for that private wealth to increase and a means for temporarily solving problems caused by the current 'spatiotemporal dynamics of capital accumulation'.[10]

This is symptomatic of a condition that I have elsewhere referred to as 'idiotism'.[11] Broadly speaking the term is used to name a situation in which the private, including economic as well as social privatisation (atomisation or individualisation), has come to dominate all aspects of life. Idiotism deploys the original Greek word for the private and the personal, idios, to speak about the pervasive workings of free-market or neoliberal capitalism. Idios refers to the private realm as well as to private property and personal belongings; to what is one's own. It also refers to what is particular or peculiar, a meaning retained in the English words 'idiom' and 'idiosyncratic'. Idios also pertains to that which is distinct and separate, to a realm that is separated or closed off. The philosophy and practice of enclosing the commons has a very significant place in the history of capitalism,[12] so idiotism is also used to register the persistence of enclosure within past and current regimes of accumulation. In addition, this sense of enclosure suggests the closing down of alternatives to neoliberalism; current thinking is so closed off to different views and approaches that it has become profoundly dogmatic.

It must also be noted that idios has an important relation to ideas about knowledge. It is from here that English derives the pejorative term 'idiot'. In Greek the idiotes primarily refers to a person of private standing, that is, someone not holding public office. The derived sense of the idiotes, as a person lacking knowledge, stems from the fact that as a layman the idiotes would not have the specialist knowledge of someone operating in a public capacity.[13] However, while my use of idiotism signifies a condition that privileges the private it is not used here to refer to a condition of stupefied acceptance or generalised ignorance. It is true that our current situation does appear to be lacking intelligence to some degree. The huge disparities in wealth, the trade imbalances on which the global flow of capital is dependent, the persistence of corporate over collective interests (especially in the areas of energy generation), the emergence of a military-industrial complex that increasingly behaves like a corporate praetorian guard, all suggest that our society is seriously out of kilter. And yet this situation has arisen not because of a lack of knowledge or the engendering of false-consciousness, at least not entirely. It can be legitimately assumed that people act the way they do because of a lack of knowledge in certain areas or that stories circulated by a media with a strong corporate bias maintain specific frameworks of knowledge that continue to serve the most powerful – as was noted above with the adroit shift from private catastrophe to public obscenity. But I would like to contend that the reason most people carry on doing what they previously did and thinking what they previously thought in the face of a crisis pertains to how we are in the world rather than what we know about it.

WE ARE THE WORLD

What interests me in Heideger's analysis of *dasein*,[14] which he describes as the being for whom its being is an issue, is that *dasein* cannot be properly understood unless our analysis begins with *dasein*'s practical engagement with rather than knowledge of the world. That our being-in-the-world is primarily practical rather than theoretical and that the means for an adequate understanding of *dasein* takes place via the analysis of tools and their use has promoted a number of Marxist scholars, most notably Lucien Goldmann[15] and Herbert Marcuse[16] to draw a link between Marx and Heidegger. Secondly, and most significantly, Heidegger's account of *dasein* and its world suggests that the discovery that the world one 'knows' is wrong will not necessarily direct *dasein* to change its world, but quite the contrary it is more likely to encourage *dasein* to defend it even more vociferously. This means that while our current predicament can in part be explained through the power of vested interests and what Johnson and Kwak call the 'Washington-Wall Street corridor',[17] the capacity for any ideology to persist needs to be understood in relation to the ontological anxiety engendered when our world begins to fall apart and the tendency for *dasein* to try to practically rebuild what is broken rather than theoretically reflect on the nature of the fault.

This is because there is no distinction between *dasein* and its world. *Dasein* is always in-the-world and cannot be otherwise. In contrast to what Heidegger would call the ontic world of material and ideational things the ontological conception speaks of a primary characteristic of human being itself: world doesn't indicate something objectively distinct from the subject, but indicates a fundamental characteristic of human existence. So while *dasein* can be said to live within specific 'worlds', i.e. regions of objects, tools and practices that distinguish the medical 'world' from the legal 'world', being-in must also be understood ontologically as how we are. Ultimately, human beings are world-creating. They invent, generate, posit, alter, repair and reinforce a meaningful totality called a world, and yet this is never a mastery of the world because *dasein* must be understood as the 'dependency of being referred'.[18] Dasein is dependent upon a set of references, understood as practices, assignments, objects, values and meanings that function as a totality in which it takes its place and from which it projects its future.

Most of the time the world is unproblematic. We go about our everyday dealings with things often without a thought. The world only appears (becomes a problem) when something disturbs its regular rhythms and patterns. This manifesting of the world as the destabilisation of its references offers the opportunity to reflect upon and possibly alter it, but what is important for Heidegger is that such a disturbance more readily induces an experience of profound anxiety that compels *dasein* to turn away from any reflection and re-immerse itself in the everyday dealings it is comfortable with in an attempt to re-establish the meaningful world it 'knows'. At times of crisis the world falls away to be replaced by a questioning that is profoundly unsettling. Such crises are endemic to capitalism, but when Marx described the constant revolution at the heart of bourgeois production – writing 'all that is solid melts into air, all that is holy is profaned, and man is at last compelled to face with sober senses his real conditions of life, and his relations with his kind'[19] – he suggested that capitalism contains within itself the revelation of a radical truth. For Heidegger, however, such moments of authenticity are so anxiety-inducing that they are especially difficult to grasp. In this analysis, knowledge does not bring about the desire for change but the desire to recover things as they were. If crises are essential to the capitalist mode of accumulation we might also say that crises are ontologically essential to the maintenance of the capitalist 'world'. *Dasein*, given no security on the basis of which it might authentically reflect, continuously sets about anxiously trying to repair what is fundamentally broken, potentially deploying every scapegoat common sense allows. In the age of idiotism with its privileging of private enclosure, personal expression and intimate desire, the need to sure up one's world at the expense of others seems even more 'natural'.

In Heidegger's analysis the individual is divided across a complex range of social, political and cultural references in such a manner that should those references be broken, the entity we refer to as the 'subject' is cut adrift, searching for the first point to anchor itself to again. Hence when the system of privatisation and deregulation collapses we deploy a range of prejudices pertaining to race, nation and class to blame the lack of money on a bloated public sector and unnecessary public spending, thereby rescuing the referential totality of privatisation, symbolic consumption, and upward mobility from being undermined. Why would we not try to re-establish a world that posits each singular *dasein* as its own guarantor? For those persuaded by the myth of sovereign individuality, the truth of our distributed social dependency is far less appealing and extremely troubling. The search for a guarantor is one reason why belief in Fate or God is so strong. Irrespective of the accident that befalls us faith in God's will or resignation to the workings of Fate allow our world to accommodate all things. This is why dogma can have such a hold.

THE POLITICS OF DESCRIPTIONS

The understanding that knowledge alone will not enable us to change our practices – or even worse, the argument that knowing something is wrong leads us to strive even more vigorously to maintain the error that sustains us – need not lead to entirely pessimistic conclusions, but suggests that part of the political response to the current fundamentalism must be to create spaces wherein the production of anxiety is permitted if not actively encouraged. One such space has been and ought to remain the university. The problem, of course, is that the university is increasingly being brought within the fundamentalist logic of neoliberalism, and the idea that it might be permitted to investigate other ways of being-in-the-world is increasingly presented as unrealistic and unproductive.

The most recent manifestation of Heideggerian Marxism is the work of Gianni Vattimo and Santiago Zabala, who have deployed Heidegger's understanding of the centrality of interpretation and hermeneutics to challenge what they call 'the politics of descriptions',[20] where any and every alternative to the currently described state of affairs is declared false. Under these conditions the hermeneutic strain in philosophy has been 'reduced to pure nihilism' simply because of its 'ineffectiveness for today's bearers of power' (*Hermeneutic Communism*, p2). Hermeneutics is central to Heidegger's thought because the worlds we build are ultimately interpretations. They are not built on an immutable and final truth, but are brought into being through *dasein*'s interpretive practices in response to the questions that concern us, and this questioning itself arises because the world is a meaningful totality continually prone to meaninglessness.

For Heidegger, this gives truth a polemical, conflictual character, split between the meaningful and the meaningless, between what has been revealed through interpretation and what remains withdrawn. This is a conflict that continually demands new interpretations. Thought historically, truth is the inception of interpretation from out of this polemical condition of our being in-the-world, and this inception takes place continuously. Post-history is utterly alien to *dasein* for whom the world will always be a project. For this interpretive and conflictual understanding of truth Heidegger used the Greek word *alētheia*, meaning to reveal or more literally to bring from out of oblivion. He argued that in the movement away from this conception through the various Latin translations of *veritas, adequatio, rectitude*, and finally the modern *certitudo* 'the conflict indigenous to the very essence of truth'[21] was lost. He goes on to say: 'For us, "truth" means the opposite: that which is beyond all conflict and therefore must be nonconflictual' (*Parmenides*, p18). The imperial tendencies in this notion of truth are set out in the only opposition that certainty permits, namely the distinction between truth and falsity. To falsify is 'to bring to a fall' and with that to command and dominate.

The certainty manifested in today's prevailing forms of knowledge of human affairs, the certainty that makes the market uncontestable, is only complete, though, once the doubt that originally determined what was certain is erased under the new descriptive regime. The sceptical turn in modern knowledge that dealt a serious blow to arbitrary authority has itself been rolled back such that society is once again seemingly ruled by an oligarchy of priests who demand acknowledgement of an invisible hand said to be the true test of, and guide for, all human endeavour. This 'realism' supports contemporary power by denying any other interpretive practice. For Vattimo and Zabala, 'the strong determine the truth, because they are the only ones that have the tools to know, practice, and impose it' (*Hermeneutic Communism*, p12).

Where the scientific demand that knowledge by authorised by proof had revolutionary social and political implications, it is possible to argue that contemporary knowledge production is no longer modern.

Where modernity can be taken to be the instantiation of new socio-political formations in keeping with the epistemological and subsequent technological revolutions, the ingenuity of current intellectual work is restricted to entrepreneurial innovation aimed at optimising the efficiency of a system already in place: one overseen by financial gurus and governmental 'technopols',[22] and deemed sufficient in terms of historical development. There are, of course, new technologies that threaten or promise to revolutionise how we think of ourselves (genetics), matter (nanotechnology), objects (ubiquitous computing), and by extension the human/non-human divide (robotics, AI), and yet it is assumed none of this will challenge the end state of civilisation understood as plutocratic, free market capitalism.

It is important to note how the radical possibilities of these scientific and technological breakthroughs continue to support already assumed descriptions pertaining to the sovereignty of individual, atomised consumers and the market that mediates between them. Exemplary in this regard is the work of MIT professor Neil Gershenfeld on 'personal fabrication'.[23] This work is extraordinary not least for the technical ingenuity of the machines he designs, machines that have more recently entered popular consciousness under the tag '3D printers', but also because of the genuinely revolutionary implications of the machines that promise to take production out of the hands of large transnational corporations and put it 'back in the hands of its users' (*Coming Revolution*, p8). To be clear, the vision is that personal fabricators will not only enable us to make the commodities we currently buy, but also the machines that make the products we currently buy. When thought in terms of its social and economic implications this technology is potentially world-shattering. This is nothing less than workers taking over the means of production or rather being able to purchase an affordable version of the means of production, and it is in this qualification that Gershenfeld's fabricators epitomise the post-historical thinking that has become so dogmatic today. The freedom offered by these machines is not rendered in terms of material independence or collective autonomy, but as the ultimate realisation of personal expression and individual choice. In other words, they reside very much within the descriptions of what is currently deemed preferable – an increasingly free, increasingly niche-oriented, personalised market.

Gershenfeld is adamant that personal fabricators will overcome the problem Marxists refer to as alienation. This future, he writes, 'really represents a return to our industrial roots, before art was separated from artisans', but quickly qualifies this by saying 'when production was done for individuals rather than masses' (*Coming Revolution*, p8). A little later his vision is clearly set out:

> consider what would happen if the physical world outside computers was as malleable as the digital world inside computers. If ordinary people could personalize not just the content of computation but also its physical form. If mass customization lost the 'mass' piece and become [sic] personal customization, with technology better reflecting the needs and wishes of its users because it's been developed by and for its users (*Coming Revolution*, p42).

In this quote it is quite clear to see how the most radical of technological innovation – that theoretically has the potential to revolutionise the spheres of production and consumption and with that the entire character of our society – is nevertheless housed within a politics of descriptions reproducing the definition of individual action based on rational choice in response to supposedly authentic needs that legitimises the entire discourse of free markets, and in turn legitimises the subjection of every aspect of social life to privatisation. In this vision of absolute and total malleability, the foundation of neoliberal dogma remains fixed, if not strengthened.

Of central importance to the established discourse of the free market, especially in times of crisis, is that it remains the best way of representing and satisfying human beings defined as self-maximising, individualised units of competing desire. In this situation the polemical is reduced to conflicting passions that can still be best served by the unitary truth of a thinly veiled, user-friendly, consumer-oriented version of the Hobbesian assumption as to the state of nature. This is the 'realism' that maintains the politics of descriptions. Underneath the talk of freedom, choice, and expression is a philosophical anthropology – a 'knowledge" of human nature – that supports the free market no matter what. This realism, and the corresponding call to 'be realistic' when proposing more fallible, communal, other-directed models of human behaviour, regularly police both popular and academic discourses in favour of the status quo. This means the old dichotomy between facts and values or facts and norms has been resolved in favour of an understanding of reality organised according to a tight set of descriptions that in turn prescribe the sort of approach to the world that will produce the next round of supportive descriptions. For Heidegger this would be the most dangerous form of nihilism; the turning away from any sense that the nature, character or shape of our being-in-the-world might still be open to interpretation. In this manner our tendency to become ontologically absorbed in the world is exaggerated by this monological realism. For Vattimo and Zabala the apparent lack of emergency within the neoliberal worldview following the crisis, or the argument that the free market remains the answer to each and every question is in fact the sign of a dire emergency (*Hermeneutic Communism*, p28): a sign that forms of social organisation lying outside the prescribed frames of reference are now practically unthinkable.

THE POST-HISTORICAL UNIVERSITY

That all university practice must be tightly woven into the politics of descriptions can most clearly be seen in a disturbing document that is currently circulating Australia and New Zealand entitled 'University of the Future'. This is a report written by the accountancy firm Ernst & Young declaring 'the current public university model [...] unviable in all but a few cases'. The fact that Ernst & Young are seen to be an authority on universities is because over recent years the complex social accountability of an institution like the university has been reduced to the one-dimensionality of economic accounting, but what is so brazen about the report is that recommendations for the future of a publicly funded institution should come from a company whose existence is premised on minimising the movement of money from private corporations to the public purse, and one that had such close relations to the financial crisis that warranted a massive bail out with public money.[24]

The point to make, however, is a simple one; the report starts from a set of descriptions, which it refers to as 'drivers' that indicate how universities should transition. These drivers are 'contestability of markets and funding'; 'integration with industry'; 'global mobility'; 'digital technologies'; and 'democratisation of knowledge and access', an issue I will return to below. At no point are the descriptions questioned or challenged. They are simply presented as a reality to which the university must conform; and it can do so in the main only by abandoning its current public status. The idea that the described reality ought to transition, that it might in any way invite let alone require fresh interpretation and alternative modelling, does not occur to the author of the report. What it sets out, therefore, are a series of templates for what Bill Readings called the 'post-historical university'[25] whose purpose and justification lies solely in concurrence with and further facilitation of the world the report describes. Like the economies in which universities operate, all the 'big' questions have been decided and the only legitimate pursuit is contributing to the efficient performance of the system taken as a given.[26]

This form of operational closure has long been known to academics through the managerial discourse of 'excellence', understood as the compliance of academic performances to a set of administratively determined targets. As Readings points out, the term 'excellence' suggests virtuous, high achievement, but in itself 'excellence' is 'entirely meaningless',[27] requiring secondary criteria and judgements to give it some content.[28] In this sense, 'excellence' is not entirely meaningless, but assumes content from the university's performance in relation to broader criteria that determine what is true and good. It is possible to see the university as a social entity automatically and necessarily adapting to changes in its environment, but it is also important not to overlook the fact that these changes are implemented as a result of the active decision-making of a class of people with significant interests in the advancement of a free market doctrine rendered ever-more sovereign. With the unions largely broken and the media having internalised the truth of formal democracy, privatisation, and trickle-down economics, the university is the only social institution that remains outside the neoliberal group-think and the 'psychology of herding'. Because the university has the capacity to produce – and I believe the moral imperative to produce – heterodox, dissenting knowledge, it must be brought into line if the wider neoliberal, corporate system is to operate as effectively as possible. Capital needs to flow. Liquidity is everything to the current system. Alternative interpretations, positing alternative worldviews, and proposing alternative practices feed friction into a system that desires to be smooth. This is the meaning of the otherwise meaningless University of Excellence and the ideology of compliance.

The university as an institution, however, has always been subject to a variety of social and political interventions. As Gordon Graham[29] clearly shows, while the medieval university was deployed by monarchs and popes to further their interests and advance their beliefs the modern university has been subject to all manner of political interventions and policy changes. For example, the goal of promoting distance learning – taken to be an essential response to the drivers described by Ernst & Young – dates back to at least 1849 when the University of London established such a provision and dis-established the requirement for residency amongst its students. As Graham notes, this means of examination not only opened up the

University of London to more students, but it also became the model of non-resident examination that enabled universities to play an important role in the education and administration of the British Empire. It would be foolish, then, to suggest that the university as an institution has an essential and immutable purpose. What has been consistent in its history has been the centrality of literacy and learning to its practices; but much like the discourse of excellence, learning needs to be shaped by evaluations of what is to be learned, for what purpose and how it is to be done. Such evaluations always take us back to socio-political determinants and the fact that the university as an institution has always had a certain plasticity, whether it was overseen by Church or State.

The specific determinants currently shaping the post-historical university are the discourse of 'impact', the practice of 'casualisation', and the over-arching disciplinary mechanism of 'customer service', something that clearly indicates how the regime of compliance couples university practice to wider neoliberal doctrine. With regard to the first of these terms the value of research in the UK is becoming increasingly judged according to its capacity to demonstrate its immediate 'economic and social impact', while Anglophone academic journals are increasingly judged in terms of a supposedly measurable 'impact factor' derived from a bibliometric measure of the speed and frequency with which their contents generate citations. In the UK, the measurement of 'impact' has become a central element of another disciplinary mechanism known as the 'Research Excellence Framework', that grades the quality of research outputs. Although impact-measurement also considers the 'reach and significance' of research in a way that enables the use of criteria traditionally used to assess scholarly importance, the demand for it remains an attempt to incrementally tie research to indicators of social utility seen to be conducive to the greater efficiency of the system. Impact-measurement still allows for some critical work, but research is increasingly being shaped by the need for immediate demonstrable outcomes, and given that university senior management are increasingly under pressure to secure extra income now that public funding of degree places has been so dramatically reduced, academic decisions about which projects to pursue are increasingly made with 'grant capture' in mind. This is a situation that directly affects the humanities, but is equally likely to be detrimental to physics departments where cosmologists may also find it hard to demonstrate how their 'star-gazing' will produce the requisite commodifiable spin-offs.

The next step will be to introduce a tenure-style system to the UK that affords a further disciplining of research in relation to the objectives of senior management.[30] Before this happens, and perhaps even pre-empting the need for it, the most likely route to ensuring academics do what is deemed necessary would be the adoption of another feature of US higher education, namely the casualisation of employment. This was an issue brought to my attention by an important article Sarah Kendzior recently wrote for Al-Jazeera entitled 'The Closing of American Academia'. In this piece Kendzior describes how a friend of hers spent almost her entire salary to get to a conference they were both attending. 'My friend is an adjunct', she writes. 'She has a PhD in anthropology and teaches at a university, where she is paid $2100 per course. While she is a professor, she is not a Professor. She is, like 67 percent of American university faculty, a part-time employee on a contract that may or may not be renewed each semester. She receives no benefits or health care'.[31]

There is no reason why academics should not be subject to the increased casualisation haunting the new 'precaritat'.[32] Precarity works perfectly well for ensuring compliance and the eradication of expensive labour rights in other areas of employment, and in all likelihood will increasingly be used to make the intellectual work force 'fit and flexible' in an age of austerity. Under the cover of not being able to afford it – or in response to drivers such as 'global mobility' – funding of full-time, permanent posts will no doubt reduce as workloads are covered by casual staff topping-up their income by working for companies such as essaysontime.com, who exemplify the opportunities in the ever-growing market for customised, on-demand essay writing. Some permanent staff will no doubt be retained. There will be the intellectual celebrities that promote a particular UniCorp brand or those that supervise PhD students, a steady flow of which will be needed to keep the pool of potential adjuncts competitive.

The casualisation of faculty will be the perfect instrument for market-supporting research delivery. It will also be affected by the move towards customer service in which it is becoming increasingly important to offer courses that students want to do, and increasingly on topics they think they already know something about. Recruitment via courses dovetailing precisely with career paths, and courses that are entertaining and user-friendly are becoming the norm. Should the adjunct professor fail to comply their contract will automatically fail to renew because failure from within this perspective can only be on the delivery side. It is a no-win situation for academics, especially adjuncts already operating from a position that is subordinate and temporary. The irony is that while student input is essential to the maintenance of good pedagogic practice, customer service is not. Customer service aims at fast, clear, efficient and accessible communication with the goal of greater immediacy in relation to the resolution of an existing problem. By contrast, communication in a pedagogic relation might require the mediation of 'noise' as a student's assumptions about the world are challenged and problems are magnified or made manifest during the learning process. This is no excuse for poor teaching, simply a recognition that the interface for student and customer can be, and in some ways must be of a completely different order.

THOUGHT BUBBLE

The Ernst & Young report quotes one anonymous university Vice-Chancellor declaring: 'Our major competitor in ten years time will be Google ... if we're still alive!' This quote supposedly encapsulates changes to our relation to knowledge indicative of the two drivers of change which the report calls 'digital technologies' and 'democratization'. The reason why these two are related is because the report understands democratisation simply in terms of 'access' and then assumes the flawed syllogism whereby because digital technologies make knowledge accessible and democracy is about access, therefore all digital technologies are democratic. It would be foolish to suggest that a report citing 'the Darwinian force of the market'[33] could countenance the idea that democracy ought to be measured by something other than consumer-style access, but access in and of itself is not inherently democratic. Much like 'excellence' it requires secondary criteria to become a meaningful concept. Admittedly the report does avoid the positivist trap that users of Google can easily fall into, of assuming that knowledge is simply 'out there', such that its acquisition is merely a matter of data retrieval. The author of the report does link knowledge to analysis and interpretation, but given that we are asked to bend our knee to 'the Darwinian force of the market', one suspects that analysis and interpretation is of a kind with that found in the pages of the *Financial Times* and will be limited to debates over best policy within a given system, rather than any ontological engagement with the character and shape of the world itself.

The Google model is, however, exemplary of the problem faced by the post-historical university and the nature of its democratic role. Leaving aside the rather obvious point that in the pursuit of profit Google have quite happily aided the Chinese government in their restriction of the democracy movement in that country, the Google model is significant because its success is based on successfully attending to and facilitating the personalisation that has come to define both democracy and knowledge in neoliberal consumer cultures. Google's success has primarily come from its ability to provide a highly individualised service, partly due to the capacity of its search engine to learn what the user likes and to display results that are closely aligned to preferences indicated through earlier 'click signals'; but this has also been a path to monetisation as the company is able to claim that it can deliver customers to companies with impressive precision. In an economy increasingly based on information, attention becomes a very rare commodity,[34] so the ability to deliver attention to advertisers becomes a highly profitable capability. The capacity for Google to archive click signals affords increasingly successful searches without additional work from the user and provides a profile that companies can attach themselves to in their search for consumers.

While this mode of information retrieval sits well with all the neoliberal markers of value – individuality, preference, choice, competition, immediacy – it gives rise to significant concerns for both knowledge and democracy that must not be ignored. In a fascinating book entitled *The Filter Bubble*, Eli Pariser sets out the implications of the Google algorithm. Initially, while the idea that what is best for one person may not be best for someone else is hardly revolutionary, the idea that a search engine is 'biased to share our own views'[35] has far-reaching consequences. In short, 'your computer monitor is a kind of one-way mirror, reflecting your own interests while algorithmic observers watch what you click' (*Filter Bubble*, p3). Here, access is instant and individualised, but Pariser is concerned that where 'democracy requires a reliance on shared facts [...] we're being offered parallel but separate universes' (*Filter Bubble*, p5). While it is important to argue that "facts" are not enough, shared or not, the problem is accentuated because the search engine, which is now a 'prediction engine' (*Filter Bubble*, p9), has a tendency to search out 'facts' you have already indicated a preference for through click signals. Ultimately the cookies and bots that aid personalised web-browsing begin to produce a filter bubble; 'a unique universe of information for each of us', but more importantly one that 'fundamentally alters the way we encounter ideas and information' (*Filter Bubble*, p9). In other words, the Google model is one in which we continually receive more of what we already know and have indicated a preference for. Ultimately, the filter bubble is 'a cozy place, populated by our favourite people and things and ideas' (*Filter Bubble*, p12).

Pariser notes that while this personalisation flatters users who believe they are in a position of control because the prediction engine appears to be giving them what they want, it increasingly subjects users 'to a kind of informational determinism in which what you clicked on in the past determines what you see next' (*Filter Bubble*, p16). This mode of personalised access means that Google does have great significance for the post-historical university, but that significance does not lie in the claim that Google University is the future as Ernst & Young would have us believe. Rather, the Google model is significant because the two forces of impact and customer service suggest that the post-historical university will increasingly take on the character of a filter bubble. As research is increasingly directed towards what are described to be the needs of the current system, and teaching is tailored to satisfying the existing desires and preferences of students refigured as customers, the university's role in the global knowledge economy will be to offer more of the same. The university has always had a major role to play in maintaining the cultural status quo and policing knowledge, but it has also historically been a major site for the social production of dissensus which is irreducible to the promotional language of 'innovation' and 'entrepreneurialism' (or any historical equivalent thereof). Ultimately the sole purpose of the Ernst & Young report is to ensure that the university of the future plays an integral part in the production of an 'identity loop' (*Filter Bubble*, p127), or what we might call a thought bubble that reproduces the truth of market logic.

In the face of this doctrinal onslaught the future of the university as a social institution looks bleak, but despite the heavy-handed ideological work that the Ernst & Young report epitomises, the future cannot be closed off in the way they hope. As was noted in the introduction, the rationality of markets was shown to be a pseudo-science by the persistence and the effects of what Besley and Hennessey called the 'psychology of herding'. First of all this produced the hysterical delusion that the business cycle had been overcome, which was then counteracted by the global loss of confidence that brought about the greatest economic crisis in living memory. The evident role played by these 'animal spirits' testifies to the importance of a non-theoretical, non-rational relation to the world, but also to a more profound ontological state of mind that Heidegger refers to as 'attunement' or 'mood'.[36] Ordinarily that attunement is an unremarkable and comfortable familiarity, but one that might become a concerted defence in times of crisis. Fluctuations in mood are usually accompanied by stories that tell us something about the world we live in. With regards to the world of economics these are stories that precipitate trust, confidence, euphoria, frenzy, fear, and anxiety.[37] These spirits and the stories that shape them are evidence of the continuing hermeneutic condition set out above. Stories make a world of sense, but they are only ever interpretations and remain subject to the vagaries of mood.

The narrative of neoliberal post-history can claim to be the rightful representation of human relations only because it is underwritten by gigantic economic, political and social power that supports and distributes its stories, not because it has discovered the truth. In such an environment, academics regularly articulate concern about the utilitarian if not instrumental mood, of managers and students alike. While the discourses of impact and customer service further support such instrumentality and suggest that the university of the future will increasingly help lock down the narrative of post-history, there is still hope. In keeping with Heidegger's (in)famous use of Hölderlin's words: 'But where danger is, grows/The saving power also',[38] the pressures on students to achieve a certain GPA or class of degree and the demands on them to be socially compliant, still does not eradicate their sense that the world is contestable. In many cases the mood of students remains one of scepticism and doubt towards the supposed common sense, coupled with a desire for change. They remain interested in the big questions and readily support courses that make great theoretical demands on them. Students tend to be of an age when the sedimented world they have inherited has not yet ossified and all kinds of malformations and reformations remain possible. This means that an important role can still be played by the university; not one that is reduced to increasing access to what is already given, but one that opens up spaces for this contestation and challenging of the world, for offering up radically alternative ways of living and being-with-others.

As was noted in the introduction, the humanities have an especially important role to play in this regard. While traditional humanities disciplines such as philosophy, English, and history have all supported social and political conservatism through, amongst other things, the defence of a canon, these disciplines have also been traditionally concerned with that gap between the meaningful and meaninglessness that defines the human condition. Whether a philosophical treatise, a work of literature, or the recovery of a counter-history, work in the humanities has always occupied that space where the meaningful totality we call our world suffers a variety of disruptions and is revealed to be inadequate. The humanities are never more alive than when faced with the loss of an established truth and the slipping away of the world. Some of the greatest works in the humanities are riddled with anxiety. It therefore falls on the humanities in a time of crisis to enable anxiety to work in the name of alternative visions, which is precisely why the humanities are under such strident attack within the marketised model. This is also a role that ought to be taken beyond the campus to form the beginnings of a new contract with a public that has just bailed out private speculators at the expense of public welfare. Turning away from the anxiety generated by the crisis will only encourage more of the same. The public role of the university should be to ensure this anxiety, understood as the re-emergence of the questioning that neoliberal post-history continually seeks to suppress, is turned to creative use.

NOTES

1. John Maynard Keynes, *The General Theory of Employment, Interest and Money*, New York, MacMillan, 1973.
2. Milton Friedman, *Capitalism and Freedom*, Chicago, University of Chicago Press, 2002, p13.
3. Friedrich Hayek freely likens the contemplation of the free market to religious experience. For him it is 'submission to the impersonal forces of the free market' that has 'made possible the growth of a civilization', F.A. Hayek, *The Road to Serfdom*, Chicago, University of Chicago Press, 2007, p212, and he goes on to write that the necessity of submitting to these forces is better served by the 'humble awe' (p212) demanded by religion than any rational understanding.
4. John Bellamy Foster and Fred Magdoff, *The Great Financial Crisis*, New York, Monthly Review Press, 2009; George A. Akerlof and Robert J. Shiller, *Animal Spirits: How Human Psychology Drives the Economy and why it Matters for Global Capitalism*, Princeton, Princeton University Press, 2009; John Quiggin, *Zombie Economics: How Dead Ideas Still Walk Among Us*, Princeton, Princeton University Press, 2010; David Harvey, *The Enigma of Capital: and the Crises of Capitalism*, London, Profile Books, 2010.
5. Harvey, op. cit; Neal Curtis, *Idiotism: Capitalism and the Privatization of Life*, London, Pluto Press, 2013.
6. Antonio Gramsci, *Selections from the Prison Notebooks*, London, Lawrence and Wishart, 1971, p423.
7. Robert McChesney, *Rich Media, Poor Democracy: Communication Politics in Dubious Times*, New York, The New Press, 2000.
8. John Lanchester, *Whoops! Why Everyone Owes Everyone and No One Can Pay*, London, Penguin Books, 2010.
9. At the same time, relatively small private companies known as ratings agencies, who make judgements regarding the quality of an economy from the perspective of investors – not workers, mothers, patients, students, or any other social category that might have a stake in the shape of an economy – held complete

sway over democratically elected officials. Do what the rating agency like and your borrowing costs remain stable; do what they don't like and your borrowing costs soar. Of course, what ratings agencies like is the liberalisation of economies because extending privatisation and the selling of public or common assets is good for investors.

10. David Harvey, *The New Imperialism*, Oxford, Oxford University Press, 2003 and 'In What Ways Is "The New Imperialism" Really New?', *Historical Materialism*, 15, 3, (2007): 57-70.

11. Curtis, *Idiotism*, op. cit.

12. Vandana Shiva, *Stolen Harvest, The Hijacking of the Global Food Supply*, London, Zed Books, 2000; Harvey, *The New Imperialism*, op. cit; Ellen Meiksins Wood, *Empire of Capital*, London, Verso Books, 2003.

13. In his cultural history of idiocy, Patrick McDonagh, *Idiocy: A Cultural History*, Liverpool, Liverpool University Press, 2008, attributes Macbeth's claim that life is a tale told by an idiot precisely to this meaning of idiots. Following his wife's suicide, even the public office of the King means nothing as, in the face of death, even he is reduced to the standing of the idiots and the finitude that is most common. In this context stupidity would be reserved for someone unable to recognise that mortality undermines earthly power.

14. Martin Heidegger, *Being and Time*, Oxford, Basil Blackwell, 1962.

15. Lucien Goldmann, *Lukács and Heidegger: Towards a New Philosophy*, London, Routledge, 1977.

16. Herbert Marcuse, *Heideggerian Marxism*, University of Nebraska Press, 2005.

17. Simon Johnson and James Kwak, *13 Bankers: The Wall Street Takeover and the Next Financial Meltdown*, New York, Pantheon Books, 2010.

18. Heidegger, *Being and Time*, op. cit., p81.

19. Karl Marx and Friedrich Engels, *The Communist Manifesto*, London, Verso Books, 2012, pp38-9.

20. Gianni Vattimo and Santiago Zabala, *Hermeneutic Communism: From Heidegger to Marx*, New York, Columbia University Press, 2011, p12, hereafter *Hermeneutic Communism* in the essay.

21. Martin Heidegger, *Parmenides*, Bloomington, Indiana University Press, 1992, p18, hereafter *Parmenides* in the essay.

22. Leslie Sklair, *The Transnational Capitalist Class*, Oxford, Blackwell Publishers, 2000.

23. Neil Gershenfeld, *Fab: The Coming revolution of your Desktop-From Personal Computers to Personal Fabrication*, New York, Basic Books, 2007, hereafter *Coming revolution* in the essay.

24. Ernst & Young were the accountants for Lehman Brothers and implicated in the 'balance sheet manipulation', Jill Treanor, 'Lehman audit investigator takes no action against Ernst & Young', *Guardian*, 22,06,2012, that took place at that now defunct organisation just before their collapse in 2008.

25. Bill Readings, *The University in Ruins*, Cambridge, MA, Harvard University Press, 1996.

26. This shift was first set out in Jean-François Lyotard's 'report on knowledge' entitled *The Postmodern Condition*. This much criticised yet visionary report, which appeared in French in 1979, the year Margaret Thatcher came to power in the

UK, presciently explained how the only narrative now legitimating knowledge was 'performativity' understood as the optimisation of systemic inputs and outputs primarily organised through the dominance of the commodity form and the social relations accompanying it. Knowledge was now legitimate only if it was commodifiable and generated surplus value. However, while Lyotard's diagnosis of the emerging condition was correct, his history of the modern university was insufficiently complex. Although this is not the place to set out a history of the university, the idea that knowledge had been legitimated by the two meta-narratives of Idealism and Republicanism was too simplistic.

27. Reading, op. cit., p22.

28. In an earlier manifestation such secondary criteria would have pertained to the institution's contribution to the culture of national life and advancement of national identity. For Readings, however, as the nation-state is no longer 'the organizing centre of the common existence of peoples across the planet, ... the University of Excellence serves nothing other than itself, another corporation in a world of transnationally exchanged capital', Reading, op. cit., p43. Although I would challenge Readings' hasty declaration of the death of the nation-state it is also necessary to challenge his argument that without the nation-state it is impossible to consider this discourse ideological. In the age of transnational capital the role of the nation-state has changed, but it remains a key element in facilitating the movement of capital through enacting local policies of privatisation, deregulation and other forms of supportive legislation. In keeping with this it is imperative that knowledge is produced that legitimises, justifies and reinforces descriptions of the world that underpin these policies.

29. Gordon Graham, *Universities: The Recovery of an Idea*, Thorverton, Imprint Academic, 2002.

30. For a discussion of how managerialism is linked to the doctrine of neoliberalism see Chapter 4 of Curtis, *Idiotism*, op. cit.

31. Kendzior continues: 'In most professions, salaries below the poverty line would be cause for alarm. In academia, they are treated as a source of gratitude. Volunteerism is par for the course – literally. Teaching is touted as a "calling", with compensation an afterthought. One American research university offers its PhD students a salary of $1000 per semester for the "opportunity" to design and teach a course for undergraduates, who are each paying about $50,000 in tuition. The university calls this position "Senior Teaching Assistant" because paying an instructor so far below minimum wage is probably illegal', http://www.aljazeera.com/indepth/opinion/2012/08/2012820102749246453.html.

32. Ivor Southwood, *Non-Stop Inertia*, Winchester, Zero Books, 2011.

33. It is interesting to note that the author of the Ernst & Young report cites this Darwinian force precisely at the point when he notes that a number of the 'industry leaders' felt the sector could 'continue with broadly similar models to those of today' (p15).

34. Christian Marazzi, *Capital and Language*, New York, *Semiotext(e)*, 2008.

35. Eli Pariser, *The Filter Bubble: What the Internet is Hiding from You*, London, Penguin/Viking, 2011, p3, hereafter *Filter Bubble* in the essay.

36. Heidegger, *Being and Time*, op. cit., p175.

37. Akerlof and Shiller, *Animal Spirits*, op. cit.

38. Martin Heidegger, *The Question Concerning Technology and other Essays*, New York, Harper Torchbooks, 1977, p34.

CAPITALIST REALISM AND NEOLIBERAL HEGEMONY: A DIALOGUE

Mark Fisher and Jeremy Gilbert

This is a dialogue conducted over email by Mark Fisher, author of the widely-read *Capitalist Realism: Is There No Alternative* and Jeremy Gilbert, editor of *New Formations*. The discussion touches on issues raised by Fisher's book, by some of Gilbert's work as a theorist and analyst, by some of the political commentary in which each has engaged at various times (online and in print), as well as by the recent prevalence of a certain identification with anarchist ideas and methods amongst activists and online commentators whose intellectual and political reference points are otherwise very close to those of Fisher and Gilbert. It considers the concept of 'capitalist realism' as a way of understanding neoliberal ideology and hegemony; the role of bureaucracy in neoliberal culture and the 'societies of control'; the types of political and cultural strategy that might be required to challenge their hegemonic position; the relationship between political strategies which do and do not focus on conventional party politics; the general condition of politics in the UK today. Although largely concerned with a specifically British (and, arguably, English) political context, its consideration of abstract issues around the theorisation of ideology and neoliberalism and the nature of political strategy have far wider applicability.

JG: Your use of the term 'capitalist realism' seems to designate, at its simplest, both the conviction that there is no alternative to capitalism as a paradigm for social organisation, and the mechanisms which are used to disseminate and reproduce that conviction amongst large populations. As such it would seem to be both a 'structure of feeling', in Williams' terms (or perhaps an 'affective regime' in a slightly more contemporary register) and, in quite a classical sense, a hegemonic ideology, operating as all hegemonic ideologies do, to try to efface their own historicity and the contingency of the social arrangements which they legitimate. Is that right? Could you correct and/or expand on that explication of the term and say a little bit about its genesis and its specific implications?

MF: I don't think there's anything to correct in your description. I think, though, that we can say that capitalist realism has effaced not only its own historicity and contingency, but also its own existence as an ideological constellation. You could say that effacement is what defines capitalist realism. The hegemonic field which capitalist realism secures and intensifies is one in which politics itself has been 'disappeared'. What capitalist realism consolidates is the idea that we are in the era of the post-political – that the big ideological conflicts are over, and the issues that remain largely concern who is to administrate the new consensus. Of course, there's nothing more ideological than the idea that we've moved beyond ideology. It has become increasingly clear over the last few years, especially since 2008, that the (essentially 1990s) idea of the post-political and the post-ideological was always a cover for neoliberal hegemony. The increased use of the term neoliberalism since 2000 is a symptom of the weakening power of neoliberalism. The more it is named, the less its doctrines can pose as post-political.

Nevertheless, the notion of the post-political isn't just an ideological ruse. Membership of political parties and trade unions really is declining. It's a commonplace that the major political parties in the UK and the US are scarcely distinguishable from one another. Very few people identify themselves as political. Given this context, there's something misleading about describing capitalist realism, as I myself often tend to, as the belief that capitalism is the only viable political economic system. Capitalist realism could perhaps better be seen as a set of behaviours and affects that arise from this 'belief'. The dominance of capitalism, the inability to imagine an alternative to it, now constitute a sort of invisible horizon. Few explicitly think about 'capitalism' as such – the disappearance of alternatives, even if only imaginary alternatives, make it much harder to apprehend capitalism as a specific, contingent system. Capitalist realism as I have understood it entails this deep embedding in a world – or set of worlds – in which capitalism is massively naturalised.

Capitalist realism doesn't appear in the first instance, then, as a political position. It emerges instead as a pragmatic adjustment – 'this is the way thing are now'. This sense of resignation, of fatalism, is crucial to the 'realism'. Here we can distinguish between neoliberalism and capitalist realism. Capitalist realism isn't the direct endorsement of neoliberal doctrine; it's the idea that, whether we like it or not, the world is governed by neoliberal ideas, and that won't change. There's no point fighting the inevitable.

It's not an accident that I came to the idea of capitalist realism while working in a Further Education (FE) college at the height of Blairism. New Labour was the paradigmatic example of a formerly left-wing party capitulating to capitalist realism. For it must be recognised that capitalist realism is a pathology of the left. It is the left which has had to tell itself the story that there's no point struggling for an alternative to capitalism. In other words, capitalist realism is the left acquiescing in the narrative that the new right so aggressively pushed in the 1980s. Thatcher was right to claim Blair as her greatest achievement. Labour's painful journey from unelectability in the 1980s to government in the 1990s ended up consummately proving Thatcher's point that there is no alternative. When Thatcher first made that remark, she was saying that there is no *viable* alternative to neoliberal capitalism. By 1997, there was no *imaginable* alternative.

In the Further Education sector where I worked, you could see the practical and existential consequences of all this. There was an acceptance amongst managers of the inevitability that education would increasingly be modelled on business. Some managers would typically introduce new procedures by explicitly saying that they didn't themselves think they were a good idea, but what could you do? This was how things were to be done now, and the easiest option all round would be for us to go through the motions. We didn't have to believe it, we only had to act as if we believed it. The idea that our 'inner beliefs' mattered more than what we were publicly professing at work was crucial to capitalist realism. We could have left-wing convictions, and a left-wing self-image, provided these didn't impinge on work in any significant way! This was ideology in the old Althusserian sense – we were required to use a certain language and engage in particular ritualised behaviours, but none of this mattered because we didn't 'really' believe in any of it. But of course the very privileging of 'inner' subjective states over the public was itself an ideological move.

Capitalist realism, then, is essentially about the depoliticisation of work and, more broadly, of everyday life. That's one of the saddest effects of the subduing of unions. At work, we learn to accept worsening pay and conditions as 'just the way things are' in a competitive, globalised world. 'Politics' becomes something that we engage in only at the ballot box, if we even consider that to be worthwhile (and many of those who vote think of it as a pointless, impotent act) or, if we're of a more activist bent, it's something that we do at protests of various kinds. In either case, work becomes decoupled from politics. (One benefit of the occupations that happened in educational institutions as part of the anti-fees movement in the UK in 2010 was that they remade the link between work and politics.)

In summary, then, I think it's best not to see capitalist realism as a political position but as something which precludes political involvement and identification. It therefore follows that one of the most effective first steps in the struggle against capitalist realism will be the invention of new ways in which people can become involved with politics.

JG: What do you see as the role of bureaucratic managerialism in the neoliberal regime?

MF: The – on the face of it – strange role that bureaucratic managerialism played in neoliberal culture was central to the formation of my thinking about capitalist realism. It became increasingly apparent to me that we were living out a cognitive dissonance. We'd internalised the idea that it was social democracy, socialism and Stalinism that were bureaucratic, and that neoliberalism was against red tape of all kinds. Yet workers, particularly workers in public services, found ourselves doing more bureaucracy than ever before. How can we make sense of this?

The first thing to say is that the nature of the bureaucracy has changed. Bureaucracy has become decentralized. It's not (just) something to which we are subject now; it's something which we are required to actively produce ourselves. In some respects, we're in a worst of all worlds scenario, in which the old, top down state bureaucratic apparatuses are supplemented by a regime of self-surveillance. We're all familiar with this regime – continuing professional development, performance reviews, log books, not to mention the whole machine of the Research Excellence Framework (REF).[1] We're also familiar with the diffuse atmosphere of light cynicism which surrounds these activities. When I was working in FE, one manager would cheerily present us with each new initiative, openly saying that he didn't think it was of much value, but that we should do it to make our lives easier. He once told our team that we weren't sufficiently critical of ourselves in one of our performance reviews – but not to worry because nothing would happen on the basis of any criticisms that we made. I don't know what was more demoralising here: the fact that we were required to denigrate ourselves as part of our job, or the fact that the criticisms we made were a purely empty exercise. Some of the affective consequences of this self-surveillance regime are amply demonstrated here: anxiety, accompanied by a sense of the meaninglessness of the activity about which one is anxious. The word 'Kafkaesque' is enormously over-used, but it fits this existential situation perfectly. So, bureaucracy becomes immanent to the fabric of work in general, not something performed by a special kind of worker. This also means that what we might call bureaucratic time has changed. In line with Deleuze's highly prescient analyses in his essay 'Postscript on Societies of Control', there is a shift from the punctuated time of the periodic assessment to the more open time of the continuous assessment. The inspection never ends. As Deleuze says, drawing on a term from Kafka's *The Trial*, we are in a condition of indefinite postponement. Our status is never fully ratified; it is always up for review. The legalese vagueness of the criteria by which we are judged intensifies the sense of uncertainty: can we be sure have we interpreted the guidelines correctly?

Rather than an elimination of bureaucracy, what we've seen under neoliberalism is just the reverse: bureaucracy's mad, cancerous proliferation. Increasingly, what this new bureaucracy measures is not the worker's ability to perform their job, but their ability to perform bureaucratic tasks effectively. This has perverse effects on the way that institutions function, which we saw demonstrated with New Labour's 'target culture'. As is now well known, the imposition of targets led to widespread gaming of the system, and also a neglect of those areas which fell outside the remit of the target. I've called this situation 'Market Stalinism'. This isn't just a joke; what it highlights is the extent to which neoliberalism depends upon authoritarian bureaucratic control systems. Again, New Labour exemplified this perfectly. The party repudiated authoritarian Stalinism at the level of ideological content, but, at the level of form, Labour became an increasingly authoritarian organisation. The concept of Market Stalinism also allows us to recognise that neoliberalism was never about reducing governmental control in order to free up the market. Market dynamics don't spontaneously appear in public services, they have to be constructed – and, as the examples I've already given show, this requires, not a trimming back of bureaucratic agencies, but the production of new forms of bureaucracy. In order that institutions and workers can be seen to be competing with one another, it is necessary to produce all kinds of spurious quantificatory data. This means that, in education and other public services, we're not dealing with 'marketization' so much as a pseudo-marketization, the *simulation* of market dynamics.

The question then arises – if this neoliberal bureaucracy is (in its own 'official' terms) dysfunctional, if it doesn't work to achieve its stated goals, then, what is its real purpose? I think there are a number of answers to this. The first is that the Market Stalinist bureaucracy has an ideological effect. If, as Althusser said, ideology is essentially ritualistic – i.e. it makes us adopt a certain language, range of behaviours etc. – then neoliberal bureaucracy is quintessentially ideological. It not only naturalises and normalises the language and practices of business; it makes the ritualised performance of this naturalisation a condition of workers retaining their jobs. The second role that managerialist bureaucracy plays for neoliberalism is a disciplinary function: it subdues and pacifies workers. The anxiety that neoliberal bureaucracy so often produces should not be seen as an accidental side-effect of these measures; rather, the anxiety is something that is in itself highly desirable from the perspective of the neoliberal project. The erosion of confidence, the sense of being alone, in competition with others: this weakens the worker's resolve, undermines their capacity for solidarity, and forestalls militancy.

So it seems to me that the politicizing of managerialist bureaucracy could be extremely fruitful from the point of view of the struggle against neoliberalism. There is a widespread discontent with managerialism, but, in the lack of any agent or organised struggle which can focus it, this discontent will remain impotent grumbling. This is just the kind of space that I was referring to in my first answer, when I was talking about the kinds of struggle which could reconnect politics to work and everyday life. For whatever reason, unions don't yet seem to have grasped the potential here. This is a catastrophic shame – the tendency of neoliberal bureaucracy is to individualise (with the threat that, if individuals refuse to co-operate with particular bureaucratic initiatives, they will lose their job). It can only be countered by the kind of collective action which unions ought to be able to organise.

JG: Your point about capitalist realism being legitimated by the idea that the interior conscience is the only true site of the authentic self seems quite crucial. I think one of the implications of a properly anti-individualist philosophy has to be at least a certain scepticism towards the assumption, inherited from the confessional tradition, from Romanticism and from depth psychology, that the interior life is the privileged site of authentic selfhood. That's hardly a new observation I know, but your point lends it a new kind of critical urgency I think. It's been clear for a long time that neoliberalism effectively offers us a bargain whereby we accept the lack of collective control over our physical or social environment in return for a very high level of personal autonomy outside the sphere of work: the logical correlate of that is to accept a mode of subjectivity which ultimately accords all value and intensity to an entirely private domain of personal consumption. But one further problem here is that many contemporary forms of labour are all about the production and reproduction of affects and relations...so to some extent there has to be an increasingly demarcated boundary, a sort of psychic *cordon sanitaire*, between this posited domain of interior authenticity, and the whole remainder of a subject's social, affective, relational and emotional life ... I wonder if what we're talking about here is something like the logic of Oedipalisation as described by Deleuze and Guattari (D&G) ... which is rather different from the classical psychoanalytic understanding of Oedipus as simply a function of all possible civilisation. Of course Zizek tries to tackle this complex of issues a bit in his interesting essay 'Whither Oedipus?' from a few years ago, but he's still, I think, coming from a perspective that doesn't quite grasp D&G's point that the experience of desire-as-lack, which is partly dependent upon the demarcation of the interiority of the subject (where lack is experienced as the truth of our experience) from the rest of existence, is actively *produced* by capitalism rather than simply being given a particular meaning by it. Any thoughts on this?

MF: This set of issues seems to me to represent a major tension in capitalist culture at the moment. On the one hand, as you say, it is increasingly difficult to separate life from work. In conditions of mandatory entrepreneurialism, where we are continually enjoined to sell ourselves, it is in one sense almost impossible to set up the *cordon sanitaire* to which you refer. This isn't only a matter of duties extending beyond the workplace – via email and the like – it is also because it is our own subjectivity that is for sale. It's not enough to just do our jobs; we have to be seen wanting to do them. What we do in our 'spare time' becomes an asset we can market at work, while activities that are ostensibly beyond work, such as updating our Facebook profiles, are work in the sense that they create value – but we are not remunerated for this value-creation.

Seen from another angle, that kind of *cordon sanitaire*, far from being impossible to maintain, loooks like a condition of work now. It's what characterises alienation in the classic sense. We acquiesce at work because work and 'what we really are' have to remain separate.

We live in a new age of Oedipus. It seems to me that the basic Deleuze and Guattari story – that capitalism actively produces neurotic individualism, that Oedipus is the reterritorialized face of a capitalism that is, at its other pole, increasingly abstract, impersonal, 'dehumanised' – has been strongly confirmed by recent political and cultural developments.

Since around the turn of the millennium, there's been a shift in culture towards a neurotic individualism. On social networks, we become anxious curators of our own identities. With reality TV such as *Big Brother*, television talent shows and business-based TV programmes such as *The Apprentice* and *Dragon's Den*, there's been a strong emphasis on individuals competing with one another, and an exploitation of the affective and supposedly 'inner' aspects of the participants' lives. This is another dimension of capitalist realism. It's no accident that 'reality' became the dominant mode of entertainment in the last decade or so. The 'reality' usually amounts to individuals struggling against one another, in conditions where competition is artificially imposed, and collaboration is actively repressed.

Now let me ask you some questions.

MF: It's hard not to have some sympathy for the anarchist critique of parliamentary politics at the moment. How can we counter this – what reasons are there to be in any way optimistic about change coming through parliament?

JG: Well firstly let's acknowledge the validity of the first part of your opening remark. It's hard not to have sympathy for a highly reductive critique of parliamentary politics – which would see it as effectively useless from a progressive, radical or democratic perspective – because representative politics across Europe, North America, Australasia, and even in South Africa, seems to have been able to deliver very little beyond various degrees of accommodation to the demands of neoliberalism for several decades now, despite the widespread unpopularity of that programme in most instances. That's the most immediately visible fact about the relationship between formal representative politics and any set of – even quite minimally – egalitarian political objectives in recent years. If we think that there's any point in getting involved with representative politics at all – and I think we both do – then initially it's up to us to respond to that observation by explaining why.

The first thing I would say is that, when thinking about this kind of question, we always have to look at actual history. What has and hasn't been achieved in the past by whatever means, that might lead us to expect certain outcomes from certain types of action in the future? On this basis it's very clear that the history of anything we could really designate as 'anarchist' politics has delivered almost nothing, or at least nothing on its own, in terms of achieving either revolutionary or reformist objectives in any sustained way, despite having been around since the 1860s at the latest. Despite the habitually self-congratulatory tone of, for example, self-styled 'anarchists' around the Occupy movement (which I think has been very important, but not because it has actually achieved anything) anyone who wants to claim that it did have any such success has to refer to the existence of a few Spanish communes during the civil war that managed to last for a matter of months each.

On the other hand, the at least partial success of parliamentary reformism is pretty palpable. I mean, in very crude terms, if you look back to the early twentieth century, and you look at the places were anarchism and revolutionary communism were strongest – Eastern and Southern Europe – and then you look at the countries of Northern and Western Europe, then on one level you have to say that the forms of social democracy that emerged in the latter context have proven ultimately more effective at protecting workers from exploitation than anarchism and communism in the former. Wages are higher, working hours are shorter, inequality is less, in countries with strong welfare states than in countries that were once soviet republics or hotbeds of anarchism; so everything I'm saying here goes very much for people who want to launch a revival of 'communism' as well. This isn't to say that the anarchist and indeed the soviet critique of both the state and traditional modes of left organisation are without validity, but it is a point worth keeping in mind.

And in terms of how we counter a naive ahistorical anarchism: to be honest I think the single most important thing we can do is to study both the recent and longer term history of radical politics and to encourage others to do the same. The worst problem which afflicts activist culture, at least in the UK, is the fact that young political activists generally know almost nothing about their immediate antecedents or about the broader political history of institutions like the Labour Party. The phrase you hear from such people all the time is 'party politics never changes anything' – but at best this assertion is normally based on disappointment with the Blair government (which did, in fact, enact a series of significant reforms such as the minimum wage, subsidised childcare, improved maternity and paternity rights, etc. which it's very clear the kind of vicious anti-welfare neoliberalism being embraced by the Conservatives would never have tolerated); at worst it's just an article of faith based on no evidence at all. Invariably, in my experience, such activists either know or remember nothing about the recent past of extra-parliamentary radicalism, and how little it has achieved (or what it has achieved when it has achieved anything). I think the most effective way to combat this kind of ignorance would be to start trying to consolidate and publicise the history of radical politics in the UK and elsewhere over recent decades. That would be the way to combat the kind of naive anarchism – a manifestation of what I've called before 'the activist imaginary' – that I think you're referring to.

Having said this I think I would want to differentiate somewhat between a very vulgar anarchist critique of parliamentary democracy – which thinks that you should simply oppose and/or ignore it *in toto* – and the kind of critique that we might associate more with the Marxist tradition, and even what we might call the left wing of social democracy (and I'm sure lots of self-professed 'anarchists' would endorse this more complex view as well).

The latter view would tend to stress the need to use the mechanisms and institutions of the existing state in order both to achieve immediate social reforms but also to create and potentiate new forms of collective power, without falling for what I've called before (I'm sure I wasn't the first) 'the Fabian fantasy' – the belief that government is simply a neutral instrument that can be used by any political group to implement any agenda. I would have to say that I think that this myth is just as dangerous as the anarchistic belief that you can simply ignore or destroy those institutions. You can't just ignore or destroy them, but you can't simply occupy them while making no attempt to transform and ultimately supplant them, and expect to achieve progressive ends, other than very short-term ones. In my experience most Labour MPs seem to be completely deluded on this point. They might recognise that New Labour got captured by neoliberalism, but they think that this happened basically because Tony Blair was persuaded by Andrew Adonis that neoliberalism was a good idea or because Gordon Brown didn't have the guts to stand up to Murdoch. They have no idea that there might be real structural impediments to using the existing institutions of the British state to do anything other than implement the interests of finance capital. They really believe that all they have to do to pursue a different agenda is to achieve ministerial office and maintain good intent, and somehow they will be able to administer social justice from Whitehall. At best they tend to think that you need to get more people 'involved' in politics, but this basically translates as attending local party meetings and participating in local campaigns around discrete issues, rather than making any substantial reform of democratic procedures and institutions themselves. In fact I think that to a large extent the popularity of a simplistic anarchism amongst activists connected with projects like Occupy is as much as anything a mirror-image of this kind of idiotic parliamentarism, which is reproduced most uncritically not by parliamentarians themselves, but by the whole profession of political journalists and professional commentators. It's worth stressing here actually that I've spoken to a number of very bright MPs who don't hold this naive view, but I think I've met even fewer professional journalists in recent years who don't.

I don't make this analysis on the basis of a theoretical position but merely on the basis of an objective consideration of the relevant history. How have political goals which effectively redistributed both wealth and power actually been achieved in the past? If you look at something like the National Health Service - it wasn't built by anarchists and revolutionaries, but it also didn't come about just because some well-meaning mandarins and ministers decided it would be a good idea (which is what your average well-meaning Oxford PPE graduate has been taught and sincerely believes). It was only an assemblage including a very well-organised labour movement – including both the trade unions and the democratic socialist wing of the Labour party led by Nye Bevan – and a certain kind of technocratic modernising tendency within the parliamentary Labour Party and even sections of the Civil Service – that made such lastingly significant reforms possible.

So the short answer to your question is that history suggests that radical and democratic politics won't get anywhere if it doesn't engage with mainstream party politics. More theoretically we could say that if we accept the basic Gramscian (and by no means only Gramscian) proposition that political change can only really be brought about by broad-based social coalitions, then it's pretty clear that right now in a country like the UK, the only organisations with anything like the necessary resources to begin to make such a thing possible are the trade unions and the Labour Party, which is why it remains the case that you can't win any serious progressive objectives without winning the argument inside Labour.

But having said all this one can equally say that another condition of possibility for political progress under these circumstances is for the leaderships of such organisations to accept their own limited capacities and the need to build up new centres of collective and democratic power. It's this that I think should actually form the core demand of the Left in relation to, for example, the Labour leadership in the UK: they don't need to have a programme for implementing radical social reform, until political conditions exist which might make a genuinely progressive project actually viable, but they at least need to have a programme aimed at trying to make such reforms politically possible in the future. I think a lot of left criticism of New Labour was very confused on this point – a lot of it was framed in terms that seemed to imply that after 18 years of Thatcherism, the demolition of the unions, the complete corporate take-over of the media, the evisceration of local government etc. it would have been possible simply to resume the post-war social democratic project, or some updated, more libertarian version thereof. That would never have been viable. But a Labour government coming to power under such circumstances *could* have implemented a programme aimed at reversing each of those trends: rebuilding local government, sponsoring the development of an alternative media sector, reinvigorating the unions. Yet they did nothing of the kind, and that's what they should have been attacked for, repeatedly and relentlessly. To answer your second question then – there is no hope of change coming through parliament alone, just as there is no hope of it coming through mechanisms which don't involve parliament at all. Radicals should engage with parliamentary politics precisely to try to ensure that time and opportunities are not wasted pursuing either of these sterile options, as well as trying to ensure that however useless the next Labour government is, pressure can be brought to bear on it take those measures that it realistically could take in order to transform the broader strategic situation.

MF: Yes, there's a sleight of hand in many anarchist lines of argument. The reformist, social democratic left is judged by what it has actually done, whereas anarchism is judged by what it would do, in some ideal society. Setting things up like this obscures what the parliamentary left actually achieved, while distracting us from anarchism's meagre achievements. There's an anarchist fatalism which is the other side of capitalist realism. According to this logic, both parliament and mainstream media are irredeemably corrupt, and we should totally disengage from them. This is given extra force by the appeal to networks and new technology, which allegedly make the mainstream media (or MSM) and the state irrelevant. I think these arguments should be rejected *tout court*. The first problem is that this view of politics and media isn't making a break from the currently dominant hegemonic position; it only echoes it. Franco Berardi said of Berlusconi that he is the clown who mocks the place of power while occupying it. We might say something similar about Boris Johnson. Johnson profits from the atmosphere of cynicism that settled over politics. His personal appeal derives in large part from his seeming distance from the earnestness of party politics. Yet this distance doesn't stop Johnson occupying a position of power. That leads to my second problem with the disdain for mainstream politics and media. Elements of the left seem to earnestly believe what they say about the irrelevance of the state. The neoliberal right has been much more pragmatic. It might have relentlessly propagandised against the state, but it also made sure that it controlled the state. (Of course, in practice neoliberalism was only ever opposed to certain state functions, such as social security, spending on public services etc.) The point is – if we withdraw from the state and the media, this doesn't mean that the state and the media will cease to have any power. It just means that we will cease to have any influence over the shape that power takes. The problem is that these critiques essentialize both media and party politics. We need to remember that neither of these spaces is fixed for all time; that they are terrains shaped by struggles. Anarchist fatalism maintains that a leftwing Labour Party is impossible – what a contrast with the ambition and can-do spirit of the neoliberals who took over the Labour Party. If only they had been so fatalistic!

All of this is meant to echo your point. It's not that only activity within mainstream media or party politics counts. On the contrary, these terrains will only change when they are put under pressure from outside. But that pressure must be exerted; and producing 'radical' networks that see their function as bypassing MSM and parliament will only allow the right to retain control of the so-called centre ground. One of the major problems with New Labour was that it never moved past stage 1 of a project for hegemonic takeover. It won power, but then – after introducing the measures that you mentioned, such as minimum wage, subsidised childcare etc. which are by no means insignificant – it became stuck on a Sisyphean wheel, where the only goal was winning re-election. Blair likes to chide 'Old Labour' for being stuck in the past, but he never really moved beyond 1996 – with power close enough to be touched, but extreme caution necessary to ensure that it was won. The contrast with the Thatcher government, or indeed the current coalition, is as striking as it is painful. Thatcher succeeded in changing the definition of the centre ground, but, after more than a decade of New Labour government, the centre remained more or less where Thatcher had left it. This failure to re-define the centre meant that, when the coalition came in, it could immediately drag everything to the right.

So let me ask a further question.

MF: What strategies can we pursue to break neoliberal hegemony?

JG: Strategically any kind of hegemonic or counter-hegemonic intervention is always about the co-ordination of interests. Exactly what form that co-ordination has to take is dependent upon the circumstances. Given that the old form of the highly uniform and relatively monolithic political party – Gramsci's 'modern Prince' – is clearly unlikely to return to efficacy any time soon, I think it's necessary to keep thinking about how the very divergent elements of an assemblage which could challenge neoliberal hegemony might work together, or at least towards mutually-supportive goals. In the context of a very diverse and fragmented culture, we can't expect any one organisation or leadership to do all or even most of the necessary work. On the other hand, given the general depoliticisation of the culture which you've referred to, it's hard to imagine this happening at all without there being a viable alternative and the will to work for it coming from a visible section of the political class. To put it crudely, without a degree of explicit sympathy for a populist anti-neoliberal position being expressed by the political leaderships of the mainstream Left, we're not likely to get very far. At the same time, I take it to be the main point of your first question that it's important for radicals to recognise that unless they themselves form constituencies to whom politicians on the mainstream Left might realistically look for support in the pursuit of such a project, then those politicians are never going to have the courage to express such sympathy.

In more substantive terms I would say that any successful strategy against neoliberalism will have to possess several key characteristics. Firstly, it has to set itself – philosophically, aesthetically, and politically – in opposition to the competitive individualist ideology which is the core of neoliberalism and its basis presuppositions (what Macpherson called 'the political theory of possessive individualism'). Secondly it has to avoid the trap of doing this simply by invoking a conservative communitarianism, be it nationalist, localist or religious in character. This is the terrible mistake being made by the current Labour leadership in the UK: trying to respond to neoliberalism with an explicitly conservative appeal to 'faith, flag and family' (in the words of 'Blue Labour' guru Maurice Glasman), conceiving these as the very entities which must be defended from the depredations of neoliberal capitalism and which only the state – or a completely undefined 'community – can protect.

The problem with this approach isn't just that it's obnoxious. It also won't work. It promises something that simply can't be delivered: a return to some unspecified, pre-neoliberal past. And above all, it makes the catastrophic mistake of adopting a purely negative attitude to the main vectors of current social change. Any successful strategy against neoliberalism surely has to try find ways to connect with those aspects and elements of such change which might be articulated to a democratic project: for example the popularity of social networking could surely be channelled into something more potent than the generation of commodifiable market data. But for this to happen would require political leaders actually to take an interest in the general project of radicalising democracy, creating new types of democratic institution which are more participatory and accountable than parliamentary institutions (as is happening today in Latin America), and this would require them to accept that the inherited institutions of parliamentary government are ultimately limited in their usefulness in the 21st century. This is a huge gulf to cross and in this country at least I'm afraid we're still nowhere close to it; but given how obvious this truth it is to the rest of the populace, it may be surprisingly easy to convince a few enterprising MPs and trade union leaders to take this line. Maybe. Probably not though.

MF: Yes. Part of the problem with the Blue Labour position is that isn't the break from the current hegemonic field that it presents itself as. 'Community' is often posited as the alternative to neoliberalism, but in actuality it has functioned as part of the same political imaginary, in which we are offered an alternative between radically isolated individuals and homogeneous, stable, communities. This pseudo-opposition is the one that Thatcherism installed. Blue Labour doesn't challenge the racism that Thatcherism required as a supplement to neoliberal economics, it further embeds it. Actually existing neoliberalism has always depended upon a commitment to traditionalism. Faith, flag and family, after all, are values that Thatcher fully supported. Reagan and Thatcher's success, in fact, was largely a consequence of their capacity to square the circle, and achieve a kind of rainbow coalition of the right, which could bring together economic liberals with the religious right. We've talked a great deal about the problems of the left, but it's worth remembering that, the parliamentary right has a very serious crisis of its own. Look at the Republicans' catastrophic campaign in the last US election, and the very tepid support that David Cameron managed to drum up at a time of deep unpopularity for Labour. The fix Cameron is in – trying to 'modernise' a party whose core support is reactionary – shows that the old Thatcherite formula of neoliberal economics plus social conservatism and authoritarian populism won't work anymore. It is the advances that the left has actually made during the period of neoliberal domination - the bringing into the mainstream of anti-sexist, anti-racist and anti-homophobic agendas – which have contributed to the crisis of the right.

JG: Good point.

MF: Blue Labour is cynical and fatalistic; it believes that racism is inevitable, especially among the working class, and its whole strategy is geared up to appealing to that racism, while dressing it up as 'community'. But there's a reason that *National* Socialism has a bad name! And there's a popular cosmopolitanism which has practically no-one in parliament speaking for it. We saw this cosmopolitanism celebrated in the Olympic opening ceremony and in the Olympics themselves last year. When Tories started grumbling about 'lefty multiculturalism', they not only came off as a racist, but out of touch. The appeal to community almost always has an anti-modern as well as an openly racist dimension to it. The left needs to argue for a model of collectivity which doesn't depend on a backward-looking and insular notion of community.

JG: I agree entirely. Having said all this about what should happen at the level of political leadership, however, I think it's also necessary to think about what would have to happen at the 'molecular' level (as Deleuze and Guattari, but also Gramsci – who uses the word 'molecular' several times in the *Prison Notebooks*, to mean much the same thing as D&G – would put it). To really make a political challenge to neoliberalism viable, we would need to see some significant cultural upswell of radically democratic, libertarian yet anti-individualist sentiment. I'm afraid it's very hard to see any sign of this right now – even in the rather banal form of something like the rave culture of our youth. The older I get, the longer I live with neoliberalism and the challenges it poses, particularly now trying to raise a family, the more convinced I become that we can't really get anywhere without a resurgence of something that would look in many ways like the counterculture of the 1960s and 1970s, (and I include in this category the most daring strands of the feminist movement, for all that they themselves were reacting against the implicit misogyny of sections of the New Lefts and Rock culture in the 1960s). Unless there's a real movement to try to put into question – from an egalitarian, libertarian, anti-individualist perspective – the basic social forms of the household, the school, etc., and the core aesthetic presuppositions of liberal capitalist culture (for example the obsession with the individual, the private and the competitive which is the basis for celebrity culture, for the dominance of TV by 'reality' formats, and for the depressing centrality of columnists and opinion-journalists even to middle-brow media output) – it's hard to imagine anything but the most timid political reforms becoming viable. This isn't something we can plan for, legislate for, or even strategise for; but we might at least try to arrive at a situation wherein the leaders of the labour movement are not so completely unable to connect with the radical energy of such a movement once it emerges – or even threatens to emerge – as they were at every previous moment of opportunity from the end of the 1960s, when Jim Callaghan's rejected 'the permissive society', right up to the 1990s, when the movement didn't have a clue what to do with the constituencies who had been radicalised by rave and *Reclaim the Streets*.

What might actually make any of this possible? Well – on the cultural, 'molecular' side, I think this is pretty well impossible to answer. We'll know when it happens, I hope. It's partly the job of cultural theorists like us to keep looking out for such possibilities and to try to persuade key sections of the political class not to be terrified of them if and when they start to emerge. I think one very interesting kind of intervention would be to make some effort to reclaim the festival form – which for decades was the key cultural form of the counterculture and its legatees – from the wholly sanitised and corporate state it's now in (there was an interesting discussion about this on the Open Democracy website last year): maybe we need something like a British Burning Man. Maybe Burning Man is itself part of the problem, given its general ethic of antipoliticality. I'm not sure.

On the 'molar' side of political leadership I think there are good things that can be done very deliberately. In Britain, the organisation *Compass* is doing great work in trying to bring together people on a spectrum of opinion that runs from radical Greens to mainstream Labour members and even Liberal Democrats in the 'social liberal' tradition. In concrete tactical terms that work probably needs to include some deliberate efforts to think about recruiting and training future political leaders, because one of the problems that we are faced with very acutely at the present time is the consequences of the narrowing and hyper-professionalisation of the

Labour party's young activist base at the end of the 80s: from that moment on, for a very long time, becoming a Labour MP just wasn't an appealing prospect for anyone who wasn't a ruthless careerist or a political geek (and the latter types tends to have no real affective instinct for shifting popular moods and their political potentialities, even if they might have a very sincere commitment to some abstract notion of social justice). That might have already changed – but we would need to make sure that it had before having any real prospect of an effective political alternative to neoliberalism crystallising in the UK. I'm not sure how these observations would translate into other national contexts, but I'm sure there are parallels as well as significant differences with what's happening in many other countries.

NOTES

1. The Research Excellence Framework, within which British university departments are subject to a cycle of regular assessments of the quality of their research output, occurring at roughly 5-6 year intervals, the results of which heavily determine the level of research funding that they will receive in coming years. While its predecessor, the 'Research Assessment Exercise', was originally conceived, in the dying days of Thatcherism, on a wholly 'open-competition' model, elite universities have increasingly lobbied government to introduce mechanisms intended deliberately to skew the distribution of research funds resulting from the exercise in their favour.

BEYOND THE ENTREPRENEURIAL VOYEUR? SEX, PORN AND CULTURAL POLITICS

Stephen Maddison

What forms of sex are fostered by neoliberal ideologies? And in what kinds of social relations do these forms of sex take place? The ongoing popularity of pornography as a subject for academic study is in part related to its status as a barometer of the changing conditions of sex in cultural politics, where the richness of its materiality lends weight to its indicative status, and helps us adjudicate practices enshrined in layers of privacy. Pornographic commodities, their content, modes and relations of production, aesthetics, affective properties, and financial value, all provide evidence of the shifting terms under which sexual intimacies are conducted, and the cultural and historical circumstances that bear upon those intimacies. Naturally, porn's barometer status is hugely problematic, as nearly three generations of feminist activism demonstrates; and yet, the continuing strength of academic porn studies attests to its significance, which has been enhanced by the intensification of work on network cultures and on theories of the relationship between bodies and sensation.

In this essay I want to consider the relationship between sex and neoliberalism, using porn as a marker of the contemporary cultural conjuncture. I hope to explore several overlapping concerns. Firstly I want to point to an impasse of constrained optimism that characterises recent work in porn studies, which has become preoccupied with the question of alternative pornographies (altporn). This is significant because it points to a residual investment in a notion of agency, as I shall demonstrate; such a notion has been politically significant for feminist and queer analysis of popular culture, but tends to collapse the possibility of a critique of the relations of capital. As a critical concept, agency allows us to access the entitlements gained by women and queers, for instance in the context of post-feminism and homonormativity, but potentially forecloses analysis of the neoliberal conditions that determine the limits of that agency.

Professional gay men and childless professional women have prospered under neoliberalism (albeit in complex and uneven ways), in terms of improving social and economic opportunities, cultural choices and economic advancement. But such entitlements, as commentators such as Rosalind Gill have pointed out, have entailed new responsibilities,[1] along with, I would suggest, new constraints associated with cultural and social assimilation. So-called 'sexualisation' may have offered a degree of what has been described as 'democratisation' in relation to access to sexual culture and visibility for minorities and women, but the terms of that 'democratisation' are at best problematic, and have been highly contested.[2] Secondly, following Lazzarato's work on immaterial labour, and work that has emerged following the publication of Foucault's lectures from the Collège de France, I want to introduce and develop two new concepts that potentially allow us to elaborate on the forms of sex fostered by neoliberalism; these are: immaterial sex and the entrepreneurial voyeur. Immaterial sex may help us to describe the creative and affective energies commodified in porn production, whilst the idea of the entrepreneurial voyeur may help us to account for the ways in which porn consumption, sexual subjectification, and the enterprise culture mutually reinforce one another. If an analysis of neoliberal governmentality and the enterprise culture leads us towards a scepticism about the transformative potential of individual agency and autonomy, this poses significant, and as yet unconsidered, problems for the frameworks in which we have tended to consider sexuality, and porn consumption in particular. And finally, I want to consider how we might identify terms for moving beyond the entrepreneurial voyeur and towards a less alienated and competitive mode of sexuality. Here I will offer an analysis of the independent film *Made in Secret* which seems to pattern a mode of porn production/consumption, and a way of thinking about porn, that is communal and confederate, rooted in reciprocal social relations and not in privatised exchange.

CONSTRAINED OPTIMISM AND THE PROBLEM OF AGENCY

To engage directly with mainstream commercial porn requires an engagement with material that is often relentlessly misogynistic, male supremacist, racially fetishizing, repetitive, predictable and unerotic; it is, in other words, to engage with a terrain which seems to offer few possibilities for surprise, change and progress. To fail to engage with that mainstream risks eliding its power and influence, as Karen Boyle has recently pointed out.[3] But to engage with it risks re-producing its authority and inevitability, closing a circuit of entrapment. It is for this reason that many scholars and activists working in porn studies have recently been preoccupied with what has been variously referred to as altporn,[4] netporn,[5] realcore,[6] indie porn[7] or amateur porn.[8] Academic work on these 'alternative' pornographies tends to demonstrate constrained optimism: looking for breakthrough trends, movements and artefacts to validate the agency of the progressive voyeur or sexual dissident against the forces of reaction and bigotry, whilst evading a direct engagement with the political implications of progressive or dissident activism based in relations of consumerism. Much porn studies work is critical of tendencies in altporn, most significantly around questions of labour and commodification. Yet the focus on alternative pornographies tends to maintain an investment in the promise of agency, where this agency is a function of the expansion of the technological resources available in a networked culture, the proliferation of choice, and the blurred boundary between consumer and producer. In this, porn studies exemplifies wider trends in popular culture analysis, as Clare Hemmings has pointed out.[9]

Florian Cramer and Stewart Home have suggested that indie porn 'is the pornography of this decade, if not of the whole century'.[10] If trends towards the mainstreaming of sex haven't yielded the 'sexual democratisation' that some commentators hoped for[11] and mainstream porn 'is sexist and disgusting' for pro- and anti-porn feminists alike[12], it is easy to see the appeal of altporn to academics, producers and activists concerned to understand the potential of porn cultures in the context of the rise of user-created content.[13] The problem of categorisation casts a long shadow here. Susanna Paasonen has rightly suggested that 'the notion of the mainstream is porous and contingent', and it's clear that the category of altporn is slippery.[14] As the description of a particular kind of online product or experience, altporn can be difficult to disaggregate from the output of an industry that depends upon continual commodity innovation[15], and where the categories of amateur and professional, producer and consumer, are in flux. And it can sometimes feel that the preoccupation with taxonomies of sexual expression has somehow become the political project of porn studies, rather than a means of gaining a purchase on the question of how porn production and consumption, and sexual practices and identities, are implicated in social relations. In terms that exemplify constrained optimism, Katrien Jacobs suggests that 'the future of uncanny cybersexuality is sparkling yet gloomy' as 'consumers, artists and activism' are set against 'corporate ownership and technological determinism' but that cyberspace retains the potential for consumption of 'sex as encounters with non-mainstream and non-commercial communities, individuals and types of agency'.[16] Jacobs suggests that amateur porn represents 'the long-awaited schooling of pornography, its rapid democratisation', and asserts that the 'sexual revolution is over' and that 'close communities' and 'remote peer networks' offer opportunities to 'maintain ourselves, as pragmatic networkers of non-reproductive sex' swimming against the tide of 'superpower politics' and 'the expansionist corporate industries'.[17] Susanna Paasonen theorises a distinction between 'porn on the net' and 'netporn', where the former caters to mainly male heterosexual consumers, is industrialised, homogenised and cross-platform, and the latter is non-normative, ethical, subcultural, resistant to commodification and net-specific in its technological realization (Labors of love, p1299). As such, netporn 'entails the blurred boundaries of porn producers and consumers, the proliferation of independent and alternative pornographies, as well as the expansion of technological possibilities brought forth by digital tools, platforms and networked communications' (Labors of love, p1298). Striving for optimism, Paasonen suggests that 'amateur productions have come to connote a better kind of porn that is ethical in its principles of production' (Labors of love, pp1302, 1299).

Drawing on both Henry Jenkins' concept of 'cultural convergence' to describe a media culture increasingly distinguished by a slippage between producers and consumers, and Katrien Jacobs' analysis of amateur porn production, Feona Attwood suggests that altporn represents a potential 'democratisation of porn'.[18] Offering an analysis of two sites, Nerve.com and SuicideGirls, she suggests that both represent 'participatory cultures which serve corporate and community needs'.[19] Attwood's work exhibits an unacknowledged tension that characterises much of porn studies engagement with altporn: whilst she recognises the ways in which both of the sites she discusses serve commercial as well as community interests, complex questions of democratisation, and community, alluded to early on, aren't developed. Cramer and Home suggest that indie porn seems to finally offer 'a non-industrial and erotically imaginative pornography for hetero- and bisexuals'.[20] But for them such promise is unfulfilled, because indie porn is effectively 'the research and development arm of the porn industry'.[21] Cramer and Home are critical of claims for the participatory nature of indie porn, suggesting that the democratising potential of user-generated content merely provides the means for 'outsourcing labour' and cutting production costs by exploiting the opportunity for consumers to display themselves.[22]

The antagonisms that inflamed feminist debates about porn are still rumbling on (as recent controversy surrounding the launch of a new academic journal, *Porn Studies*, makes clear[23]), making the articulation of female agency in sexual cultures, and in porn in particular, strategically appealing for what we would once have called pro-porn, anti-censorship feminists. Yet in the context of sexualisation, which Rosalind Gill suggests offers women new forms of empowerment but also new forms of containment, and neoliberalism, where agency, choice and freedom proliferate conditions of alienation and competition from within the experience of entitlement, we urgently require new terms for elaborating a politics of pornography and of sexuality.[24] This problem isn't confined to porn studies: as Clare Hemmings has suggested in her critique of theories of affect, it is played out across media and cultural studies. Hemmings suggests that affect has been proposed as a solution to the 'impasse' arising from recognition of the limitations of social constructionism as an account of subjectivity, the limitations of textual analysis for capturing the texture of the social world, and the limitations of binary models of power/resistance and repression/subversion.[25] Hemmings concludes by re-stating the efficacy of poststructuralist theory, in which affect can be a useful tool; but she asserts the critical importance of 'social meaning'.[26]

Much writing on altporn implicitly or explicitly positions it as resistant to the mainstream of pornography, in a variety of ways, and the analytical process of articulating this resistance is itself a form of resistance (and no less so than anti-porn writing). But the specific forms of this resistance privilege either a notion of affect that tends to come adrift from 'social meaning', or a residual investment in the notion of sexual democratisation and agency. Thus, Niels Van Doorn rightly concludes his analysis of YouPorn clips by cautioning against 'falling for binary oppositions such as "emancipation" versus "discipline"... scopic regimes do not exist as airtight, monolithic structures'.[27] Nevertheless, in terms that exemplify the idea of constrained optimism, Van Doorn celebrates YouPorn for its bodily diversity, despite the homogeneity of its genital play, and yet is constrained by his recognition that YouPorn's participants explore their sexuality 'in the heterogeneous pursuit of a hedonistic, narcissistic form of individuality and pleasure' and that they realise their sexual self 'by making it available for continuous surveillance' (Keeping it Real, p426). To resolve this deadlock, Van Doorn concludes with the suggestion that despite user-generated altporn demonstrating an adherence to the normative pornoscript, some of the clips he analyzed contained a variety of 'slips, discontinuities and interruptions' which he argues 'have the potential to figure as multiple fissures in YouPorn's scopic regime and the essentialist gender ideology it perpetuates' (Keeping it Real, p426). Can such slips and interruptions bear the weight of the optimism invested here? If the conditions imposed on a realisation of the sexual self, of achieving a sense of agency, entail 'continuous surveillance', as Van Doorn suggests, we should note that this surveillance is not merely confined to the participatory community of YouPorn's self-display and user-generated content, but expresses wider conditions in which the enterprising of ones sexuality is but a small part of the prevailing disciplinary dispositif of neoliberal governmentality. If we are to make sense of how power circumscribes sexuality and gender, and how resistance may be formulated and enacted, we need to consider the implications of the notions of agency and democratisation that underpin the prevailing politics of altporn and porn studies.

THE ENTERPRISE SUBJECT AND IMMATERIAL SEX

What writers like Jacobs, Attwood, Paasonen, Boyle and Van Doorn seem to implicitly seek is not a sexual rupture or emergence, but a social and political one; similarly, Cramer and Home have called for 'a radically populist pornography of collectively produced, purely formal codes'[28] which describes a political formation, rather than a sexual or aesthetic one. These are questions about what altporn, and the wider mainstream porn industry, tell us about the relationship between sex and neoliberal ideology, and in answering them, we need to turn away from porn studies.

In *The Birth of Biopolitics* Foucault takes up the figure of homo oeconomicus, which first emerged in the philosophy of Hume and Smith. For Foucault, homo oeconomicus represents an intensification of economic interest that adopts its most radical form in contemporary neoliberalism, where governmentality is concerned less with the project of establishing a market society as conceived by classical liberalism, and more with establishing 'mechanisms of competition' and 'an enterprise society'.[29] For Lazzarato the organisation of labour in neoliberalism works to maximise polarisations of income and power whilst working to prevent these inequalities becoming 'irreducible political dualisms': in this way neoliberalism effects a depoliticisation of labour (*The Birth of Biopolitics*, p120). The enterprise society involves the 'generalization of the economic form of the market ... throughout the social body and including the whole of the social system not usually conducted through or sanctioned by monetary exchanges' (*The Birth of Biopolitics*, p243). This extension of market rationality to delineate all social forms also extends to what Foucault describes as 'human capital' or 'abilities-machines'. This is the value that humans accrue as a function of the marketisation of their biological and social capacities, such as: heredity (in terms of susceptibility or resistance to disease and related exposure to economic risk), possible genetic enhancement, the affective labour of parents, and the potential value inherent in mobility and migration (*The Birth of Biopolitics*, pp226-230). Lois McNay has emphasized several features of neoliberalism's construction of the self-as-enterprise. Critically, the organisation of self around a market logic 'subtly alters and depolitizises conventional conceptions of individual autonomy' foregrounding choice, differentiation, and 'regulated self-responsibility'.[30] This has profound effects for sociality: quoting Donzelot, McNay suggests that the entrepreneur of himself 'has only competitors'. Neoliberalism proceeds on the basis that these 'competitors', alienated from one another by the governmental maximisation of the inequalities between them, should seek advancement through the acquisition and exploitation of individual freedoms, which are proliferating constantly. Class and other forms of solidarity are discouraged precisely because these 'competitors' are constantly differentiated from one another, and because the 'idea of personal responsibility is eroded' (Self as Enterprise, p65) by the outsourcing to individuals of 'rights' and responsibilities previously secured by the social contract. Lazzarato elaborates the idea of human capital in his formation of the concept of immaterial labour, as a way of accounting for changes in the nature of work and professionalism, and where neoliberal markets extract capital value from intellectual, creative and emotional effort in ways that exceed traditional accounts of exploitation and alienation.[31] Lazzarato suggests that in the context of precarity, just in time production and project-based employment and consultancy work, immaterial labour is 'the labour that produces the informational and cultural content of the commodity'.

These theories of labour and power may help to account for the constrained optimism porn studies writers have exhibited about altporn. On the one hand we can see the work of altporn entrepreneurs as expressions of the post-Fordist multitude: emergent expressions of creativity and sociality, arising from the articulation of communities of interest, where inter-dependence and co-operation is expressed by user-generated content and interactivity in forums, blogs and reviews, as a function of new technological possibilities. On the other hand, we can see altporn entrepreneurs as immaterial labourers for whom the distinction between life and work, and work and leisure, has collapsed, and for whom the opportunity to comply with the requirement to enterprise themselves arises from an exploitation of their latent immaterial creativity.

We might describe what emerges from such transactions as immaterial sex, where libidinal, emotional and physiological energies, desires and sensations are a function of human capital. Porn exploits the immaterial sex of performers and actors, who represent a post-human elite: sexual 'cyborgs'[32] and 'athletes'[33] with outsized genitalia, and bodily and affective capacities elaborated by the technical capacity of digital video production, and by surgical and pharmacological enhancement, who perform acts that express a post-Kinseyian logic of sexual pleasure.[34] The labour conditions experienced by this elite are likely to be far from commensurate with the privileged status of their sexual immateriality.[35] This immaterial sex is the property of the commodities which it produces, but it is also a function of the post-Fordist working experiences of porn consumers seeking pleasure in terms that replicate and facilitate work patterns[36] or that offer compensations for the privations of neoliberalism.[37] Here porn consumption offsets the impossibility of the sexual standards it installs: impossible to achieve because we don't have enough time for an elaborate recreational sex life, or at least one that patterns the affective capacity of the sexualised society; impossible to achieve because we are unable to autonomously realise our libidinous capacity, because we're too tired, alienated, socially inept, or domestically and socially compromised; or because our sensory and affective responses might relate more to mediated, networked interactions than to 'meat' intimate bodily ones. To be clear, immaterial sex suggests both the creative, bodily and affective capacity derived from the 'carnal resonances'[38] associated with pornographic genital play, and the exploitation of such capacity through the processes of production and consumption that characterise capital valorisation and exchange in the porn industry.

One frequently cited example of an altporn site, FuckForForest, offers a novel approach to the conventional business model of online porn sites, in which pay-per-view subscriptions for video clips featuring performances by the site's collective of eco-activists are used to fund ecological activism.

In this, FuckforForest may offer a partial realisation of what Mark Coté and Jennifer Plybus describe as the 'always already liberatory potential of immaterial labour', what I'm describing as immaterial sex.[39] Here we may identify something akin to the 'radically new collective possibilities' that Coté and Plybus suggest it is the project of neoliberal capital to exploit, but which also threaten its authority.[40] FuckforForest articulates and exploits immaterial sex, the human capital inherent in the desires, affects and practices of its activist/performers, in ways that both mimic the prevailing commercial form of online pornography, and resist its corporate fetishism of profit. The form of FuckforForest's venture is entrepreneurial, and appropriated from mainstream 'amateur' porn sites: free images solicit desire, at which point you have to get your credit card out to have that desire fulfilled. Yet here profit is ambiguously associated with commodity: the financialisation of immaterial sex produces charity donations, not surplus value. Similarly, as other commentators have noted, FuckforForest stages the performance and display of immaterial sex as a collective enterprise, arising from its proximity to anarchist politics and its solicitation of user-generated content in lieu of subscription fees. This needs not to be over-stated: there is no self-conscious articulation of non-competitive social relations on FuckforForest, and immaterial sex is still circulated as a route to self-actualisation and autonomy that are in keeping with the structure of homo oeconomicus. Subscriptions may be donated to charity, but the organisation of exchange and immaterial sex still equates affect and desire with money in a manner consistent with the logic of capitalist valorisation. And from the perspective of a consumer who chooses to exchange money for FuckforForest's sexual content, there may be an affective thrill attached to the promise of consuming ethical porn, but otherwise the experience is remarkably similar to that of consuming other kinds of online porn: the porn consumer is still constituted as an entrepreneurial voyeur.

THE ENTREPRENEURIAL VOYEUR

In 2012 Cindy Gallop, a former brand consultant for Coca-Cola and Levi's, launched a pay porn site, MakeLoveNotPorn.tv (MLNP.tv), which at the time of writing is still in beta. MLNP.tv follows an earlier venture launched in 2009 by Gallop, which aimed to debunk porn 'myths' and assert 'real world' 'truths' about sex (examples include: women don't enjoy men ejaculating on their faces, women don't enjoy being choked performing oral sex) and which leveraged Gallop's persona and business acumen in order to attract investors to the pay porn venture. The MakeLoveNotPorn sites self-consciously resist a mainstream of porn that Gallop fears for its 'creeping ubiquity' which is influencing how a generation is learning to have sex.[41] MLNP.tv offers a familiar altporn experience that exhibits many of the characteristics Feona Attwood identifies in the new taste cultures: an appeal to community and authenticity, a self-consciousness about resisting familiar porn tropes, and an aestheticisation of sex that accords with the apparent bourgeois bohemianism celebrated by the popular TV drama *Sex and the City*.[42] Unlike Nerve.com or SuicideGirls, however, MLNP.tv focuses on hard core clips, rather than soft core images, and critically, its unique selling point rests on the visibility of Gallop's own affectivity, through the site itself, and in the wider culture, where she has been able to generate significant public relations momentum for MLNP.tv. The site proclaims 'we are pro-sex, pro-porn and pro-knowing the difference'.[43] An interview with the *Guardian* newspaper in the UK, illustrated with a photograph of Gallop reclining vamp-like on a rather fabulous animal print chaise, makes explicit the correlation between the distinctiveness of MLNP.tv and Gallop's persona. So, if MLNP.tv is 'an elevated style of adult video' which offers 'tasteful erotica' that will be 'the sex education of the future', Gallop herself is 'enthusiastically single and unashamed to date men less than half her age', despite being 52 years old, and 'wears figure-hugging black ensembles, attends glamorous parties and is not shy in correcting her aggressive young lovers'.[44] Here Gallop's lust, her taste for young men and her sexual promiscuity, her charisma, her class and wealth, her liking of porn despite her distaste for its apparent 'myths', and her greed/agency/business acumen represent both her affective labour as owner of a website looking to attract more users, enterprising her tastes and desires, as well as a promise of our potential pleasure and fulfillment in purchasing porn clips. The business model of MLNP.tv rests on sharing profits from pay-per-view subscriptions with apparently 'amateur' uploaders who are encouraged to use the site to enterprise their sexual immateriality. A prominent graphic of interlocking hearts and circles illustrates the structure of MLNP.tv: 'SUBMIT your #realworldsex video $5 curation fee RENT $5 per video rental 3 wks unlim. viewing EARN 50% of the profits PLAY whatever you want w/ your earnings'. MLNP.tv emphasises its 'realness', a quality it differentiates from both (so-called) amateur and professional porn. This 'realness' is authenticated by the site's aesthetics, along with its arch text, which eschews both the rigid categorisations of mainstream pay and 'free' (advertising funded) porn sites (anal, Asian, blowjob, creampie, cumshots, interracial, and so on) and the DIY aesthetic of some amateur sex blogs. And in a critical innovation to the pay porn format, MLNP.tv foregrounds a 'peek' preview which features a range of intimate contextualisations of the videos offered for rental. The importance of these 'peeks' to the economic success of posters, is foregrounded in advice on the site. The 'peeks' comprise a range of different formats and content, from voice-over commentary that offers reflexive and intimate insight into the participants' body image and domestic décor, through to filmed interviews of participants, who variously talk about the backstory of their relationships, their investments in specific kinds of sexual practice, and the limits of their desires and tastes in busy lives.

Does MLNP.tv represent sexual democratisation? As Jenkins suggests, the facilitation of user-produced content and user-participation 'has become a corporate strategy in a new affective economy'.[45] Moreover, in an exemplification of McNay's argument that 'individual autonomy becomes not the opposite of, or limit to, neoliberal governance, rather it lies at the heart of its disciplinary control' (Self as Enterprise, p62), MLNP.tv stages resistance to porn in precisely the terms in which porn, mainstream and alt, solicits user engagement and participation: in largely individualised ways that do little to engender social confederacy. The sexual entrepreneurs who upload their content to MLNP.tv exchange their creativity, their emotions, tastes, desires, opinions, social interactions, domestic practices, their bodily reactions, sensations and capacities for money in a competitive commercial environment. Their products – their sexual immateriality – are in direct competition with other content on the site, hence the importance of the 'peek' as a marketing tool. This 'peek' designates an extension of the terms of pornographic immateriality, commodifying moments of intimacy and intensity that exceed the conditions of generic genital play in pay porn.

MLNP.tv, in its tasteful and glossy way, makes explicit the post-Fordist mode of sexual production in contemporary network porn. Participation is competition, sharing is self-exploitation, and resisting the normative pornoscript is a business venture dependent for its economic success on extending the terms of affective labour. In this we can see a correlation between the mode of production and the mode of consumption. Successful consumption of porn in an increasingly stagnant market, defined by a demand for high volume of content throughput, depends upon restively browsing through a lot of material, with hands occupied not only in stroking the body, but the mouse or trackpad, opening and scrubbing through files to patch together a bricolage of potentially quality pornographic moments. Access to porn, often especially altporn, is dependent on managing networks and social media where we must demonstrate entrepreneurial skill, choosing appropriate contractual subscriptions, following links and recommendations to new sites of free content, keeping up with chat rooms, torrent lists, blogs and feeds to ensure we aren't missing out on opportunities to realise our desires, and demonstrate our self-management. These patterns of entrepreneurialism of the self mirror the practices necessary to maintain professional success as an immaterial labourer. These are the conditions described by Mark Fisher's notions of 'reflexive impotence' and 'depressive hedonia',[46] where pornographic pleasures, in all their accessibility, standardisation and dependability, satisfy the need for work-centric patterns of social relations. This is the moment when the search for pleasure, as Nina Power notes, becomes another form of work.[47]

'THIS IS WHAT DEMOCRACY LOOKS LIKE NAKED'

The breakthrough we need is not more pornography, more choice, new terms and conditions for demonstrating our ability to self-regulate, but new social forms through which to imagine what pornography, and the erotic affects it solicits and represents, might be for. This is an ambitious, idealistic agenda, but not an unrealistic one. Whilst much academic writing on altporn is characterised by constrained optimism, that optimism resides at its best in an expectation that new technologies and new articulations of creativity may facilitate new forms of sociality.

Adam Arvidsson notes Laqueur's assertion that historically the danger of masturbation was seen to be social, not physical; masturbation 'risked deviating psychic energy away from the moral project of the social towards the individualistic pursuit of fantasy'.[48] This notion of masturbation as asocial persisted until the 1970s when it was appropriated by the feminist movement as a consciousness raising technique. Arvidsson suggests that 'the internet realizes the hidden potential of the masturbatory economy' but by offering fantasies that are more interactive than was hitherto possible.[49] We have seen that this interactivity does not necessarily guarantee the liberation of immaterial sex from commercial exploitation or from forms of subjectivity and political framing derived from the enterprise society;

indeed much 'netporn' secures the subject position of the entrepreneurial voyeur, even, and perhaps most especially, at those moments of greatest interactivity where we strive for autonomy and agency. And yet we cannot foreclose the potential of the experimentation in immaterial sex that altporn represents, especially as such foreclosure simply reproduces the binary poles of resistance and domination.

McNay is critical of the way in which some of Foucault's writing that came after his lectures printed in *The Birth of Biopolitics*, continued to foreground the idea of an ethics of the self as a form of oppositional political agency, and failed to take account of the insights he had developed in the lectures at the Collège de France in 1978-9; she says:

> it is questionable whether an ethics of self can withstand co-optation into the flexible, depoliticizing spirit of capitalism ... as a model of political action, an individual ethics of the self appears to be relatively ineffective because its radical energies seem too vulnerable to re-privatization by the assimilating force of the self as enterprise (Self as Enterprise, p68).

However, McNay identifies two sets of ambiguities in Foucault's work that offer more promising possibilities; the first concerns the tension between the idea of neoliberalism as a theory 'which is intellectually hegemonic' and as a 'practice of governance which is never ... complete'; and the second concerns the residual function of juridical power and the concept of rights in a civil society otherwise dominated by the utility of economics (Self as Enterprise, p69). Foucault's analysis of rights, rooted in his deep skepticism about their fetishisation in liberalism, but also acknowledging of their temporary value as a pragmatic utility, is suggestive to McNay of a form of political strategy rooted in 'association' and symbolically powerful as a counter to the individualising tendencies of neoliberalism. McNay suggests that Foucault alludes to a 'power of collective action' that consolidates 'marginal practices' and creates 'solidarity' (Self as Enterprise, pp71-72). Synthesising these interpretations, McNay proposes a concept of radical equality, as a way of understanding opposition to neoliberal governance (Self as Enterprise, p73). What might this radical equality look like? McNay's article doesn't have the scope to map this out, but we can start to develop its shape from the imperatives her analysis gives it.

In an interview in 1981 Foucault famously suggested that 'the problem is not to discover in oneself the truth of one's sex, but, rather, to use one's sexuality henceforth to arrive at a multiplicity of relationships'.[50] This simple formation describes a complex contrapuntal move, in which we resist dispositifs of truth that discipline our subjectivities, at the same time as strategically embracing their ability to define conditions of 'association' and solidarity, so as to proliferate, in that communal space, alternative and resistant modes of being. This seems resonant of a 'radical equality' that may stand in opposition to the 'equality of inequality' reproduced by neoliberal governmentality, in order to secure conditions of competition in every social sphere. In the context of the question of altporn, I would suggest that this radical equality would need to resist the competitive structure of the entrepreneurial voyeur of porn, and displace conventional forms of capitalist valorisation with forms of association and solidarity that aren't organised to commodify immaterial sex.

I want to offer a sustained analysis of the film *Made in Secret: The Story of the East Van Porn Collective* (2005, director One Tiny Whale) as a way of thinking about how pornography can engender forms of sociality that unleash the creative potential of immaterial sex, whilst potentially resisting exploitation as immaterial labour, and offering an alternative form of subjectification to that of homo oeconomicus.

Made in Secret is a low budget film produced over three years that apparently documents the activities of a collective of seven well-educated white people living in East Vancouver, Canada, as they attempt to make porn. It mixes hand held documentary with interview footage, and shows the work of the collective on the set of one of their movies, *BikeSexual*, as well as showing them in meetings thrashing out the way in which the collective will work. The film was shown on the international film festival circuit in 2005, including at the nineteenth London Lesbian and Gay Film Festival, and was subsequently released on region-free DVD, available through the collective's website. Marketing of the film, which consists of copy on the DVD sleeve and on the website, as well as a flier that was distributed when the film was shown on the festival circuit, emphasises the self-consciousness with which the documentary was made. Several extras on the DVD release heighten and foreground this effect. The collective note that,

> Made in Secret is a pure labour of love, made over the course of three years by a group of friends who wanted to see a documentary made about our local anarcho-feminist porn collective. The only problem was, that collective didn't exist. And so, in a post-modern twist that Gandhi may never have foreseen, we became the anarcho-feminist porn collective that we so dearly wished to see in the world, simply

in order to make a film about it. In other words, we didn't document what we were doing; we did the things we wanted to document. Or, it's equally true to say, we set out to make a fictional film and in the process, ended up living the story we were trying tell (East Van Porn Collective, nd).

And they go on to suggest that, 'as we grew more and more immersed in the constructed reality of the film, the layers of reality and meta-fiction began to feed off each other. Eventually the process and the product became so conflated that it was no longer possible to distinguish between the movie and real life'. The collective suggest that: 'Made in Secret is an ambiguous, but undeniably genuine artifact of this life- transforming experiment. Which is why, whether the movie is perceived as fact or fiction or none of the above, ultimately it's all true'. The self-conscious deployment of the de-familiarisation devices draws attention to both the privileged status of the real, and the artifice on which it is based, in generic and technical terms. Even if *Made in Secret* had been a 'straightforward' documentary, its depiction of the collective's activity would have been narrativised, with editing and other resources used to construct relationships, themes and characters from raw footage. In the extra material on the DVD, the collective claim that they were making a film about a collective making a documentary about making porn. But they did make porn, and they did form a collective.

Made in Secret opens with the caption, 'the following film is neither fact nor fiction', followed by grainy, lo-fi footage of one of the collective's members, Monster, performing a comic poetry reading of a work entitled 'Draft Manifesto of the East Van Porn Collective':

We're turned off, and we want an apology
For shot after shot
Of slot after slot …
We want to get off
But we grow soft
Watching well-hung apes
Thrusting grey wet steak …
We propose a solution
A home-made, grass roots
Pervert Revolution
We want to see movies

Full of arty cuties making out
And enjoying it …
I want to see something that won't bore me
Something with a story
So far from dumb
That I'll sit in the wet spot
After I cum
To see how it ends
Friends, that is the porn revolution
I want to watch
With one fist in the air
And one in my crotch.

Her performance is arch, charismatic, and greeted with riotous laughter, hooting and applause by the audience. What follows takes place three years later. A member of the collective arrives at a house with the finished videotape of their most recent movie where the rest of the members are waiting for a screening party. But there's a problem: the collective have failed to tell one of their members, nerdGirl, that Godfrey will be filming the screening party. The action breaks whilst the collective meet to discuss the situation; Godfrey films the meeting through the window from the outside. Action commences when Godfrey is admitted, but is told that he cannot film the screen on which the movie is playing, only the members of the collective as they watch it. We as the audience are unclear whether the dispute has been staged for the documentary. We also remain uncertain about the content of the collective's porn movie, aside from the intimate sighs and groans we can hear on its soundtrack, and the reactions of the members of the collective watching it, which stage a range of affective responses, including coyness and laughter, which is suggestive of the idea that some of them are watching themselves on screen.

This forms the pattern for the rest of *Made in Secret*, which strives to represent the affectivity of the collective's social and creative process, a process that has no tangible commodity output: the collective's films, if they even exist as discrete objects, can't be shown outside the collective, and have no financial value. The work of the collective isn't geared to commodity production, despite drawing on immaterial effects: the desires and fantasies of the collective, their bodies and time, and the social network, affinity and process of the collective itself. As hardcore porn strives to elicit from its spectators affective responses equivalent to, and synchronised with, those of the performers on screen, so *Made in Secret* solicits engagement from its spectators with the affective energies and moral purpose of the collective in its commitment to generating internal consensus. The self-conscious tension the documentary produces around the fiction/reality dichotomy increases the sense of complicity that spectators have with the conditions of production.

As a spectatorial experience (for this spectator at least) *Made in Secret* turns on the way it synthesises a compelling narrative of egalitarian social process, with a correlative production of affects related to that sociality: desire, belonging, frustration, impatience, affection. Writer and activist Mattilda Bernstein Sycamore suggests that a scene in which one of the members of the collective blocks consensus about whether to show their work at a DIY porn festival, offers an 'exposé of power dynamics within the consensus process [that] is the core of the movie, and I can't say that I've seen this portrayed so clearly, honestly and intimately before'.[51] Noting that the collective eventually agrees (ten hours later) not to show their work, Sycamore argues that this is 'where the politics come together so explosively with the process, which isn't only the process of making art but the process of their relationships and their political, emotional, cultural and sexual engagement with the world'. Sycamore concludes,

> So I find myself inspired. Inspired because here is a group of people so excited about the potential of their own sexualities and the possibilities of a collective process of desire. I start to wonder what my own collective would look like, maybe not a porn collective but a collective of people (maybe fags, I don't know) trying to regain a sense of liberation and excitement in our own sexual lives.

Here immaterial creativity, human capital, works to undermine the inevitability of competition, at the same time disconnecting value from the principle of commodity exchange.

The value of *Made in Secret* lies in part in its rejection of money as the governing logic of porn production (of cultural production), and the concomitant exploitation of sexual affect as immaterial sex, exploitable value, and the circumscription of sexual subjectivity by self-entrepreneurialism. By denying us access to visual spectacles that conform to the normative pornoscript, and yet by teasing us with erotic scenarios suggested, but not documented, by the documentary's narrative (a lesbian masturbates in the shower, having discovered her desire for a bisexual woman whose bike she was fixing; a straight couple hook up in East Vancouver's cycle lanes and then take a room on a ferry where she fucks him with a strap-on; two straight men have their first homoerotic experience in a cycle park; two men and a woman taking a cycle ride through a park become entangled in a pansexual, cross-orientation romp in the mud) *Made in Secret* pricks desire, and proliferates possibility, rather than offering predictable scenarios that arise from market segmentation. Consequently we are unable to take up the familiar position of entrepreneurial voyeur; each erotic scenario is framed as a scene being shot for a porn film called *BikeSexual*, the production of which is itself being filmed for a documentary called *Made in Secret*. Our spectatorial experience offers little scope for expressing our sexual autonomy through the appropriate, and competitive articulation of choice. In its refusal of the horizontal branding of sex, where commercial porn apparently diversifies sexual tastes and possibilities as commodity categories, whilst in fact producing standardisation, *Made in Secret* instead offers a post-queer conjunction of diverse erotic possibilities (lesbianism, male homoeroticism, submissive male heterosexuality, dominant female heterosexuality, autoeroticism, voyeurism and exhibitionism) in a context where the proposition is that the collective, and the couples and single people within it, offer their sexuality to one another as a means of, variously, 'reclaiming their sexuality', inspiring 'people to do similar things in their communities', and making 'positive propaganda ... against the hegemony of porn'.

There's no doubt that at times the self-consciousness of *Made in Secret* is tiring, and verges on a kind of tricksy postmodernism. But this effect is minimised by the rich affectivity of its depiction of social relations: ultimately, what is so noteworthy about *Made in Secret* is how it models the disconnection of agency from individual autonomy and self-enterprise. Here, narratively and affectively, in the pursuit of 'sexy movies' that aren't 'creepy and weird and oppressive' but which make 'you want to watch ... and then go home and hump the furniture', is a pattern of agency that is a function of collective, consensual, non-competitive social relations, imprinted with powerful affective experiences related to the vicarious participation in those relations, that are strengthened by a de-centring of the commodity, the provocation of desire and an alternative sexual aesthetic. Whilst *Made in Secret* mobilises postmodern devices, its significance isn't limited to the kinds of individualised reading strategies Boyle decries.[52] If *Made in Secret* inspires DIY porn production, it also models a social form that offers that porn as political resistance of the enterprise culture.

CONCLUSION: BEYOND THE ENTREPRENEURIAL VOYEUR?

Pornography is, or should be, a compelling subject for academic study, because it straddles the shifting boundary between public and private at a moment in history when the tension between the two has never been more urgently in need of critical engagement. Porn cultures stage the scene of sexuality, disclosing both the discipline of bodies and the biopolitics of population: 'meat' and 'plant' embodiment and the organisation of sexuality as fragmented, competitive articulations of neoliberal subjectivity. The atomised and alienated nature of the sexual entitlements offered by the mainstreaming of sex and the sexualisation of culture, for those of us whose sexual politics were forged in the aftermath of second wave feminism and gay liberation, feels both unsatisfying and yet hard won. Meanwhile, if sexualisation by definition depoliticises sex, sex nevertheless remains relentlessly politicised by hard line right-wing constituencies for whom it is a rallying point, a bulwark against secularisation and the flattening of traditional stratifications in the face of neoliberalism's determinist equality of inequality. In this context it's worth recalling Foucault's suggestion that 'if sex is repressed ... then the mere fact that one is speaking about it has the appearance of a deliberate transgression'.[53] Sexualisation has undoubtedly advanced the material circumstances of many kinds of queers (most especially professional gay men) and many women (most especially middle class professionals without children), offering increased cultural and social choices, legal entitlements, and a greater range of pleasures and professional opportunities. The proliferation of forms of pornography, including altporn, have offered consumers greater choice, whilst digitisation and networked cultures have enabled the emergence of new taste cultures and a hitherto unprecedented degree of interactivity. But these choices and freedoms are available only within an increasingly privatised zone of entitlement, the desirability of which is used to legitimate the radical abandonment of the public sphere by state governments of the so-called advanced democracies. In this context, academic porn studies has reached an impasse of constrained optimism. The enthusiastic engagement with altporn represents a circling of the wagons, and signifies the extent to which pro-porn positions necessarily mediate the hostility of radical and anti-porn feminisms, and right-wing anti-feminist and anti-gay activism, at the same time as acknowledging the seemingly unassailable power of capital and business. The effect of this set of mediations is an over-emphasis on agency, a preoccupation with classification that strives to identify the breakthrough artifact in the midst of unruly choice and segmentation, and an over-investment in the possibility of technological democratisation. Coming to terms with the implications of the enterprise society, as Lois McNay suggests, requires a reconfiguration of our notions of autonomy and agency, and in relation to porn, it requires us to come to terms with the limits of our entitlements, and the effects of our immaterial labour, as entrepreneurial voyeurs. The celebration of choice, even where that choice offers apparently ethical forms of commodity, works to re-confirm the logic of neoliberalism. Framing progress or resistance outside these terms isn't easy, and in a climate where academic output is a function of our personal profiles as enterprising subjects, and often works to solidify competitive conditions of productivity, we are especially, if not predictably, constrained. This is one of many reasons why the affective pleasures of *Made in Secret* are significant at this juncture. The film depicts in representation the difficult and traumatic nature of yielding personal agency to collective process, and of de-privatizing sexual autonomy. It also solicits affective intensities connected to social processes in ways that animate them. New modes of collectivity that resist the competitive individualism of the enterprise culture are increasingly defining a range of political activisms, utilizing social media, funding models, forms of address and branding strategies appropriated from commodity culture. Yet, the entrepreneurial voyeur remains alienated by the privatisation of sex and the asocial framing of masturbatory activity and the fragmentary nature of fantasy. *Made in Secret*, in fact or fiction, models an alternative, where pornographic pleasures and collective endeavor validate and reinforce one another. If porn studies, and the fields of sexuality and gender on which it draws, are to regain a sense of relevance and urgency, then we need to reframe our critical perspective in order to facilitate the articulation of such possibilities.

NOTES

1. Rosalind Gill, 'From Sexual Objectification to Sexual Subjectification: The Resexualisation of Women's Bodies in the Media', *Feminist Media Studies*, 3, 1, (2003): 100-106.
2. See, amongst others: Laura Harvey, Rosalind Gill, 'Spicing it up: Sexual

entrepreneurs and The Sex Inspectors' in R. Gill & C. Scharff (eds), *New Femininities: Postfeminism, Neoliberalism and Subjectivity*, London, Palgrave, 2011; Rosalind Gill, 'Beyond the `Sexualization of Culture' Thesis: An Intersectional Analysis of 'Sixpacks', 'Midriffs' and 'Hot Lesbians' in Advertising', *Sexualities*, 12, (2009): 137; Feona Attwood, 'Sexualisation, Sex and Manners', *Sexualities*, 13, (2010): 742; Feona Attwood, 'Sexed Up: Theorising the Sexualisation of Culture', *Sexualities*, 9, (2006): 77.

3. Karen Boyle, 'Epilogue: how was it for you?' in Boyle (ed), *Everyday Pornography*, Routledge, Abingdon & New York 2010.

4. Feona Attwood, 'No Money Shot? Commerce, Pornography and New Sex Taste Cultures', *Sexualities*, 10, 4, (2007): 441-456; Katrien Jacobs, 'Pornography in Small Spaces and Other Places', *Cultural Studies*, 18, (1): 2004, available at http://libidot.org/katrien/tester/articles/pornsmallplace.pdf; Katrien Jacobs, 'Negotiating contracts and the singing orgasm', *Spectator*, 24, 1, (2004), available at http://libidot.org/katrien/tester/articles/negotiating-print.html.

5. Susanna Paasonen, 'Labors of love: netporn, Web 2.0 and the meanings of amateurism', *New Media & Society*, 12, 8, (2010): 1297-1312, hereafter Labors of love.

6. Messina, quoted in T. Gemin, 'Realcore: Sergio Messina and Online Porn', *Digimag*, 19, 2006, http://www.digicult.it/digimag/article.asp?id=675, accessed November 2011.

7. Florian Cramer, 'Sodom Blogging: Alternative Porn and Aesthetic Sensibility' in Katrien Jacobs et al. (eds), *C'Lick Me: A Netporn Studies Reader*, Amsterdam: Institute of Network Cultures, 2007, http://www.networkcultures.org/_uploads/24.pdf; F. Cramer, & S. Home, 'Pornographic Coding' in K. Jacobs et al. (eds) *C'Lick Me*, op. cit.

8. Jacobs, 'Pornography in Small Spaces', op. cit.

9. Claire Hemmings, 'Invoking Affect: Cultural Theory and the Ontological Turn', *Cultural Studies*, 19, 5, (2005): 548-567.

10. F. Cramer & S. Home, 'Pornographic Coding' in K. Jacobs et al. (eds), *C'Lick Me*, op. cit.

11. Brian McNair, *Striptease Culture: Sex, Media and the Democratisation of Desire*, London & New York, Routledge, 2002, p207; Attwood, 'Sexed Up', op. cit., p81.

12. Cramer, 'Sodom Blogging', op. cit.

13. Attwood, 'No Money Shot', op. cit; Jacobs, 'Pornography in Small Spaces', op. cit; Jacobs, 'Negotiating Contracts', op. cit.

14. S. Paasonen, 'Epilogue: Porn Futures' in Paasonen, K. Nikunen & L. Saarenmaa (eds), *Pornification: Sex and Sexuality in Media Culture*, Oxford & New York, Berg, 2007, p163.

15. Enrico Biasin & Federico Zecca, 'Contemporary Audiovisual Pornography: Branding Strategy and Gonzo Film Style', Cinema&Cie, *International Film Studies Journal*, 9, 12, (2009): 133-50.

16. Jacobs, 'Pornography in Small Spaces', op. cit., p80.

17. Jacobs, 'Negotiating Contracts', op. cit., p14.

18. Henry Jenkins, *Convergence Culture: Where Old and New Media Collide*, New York & London, New York University Press, 2006; Jacobs, 'Pornography in Small Spaces', op. cit; Attwood, 'No Money Shot', op. cit., p442.

19. Attwood, 'No Money Shot', op. cit., p443.
20. Cramer & Home, 'Pornographic Coding', op. cit., pp164-5.
21. Ibid., p165.
22. Ibid.
23. Carole Cadwalladr, 'Porn wars: the debate that's dividing academia', *Observer*, 16 June 2013, http://www.guardian.co.uk/culture/2013/jun/16/internet-violent-porn-crime-studies, accessed June 2013.
24. Rosalind Gill, 'From Sexual Objectification to Sexual Subjectification', op. cit., pp100-106.
25. Hemmings, 'Invoking Affect', op. cit., pp549-550.
26. Ibid, p565. C.f. Jeremy Gilbert, 'Signifying Nothing: 'Culture', 'Discourse' and the Sociality of Affect', *Culture Machine*, 2004, p6.
27. Niels Van Doorn, 'Keeping it Real: User-Generated Pornography, Gender Reification, and Visual Pleasure', *Convergence*, 16, 4, (2010): 426, hereafter Keeping it Real.
28. Cramer & Home, 'Pornographic Coding', op. cit., p165.
29. Michel Foucault, *The Birth of Biopolitics: Lectures at the Collège de France*, Basingstoke, Palgrave, 2008, pp146-7, 225-226, hereafter *The Birth of Biopolitics*.
30. McNay, 'Self as Enterprise: Dilemmas of Control and Resistance in Foucaults's *The Birth of Biopolitics*, *Theory, Culture and Society*, 26, (2009): 55-77, hereafter Self as Enterprise.
31. Lazzarato, 'Immaterial Labor', http://www.generationonline.org/c/fcimmateriallabour3.htm, 1999.
32. Mark Davis, *Sex, Technology and Public Health*, Houndmills & New York, Palgrave Macmillan, 2009.
33. Tristan Taormino, 2008, quoted in S. Paasonen, *Carnal Resonance: Affect and Online Pornography*, Cambridge, MIT Press, 2011.
34. Stephen Maddison, '"The Second Sexual Revolution": Big Pharma, Porn and the Biopolitical Penis', *Topia: Canadian Journal of Cultural Studies*, 22, Fall 2009.
35. Catherine Waldby & Melinda Cooper, 'The Biopolitics of Reproduction: Post-Fordist Biotechnology and Women's Clinical Labour', *Global Biopolitics Research Group Working Papers*, 2006, URL (consulted 21/11/07) http://www.ioh.uea.ac.uk/biopolitics/networks_publications_working.php.
36. Nina Power, *One Dimensional Woman*, Winchester & Washington, Zero Books, 2009.
37. Lauren Langman, 'Grotesque Degradation: Globalization, Carnivalization, and Cyberporn' in Dennis D. Waskul (ed), *net.seXXX: Readings on Sex, Pornography and the Internet*, New York, Peter Lang, 2004.
38. Paasonen, *Carnal Resonance*, op. cit.
39. Mark Coté & Jennifer Plybus, 'Learning to Immaterial Labour: MySpace and Social Networks', *Ephemera*, 7, 1, (2007): 104.
40. Ibid., p94.
41. See footage of Gallop's presentation at the TED conference of 2009, http://blog.ted.com/2009/12/02/cindy_gallop_ma/; see also Gallop *Make Love Not Porn: Technology's Hardcore Impact on Human Behavior*, TED Books 2011.
42. Attwood, 'No Money Shot?', op. cit.
43. https://makelovenotporn.tv/pages/about/how_this_works, accessed January 2013.

44. Joanna Walters, 'Make love not porn, says Oxford graduate on a mission to make sex more erotic', *Guardian*, 15.09.2012, http://www.guardian.co.uk/culture/2012/sep/16/make-love-not-porn, accessed January 2013.

45. Jenkins 2006 in Paasonen, 'Labors of love', op. cit., p1306.

46. Mark Fisher, *Capitalist Realism: Is There No Alternative?* Winchester & Washington, Zero Books, 2009, p21.

47. Power, *One Dimensional Woman*, op. cit., p51.

48. Adam Arvidsson, 'Netporn: The Work of Fantasy in the Information Society' in Jacobs et al. (eds), *C'Lick Me*, op. cit., p73.

49. Ibid, p74

50. Michel Foucault, 'Friendship as a Way of Life' in P. Rabinow (ed), *Michel Foucault Ethics: Subjectivity and Truth. Essential Works of Foucault 1954-1984, Volume 1*, London, Penguin, 2000, p135.

51. M.B. Sycamore, 'Made in Secret: the story of the East Van porn collective, and me', 2008, http://www.bilerico.com/2008/03/made_in_secret_the_story_, accessed November 2011.

52. Boyle, 'Epilogue', op. cit., pp203-4.

53. M. Foucault, *The History of Sexuality Volume 1: An Introduction*, New York, Pantheon Books, 1978, p6.

FEMINISM, THE FAMILY AND THE NEW 'MEDIATED' MATERNALISM

Angela McRobbie

In this essay I trace a line of development from liberal to neo-liberal feminism which is, I claim, being at least partly realised and embodied through the ubiquitous figure of the middle-class, professional, wife and mother. Following on from a comment by Stuart Hall on the centrality of the 'middle class' to the neoliberal project, I overlay this with the additional categories of gender and maternity.[1] This image of motherhood not only displaces but also begins to dismantle a longstanding political relationship which has linked post-war social democracy with maternity, while simultaneously providing the political right with a new, more contemporary script which allows it to take the lead in the current debate on family life. My tone is somewhat tentative for the reason that what I am referring to seems, at present, more like a strong undercurrent than a fully-fledged sociological phenomenon. The analysis I offer is also restricted, more or less, to contemporary Britain, with several references to US popular culture and to US liberal feminism for the reason that these have provided so much of a steer for the way in which the neoliberal agenda in the UK has addressed motherhood and domestic life. This agenda is quite different from the now out-of-date conservative mantra of 'family values'. The right-wing newspaper the *Daily Mail* in its *Femail* Section has been particularly forceful in its championing of a style of affluent, feminine maternity. This idea of active (i.e. *en route* to the gym), sexually confident motherhood marks an extension of its pre-maternal equivalent, the ambitious and aspirational young working woman. It is also consistently pitched against an image of the abject, slovenly and benefit-dependent 'underclass' single mother, the UK equivalent of the US 'welfare queen'. Only in academic feminism do we find a more critical and empathetic response to the difficulties faced by out-of-work single mothers[2].

While feminism has for many decades been a political formation with historic connections closer to the left than the right, this alignment is now undergoing change, with substantial gains for the right should it manage to develop further what is at the moment merely a kind of feminist flourish. Within and alongside the UK Coalition government we can see a fledgling feminist strand led mostly by an urban, upper-middle-class, cosmopolitan elite including former Cabinet Minister Louise Mensch, Home Secretary Theresa May, Lib Dem MP Jo Stimson as well as a number of influential young spokeswomen from right-wing think tanks such as Policy Reform.[3] This endorsement is informed by 1970s US liberal feminism, with an emphasis on equal rights, condemnation of domestic and sexual violence, and action against genital mutilation. It is drawn into the field of popular neoliberal hegemony which the Tory Party is intent on building particularly through the idea of 'welfare reform' and in this realm it takes the form of an unapologetically middle-class feminism, shorn of all obligations to less privileged women or to those who are not 'strivers' (a favoured term within welfare reform discourse). The task I undertake here is to somehow clear the pathway so that a fuller understanding of these quite complex processes can be arrived at.

In what is I hope a continuation of feminist discussions on the rise of neoliberalism led by Wendy Brown on the 'end of liberal democracy,[4] and followed through by my own recent writing on young women as subjects of the new meritocracy under New Labour[5], and by Nancy Fraser in her provocative argument that there has been 'feminist complicity',[6] I aim to show how a new momentum for the political right comprises a careful claiming of progressive heterosexual maternal womanhood. What has emerged recently is a perhaps unexpected rehabilitation of feminism as a broad constellation of progressive socio-political interests converging around the category of woman, which can be usefully deployed by those modernising forces of the right, centre and also centre left, where previously such an association would be shunned. The very words 'conservative feminism' are now common-place, part of the everyday vocabulary of Louise Mensch in her newspaper articles, blogs and TV appearances[7] and a lively 'talking point' across contemporary political culture in the UK. Feminism is no longer despised but given some new life through an articulation with a specific range of values pertaining to the project of contemporary neoliberalism. This connection is confirmed towards the end of the best-selling book titled *Lean In: Women, Work and the Will to Lead* by the Chief Operating Officer (COO) of Facebook Sheryl Sandberg where she unashamedly declares herself a feminist. I will return to Sandberg's book and its significance in the final section of this paper, but for the moment I want to highlight this take-up of feminism as an aspect of the ambitious reach of neoliberalism such that its principles have become not just a new kind of common-sense, but also an active force-field of political values, at a time when the political left has been crushed or at least subdued. Others would remark that parties of both the left and (centre) left have in any case already conceded to these same goals, such that there is not a great deal of difference in the UK between the modernising agenda of New Labour and the austerity-driven policies of the Coalition government. In each case there has been a commitment to privatisation of the public sector, the denigration of welfare regimes as producing unaffordable dependencies, the emphasis on self-responsibility, entrepreneurialism and constant advocacy of stable (if also now flexible and gay) forms of family life.

As a starting point then I would say that there is something of a feminist endorsement detectable in the political air. The animosity and repudiation which was a feature of the Blair government and the popular culture and media of the time, has receded. Support for 'hard working families' – a phrase first coined by Gordon Brown during his time as Chancellor of the Exchequer – is retained by both leaders of the Tory Party and the Liberal Democrats but this now incorporates a more engaged and sympathetic dialogue with mothers (stay at home and working) with some indication that this is a 'feminist issue' for today.[8] This promulgating of women seems like more than just a pragmatic move to secure the female vote, and more than a knee-jerk response to the vocal presence of online campaigners and new female constituencies.[9] Instead it is arguably part of a process of inventing a repertoire of woman-centred positions which will confirm and enhance the core values of the neoliberal project. So much of this ideological work takes place outside, but in close proximity to, the field of formal politics, in culture and in particular within the various forms of feminine mass media[10] including BBC Radio 4 *Women's Hour,* the *Femail* Section of the *Daily Mail* mentioned above, the women's pages (or lifestyle sections) of all the national quality daily newspapers such as the *Guardian,* the *Independent, The Times* and the *Daily Telegraph,* some key daytime TV programmes such as *Loose Women,* and of course the range of women's magazines from the fashion-oriented *Grazia* to *Red,* a monthly publication, for one generation older than *Elle* and therefore targeting middle-class mothers (stay-at-home and in employment), to the traditional *Women's Own.* Where in the early 2000s an invitation to female empowerment seemed to require a ritualistic denunciation of feminism as old-fashioned and no longer needed, (with the exception of the left-leaning *Guardian* newspaper and BBC Radio 4s *Women's Hour*), the current repertoire now feels able to make a claim, of sorts, to a feminism, of sorts. The observations I offer in the pages that follow suggest the value of a feminism (with roots in the US liberal feminism tradition) for the neoliberal regime, offering a distinctively gendered dimension to the mantra of individualism, the market and competition as well as updating the now old-fashioned 'family values' vocabularies associated with social conservatism. These are old-fashioned for a number of reasons. For a start female labour power is far too important to the post-industrial economy for anyone to be an advocate of long-term stay-at-home wives and mothers. Moreover spurred on by the rise of feminism from the mid 1970s onwards, women expressed a strong desire to work. With the high rate of divorce, having a career does not just provide women with an income and independence, it also reduces the cost of welfare to government. It thus makes sense for government to champion women who will enter the labour market and stay in it. In this context the new 'corporate' feminism supports and extends the dominance of contemporary neoliberalism. If it runs into some difficulties when confronted, for example, by religious lobbies and by individual politicians of both sexes opposed to abortion, (or similar issues), these are surmountable obstacles, where choice, empowerment and a commitment to 'planned parenthood' are uppermost. Imperative to this new neoliberal feminism is its stand and status in regard to its imagined other, the Muslim woman assumed to be oppressed and subjected to various forms of domination and control. Various feminist scholars writing in the context of the post 9/11 world have referred to this as the instrumentalisation of feminism, and Jasbir Puar has reflected on the strategic value of homonationalism, and the instrumentalisation of gay and lesbian rights as a means by which western governments, particularly the US, can assert a kind of global progressive superiority.[11] What I am interested to chart here is the way in which, working through a number of powerful media channels, political parties and forces of the mainstream right (primarily, in my account, the British Conservatives, but also elsewhere in Europe – the German Christian Democrats for example), are able to re-vitalise and modernise the conservative agenda through adopting a weak version of feminism which in turn permits a new kind of more attentive address to women.[12]

REVOLUTIONARY ROAD?

In what follows I introduce the analysis of family values and neoliberal feminism by briefly considering the 2009 film *Revolutionary Road* (dir. Sam Mendes). I then look back at some strands of (second wave) socialist-feminist writing on the family from the late 1970s. This is followed by a section on the Foucault tradition, especially the late 1970s biopolitics lectures and the concept of human capital. And then as a tool for understanding the new address to mothers as active sexual subjects (expressed through body culture), as well as them being pro-active in the economic sense (in the workforce), I propose 'visual media governmentality' as a regulatory space for the formulation and working through of many of these ideas. It is here that the benchmarks and boundaries of female success are established; it is here that new norms of failure symbolised in the abject body of the 'single mother' and in the bodies of her untidy children or 'brood' are to be found. In this visual field vulnerability and dependency are graphically equated with personal carelessness, with being overweight, and badly dressed, and these in turn become 'performance indicators' signalling inadequate life planning, and what Wendy Brown calls 'mismanaged lives'.[13]

Why *Revolutionary Road?* This is a film positioned somewhere between the popular, middlebrow, quasi-independent films associated with the Working Title productions of Richard Curtis (films often appealing primarily to women), and a more art-house genre. This generic slot promises a largely female, middle-class, possibly university-educated audience. Such are the complex economies of film production and distribution today that there are multiple strands of accompanying publicity and snippets of information widely disseminated across a range of media forms, at the time of the cinematic release, with the result that films become remarkably open-ended, cultural objects. *Revolutionary Road* re-united two of Hollywood's most famous actors already known for their previous performance in *Titanic*, and in this sense the stars Kate Winslet and Leonardo DiCaprio bring to the film a whole set of both sexual and romantic expectations. The director Sam Mendes was at the time married to Kate Winslet and the film itself is about marital discord. Mendes is known for his directing of *American Beauty*, and he is regarded as someone with a liberal sensibility. Both *American Beauty* and *Revolutionary Road* have small casts, like stage-plays, and they are prepared to tackle difficult emotional situations, underscored by a recognition of the place for, and impact of, sexual politics. If *American Beauty* told a

story of post-feminist heterosexual family life, *Revolutionary Road* turns
the director's gaze back in time to pre-(liberal)-feminist USA. Based on
a highly regarded novel published in 1962 by US writer Richard Yates,
Revolutionary Road offers the opportunity to reflect on a move from the
founding moments of white, middle- class, US liberal feminism, to its
contemporary transformation into neoliberal feminism. It is a film which
has as its subtext a range of feminist issues, serving as a reminder of the
gains made in the moment coming directly after the period in which
the film is set. It is not so much that it anticipates feminism; rather, it
shows why US liberal feminism, when it finally exploded into being,
took the shape it did. It is therefore an immanent narrative fuelled by an
unspeakable desire for something, which could only be a sexual politics to
come. The timing of its production, the themes which the director does
not quite bring to the surface but leaves to audience inference, as well
as a press comment by Kate Winslet that she read *The Feminine Mystique*
in preparation for the role of April, suggest that the producers of such a
multi-million dollar production as this could be persuaded that it would
be a box-office success.[14] Set in the mid-1950s there is however no evoking
of nostalgia. Winslet's wardrobe is carefully chosen to both constrain her
within that pre-feminist moment of conservative femininity while also
suggesting her pushing at the boundaries of convention. She is more
urban and elegant than her neighbours, and her clothes encapsulate her
yearning to be somewhere else. This is a film located in that US post-war
suburban moment as a pre-feminist stage before the storm bursts, and it
depicts a litany of feminist concerns explored through the character of
April, but without naming them as such.

  The couple April and Frank find themselves locked into a lifestyle which
bears all the marks of post-war American affluence, and all the rigidities
of gender and sexuality which underpinned the new nuclear family of the
period. April's hopes for a career in acting are dashed after a humiliation
in a local amateur dramatics; she also sees that her husband is unfulfilled
in his desk job and so she proposes a move to Paris. April's enthusiasm is
first curbed by the hard work she has to do to win her husband over to this
plan, and then extinguished when two events follow each other in quick
succession: she gets pregnant with a third child and wants an abortion,
which shocks Frank; and he in turn gets an unexpected promotion at work,
while also compensating for suburban boredom by enjoying the frisson
of adultery with a girl from the office pool. As the relationship crumbles
April flirts with one of the neighbours when they find themselves alone

together after a couples' night out, and she has sex with him in the car, rejecting him a few days later. She then infuriates her husband by getting hold of an obstetric vacuum to carry out an abortion and when he confesses to having had an affair, she merely asks him angrily why he bothered to tell her. Paris is no longer an option and in despair April aborts herself, rupturing her womb and haemorrhaging to death. The film closes with shots of the bereaved father Frank now moved to New York City watching his kids play in the park, and the realtor neighbours back in the suburbs commenting that the couple did not really ever fit in.

These are the years before easily available birth control, never mind safe abortions, when ambitious women, with the onset of motherhood, were rarcly able to fulfil themselves with a career. The film shows the claustrophobia of family life and motherhood as triggers for what was to come, i.e. the women's movement (or revolution) of the mid-1960s. There is a catalogue of soon-to-be feminist issues. The question of female sexual pleasure is explored when April enjoys seducing her neighbour, but the sex act itself only lasts a few seconds. Once it is done it is over. Nor does April display any significant affection for her children: maternity is simply something that happened to her unbidden. Overall, the film implicitly makes the strongest argument in favour of divorce. The narrative suggests that female mental health and well-being can depend on being able to exit a marriage, and gain independence, a life of one's own.

It is the timing of the film that is significant in the context of its reception in the UK and US. The film feeds into current anxieties about the breakdown of marriage and the de-stabilising of family life. It introduces feminist issues for a middle-class audience segment unused to the intrusion of angry sexual politics within the landscape of contemporary cinema. Maybe it introduces gender discord and sexual politics within the ranks of the political right, if the review by Charles Moore in the *Daily Telegraph* is anything to go by.[15] In any case my argument here is that the film marks a point of contestation in a popular-film culture which for the previous decade has celebrated weddings, and which has humorously portrayed young women's fears of missing out on marriage and children, and of 'always being the bridesmaid and never the bride'.[16] *Revolutionary Road*, with its Hollywood stars, demonstrates it liberal credentials by contesting the sanctity of marriage. The film serves as a reminder of the contribution of liberal feminism to contemporary western women's freedoms. Through the narrative of April, the film anticipates progress and the 'revolutionary' change which was just round the corner. The film reminds its viewers of the idea of progress – there can be no return to a time when married women were trapped in the home with only the chores of babies and housework to punctuate the day. The narrative bolsters a linear model of progress along with the idea of personal or individual liberation. There is a profoundly liberal feminist 'structure of feeling' running through *Revolutionary Road.* Kate Winslet, in and out of character, offers a powerful point of identification for young, middle-class women today. She is beautiful and successful, and she exudes an aura of being a passionate and independent woman As the *Daily Mail* sourly notes, following the recent announcement of her pregnancy, she will soon be the mother of three children, all of whom have different fathers: a '3x3'.

THE NURSERY AS SOCIALIST IDEAL

I have argued that contemporary neoliberalism in its bid for deeper embedding as a new kind of common-sense, enters into a kind of symbiotic relationship with liberal feminism. I have also pointed to the significant role allocated to the professional middle-class mother in this hegemony-building exercise. But who exactly is she? We could point to the modes of visibility and publicity management which surround leading politicians' wives, such as Michelle Obama, Samantha Cameron and Miriam Clegg. We could also include COO of Facebook Sheryl Sandberg in this list of female 'highflyers' (as the press describes them) – mothers who, whether temporarily on sabbatical from their careers, or else 'juggling' and combining work with motherhood, nevertheless embark on the latter with professional attention to duty, responsibility and all the skills required to ensure a stable upbringing for children. In effect they are called upon to be 'exemplary' mothers within a political culture intent on reversing family breakdown, and on encouraging better and more effective parenthood. But it is the website www.mumsnet.com which most precisely embodies this new role of professional middle-class maternity, and which now has achieved the status of a mother's lobby.[17] This model of maternal citizenship is counter-posed in the popular press and tabloids, as I have already noted above, by an abject maternal figure – typically a single mother with several children fathered by different men, reliant on benefits, living in a council house, and with an appearance which suggests lack of attention to body image, all of which within today's moral universe imply fecklessness, promiscuity and inadequate parenting. The *Daily Mail* once again takes the lead in exposing these examples of bad mothering, many of whom are shown either to be cheating the welfare system, bringing up delinquent children, never having had a job or else having failed to provide their children with reliable father figures. In a recent edition the *Daily Mail* commissioned respected British Asian writer and broadcaster Yasmin Alibhai-Brown to spend a day in a neighbourhood known colloquially as a 'man desert' given the disproportionate number of single mothers, many of whom in this case were black.[18] More often, articles like this rely on photographs of unruly-looking children alongside a tired and 'ungroomed' mother, where, as Bev Skeggs would argue, ungroomed has become synonymous with unrespectable and morally deficient working class femininity.[19]

This whole vista of information, publicity and 'news' exists within a frame where social and political affairs merge into, often to be overtaken by, the world of entertainment and celebrity culture. In effect some of the most pressing social issues of our times such as 'welfare reform' are wrapped up in a confection of what used to be known as 'tit-bits', gossip, in a contemporary version of what Richard Hoggart in 1957 referred to as the traditional 'Peg's Paper' style of reading material designed for a large popular female readership and audience.[20] An allusion to Hoggart is actually appropriate because what is also entirely missing from this new world of either exemplary or shameful maternity is the figure of the strong, working-class mother, the kind of stalwart of the community which Hoggart described so vividly and before him DH Lawrence. Not particularly concerned about her appearance, often tired, sometimes holding down several poorly paid jobs at once, making sure her children were well fed and got the best opportunities, this figure has almost gone from the popular imagination. She lingers on only as the occasional character in TV soap opera such as *Coronation Street*, and when she does make an appearance in other TV genres, it is as the hard-pressed Mum in need of a make-over, whose children or husband will connive with the TV presenters to offer her the chance for some radical transformation which will bring her up to the standard of glamorous visual appearance now required to count as a woman today; in short, she is subjected to the normalising horizon of beauty culture which brings working-class women somehow within reach of middle class aspiration, sexual attractiveness and hence social acceptability.[21] The disappearance of the working class mother, as someone with any public voice or visibility, never mind the respect and dignity such a figure once had in leftwing thought as well as in literature, in drama and in cinema, is instructive in this shifting political universe where social democracy is in decline, where welfare is widely targeted as wasteful and where there are fewer voices in politics, media or in public policy fields defending these principles.

To unpack further the starkness of this transformation and the withdrawal of compassion and support to women who as mothers find themselves trapped in welfare dependency, we need to reflect on the historical relationship which existed between both radical and social democratic politics and feminism, especially with regard to maternity, for the reason that it is this set of intersecting political forces which has been trounced and overshadowed by the ascendancy of the new right, the centre right, and the centre left inaugurated by the Clinton government in the US (with its singling out of 'welfare queens' as the focus of attention in the bid to make workfare the only option) and followed up as the Third Way during the Blair years. Indeed we cannot under-estimate the zeal with which the Blair government set about dismantling old Labour allegiances, including the perhaps romanticised place occupied by the working-class mother. This also involved a scornful repudiation of feminism and a discarding of the value of and place for labour history. Of course it is not as though feminism had ever existed in comfortable harmony with the Labour Party. The schisms between Labour and the extra-parliamentary left, including the socialist-feminists, from the 1970s through to the 1990s, are well documented. Most of the best known writing on feminism and the family emerged from Marxist-feminist scholarship including the work of Elizabeth Wilson, Michele Barrett and Mary McIntosh, and also the historical writing of Denise Riley and Anna Davin.[22] None of these writers were directly connected to the Labour Party and many were fiercely critical of the reformist tendencies of social democracy. Yet this divide was not entirely impermeable: by the mid-1980s several Marxist groups had dissolved and entered the Labour Party (the influential International Marxist Group), while the British Communist Party, including the well-known feminist journalist Bea Campbell, shared many political platforms and indeed journals with prominent figures inside Labour, especially as it moved to embrace the more mainstream Euro-communism. If the heroic years of the Labour Party was the post-war period, then it is also the case that through these decades, inside and alongside the party, there were many activists and campaigners committed to improving living standards for families, especially those who found themselves in financial hardship. It was women inside Labour who also lobbied to ensure that Child Benefits could be paid direct to the mother, and who fought hard to establish pre-school provision, especially in low income neighbourhoods. The Child Poverty Action Group was influential for many years and for a period was headed by Ruth Lister, a highly regarded feminist scholar as well as campaigner who for decades has been involved in (among other things) defending poor, single mothers against attempts by government to push them into work despite the difficulties in securing good quality full time nursery provision.[23] The Blair period of modernisation set in place a momentum which marginalised, discredited or cast as old-fashioned this kind of feminist policy work, with the result that apart from the Women's Budget Group and the 'gender mainstreaming' (i.e liberal feminist) platform led by feminist sociologist Sylvia Walby, women's voices were muted and more or less ignored.[24] This demise is arguably a key factor in the rise of the new binaries of good and bad motherhood which now litter the popular press and media. Despite the emergence of new feminist online campaigners and activists in the last five years, little of their attention has been paid to defending poor women against cuts to welfare. Nor have these online organisations tackled the disapproval and disapprobation of poor, single mothers, or challenged the glamorisation of motherhood found across the popular media which concentrates only on the super-wealthy and celebrities who have access to as many nannies as they need. Feminist public policy research in journals such as *Critical Social Policy* does span this range of topics, interrogating for example the wider impact of this negative stereotyping of single mothers, and there have also been a number of articles in *MAMSIE* challenging the new moral landscape of motherhood.[25] What is missing is a wider contextualisation of the demonisation of the disadvantaged within a socio-cultural framework which charts not just the decline of social democracy, an enormous loss to British political life, but also the fact that this passing away is strangely unmarked and hence unmourned.

If we do pay attention to what was a defining feature of the UK welfare state in the early years, i.e the important place occupied by women and children as rightful subjects of entitlements and benefits, we can also be reminded nevertheless of how the social security system was predicated on a male breadwinner model, which by the late 1970s was being challenged by socialist feminists who argued for women to participate fully in the labour force as a means of gaining and retaining economic independence. With this the question of childcare provision suddenly comes to the forefront. Three key texts of this period reflect exactly the terrain of debate: Elizabeth Wilson's *Women and the Welfare State* (1977), Michele Barrett and Mary McIntosh's *The Anti- Social Family* (1982), and Denise Riley's *War in the Nursery* (1987).[26] Riley's rich historical account charted the angry debates that raged within the ranks of the medical experts, psychoanalysts and other professionals about the role of nursery care, and this in turn brought to the attention of feminists the idea of 'socialised childcare', something also associated with Communist states. This idea found great favour within different strands of feminism in the UK for various reasons: first, that only full-time nursery care freed women to enter employment, gain economic independence, and pursue uninterrupted careers, thus fulfilling their potential as equal to men in work and in professional life; second, that the nursery environment was beneficial for children allowing them to gain social skills and escape the over-heated and exclusive emotional connection with the mother; and third, that exclusive motherhood was in any case a trap for women, an exhausting, unrewarding role, one of servitude without pay. Well-organised nursery provision was a socialist idea, almost from the start. Nursery provision was a key feature of both feminist discourse and of wider public policy discussion for more than forty years. Labour governments had seen nursery care as a way of improving the health and well-being of children from poor families while also allowing women to work and hence contribute to family incomes. While feminist theorists, especially Elizabeth Wilson, pointed to the policing role of welfare as it intruded into the lives of working-class families, there was nevertheless a consistent support within feminism for state-provided nursery care alongside paid maternity leave, and other related provisions.

The Anti-Social Family is also instructive to look back at, not just because it tackles the oppressive aspects of domesticity and the 'tyranny of maternity' but because it acknowledges the exclusions for lesbian women who at the time had few possibilities for maternity and who also suffered the stigma of childlessness. In many ways this book articulates the divide between the perceived privileges of heterosexual feminism and its championing of motherhood as a priority within feminism, and the pre-queer dynamics of marginalisation from normative family life. At the same time Michele Barrett and Mary McIntosh fully recognise the apparently endless 'popularity' of the family in everyday life and the unlikelihood of its demise. In the light of this seemingly consensual enjoyment of the domestic sphere, feminists arguably withdrew from extreme anti or alternative-family positions and instead became involved in campaigns which supported mothers through a range of measures, notably maternity leave, flexible working hours, as well as access to affordable childcare. I stress this historical trajectory not as an uninterrupted pathway, but rather to emphasise the troubled but nevertheless anchored connection between feminism and the pro-active policies associated with social democratic governments which supported women's movement into work from the early 1970s onwards, and, concomitant with this, recognised pre-school childcare as socially as well as financially beneficial.

What has happened in the last decade in regard to this configuration of once powerful forces is instructive. The feminist emphasis on the 'tyranny of maternity' as Barrett and McIntosh put it, is wildly unspeakable, as is the portrayal of housework and childcare as drudgery. It would be interesting to speculate as to why there is at present, despite various other feminist actions, no organisation or campaign which addresses the oppressive, repetitive, exhausting nature of daily housework and childcare and the extent to which women are still disproportionately responsible for these daily responsibilities. Perhaps this can be attributed to the legacy of a post-feminist culture which emphasises responsibility and choice. As various sociologists have argued, structural issues are transformed into personal matters for which private solutions must be found.[27] The ideological force of choice has a de-socialising and de-politicising function. But more emphatically the idea of affordable socialised childcare (ie mass nursery care) as a universal provision is also unthinkable, for the reasons of its socialist, communist and welfare-ist heritage, and thus its cost to the state. In this context the idea of full time nursery provision for babies and toddlers, has been conveniently discredited as harmful to children.[28] And yet this model provided the single most effective route out of poverty for disadvantaged and single parent households. For mothers to be fully participating in the labour market there has to be an extensive and well run programme of child care and after school care. Without this working mothers will always have mixed feelings about prioritising wage labour.

The nexus of social democratic and feminist politics which was for many years a defining feature of Labour policies in the UK, shaping the nature of thinking on families, welfare and maternity, found itself at least by-passed, if not thrown out by the forces of modernisation associated with the Blair period. Banal phrases like the 'work-life balance' came to replace more sustained debate about how motherhood and work could realistically be combined, without women jeopardising their opportunities in the workplace. Implicitly, as Rosemary Crompton suggested, there was a return to gender traditionalism as women were urged to compromise in the workplace so as to maintain a dual role, this being a step back from all feminist arguments for gender equality and the equal sharing of domestic roles.[29] No one at the time was prepared to argue loudly for men to compromise on their careers or prospects for promotion in favour of sharing all household responsibilities, as to say such a thing would merely confirm a feminist anti-men stance which during the Blair years was quite unacceptable within the landscape of Westminster politics.[30] To sum up, to understand the new family values of the present moment it is necessary to look back to the New Labour period and to the way in which previous historical affiliations between social democracy and feminism which aimed to support women as mothers were dismantled and discredited. This opened the pathway for the present day demonisation of welfare which suggests that relying on support or subsidy is somehow shameful. Thus families need to take responsibility for their own affairs and not look to the state for 'hand outs'. At the same time there is a widely disseminated discourse which celebrates choice and the privatisation of childcare through the use of nannies. The granting of marital and parental rights to lesbian and gay couples, while important and just, has consolidated a kind of hermetic ideal of family life which undercuts the older social democratic systems of provision for families outside the family such as youth clubs, girls groups, and a wide array of leisure facilities such as municipal swimming pools, tennis courts, libraries and community centres.

GOOD HOUSEKEEPING: THE BIOPOLITICS OF THE FAMILY

Feminist historians, such as Anna Davin, Catherine Hall and Leonore Davidoff have investigated the entanglements of class, race and sexuality which have accompanied the politics of maternity and family life over a period of more than two hundred years.[31] This influential work has pinpointed, among other things, the exemplary status accorded to the middle-class family, especially in the Victorian period, and the maternal citizenship role allocated to the virtuous mother who was also the 'angel in the house'. To the feminist sociologist, however, the writing of Foucault and scholars influenced by him allows for an extrapolation from history so that certain reiterated processes can be gleaned as central to the 'birth of the social' and to contemporary modes of managing the family. The disciplining of unruly, excessively fertile, female, working-class or colonial bodies entailed, for example, an accumulation and organisation of knowledge, as well as the training of experts to administer various techniques designed to rein in and control this sexual activity. As we know from Foucault, huge apparatuses of the state came into being to form a government of populations with the nuclear family unit replacing the proliferation of wild and deviant sexualities, all of which were to be censored as the 'parental bedroom' took precedence as the sanctified space for the satisfaction of desires.[32] Donzelot, writing about nineteenth-century France, followed this line of argument showing how the new administrative class struggled with the unruly habits of working class women who on the one hand too easily abandoned their own babies into the care of the state, while at the same time provided defective or inadequate care to their middle-class charges who they were paid both to wet nurse and to look after through childhood. The fear of inculcation of bad habits to the future dominant class led to action being taken to give new status and responsibility to the middle-class mother herself, to in effect make official her role, encouraging a close relationship with the medical profession and thus putting her in charge of the 'future of the race'. Neither Foucault nor Donzelot draw attention to the historical genre of the women's magazine as the point of dissemination for this educative and instructive activity. It has been the task of feminist scholars to undertake this work, looking at the various technologies of the 'advice column' or the 'problem page' as instrumental in the training of middle class young women. Practices of cleanliness, hygiene, and the whole business of good housekeeping were the focus of attention in these pages, and this was extended, according to the precise class location of readers, to include fashion, beauty and rituals around the social calendar and courtship. Not only has this genre provided the format for modern-day women's magazines and TV programmes, it has also demonstrated the centrality of looking, as well as reading to this realm of informal domestic and personal pedagogy. The question remains however as to how these forms functioned as 'dividing practices' demarcating and policing the boundaries of class and ethnicity, censoring inappropriate knowledge and removing from the gaze of the middle class readership unsuitable material. Here we could point to the editor emerging as an important figure within the ranks of the professional-managerial class, the person who both exemplifies and oversees this field of feminine taste and decorum. A strong argument could be made that the intoxicating pleasures of fashion, fabric and home-making found inside these pages came to the attention of the lower classes and subsequently had a powerful impact in diverting working class girls and women's desires in the direction of emulating middle class lifestyle, with the result that female working class identity came to be experienced as inferior rather than being a site for political consciousness. From the work of Carolyn Steedman to Beverly Skeggs to bell hooks writing about black women's desire for finery, this realm of anxiety and desire emerges as a defining feature of normative and lived femininity, taking the form of a yearning to be middle class and thereby suggesting that the power of popular media succeeds in its attempts to 'de-proletarianise' society[33].

Foucault's Biopolitics Lectures delivered in the mid-1970s also focus on good housekeeping as part of the neoliberal programme developed through the writing of the Ordoliberals in Germany in the early 1930s. Roepke for example saw the family as to be managed along the lines of a small business or enterprise, and Foucault describes the human capital of the child as an 'abilities machine'. This notion of enterprise is, argues Foucault, central to the programme of neoliberalisation, and if we move away from these historical examples to the present day it is possible to see that by casting the family as a small business a new rationale for 'gender re-traditionalisation' emerges, as Lisa Adkins has persuasively shown.[34] The family becomes a kind of unit or team, a partnership of equals, even if this means a stay-home Mum and full-time working father. In contemporary parlance such a traditional arrangement reflects a team decision, one which could be easily reversed. Once again the emphasis Foucault places on human capital permits an account of how new norms of middle-class life are directed towards young women. There is, for example, a more intense investment in marriage, motherhood and domestic life, as a benchmark of successful femininity. This validates at least a retreat from the idea of combining full-time successful careers with motherhood, and it gives new, more professional status to full-time mothers while opening up avenues for extensive media discussion of 'intensive mothering' and at the same time creating new markets (child-friendly coffee shops and so-called 'school run fashion' for the so-called 'yummy mummies'). These markets also extend to push-chairs which double as jogging machines, sexy underwear ranges for pregnant women,[35] new more fashion-oriented parenting magazines, as well as a host of website organisations. The professionalisation of domestic life forcefully reverses the older feminist denunciation of housework as drudgery, and childcare as monotonous and never-ending, by elevating domestic skills and the bringing up of children as worthwhile and enjoyable. The well run 'corporate family' endorses the 'intensification of mothering' as a mode of investment in the human capital of infants and children, while also countering any presumed loss of status on the part of the stay-home mother who now directs her professional skills to ensuring the unassailable middle class status of her children. She will not be a complainer, nor will she be 'down among the woman' as Fay Weldon darkly put it.

Contemporary neoliberal discourse as it is addressed to young women (for example in the words of Sheryl Sandberg) emphasises the importance of planning well for marriage and motherhood, and this now includes, in a gesture towards liberal feminism, finding the right kind of partner who will be prepared to consider his wife as an equal. The *dispositif* of new maternal-familialism is inextricably tied up with expansive norms of respectable middle-class life, which in turn entails careful financial planning, good self-governance to insure against family breakdown, along with the increasing professionalisation of motherhood which sets new horizons for middle-class status on the basis of aspirational lifestyle, non-reliance on the state or on benefits and a female head of household who can 'do it all' even if she cannot quite 'have it all'.[36] There is frequently some irony and 'feminist' self-consciousness in the recounting of the rewards of good housekeeping. The UK popular press and TV function as the debating chamber for these maternal transformations; the luminosities of visual culture show again and again, day in and day out, the triumph of the 'post baby body', or the favoured looks for the 'school run' – the modern woman is not 'that name' unless she is in possession of a well-dressed toddler or 'mini me'. We could go further and say that cultural intelligibility as a young woman is now tilted towards the achievement of 'affluent, middle-class maternity' with its many accoutrements, in particular a spectacularly slim body, a well groomed and manicured appearance, with an equally attractive baby and husband. Motherhood no longer offers a short time-off period of respite from those forms of social power which comprise incitements and persuasions to get back in shape and to resume the work of achieving the highly sexualised body image which is now a hallmark of successful womanhood. Quite the opposite: as Jo Littler points out the young mother must now avoid at all costs the danger of 'dowdiness', and this requires many hours of hard work in retaining her sexual desirability at all times.[37] It is almost too obvious a point to make that the emphasis on vigilant attention being paid to heteronormative desirability on the part of the wife and mother also functions to encourage marital fidelity and hence family stability. The wife is expected to remain highly desirable at all points in time during and after pregnancy, while once again, just to stress the asymmetry of these norms, no such constant and repeated addresses are made to the male partners. The post-feminist masquerade of maternity re-assures the social structures of domination by constraining young mothers in a field of anxieties brought about by the promise of 'complete perfection'.[38] This luminosity of contemporary femininity shines its light unsparingly;

its significance stretches well beyond the pages of the women's magazines because at stake in these practices are matters of state, undertaken within the new moral economy of the family.

VISUAL-MEDIA GOVERNMENTALITY, MATERNITY AND 'NEOLIBERAL FEMINISM'

With the evisceration of the public sector and the slimming down to the point of extinction of a range of family services, the expectation is that the family steps forward to look after itself and to inculcate the right kinds of self-responsibility in its children while at the same time financially mopping up those costs which in the past would have been at least partially covered by the state. The middle-class family, as it was in the nineteenth century, becomes a more self-contained, complex financial unit requiring extensive lines of dependency and obligation, in the form of loans, bequests, gifts and underwriting. This reverses some of what Ulrich Beck wrote about in his theory of reflexive modernisation[39] wherein individualisation was made possible by the expansive welfarist undertakings (education, social services, public housing, employment benefits) which freed the young to make a life for themselves often far away from the close ties of family and community associated with first modernity.[40] It is incumbent on the now professional mother to stage-manage and oversee the success of this kind of family enterprise. There is a prevailing sense that suggests this scenario is bound to be beneficial to children, ensuring a better outcome, a good university place and thus a well-paid job. There is also an insinuation echoing across the media that the feminist generation prioritised their own careers at the expense of their children, 'farming them out' to full-time nurseries. Unsurprisingly, there is no mention here of those women who cannot afford not to work, never mind the huge numbers of single parent families where the mother is the sole breadwinner. Such women as these make almost no appearance in the public debates which have taken place in recent years. This is also true of women from black and ethnic minority backgrounds, with the result that the discussion about maternity is almost wholly conducted by white women.[41] The key role in recession times of families being more responsible for themselves, more enterprising and taking over the costs which in times of more extensive social democratic government would have been covered by the state, is then an important aspect of neoliberalism within the domestic sphere.

In the light of the above discussion, and moving towards a conclusion, it becomes apparent that there needs to be a more developed theorisation of media (and social media) in relation to the question of neoliberal feminism and 'mediated maternity'. By introducing the phrase 'visual-media governmentality', I want to conjoin the biopolitical model of governmentality developed by Foucault, with its attention to spaces, gazes, bodies, populations, and the overseeing of conduct and activity, with the specific dimension of gender and media. In the first instance this would mean returning to Jacqueline Rose's psychoanalytic account of how the girlhood acquisition of femininity is never fully achieved, can always be somehow distracted from its point of fixity, which in turn accounts for the wide range of regulative mechanisms put into place to ensure that normative femininity is indeed achieved.[42] Rose's Lacanian account stresses processes of repetitive looking. The girl must be constantly looking at images which confirm her otherwise uncertain sense of self. Alongside this we could pose Butler's queer theory of gender performativity in such a way that it does not supplant or negate Rose, but instead accents the crafting, scripting and repetitive inciting of gender norms as fictitious, but institutionally embedded, social practices, required so that heterosexual domination can be instated and maintained.[43] Femininity exists then as a seemingly fundamental and universal dividing practice, one which within the time and space of western modernity has been constantly produced and reproduced by the various offices of the state and by the giant media corporations. The history of girls and women's magazines as social institutions, stand as a shining example of how femininity has been created as a seemingly distinctive separate space, one which charts the chronology of women's lives for them, while also punctuating the week or month with repetitive familiarity.[44] It is this format which is both expanded and more intensively visualised in the age of online communications: Instagram, Facebook, and the *Daily Mail's Femail* section which reproduces and in many ways replaces the traditional format of the women's magazine, now available as a constant feed of images, updated hourly, and in recent times, concentrating almost exclusively on showing pictures of glamorous and famous young women either in stages of pregnancy or just after the birth when they are displaying their slim, 'toned' 'post-baby' bodies. Female viewers are invited into this mode of repetitive looking, well beyond the years of girlhood. This landscape of power is intensified and made more complex in the age of digital and social media, but also by the way in which neoliberal governmentality inserts itself firmly within the domestic sphere, eroding the previous boundaries of public and private, of politics and entertainment, by establishing a site of cosy convergence, a politics of 'daytime TV' expressed, once again during the Blair period, in his preference for interviews being conducted 'on the sofa'.

Deleuze described the 'control of communications' as the most forceful modality of biopolitical power.[45]

Within the spaces of contemporary communication, flows of gossip intersect with and coincide with matters of great urgency, to the point that the 'fun effect' often seriously compromises and detracts from questions of gravity. Boundaries are eroded and moral confusion sets in. Political discourse cannot be separated from trivial comments about the appearance, age or sexual desirability of key protagonists. At the same time the old-fashioned more anonymous and formal modes of political engagement such as those associated with the bureaucratic years of social democracy, where women often worked behind the scenes quietly pursuing a feminist agenda, are now replaced by the need to personalise all activities, put a name on and a face to everything one does, to gain publicity or followers, likes or dislikes, in the full glare of the global media. To be effective requires going public, being constantly available and highly visible and this in turn requires modes of self-branding and self-promotion which lessens the public service dimension of traditional political activity. There is no option it seems but to launch oneself into this sphere of entertainment if one wants to take part in public debate. Few aspects of everyday life and working life are now exempt from this requirement to self-promote. This has consequences for the more branded and personalised feminism which has surfaced in recent years and which comes immediately to be attached to certain names and careers. Feminists speaking out become immediately identifiable. Feminism is now a heavily named or signatured activity, where in the past the 'collective' sufficed.

This is the context within which Sandberg's book *Lean In* has been published, attracting enormous publicity across most of the quality press and TV on the basis of her position as the Chief Operating Officer at Facebook in California. Using the term lean-in as a rejoinder to women not to psychologically disconnect from work and from the career path at the point at which motherhood beckons, and more generally as a call to women in the workplace to position themselves close to those who are in leadership positions, so that they will be noticed, the book has given rise to so-called *Lean In* circles taking place in many US cities, a ghostly version of its more overtly feminist predecessor the consciousness-raising group of the 1970s. Likewise the TED talks she has given have attracted more than

1 million viewers on YouTube (see www.youtube/TED).The singularity of Sandberg's account is that it brings an unashamedly feminist voice to a genre of writing which is associated with top US business schools and MBA courses, which despite the high status of such institutions, relies on a writing style which eschews conventional scholarship, or for that matter reportage, in favour of cheerful and uplifting anecdotes, helpful tips, homilies, sentimental eulogies to mentors and others who have helped the author in the course of her career, while also name-dropping the litanies of impressive friends and acquaintances within the ranks of the rich and powerful, all of which is set within a format which carefully avoids saying anything mildly critical of, or detrimental to, her employer. The adoption of the business manual format is certainly almost risible from the perspectives of most women who would define themselves as feminist, and who have taken part in any form of feminist politics over the years, and this accounted for the hostile or dismissive reviews of the book which appeared in liberal newspapers such as the *Guardian* and other similar newspapers and online sites across the world.

The simple use of a vocabulary drawn from the world of business and then applied not just to how women can do better in the world of work but also in home life, suggests the extent to which corporate values have achieved a fundamental centrality and seemingly incontestable as well as uncontroversial status. Where in the past almost all strains of feminism, including liberal feminism, would have found just cause to challenge the culture of the male-dominated business world, in Sandberg's case this is no longer the case. From her perspective feminism means finding better ways of adjusting to this business culture, not to try to change it, and when change is proposed it must always also be good for business, at least insofar as it extracts better performance from the workforce. The most significant point the book makes is that women in the organisations for which Sandberg has worked, no matter how well qualified, anticipating the difficulties they will encounter when they have children, begin to detach from the job in advance of the time at which they will become pregnant and then have some time off (though barely more than a few weeks in the US). In doing so women needlessly jeopardise their chances for re-gaining their roles and promotional prospects, where with greater confidence and self-belief they could somehow manage the transition to combining work and motherhood. Sandberg argues then for 'leaning in', and this in turn becomes a wider metaphor for women who, in the context of corporate life, still show signs of insecurity and lack of confidence. Much of the book repeats the early feminist observations, cast in terms of a social psychology of gender, where women fear disapproval or fear being seen as aggressive and unfeminine because they want to be liked. Instead of rounding in on the rituals of male corporate bonding and the deep-rooted sexism which thrives on stereotypes about 'scary women', Sandberg's advice is typically to find ways of outmanoeuvring these obstacles, through such strategies as smiling while also 'staying focused'. Her own career from Harvard onwards and then working her way through some of the key companies and organisations in the US, including the World Bank, the US Treasury, McKinsey, Google and then Facebook, means that she is now one of the most powerful (and well paid) businesswomen in the US, if not in the world. What she says to other women is to learn how to play the corporate game more deftly; this may mean being willing to take on new challenges rather than saying 'Im not ready'; it will also mean being willing to re-enter the labour market after a period out for children, at a lower scale, on the basis that this can then be a stepping stone for re-gaining the status or pay point lost on taking time out.

Sandberg shows her liberal feminist credentials by describing her own modest background and the sheer hard work and long hours she put in to make her way to the top. Prior to having children she routinely did more than fourteen-hour days in the office, and even though she also learnt how to be more productive on fewer hours in the workplace following motherhood, she repeatedly talks about how she still returns to the laptop after reading her children their bedtime stories. She insists that children do not suffer from having a hard-working mother; she admits to 'feeling sad' when she doesn't see enough of her kids; she makes the point that she does her best to get home in time for the evening meal (though she does not mention the routines of shopping, cooking and clearing up, such that the reader can only infer she has staff). Having 'good help' is essential and she is also in the fortunate position of having extended family close by in the same neighbourhood. She counsels women to look for the right kind of husband who will willingly share the housework and childcare, and she also suggests bringing 'negotiating strategies' to the marriage and home front when it comes to trying to find a way to combine successful motherhood with 'workplace success'. The liberal feminist message delivered to the heartland of this neoliberal world is that women can continue to be economically active, and highly successful, during the early years of having children; they need not lose out as long as they learn how to 'lean in'. The words 'daycare', never mind 'state provided nurseries', do not appear across the pages of the book; instead there is simply a reference or two to the need for getting 'good help'. Sandberg's tone is positive, cheerful, uplifting and wholeheartedly feminist in that she earnestly wants to improve women's lives. But there is a whole vocabulary which describes the world of non-elite labour which is totally missing from her writing. This includes such words as poverty and unemployment, the high cost and often low quality of childcare, the reliance of white, middle-class, elite women on the low-paid domestic labour of migrant women, many of whom will be separated from their own children in order to earn a living and hence unable themselves to provide 'quality parenting', and so on. Nothing at all is said about the non-existence of paid maternity leave for women in the US, or about the need for employer-provided crèches and nurseries, as if that would be a step too far in the direction of criticism of corporate culture and the business world. Sandberg does not even suggest local neighbourhood, or self-help nursery care; instead there is a doggedness about putting in the long hours and working one's way up the corporate ladder. Implicitly, Sandberg is talking to young women like herself, who are attending prestigious universities. This means her address is exclusively to a privileged, largely white, middle-class sector of the population. What Sandberg describes as feminist she also inaugurates as a comfortable neoliberal feminism, a political force which is defined in such terms as to protect and enhance the already existing privileges of a relatively select sector of the female population, whose position, especially as they enter into motherhood, is now charged with even greater moral responsibility than before, in times of withdrawal of the state and reduction in all public spending. This is a radically de-politicised and accommodating feminism; its conservatism is most apparent in its shying away from argument and confrontation; it merely requests a place at the table. This then has emerged as the public face of neoliberal feminism. Sandberg herself has stayed close to power since her earliest days at university, becoming the research assistant and later close friend of Obama advisor and former Chief Treasurer Larry Summers. Her narrative, scattered as it is with personal biographical details can be seen also as a kind of answer to the question implicitly posed by *Revolutionary Road* and by Betty Friedan as the 'problem with no name'. By proudly re-claiming the word feminism and bringing it back into use in the world of business as well as in the home after a long period during which it was cast aside as irrelevant or no longer needed, Sandberg also re-invents an American formation of liberal feminism so that it even more fully complies with the values of the corporate environment.

What I have laboured to argue across these pages is that a new maternal-feminine performs a double function for the neoliberal hegemony of the present: by endorsing liberal feminist principles it provides the centre right and the centre left with a more up to date way of engaging with women and women's issues while simultaneously expunging from popular memory the values of the social democratic tradition which had forged such a close connection with feminism through the pursuit of genuine equality and collective provision for families as a public good. The more professional status accorded to mothers, especially those who for perhaps pragmatic reasons choose to stay home while their children are of pre-school age, likewise fulfils a double purpose in that it brings up to date (if with some disruptive effect) the family values agenda, so dear to conservative thinking, while at the same time, in a context where austerity conditions cannot be questioned, it encourages family life to be considered in terms of an enterprise or small business led by the wife and mother who provides strong leadership and demonstrates the right kind of managerial skills. Once again what this strenuous ideological activity forecloses and seeks to forget is the very possibility of socialised childcare, including after-school care, youth clubs and publicly provided leisure facilities as a social investment and a public good. The bombardment of images showing super-wealthy mothers enjoying their luxury lifestyles introduces new forms of consumer hedonism into the hard work of motherhood, distracting attention away from what feminists in the past named as drudgery and as chores. This palliative effect, even in its trickle down version, involving routines of play dates, coffee shops and jogging buggies, re-instates new norms of middle-class hegemony against which less advantaged families can only feel themselves to be inferior or inadequate or else judging themselves as having not tried hard enough. What was in the Victorian era a moral high ground of maternal citizenship is now re-cast as a no- less-moralistic playground of lifestyle and consumer culture, predicated on young women making the right choices and adopting, at an early age, the right kind of lifeplan.

NOTES

1. Stuart Hall, 'New Labour's Double Shuffle', *Soundings*, 24, (2003): 10-24. This importance of the middle class echoes Foucault's account of the German Ordoliberal thinker, a man called Roepke, who likewise saw the importance of de-proletarianisation of society as a means of vanquishing the spectre of working-class struggle, (*The Birth of Biopolitics*, Basingstoke, Palgrave, 2006).

2. See for example *MAMSIE: Studies in the Maternal*, 5, 1, (2013), 'Austerity Parenting: Economies of Parent-Citizenship', Tracey Jensen and Imogen Tyler (eds).

3. For example, Policy Exchange think tank, including Charlotte McLeod.

4. Wendy Brown, 'Neoliberalism and The End of Liberal Democracy' in *Edgework*, NJ, Princeton University Press, 2005.

5. Angela McRobbie, *The Aftermath of Feminism: Gender, Culture and Social Change*, London, Sage, 2008.

6. Nancy Fraser, 'Feminism, Capitalism and the Cunning of History' in *New Left Review*, 56, (2009).

7. See unfashionista.com/2013/05/29/reality-based-feminism/.

8. David Cameron on BBC Radio 4 Women's Hour, 27.07.2013. See www.BBC/Radio 4/Women's Hour/ Episode Guide/July 27 2013

9. See for example www.thefword.org.uk/.

10. These institutions speak to and across each other on an almost daily basis. a story in the *Daily Mail*, for example, will often be picked up and referred to by the PM in the House of Commons in the following days.

11. Jasbir Puar, *Terrorist Assemblages*, Durham, NC, Duke University Press, 2007.

12. Though on the part of Angela Merkel there is resistance to accepting a direct connection with feminism, see www.thetimes.co.uk/tto/news/world/europe/article3756129.ece.

13. Brown, 'Neoliberalism and The End of Liberal Democracy', op. cit. So frequent and repetitive are the articles about 'single mothers on benefits' that they become almost unnoticeable. For example, the *Daily Mail*, 11 June 2013, ran a feature on a mother of seven, with her benefits itemised; allusions are made to absent fathers and attention drawn to her unkempt body and appearance

14. See bitchmagazine.org/post/re-imagining-revolutionary-road.

15. See review of the film 26.01.2009 by Charles Moore in the *Daily Telegraph*, www.telegraph.co.uk.

16. From *Four Weddings and a Funeral* (director Mike Newell, 1994) to *Bridget Jones* (director Sharon MacGuire, 2001) to *Bridesmaids* (director Paul Fleig, 2011).

17. A detailed piece of feminist ethnographic research on this website would be both timely and useful.

18. See the *Daily Mail* online www.dailymail.co.uk/femail/.../My-week-man-desert-In-parts-Britain-70-ch.

19. See Bev Skeggs, 'The Making of Class and Gender Through Visualising Moral Subject Formation' in *Sociology* 39, (2005): 965.

20. Richard Hoggart, *The Uses of Literacy*, Chatto and Windus, London 1957.

21. Skeggs, 'The Making of Class and Gender', op. cit; and McRobbie, *The Aftermath of Feminism*, op. cit.

22. Elizabeth Wilson, *Women and the Welfare State*, London, Virago,1977; Michele Barrett and Mary McIntosh, *The Anti-Social Family*, London, NLB, 1982; Denise Riley, *The War in the Nursery*, London, Virago, 1983 (first published in 1979 in *Feminist Review*, 2: 82-108); Anna Davin 'Imperialism and Motherhood', *History Workshop Journal*, 5, 1, (1986): 9-66.

23. Baroness Ruth Lister of Burtersett, Emeritus Professor of Social Policy at

Loughborough University School of Social Sciences and author of *Poverty*, Cambridge, Polity Press, 2004.

24. Patricia Hewitt meeting at House of Commons, see note 30.

25. See articles by Imogen Tyler, Kim Allen and Yvette Taylor in *Studies in the Maternal*, op. cit.

26. Wilson, *Women and the Welfare State*, op. cit; Barrett and McIntosh, *The Anti-Social Family*, op. cit; Riley, *The War in the Nursery*, op. cit. See also L. Segal (ed), *What Is to Be Done about the Family?* Harmondsworth, Penguin, 1983.

27. See Z. Bauman, *The Individualized Society*, Polity, Cambridge 2001, and U. Beck, *Individualization*, London, Sage, 2001.

28. Oliver James in the *Guardian*, 8 January 2005, 'Putting Under 3s in Full-time Daycare Can Promote Aggressive Behavior', www.guardian.co.uk.

29. R. Crompton, 'Employment, Flexible Working and the Family' in *British Journal of Sociology*, 53, 4, (2002): 537-558; see also Nancy Fraser, 'Feminism, Capitalism and the Cunning of History', op. cit., and McRobbie, *The Aftermath of Feminism*, op. cit.

30. I attended a roundtable meeting hosted by Patricia Hewitt MP (and at the time Cabinet Minister) at the House of Commons in 2002 to discuss the place of feminism in labour politics. Hewitt commented on the difficulties of being heard on this issue by the PM Tony Blair and those close to him. See also Claire Annesley *et al* (eds), *Women and New Labour: Engendering Policy and Politics*, London, Policy Press, 2007.

31. See Davin, op. cit., and Leonore Davidoff and Catherine Hall, *Family Fortunes: Men and Women of the English Middle Class 1780-1850*, London, Routledge, 2002.

32. Michel Foucault, *History of Sexuality Vol 1*, London, Allen Lane, 1978.

33. See Carolyn Steedman, *Landscape for a Good Woman*, London, Virago, 1986; Skeggs, op. cit; bell hooks, *Ain't I A Woman? Black Women and Feminism*, New York, The South End Press, 2007.

34. Lisa Adkins, 'Community and Economy: A Re-Traditionalisation of Gender', *Theory Culture and Society*, 16, (1999): 119-139.

35. See Imogen Tyler, 'Pregnant Beauty Maternal Femininity under Neoliberalism' in Rosalind Gill and Christina Scharff (eds), *New Femininities*, Basingstoke, Palgrave,2011.

36. For a detailed discussion of the ways in which these concerns are played out across the narratives of the successful chick lit and then mumslit or so-called 'hen lit' genres see Jo Littler, 'The Rise of the "Yummy Mummy": Popular Conservatism and the Neoliberal Maternal in Contemporary British Culture', *Communication, Culture and Critique*, 6, (2013): 227-243, http://doi.org/n5h.

37. Ibid.

38. Joan Rivière, (1926/86) 'Femininity as Masquerade' in Victor Burgin, James Donald and Cora Kaplan (eds), *Formations of Fantasy*, London, Routledge, 1986 quoted in McRobbie, *The Aftermath of Feminism*, op. cit.

39. Ulrich Beck and Elisabeth Beck-Gernscheim, *Individualization: institutionalised individualism and its social and political consequences*, London, Sage, 2001.

40. Free childcare provided by grandparents for example is only possible if the children to be cared for live close by.

41. In academic feminism there is thankfully a different story to be told. See the

extensive work by Ann Phoenix and also the recent publications of *Mamsie* based at Birkbeck College London, especially the writing of Lisa Baraitser, *Maternal Encounters: The Ethics of Interruption*, London, Routledge, 2009.

42. Jacqueline Rose, *Sexuality in the Field of Vision*, London, Verso, 1986.

43. Judith Butler, *Gender Trouble: Feminism and the Subversion of Identity*, New York and London, Routledge, 1990.

44. The titles of magazines, from *Just 17, 19, Elle*, to *Good Housekeeping*, tell us something about this chronologisation of women's lives.

45. Gilles Deleuze, *Foucault*, Sean Hand (trans), Minneapolis, University of Minnesota Press, 1988.

COMPLEXITY AS CAPTURE – NEOLIBERALISM AND THE LOOP OF DRIVE

Jodi Dean

Real existing neoliberalism reconfigures elements of multiple discourses. By neoliberalism, I mean not simply the ideological program of the Chicago school and its adherents in government and business but rather the broader cloud of distributed suppositions and practices through and within which capitalist reality takes its particular neoliberal format. Some of the elements from differing discourses that neoliberalism configures include frontier myths of heroic individuals, new media celebrations of fast and fluid networks, fantasies of free markets, misplaced critiques of collective ownership and government regulation, as well as confusions between the economic concept of competition and competition understood as a rivalry or contest. There are others.[1] In this essay, I highlight two additional components of the neoliberal atmosphere – reflexivity and complexity.

Reflexivity and complexity show up as assumptions regarding neoliberalism's basic setting. Insofar as these assumptions traverse politics, economics, science, philosophy, and media theory and insofar as their academic and popular applications crisscross, reflexivity and complexity seem to point to fundamental truths about thinking and being. They seem so obvious and uncontestable that only an idiot would question them. Since at least Descartes (though some might say Socrates), reflexivity has been a primary feature of reason (not to mention a necessarily constitutive element of critiques of reason).[2] Most critical academics as well as most economists and financial analysts link reason to self-consciousness and give this link a moral valuation. Most critical academics as well as most economists and financial analysts likewise embrace a general notion of complexity (if not all the specifics of complexity theory). Even as they may differ on the relative power of models and abstractions (and hence of the explanatory value of cellular automata and similar computer experiments), these academic and financial types share a weak ontology of interconnectivity, mutual causality, contingency, and singularity (the unique qualities of individuals, persons as well as non-persons). Everyone knows that there are always exceptions, different experiences, improbable results. The world exceeds our attempts to explain it. It's complex.[3]

To consider the ways assumptions of reflexivity and complexity contribute to the configuration of neoliberalism, I use the psychoanalytic category of 'drive'. In so doing, I employ and extend some ideas from Slavoj Žižek, specifically, his upgrade of ideology critique via the later seminars of Jacques Lacan. As is well known, Louis Althusser taught that the category of the subject is constitutive of ideology. But what kind of subject or the subject in what sense is constitutive? Perhaps the most widely accepted answer to this question emphasises the subject of desire, particularly as theorised by Lacan. The subject emerging through ideological interpellation is said to be a desiring subject, its desire a product of the intervention of the law that prevents it from getting what it wants, thereby insuring the openness of desire. Žižek's version of ideology critique reaches beyond the subject of desire to consider the subject of drive. Here the subject is understood as a remnant or effect of the failure of ideological interpretation, the ineliminable gap exceeding ideology's efforts to determine its subjects.[4]

One way to get at the difference between the subject of desire and the subject of drive is to highlight each's relation to the object. As Žižek explains, desire is for a lost object. In contrast, in drive loss itself is an object.[5] Drive, then, is the force of loss. For example, capitalism expresses this force of loss as an absence of completion or limits. Capital is only capital through the loss of a capacity to be at rest (money under a mattress, money that can't be invested or put to work, isn't capital). Lacking an end or a limit, capitalism pushes on, in a relentless, nonsensical circuit. The theoretical benefit of the move from the concept of desire to the concept of drive is that critique can explore not just what we want but can never attain (the economy or logic of desire), but what we cannot avoid, no matter how hard we try (the economy or logic of drive).

Desire alone can't account for the persistence of capitalism. Capitalism cannot be reduced to our desire for it. Rather, capitalism persists as a system of practices in which we are caught. Žižek writes, 'Drive inheres to capitalism at a ... *systemic* level: drive is that which propels the whole capitalist machinery, it is the impersonal compulsion to engage in the endless circular movement of expanded self-reproduction'.[6] Capital strives to accumulate, to reproduce itself. It circulates, ceasing to be capital if this circulation stops. I use drive to analyse the extreme capitalism of neoliberalism, a specific historical formation in which the limits to capitalism brought about through a century of working class struggle have been undone in the course of political victories by capitalists acting as a class. By exploring reflexivity and complexity in terms of drive, I hope to illuminate some of the specific ways neoliberalism captures its subjects and thus formats the terrain of contemporary class struggle.

DRIVE

I begin with a brief sketch of drive. In his classic work on drive, Sigmund Freud attributes four vicissitudes to the drives (unfortunately translated as 'instincts'): reversal into its opposite, turning round upon the subject's own self, repression, and sublimation.[7] Freud uses scopophilia, voyeurism, as an illustration. More than just a desire to look, scopophilia is accompanied by a drive to be seen. Looking or seeing reverses into exhibitionism. The voyeur doesn't get off just by seeing. The voyeur wants *to be seen* seeing. This reversal into 'being seen' converges with the second vicissitude: it is a 'turning round upon the subject's own self'. The self becomes the object (what is seen). As it does so, its activity is transformed into passivity. The object to be seen is replaced by the subject who is seen (and who is now the object being seen). Holding onto a conception of the object *qua* object thus misses the point. What matters is the reversal, the reflexive turning round back onto the subject.

Freud's third and fourth vicissitudes likewise converge. The third, repression, is a kind of dam. Dammed up water can overflow into a network of tributaries, breaking out in multiple directions. Like water creating new channels, the drives, Freud explains, are 'extraordinarily plastic'. 'They may appear in each others' places. One of them may accumulate the intensity of the other'.[8] Sublimation, the fourth vicissitude, is this finding of new outlets, new paths of expression, for the repressed desire. Indeed, drive is only expressed as sublimated, as an effect of repression. And while this effect takes the form of a circuit (turning round upon the subject's own self), the circuit isn't closed; it's open, plastic, capable of moving among and attaching to different objects as so many outlets or opportunities for enjoyment (sublimation). Drive is a circuit that in the course of its movement outwards and back can alter, shift, disperse and branch.

The reflexive movement drive designates is a loop, a loop that is less a circle or oval than a messy spiral or fractal. Similarly, the loop of drive isn't fixed or balanced; it's an uneven repetition and return that misses and errs. As Lacan explains, drive is 'beyond the instinct to return to a state of equilibrium'.[9] In other words, drive isn't a force through which the subject achieves some kind of steady-state. Stuck in the loop of drive, the subject tries to get the same result by doing the same thing over and over, but fails. Still, the subject gets something, a little bit of enjoyment (*jouissance*), in the repeated effort of trying. This little enjoyment is enough of a payoff for the subject to keep on keeping on, although each moment is a little different. Why is each moment a little different? Because it comes next; it adds itself and thereby changes the setting of the next circuit. So in addition to reversal and dispersion, the movement of drive involves accumulation, amplification, and intensification.

Consider slot machines. People ostensibly play the slots because they desire to hit the jackpot. This desire alone, however, can't account for the appeal of slot machines, as if slot machines were vehicles for players' rational calculations of expected financial return given a specific expenditure of capital. Instead, slot machines are assemblages for and of the drive. They rely on little pleasures of anticipation, seeing pictures disappear and appear, experiencing the little rush of noise and lights, being seen by others as one who might be the big winner. Each pull of the handle occurs at a different moment, so no pull is exactly the same. Our anticipation with the fourth pull may be invested with more excitement and delight than we have at the ninth one, when we might be anxious, worried about how much we've put in the machine. By the fortieth pull, our attachment to the machine, our capture in the circuit of drive, has disruptive effects of its own, making us late for dinner or unable to pay our phone bill. What we started for pleasure, perhaps as a way to escape from the constraints of pragmatic day-to-day responsibilities, reverses into something from which we want to escape but can't (which is why, incidentally, Lacan rejects Freud's distinction between *eros* and *thanatos*; drive is a loop rather than something that can be bifurcated into a positive and negative force).

Because drive designates a turning back upon one's self, it provides a concept for theorising reflexivity at the level of the subject. A keeping on beyond pleasure, beyond use, beyond desire, drive makes reflexivity appear as a circuit or loop in which the subject is caught, thereby disrupting the assumed coincidence of reflexivity and reason. Mark C. Taylor's definition of reflexivity is helpful here: 'Reflexivity is a nonlinear relation in which cause and effect are interdependent: the thoughts and actions of agents influence the operation of the system, which, in turn, influences the thoughts and actions of agents'.[10] Just as scopophilia becomes exhibitionism and the subject becomes the object, so does reflexivity involve a loop or turn. This looping or turning marks an unpluggable, unavoidable gap, a kind of 'halting problem' as an irreducible feature of a consciousness conscious of and anxious before its constitutive limit (in computer programming, a halting problem arises when a program gets to a point where its only options are stopping arbitrarily or running infinitely; children play with this problem when they invoke reflexive loops like 'I know that you know that I know that you know that I know ...'). Conceiving the reflexive turn via the loop of drive draws our attention to our capture in the picture we ourselves draw, the loop we ourselves designate. Rather than being an operation that can come to an end or answer, reflexivity oscillates between the arbitrary and the infinite. Drive marks our enjoyment of this oscillation (and, conversely, oscillation here points to the fact of enjoyment). It indexes not only the inclusion of the observer in the system but the entrapment of the observer as a somatic and mental entity that enjoys. We constitute the circuits, processes, tactics, operations, and systems that constitute us even as this constitution is less a matter of choice than a matter of dynamic fixation. We are features of self-constituting systems. The emphasis on drive is thus a way to retain knowledge, knowing, and enjoyment as effective components of material networks.

REFLEXIVITY

Although analysts of the recent expansion and collapse in the finance sector rarely use Lacanian psychoanalysis to explain why it happened, they frequently invoke bubbles, feeding frenzies, and feedback loops. They appeal, in other words, to the extremes and ruptures brought about by reflexivity in complex networks. Financier George Soros is most explicit on this point, theorising reflexivity as the two-way connection between participants' views and their situation and analysing the crisis in terms of this two-way connection.[11] As he makes clear, reflexivity contributed to the recent financial crisis in multiple, reinforcing ways. I emphasise three: risk management, derivatives, and poverty.

1. *Risk management.* In the nineties, financial firms began to assess the amount of capital that they needed to have on hand to back up their

COMPLEXITY AS CAPTURE 197

investments in terms of 'value at risk' (VAR). VAR is a single number that lets a bank determine how far its portfolio can drop in a single day.[12] VAR is calculated in terms of asset volatility – how much an asset's price jumps around in a given time period. The assumption is that price movements vibrate within a standard deviation; their distribution takes the form of a bell curve. Armed with their VAR, banks can calculate how much capital they want to carry in light of their overall risk exposure. Seeking to escape from government-determined standards of acceptable risk, financial firms in the nineties argued that their investment strategies were better pegged to the market.[13] Rather than sitting dormant as an unnecessary back-up or safety measure, their capital could be leveraged to create more opportunities for the generation of wealth. VAR would let them know what they could reasonably risk.

One problem with this approach to risk arises from its adoption by numerous parties.[14] Presuming that they and their trading partners have taken appropriate measures to insure against risks, firms and money managers are likely to think they are more secure than they actually are (and, indeed, some blamed portfolio insurance for Black Monday, the 508 point drop in the Dow on October 19, 1987).[15] For example, they may assume that diversifying their holdings provides sufficient protection against declines in a particular asset class since prices of different assets tend to move in opposing directions (they are negatively correlated). In extreme circumstances, however, everything might start to drop. Why? Because a firm trying to protect itself from losses in one area starts selling assets in a second area in order to maintain its VAR. This selling pushes down the price of this second area, which begins or can begin a further downward cascade, particularly insofar as other firms see prices falling in this new area and don't want to get slammed there as well as in the first area. The dynamic is reflexive in that it relies on the fact that observers of the system are agents in the system. So it's not only a matter of what a given firm is doing. It is also a matter of the firm's (always partial and distorted) knowledge of what it is doing, its knowledge that others have knowledge or expectations of what it is doing, and its entrapment in the loop of this knowledge of knowing.

2. *Derivatives*. Closely linked to risk management are derivatives, the class of custom-made financial tools such as commodity futures, stock options, currency swaps, credit default swaps, and collateralised debt obligations that let traders insure or bet against movements in other financial instruments.[16]

As a class, derivatives have three key attributes: they are limited term contracts to exchange capital in an agreed-upon description of the future on the basis of the price of the underlying asset at that time ('limited term' here means that the contract has an expiration date.)[17] Most derivatives trade privately in the unregulated over-the-counter or OTC market. The face value of derivates rose from 866 billion dollars to 454 trillion dollars between 1987 and 2007.[18]

Derivatives exemplify reflexivity in a number of ways. First, the derivative instrument itself is reflexive: it steps back from an asset's relation to its setting to bet on how investors will assess that relation in the future. It's not just a bet; it's a bet on how others will bet.

Second, this reflexivised bet itself contributes to the production of the future on which it is betting. Derivatives enable enormous leveraging. Small outlays of capital can have huge pay-offs or pay-outs in the future. Because the immediate cost of risk is comparatively small, firms can undertake more investments than they would with regular stocks and bonds.[19] Derivatives also contribute to the future on which they are betting insofar as they require counterparties. Someone has to be on the other, losing, side of the deal. Complex derivatives combine, slice up, recombine, and sell bundles of assets and/or swaps (J.P. Morgan designed synthetic CDOs; there were also CDOs of CDOs and CDOs of CDOs of CDOs).[20] From one perspective, these recombinant financial instruments distribute risk so broadly that no one firm suffers too badly when an investment sours. From another perspective, the multiplication of counterparties exposes more firms to investments gone wild. Because derivatives 'tighten intermarket connectivities,' turbulence more easily flows from one market into another, making it 'increasingly difficult to inoculate a market against potential damage'.[21]

A third way that derivatives exemplify reflexivity is in their relation to their setting in the circulatory regime of global capital. Derivatives emerge out of the perceived need to protect against the risks involved in complex speculative financial transactions even as they make these transactions possible and thereby produce, retroactively, their own conditions of emergence. In the words of LiPuma and Lee, 'once the speculative capital devoted to financial derivatives becomes self-reflexive and begins to feed on itself, it develops a directional dynamic toward an autonomous and self-expanding form'.[22] The circulation of money detaches itself from production; money is purely self-mediating. Since abstract financial relations are themselves treated as underlying assets, money markets can expand seemingly without limit – that is, as long as everyone involved believes that they will, as long as the circuit keeps on going on and no one tries to cash in or call.

Consider the synthetic collateralised debt obligation. This is a CDO comprised of credit-default swaps, insurance on tranches of bonds that pays when the bonds' prices decline. As Michael Lewis explains, 'The market for "synthetics" removed any constraint on the size of risk associated with subprime mortgage lending. To make a billion-dollar bet, you no longer needed to accumulate a billion dollars' worth of actual mortgage loans. All you had to do was find someone else in the market willing to take the other side of the bet'.[23] For derivatives such as synthetic CDOs, risk is not primarily a side effect of complex, interlinked market transactions. Rather, risk is deliberately and intentionally configured into a securitisable object.

When a market is made for a specific designer instrument, like a CDO or a credit default swap, the surplus risk shifts from being a by-product to being *the product*; it occupies the place previously held by the asset. Thomas Adams and Yves Smith bring the point home as they trace the incentive to make bad loans that drove the massive expansion of the CDO market. The riskiest tranches of a CDO are the ones with the highest potential reward. Investors, particularly hedge funds and others looking for something to short, wanted them, so banks looked for more bad loans to buy, which stimulated more brokers to issue more mortgages to anyone who would take them. In the words of Adams and Smith:

> Dozens of warning signs, at every step of the process, should have created negative feedback. Instead, the financial incentives for bad lending and bad securitizing were so great that they overwhelmed normal caution. Lenders were being paid more for bad loans than good, securitizers were paid to generate deals as fast as possible even though normal controls were breaking down, CDO managers were paid huge fees despite having little skill or expertise, rating agencies were paid multiples of their normal MBS fees to create CDOs, and bond insurers were paid large amounts of money to insure deals that 'had no risk' and virtually no capital requirements. All of this was created by ridiculously small investments by hedge funds shorting MBS mezzanine bonds through CDO structures.[24]

The financial crisis that started in the housing market and spread throughout the finance sector and into the broader economy was an effect of reflexivity – reflexivised risk.

3. *Poverty*. My third example of the role of reflexivity in the recent crises in the finance markets concerns poverty, inequality, and debt.[25] Although per capita GDP in the US nearly doubled between 1976 and 2005, about half the gains went to the top one percent of the population. [26] Real median wages remained stagnant. Any small increase to middle class households during the 'lost decade' was the result of more hours worked, whether as an effect of the increase in dual income households or of declines in vacation time. Debt addressed the decline in purchasing power experienced by the majority of people.

As I've mentioned, debt also had the benefit of being securitisable and thus available as an investment vehicle for the excess of capital at the top. In Michael Lewis's words, 'Complicated financial stuff was being dreamed up for the sole purpose of lending money to people who could never repay it'.[27] The expansion in the number of subprime mortgages, their bundling into bonds, the bonds' dividing into tranches, the tranches' repackaging into CMOs (collateralised mortgage obligations) and CDOs (which included debts besides mortgages such as student loans and credit card debts) resulted from demand for these massive financial instruments. Working people's desire to purchase homes they could not afford did not create CDOs (as media accounts blaming mortgage defaults on low income people sometimes make it sound). Investment banks did. Scott Patterson puts it bluntly, 'without the demand from the investment banks, the bad loans would never have been made'.[28] Michael Lewis agrees: the mortgage holders 'existed only so that their fate might be gambled upon'.[29]

Investment banks used CDOs to remove debt from their balance sheets. They sold this debt to investors in the form of tranches of the CDOs. Most investors thought they were buying measurable risk. Those who purchased tranches with AAA ratings from Moody's or Standard & Poor's thought they were investing in something pretty secure with a very, very low likelihood of failure, primarily because the likelihood of default on a large number of mortgages was very, very low. AAA tranches were particularly attractive for pension funds and university endowments required to keep their risk exposure low.

The problem was that the models used to figure out the correlations between the tranches not only assumed predictable, bell-curve like patterns in the data, but also ignored the fact that the price information fed into the models was coming from a bubble in the housing market. The housing bubble was inflated by historically low interest rates after 9/11, the rush of investors wounded in the burst of the dotcom bubble into ostensibly secure real estate, banks' enthusiasm for mortgages and other loans that generated lots of fees, and the rise of derivatives themselves.[30] Scott Patterson explains that the result was 'a vicious feedback loop – an echo chamber, one might say, in which enthusiastic investors snapped up tranches of CDOs, creating demand for more CDOs – and that created a demand for more mortgage loans'.[31]

Demand for CDOs corresponded to the rise in inequality. Prior to the subprime mortgage boom, subprime mortgage lending was a fairly sleazy business, selling off its loans with little to no regard for whether they could be repaid, charging lots of fees to its high-risk customers, relying on teaser rates that would balloon up after a couple of years. Most of these early lenders went bankrupt in the mid-nineties. Less than a decade later, the subprime market was larger than before, offering even lower quality mortgages to people who, facing a decade of stagnant wages and maxed out credit cards jumped at the chance of no money down, interest only mortgages.[32] The debts of poor and working people were useful: fodder for the Wall Street finance machine. So even though adjustable-rate mortgages were defaulting at epic rates in 2005, the price of houses continued to rise, the subprime mortgage market continued to expand, and the price of credit default swaps fell. The massive financial boom required, was made possible by, the debts of the people seemingly furthest from Wall Street, those considered the least credit-worthy. At this interface of the extremes of profit and loss, poverty (like risk) isn't an unavoidable by-product of financial, speculative capitalism but its condition and content. In the circuit of amplified inequality, the increase in the number of poor people isn't a social problem, it's an investment opportunity. The system turns in on itself and feeds on its own excesses.

Even in the last months of the bubble in subprime mortgage bonds (between February and June of 2007), the market in CDOs continued to generate billions. In the words of one analyst (and short-seller): 'it was like watching an unthinking machine that could not stop itself'.[33] To be sure, there was ever increasing turbulence as banks tried to get rid of bad investments before they collapsed. But insofar as buyers kept purchasing them (and firms like Bear Stearns and Lehman Brothers continued to emphasise the soundness of the bonds), the market remained afloat. Michael Lewis's description suggests the trap of drive: 'it was as if an entire financial market had tried to change its mind – and then realized that it could not afford to change its mind'.[34] The interconnected banks were caught in a circuit beyond their control. If there were no buyers for the

CDOs, and the mortgages deep in their bowels were defaulted upon as house prices continued to drop, the CDOs would be worth nothing. The credit-default swaps were ostensibly a kind of insurance, a way to hedge against massive losses, but that hedging depended on the seller's ability to pay. If the seller couldn't pay, then the insurance wasn't worth anything either. In effect, the over-leveraged derivatives market, a substantial component of Wall Street's exorbitant profits and bonuses, led the financial system to deceive itself.

The effect of the assemblage of incentives, rewards, penalties, egos, debts, mortgages, models, computers, hormones, and wagers was a financial crisis of epic proportions. The global financial meltdown and resulting recession, unemployment, and indebtedness – particularly of governments, who were subsequently pressured to eliminate social services – expose the specificity of neoliberal capitalism as a circuit in which reflexivity is a mechanism of capture rather than reason, where the loop of drive amplifies the worst tendencies rather than employs feedback as a mechanism of self-correction. Neoliberalism is thus neither a formation well-defined in terms of free, unregulated markets nor one well-understood in terms of competition as a moderating force.

As Michel Foucault explains already in his lectures on the birth of biopolitics, neoliberalism is a governmentality that intervenes in markets, that creates them, that governs on their behalf.[35] Its conceit is not liberalism's *laissez faire* approach to markets but instead an ensemble of policies and interventions resulting from the subjection of the state to the market.[36] Foucault is less accurate when he describes these interventions as attempts to induce and protect competition (neglecting capitalism's already well-documented tendency toward monopoly). Contemporary financial markets might be cut-throat, blood-thirsty, but they aren't competitive, not if by competitive we imagine some kind of open contest with clear, fair rules. I should add here the mistake with another assumption regarding neoliberalism, namely, that it is linked to consumerism. The emphasis on consumption might have highlighted a feature of Fordism, particularly insofar as Fordist economic strategies depended on keeping wages high enough for consumers to purchase the goods they produced. In contrast, neoliberalism relies on the inequality of rich and poor – a point explicitly acknowledged in the notorious Citigroup report, '*Revisiting Plutonomy: The Rich Getting Richer*'.[37] A set of recommendations for investors to buy stock in luxury goods, private banks, and financial services (a group of stocks the authors refer to as the 'plutonomy basket'), the report points out the insignificance of poor and middle class consumers. The only consumers who matter are rich ones, the ones who have been benefiting and can be expected to continue to benefit from neoliberal globalisation. The rich drive demand (not the mass of middle and working class consumers). The rich have an increasingly larger share of income and wealth and thus greater proclivity to spend. In the words of the report, 'Asset booms, a rising profit share and favourable treatment by market-friendly governments have allowed the rich to prosper and become a greater share of the economy in the plutonomy countries'. The super-rich purchase luxury items and investment vehicles. The poor rely on cheap, low quality goods and massive amounts of corn, that is, the sub-standard food of corporate agriculture. For everything else, there is debt, the debt the finance sector needs to function.

COMPLEXITY

We are regularly told that financial instruments like collateralised debt obligations and credit default swaps are beyond our comprehension. Not only are they too hard for average citizens to understand, but Alan Greenspan couldn't even understand them. In fact, as hundreds of lobbyists for the finance sector have ceaselessly worked to teach US members of Congress, derivatives *can't* be regulated, precisely because *no one* understands them. Beyond comprehension, they are beyond control. Complexity disposes of politics because nothing can be done.

Initially, finance porn (I have in mind here mainstream media treatment of the finance sector as well as the multiple books on the subprime mortgage crisis) lauded 'quants' (quantitative analysts) as the ones who actually knew what was going on. These nearly magical geeks, siphoned off from academe, used their advanced mathematics and high powered computers to identify statistical anomalies and price differentials and quickly capitalise them. The economic theory at the basis of their calculations, the Efficient Market Hypothesis, cast these profiteering moves as necessary and ethical: buying up underpriced assets helped move their prices to their proper place, back to equilibrium.

Other wizards then came up with alchemical strategies for managing risk, strategies that involved lots of borrowing (leverage) and shifting (structural investment vehicles). Many CDOs were new combinations of slices of other CDOs that a bank had created but had been unable to sell. CDOs' interrelation was circular; they contained each other yet were somehow able to transform this mutual containment into gold (with regard to the CDOs built out of subprime mortgage bonds, the supposition was that real estate would nearly always rise in value, that any declines in the housing market would be local rather than national, and that mortgage backed securities distributed risk so broadly as to dissipate it almost completely; each one of these assumptions ended up being wrong). The CDOs' opaque, exotic names, names that refuse any concrete relation with their contents – Abacus, Carina, Gemstone – heighten the sense that one is approaching the inner sanctum of finance's arcane mysteries.[38] At the heart of finance are impossible objects that create money. A Goldman Sachs trader described them in an email to his lover as 'a product of pure intellectual masturbation, the type of thing which you invent telling yourself: "Well, what if we created a 'thing,' which has no purpose, which is absolutely conceptual and highly theoretical and which nobody knows how to price?"'[39] A financial product that exceeds the market, a product beyond valuation, the synthetic CDO is a real abstraction (particularly when one keeps in mind that investors' demand for CDOs created banks' demand for mortgages to back them which led to the issuing of ever more sleazy and predatory loans to vulnerable and low-income people).

The powers that be allegedly at the helms of the big investment firms – Bear Stearns, Lehman Brothers, Merrill Lynch, Citigroup, Goldman Sachs – have claimed that they both knew and didn't know what was going on as the financial markets heated up and burned out. On the one hand, their risk management strategies necessarily involved all sorts of bets and plans on what could happen. Their justification for the creation of credit default swaps (CDSs) was protection, security, prevention of the worst. On the other hand, the bankers and regulators have all claimed that the crisis was the once in a century event that no one could have predicted. Under questioning at the Congressional hearings on the financial crisis, legendary investor Warren Buffett (chief shareholder in Moody's ratings agency) said that he didn't know what Moody's was doing. He didn't know that the agency was making massive mistakes in rating mortgages and bonds before the crisis. Neither he nor anyone else could be expected to know. His own business is too complex for him to understand.[40] Overrun by mutually influencing dynamics, expectations, unintended consequences, and unknown unknowns, contemporary finance is a domain so complex that no one should even be expected to be able to understand it. The hand of the market isn't simply invisible. It cannot be known or understood by mere mortals (although sometimes those with the right stuff, Tom Wolfe's 'masters of the universe',[41] might be able to ride it successfully for a while).

The appeal to complexity displaces accountability. The big banks claimed they were not accountable because there were all sorts of things they couldn't account for. They could, nevertheless, enjoy complexity, getting off on the obscure objects they created as they abstracted themselves from the debts out of which the objects are made, from the risks that are taken with pension funds and municipal bonds, and revelling in a sense that their power puts them above it all. This is the sense, incidentally, at the heart of the culture of extreme bonuses, the only sense such excess makes. Outlandish bonuses inscribe the surplus inequality before which politicians and press bow down. Merely grossly unequal salaries would confine bankers to the world of politicians and regulators, an economic world based on labour, production, and commodities rather than a financial world based on fantasies, bets, risks, and will.

The appeal to complexity is a site of convergence between despotic financialism and critical theory (I'm using the term broadly here to encompass contemporary continental and post-Marxist developments in philosophy and political theory). Some critical theorists associate responsibility with sovereign subjectivity and moralising impulses to punish. The mistake both they and the bankers make is assuming that responsibility implies total knowledge, total control, or total determination of outcomes. Both argue that since the world is more complicated than this, since our networked interactions implicate us in relations and outcomes beyond our knowledge and determination, accountability cannot rightly be localised.

Jane Bennett is attuned to the complexity of assemblages constituted out of human and non-human actants, assemblages like those mixing 'coal, sweat, electromagnetic fields, computer programs, electron streams, profit motives, heat, lifestyles, water, economic theory, wire, and wood' into an electrical grid.[42] Given this complexity, she finds the invocation of agency and strong responsibility to be 'tinged with injustice'. 'In a world of distributed agency', Bennett argues, 'a hesitant attitude toward assigning singular blame becomes a presumptive virtue'[43] As I see it, this hesitation corresponds with attitudes dominant in the neoliberal cloud. For examples, we might add to the abundant and proliferating crises in the finance sector the strings of failure dispersed in the wake of Hurricane Katrina, connected with the ill-conceived and aggressive war in Iraq, and gushing from British Petroleum's Deepwater Horizon oil rig in the Gulf of Mexico in 2010. Even as each instance resists confinement into a singular moment or single individual decision, decisions of boards, regulators, investors, voters, politicians, consultants, and officials are made, nonetheless. The oil rig didn't emerge spontaneously out of the ocean. The city of New Orleans didn't somehow lose organisational capacities previously put to use in coordinating Super Bowl football games and Mardi Gras celebrations.[44]

Some decisions are rightly described as bets or gambles, wagers for one future rather than another. Winners commend themselves for their prescience, presenting their good fortune as grounds for promotion, re-election, praise, a generous bonus. This commendation seems almost appropriate because of the risk of error – they could have been wrong. Correspondingly, blame, condemnation, and punishment likewise appear to be appropriate for those on the losing side of the bet. They, too, had to make a judgment under conditions that were fluid, changing, interconnected, and uncertain. These are the conditions of any human judgment, which is always part of the conditions out of which it arises: always, in other words, ideological. A judgment affirms some ways of thinking and being and rejects others. It accords with some account of fairness and equity, drawing on its embeddedness in assumptions that may remain unexplored, even repressed. One – whether individual or association – is rightly held accountable for a decision because of this embeddedness. A decision incorporates an ideology. In politics, we rightly judge, blame, condemn, and fight against those who are ideologically mistaken. Rather than 'tinged with injustice,' blame is an element of political struggle.

Franco 'Bifo' Berardi takes a view of complexity in line with Bennett's: 'the complexity of the global economy is far beyond any knowledge and possible governance'. Accordingly, he argues that 'the political and economic knowledge we have inherited from modern rationalist philosophy is now useless, because the current collapse is the effect of the infinite complexity of immaterial production ... '[45] I disagree. To say that the global economy is beyond knowledge and governance cedes in advance a terrain of struggle, a terrain that banks and corporations find important enough to spend millions upon millions to defend. Regulating derivatives isn't impossible – make them illegal. Treating food as a commodity to be speculated upon isn't necessary and unavoidable – forbid it. Banks can be nationalised and required to back permitted investment with adequate capital reserves. Whose purpose does it serve to pretend that this can't be done? Bankers benefit from our thinking that there are operations and processes that compel our obedience, like so much absolutist mystical arcana. They also benefit when we slip into thinking primarily in terms of immaterial production, a kind of derivative thinking that fantasises value in the absolutely conceptual and without price, in the enjoyment that accrues through adding, repeating, and circulating.

Given the convergence between finance and critical theory around the notion of complexity, it's not surprising to find an overlap with Friedrich Hayek. The rejection of accountability, of politics, repeats his argument against economic planning: we cannot know. For Hayek the problem of the economy is a problem of knowledge. As he points out, economic knowledge is widely distributed; much of it is local, a matter of the availability of materials and workers and infrastructure. Economic knowledge is also subject to constant change. Infinite particulars of time and place, chance and circumstance, call for constant modulation. 'It would seem to follow,' Hayek concludes, 'that the ultimate decisions must be left to the people who are familiar with these circumstances, who know directly of the relevant changes and of the resources immediately available to meet them'.[46] His argument against central economic planning, then, is that it is impossible because knowledge cannot be totalised. Total knowledge, complete knowledge, is unobtainable.

Foucault specifies the idea that limits on knowledge are limits on government as the economic rationality of liberalism. Liberalism extends the problem of economic knowledge into a more fundamental incompatibility between 'the non-totalizable multiplicity of economic subjects of interest and the totalizing unity of the juridical sovereign'.[47] Insisting that the totality of economic processes cannot be known, liberal economics renders a sovereign view of the economy impossible. In other words, for the liberal, the limit of sovereign knowledge is a limit on sovereign power. As Foucault puts it, *homo economicus* tells the sovereign, 'You must not because you cannot. And you cannot in the sense that "you are powerless". And why are you powerless, why can't you? You cannot because you do not know, and you do not know because you cannot know'.[48] Just as the impossibility of complete knowledge serves as a wedge against sovereign power, so does the inability to know emerge as an attempt to block or suppress politics, to displace matters of will and action onto questions of knowledge.

Foucault's historical account of the links between the rise of economics as a discipline and the liberal political challenge to absolutism is compelling, particularly as it situates liberal and neoliberal approaches to the market in the context of struggles and debate. He provides a potent reminder of the fact that attempts to limit the power of the sovereign shift over the nineteenth and twentieth centuries from limitations on the sovereignty of the king to limitations on the sovereignty of the people. This shift displaces our attention from the ways law, legitimacy, and sovereign authority have never been fully grounded in knowledge but have to appeal to an addressee capable of responding to and as a collective.

Complexity displaces accountability onto knowledge. In documents that Goldman Sachs made available to the Senate Permanent Subcommittee on Investigations, the firm stated that it 'did not have access to any special information that caused [it] to know that the US housing market would collapse'.[49] It explained that its risk management decisions

> were not motivated by any collective view of what would happen next, but rather by fear of the unknown. The firm's risk management processes did not, and could not, provide absolute clarity; they underscored deep uncertainty about evolving conditions in the US residential housing market. That uncertainty dictated our decision to attempt to reduce the firm's overall risk.[50]

It's hard to know what would count as such special information, information that could itself be a cause of knowledge of the future rather than one of its multiple possible contents (perhaps predestination understood as God's foreknowledge would be an example of this kind of information). The Goldman Sachs' report presumes a binary of absolute clarity versus deep uncertainty, of knowledge of what would happen next opposed to fear of the unknown. It's as if Goldman Sachs' defence is that it is not God. It does not have divine knowledge. Lloyd Blankfein's testimony that the firm does God's work suggests that a megalomaniacal sense of its own importance is part of Goldman's corporate culture. Absence of absolute clarity is no excuse, no defence, but it is evidence of an other-worldly self-concept, an epic sense of power. Only someone who presumes that others think he has absolute knowledge would have to explain that he lacks it.

Some commentators and analysts have blamed the discipline of economics for the financial crisis. One of their arguments turns on one of the discipline's primary assumptions, namely, that economics is a science that can and does know that markets are efficient. The efficient market hypothesis (EMH) is the supposition of an underlying balance or best distribution. It turns on the idea of price, that prices reflect all available relevant information. Because this information is built into a price, what will happen to that price in the future is impossible to predict. If it were possible, the predicted future would already be reflected in the price.[51] So even though no one agent can know the truth of the economy, even though this truth eludes the sovereign, market equilibrium (as embodied in each price at a given moment) must be presupposed as the sum total of the knowledge of each actor.

The interesting twist here is that if the EMH designates a truth embodied in prices, then it can be measured or, at the very least, modelled with a high degree of assurance. This supposition of the accuracy of economic models fuelled the calculations of the 'quants' or experts in mathematical approaches to finance who played major roles in hedge funds' and investment banks' approaches to risk over the last decades. Their models identify deviations and discrepancies in prices. These discrepancies show up as volatility, where volatility designates movement around an expected price, that is, more or less probable chances. If gas prices are normally between three dollars and three dollars and fifty cents a gallon, prices over four dollars a gallon suggest that something is going on and this something can then be an opportunity to bet or trade. At any rate, the underlying idea here is that contingency in prices admits of predictability. Rather than indexing the incalculable or unknowable, it points to states of affairs with varying degrees of probability. Even if we don't know exactly what will happen at a certain point in time, we do know that some outcomes are more likely than others.

In the wake of the collapse of the subprime mortgage market (and repeating insights ostensibly gained in the wake of similar collapses in recent decades), vocal economists and commentators have reasserted the falsity of the efficient market hypothesis, its untenable premises, and the impossibility of applying it to real existing markets. Blame for the collapse rests on economic models' abstraction from their contexts (for example, the divergence of a statistical approach to mortgages from its setting in a housing bubble amidst rising inequality). A particularly powerful version of the argument comes from Nicholas Taleb's account of black swans, or low likelihood/high impact events capable of setting off chain reactions as they cascade through the markets.[52] Yet these and similar emphases on unknowability end up resonating with the excuses of bank regulators and executives: they did not know (what was coming); and, they did not know, because they could not know. These accounts, too, get caught up in expectations and bubbles. As Charles Prince, then CEO of Citigroup, said in July 2007, 'As long as the music is playing you've got to get up and dance'.[53] Activity converges with passivity. Bankers had no other choice;

they could not do otherwise. Consequently, they offer excuses for their inability to act even as they relied, momentarily, on a powerful sovereign capable of rescuing them.

The back and forth between knowing and not-knowing, the fragmentation of knowledge into information that disperses into networks only to be abstracted, aggregated, and amplified and then chaotically dissolved at points of crisis, suggests the utility of analysing neoliberalism and its vicissitudes in terms of the oscillations of drive. Partial knowledge may be a limitation, but it is more importantly a condition. The partiality and fallibility of knowledge, the complexity of its interconnections, does not excuse inaction. It is the setting of action (and should be understood as its ground). We have to act because we do not know.

***

I've argued that reflexivity and com-plexity are key components of neoliberalism as an ideological formation. Rather than configuring desire, however, they run a circuit of drive, capturing subjects in patterns and loops and practices from which it seems there is no escape. While my focus has been on the more obscene components of speculative finance, I don't want to leave the impression that the work of reflexivity and complexity in contemporary ideology is somehow pre-political or post-political. On the contrary: in our current formation, appeals to both notions support the very, very rich while undermining the rest of us.

First, reflexivity's displacement of politics into narcissistic circuits of self-absorption dominate what passes for political commentary throughout the tumultuous and varied terrain of contemporary media. Bloggers blog and commentators comment on blogs and bloggers comment on commentators. A similar transfer of intensity animates Wall Street as the never-ending pursuit of profit animates efforts to produce, commodify, and bet on risk. The academic version recedes in levels of increasing meta-ness, commenting on discourses and practices and alternatives and limits until the need to act loses its force and urgency. Freud's observation that the objects of the drive can appear in each others' places, accumulating the others' intensity, alerts us to the ways that multiple, minor achievements (more hits on my blog, a higher daily book value) can well be moments in larger circuits of failure and defeat, acquiescence and accommodation. Approaches to risk that highlight possible perverse effects of regulation demonstrate the same logic. The big banks successfully fought against serious regulation of derivatives with the argument that banks would just come up with even more complex and dangerous ways to transfer risk from their books and produce new sources of profit. The ostensible reality of reflexivity in markets is that agents will incorporate changes in their setting into the behaviour, and so just work around any changes (like water going downhill). We should immediately be suspicious of such an appeal to reality as indicative of what Mark Fisher theorises as 'capitalist realism,' the excuse for capitalist excesses offered as if there were no alternative.[54] What does it mean when criminals say there is no need to define and punish crimes because they will just think of new ones – that's what the banks say. But there are alternatives. Don't regulate derivates – eliminate them. Don't supervise speculative finance – abolish it. Don't expend bizarre amounts of time and resources on an elaborate banking system – have one state bank. There are alternatives.

Second, just as reflexivity displaces politics, so does complexity. Invocations of complexity induce us, the people, to think that self-governance is impossible, too hard, over our heads. It's like an excuse for avoiding responsibility, an infantile fantasy that somehow we can escape politics. Global networks, neural networks, financial networks – if it's all just too complex for us to understand we are left off the hook for our abdication of political responsibility (no wonder the education system has been left to rot; no wonder higher education is a major front of political struggle – the more people believe the lie of 'too complex to understand,' the more they concede). Unfortunately, academics contribute to the ideological effects of complexity. We emphasise that there is always more that needs to be known, that there are unknown unknowns and unintended consequences of whatever it is that we end up doing. Complexity's tagging of the multiplicity of interrelated and unpredictable effects presents us as so deeply enmeshed in our situations that we can't assess them; we can only react, and just in time, in a 24/7 ever-faster market.

But notice: at this point, the excuses we can't predict what will happen, we can't know – turn back in on their reflexive partner: we are compelled to react, not reflect, even as we are enjoined to think more, think more thoroughly, consider all the options. We are pushed in conflicting directions, with full force, told that each is necessary, unavoidable, realistic. These injunctions, impossible to realise, impossible to avoid, signal that the neoliberalism entrapping us is ideology, not necessity.

NOTES

1. For a more thorough discussion of neoliberalism see Jodi Dean, *Democracy and Other Neoliberal Fantasies*, Durham, Duke University Press, NC 2009.
2. See Slavoj Žižek, *The Ticklish Subject*, London, Verso, 1999.
3. For example, see M. Mitchell Waldrop, *Complexity: The Emerging Science at the Edge of Order and Chaos*, Simon and Schuster, New York 1992 and Grégoire Nicolis and Ilya Prigogine, *Exploring Complexity*, New York, W.H. Freeman and Company, 1989.
4. For a more thorough account of Žižek's approach to ideology, see Jodi Dean, *Žižek's Politics*, Routledge, New York 2006.
5. Slavoj Žižek, *In Defense of Lost Causes*, London, Verso, 2008, p328.
6. Slavoj Žižek, *The Parallax View*, Cambridge, MA, The MIT Press, 2006, p61.
7. Sigmund Freud, 'Instincts and their Vicissitudes', pp109-140, *The Standard Edition of the Complete Psychological Works of Sigmund Freud, Volume XIV (1914-1916): On the History of the Psycho-Analytic Movement, Papers on Metapsychology and Other Works*, James Strachey (ed), London, Hogarth Press, 1915, p126.
8. Quoted in Jacques Lacan, *Seminar VII: The Ethics of Psychoanalysis*, Jacques-Alain Miller (ed), Dennis Porter (trans), New York, Norton, 1997, p71.
9. Ibid., p212.
10. Mark C. Taylor, *Confidence Games*, Chicago, University of Chicago Press, 2004, p285.
11. George Soros, *The Crash of 2008 and What It Means*, New York, Public Affairs, 2008, pp8, 10.
12. Justin Fox, *The Myth of the Rational Economy*, New York, Harper Business, 2008, p238; John Cassidy, *How Markets Fail*, New York, Farrar, Straus, and Giroux, 1999, pp274-275.
13. Basel II accords let this self-determining standard suffice for international banking.
14. Fox, *The Myth of the Rational Economy*, op. cit., p238.
15. Scott Patterson, *The Quants*, New York, Crown Business, 2010, p53.
16. Fox, *The Myth of the Rational Economy*, op. cit., pxii; Edward LiPuma and Benjamin Lee, *Financial Derivatives and the Globalization of Risk*, Durham, NC, Duke University, 2004, p35.
17. LiPuma and Lee, *Financial Derivatives*, op. cit., p34.
18. Fox, *The Myth of the Rational Economy*, op. cit., pxii.
19. LiPuma and Lee: 'A critical dimension of derivatives is that they do not involve the immediate exchange of principal and, accordingly, are not immediately counted on financial balance sheets, so that especially when financial agents combine different types of derivatives they allow for an extraordinary and unprecedented degree of leverage', *Financial Derivatives*, op. cit., p108.
20. Patterson, *The Quants*, op. cit., p190.
21. LiPuma and Lee, *Financial Derivatives*, op. cit., p105.
22. Ibid., p118.
23. Michael Lewis, *The Big Short*, New York, W.W. Norton and Company, 2010, pp77-78.
24. Thomas Adams and Yves Smith, 'FCIC Report Misses Central Issue: Why was

there Demand for Bad Mortgage Loans,' *Huffington Post*, posted 31 January 2011, available at http://www.huffingtonpost.com/thomas-adams-and-yves-smith/fcic-report-misses-centra_b_816149.html.

25. See Giovanni Arrighi, 'The Social and Political Economy of Global Turbulence', *New Left Review*, 20, (2003): 5-71. On US as debtor, p70.

26. For a detailed discussion, see Paul Pierson and Jacob S. Hacker, *Winner Take All Politics*, New York, Simon and Schuster, 2010.

27. Lewis, *The Big Short*, op. cit., p179.

28. Patterson, *The* Quants, op. cit., p197.

29. Lewis, *The Big Short*, op. cit., p77.

30. I don't refer here to specific US policies to enable low-income people to purchase homes because housing bubbles occurred in eleven countries during the period of the US bubbles. See George Soros, *The Crash of 2008 and What it Means*, New York, Public Affairs, 2009, p84, noting bubbles in the UK, Spain, and Australia.

31. Patterson, *The Quants*, op. cit., p 194.

32. Lewis: 'In the second quarter of 2005, credit card delinquencies hit an all-time high – even though house prices had boomed. That is, even with this asset to borrow against, Americans were struggling more than ever to meet their obligations. The Federal Reserve had raised interest rates, but mortgage rates were still effectively falling – because Wall Street was finding ever more clever ways to enable people to borrow money', p54.

33. Quoted in Lewis, *The Big Short*, op. cit., p151.

34. Ibid., p165.

35. Michel Foucault, *The Birth of Biopolitics*, Graham Burchell (trans), New York, Palgrave Macmillan, 2008.

36. For a more thorough discussion, see Jodi Dean, 'Drive as the Structure of Biopolitics', *Krisis* 2010, 2. Available at http://krisis.eu/index_en.php#htmlpart=issues.php?issue=2010,%20Issue%202. Accessed 22 June 2011.

37. Ajay Kapur, Naill Macleod, and Narendra Singh, 'Revisiting Plutonomy: The Rich Getting Richer', 5 March 2006, available at http://jdeanicite.typepad.com/files/101001citigroup-plutonomy-report-pt2.pdf, accessed 22 June 2011.

38. Lewis, *The Big Short*, op. cit., p131.

39. Email extracts available at 'What the trader said: "in the middle of complex trades without understanding them"', *Independent*, 26 April 2010. Available at http://www.independent.co.uk/news/business/news/what-the-trader-said-in-the-middle-of-complex-trades-without-understanding-them-1954288.html. Accessed 22 June 2011.

40. Zach Carter, 'Live Blogging the Ratings Agency Hearing,' 2 June 2010, available at http://www.ourfuture.org/blog-entry/2010062202/liveblogging-rating-agencies-hearing. Accessed 22 June 2011.

41. Tom Wolfe, *The Bonfire of the Vanities*, New York, Farrar, Straus & Giroux, 1987.

42. Jane Bennett, *Vibrant Matter*, Durham, NC, Duke University Press, 2009, p25.

43. Ibid., p38.

44. See Paul A. Passavant, 'Mega-Events, the Superdome, and the Return of the Repressed in New Orleans' in Cedric Johnson (ed), *The Neoliberal Deluge: Hurricane Katrina, Late Capitalism, and the Remaking of New Orleans*, Minneapolis, University of Minnesota Press, 2011, pp87-129.

45. Franco Berardi, *The Soul at Work, Semiotext(e)*, 2009: 211. The sentence continues 'and of the incompatibility or unfitness of the general intellect when confronted with the framework of capitalist governance and private property'. I am not disagreeing here with the claim that there is an incompatibility between the general intellect and the capitalist system (although I would want to emphasise the antagonism disrupting, constituting, and imbricating both). Rather, my point here is that it is precisely the antagonism that should be emphasised, not complexity.

46. Friedrich Hayek, 'The Use of Knowledge in Society', first published September 1945, *American Economic Review* 35, 4, (519-30), available at http://www.econlib. org/library/Essays/hykKnw1.html, accessed 22.06.2011.

47. Foucault, *The Birth of Biopolitics*, op. cit., p282.

48. Ibid., p283.

49. Goldman Sachs document, p11, available at http://documents.nytimes.com/goldman-sachs-internal-emails#document/p11, accessed 22.06.2011.

50. Ibid., p12.

51. Patterson, *The Quants*, op. cit., p82.

52. Nicholas Taleb, *The Black Swan*, New York, Random House, 2007.

53. Quoted in Cassidy, *How Markets Fail*, op. cit., p296.

54. Mark Fisher, *Capitalist Realism*, London, Zero Books, 2009.

Neoliberal Britain's Austerity Foodscape: Home Economics, Veg Patch Capitalism and Culinary Temporality

Lucy Potter and Claire Westall

The 'new age of austerity', as invoked by David Cameron in 2009, has seen Britain's Conservative-Liberal Democrat coalition government pursue new and existing neoliberal policies in the name of crisis management and deficit repayment. A legitimising narrative of austerity as financial and even moral compensation for the preceding debt-based bubble has intensified political demands for austere lifestyles marked by spending cuts, hard graft, individual 'responsibility', and a new 'culture of thrift'.[1] Despite reprimanding New Labour profligacy, this austerity narrative cogently reinvigorates neoliberalism's aspirational promises and remains beholden to capitalism's unstable and unsustainable growth paradigm. The British state's self-protective allegiance to capital's perpetuation means that it insists that its consumer-citizens continue to perform their consumptive duties in order to aid economic recovery, at home and internationally, but that they do so with austere self-restraint. This paper explores this austerity narrative, its home-economic messages, and the aesthetic dimensions of its deployment within contemporary Britain's foodscape. We argue that the media-led food culture that took hold during the Cool Britannic[2] 'boom' has continued to expand during our 'bust' times, in large part by maintaining its pleasure-based consumptive appeal and mutating into forms entirely consistent with consumptive-austerity. Specifically, we read the culinary encoding of austerity through the aesthetic motifs, participatory claims and nostalgic imaginary of the British foodscape of 2012. With media coverage of state-endorsed, corporate-sponsored celebrations invoking thrifty wartime resilience and postwar austerity-as-recovery, Britain's 2012 'moment' helped underscore the longstanding, but increasingly critical, disparity between the experience of food as economic burden and the culinary pursuit of frugal pleasure as consumptive self-fulfilment. The 2012 foodscape thereby enabled, and now requires, a provocative re-reading of the lifestyle programming, public-private interactions and labour-time relations that have structured British food culture and consumption patterns since the late 1990s.

The socio-cultural importance of food has become an area of burgeoning academic concern, especially within cultural studies, the sociology of food and the interdisciplinary field of food studies. A number of works have been influenced by Pierre Bourdieu's *Distinction* (1984), with its emphasis on cultural capital and class-based consumption; yet, following Zygmunt Bauman's *Freedom* (1988), consumption studies commonly connects food habits with post-Fordist mechanisms of 'individuation', enhanced consumer 'agency' and self-narrating 'lifestyle choices' within what Anthony Giddens has called a 'post-traditional order'.[3] As Alan Warde notes, a key tension has arisen between such claims for self-actualising practices and the (often class-bound) ways in which 'tastes are still collectively shared to a very significant extent'.[4] Recent discussions have examined this tension in relation to both 'alternative' consumption habits,[5] and the increasing prevalence of largely privileged forms of food-based activism.[6] Discussions of international food activism and culinary diaspora also sit alongside interrogations of today's globalised food system – often highlighting structural unevenness, agro-ecological (un) sustainability and resource (mis)management – as well as examinations of the multi-layered tensions surrounding local-global foodways.[7] The 2011 'Food on the Move' special issue of this journal marked the 'troubled cosmopolitanism' of food-based relations by navigating food's 'mobility in a lived multi-culture' and as a 'dynamic agent in the world'.[8] Taking heed of Ben Highmore's editorial, our discussion works from a similar understanding of food's 'at once revealing and concealing' potential, but occupies a space left open by the issue as a whole; namely, the investigation of contemporary Britain's foodscape and the multifaceted ways in which food, food culture and foodism are aestheticised and sold through British media, particularly the televisual, in accordance with the priorities of the state and its commitment to capital.[9] This approach notably resonates with Tracey Jensen's understanding of the government's affective austerity rhetoric, especially its retrogressive and hypocritical 'tough love' claims and its role within the media-led inculcation of 'austerity chic'.[10] Our discussion also stands in close proximity to recent debates about food-based television,[11] including Heather Nunn's conception of 'retreat TV' and Lyn Thomas' analysis of the 'downshifting' and 'good life' narratives circulating in contemporary British 'lifestyle television'.[12] Like Thomas, we recognise that food has played a significant role in UK televisual culture and its advocacy of the consumptive 'good life' since the 1970s, and similarly foreground the visible growth of prime-time food programming from the late 1990s – most notably via the 'public-service' state broadcaster, the BBC, and the 'publicly-owned, commercially-funded' terrestrial broadcaster, Channel 4.[13] This growth has expanded the range, quality and personalities involved with food presentation, established a cacophony of celebrity chefs, personalities, critics and food enthusiasts, and created a plethora of notably formulaic and often highly didactic food-formats. Where Thomas suggests that the self-fulfilment quests of DIY, fashion, health and 'heritage cooking' shows reveal recession-based ambivalence towards consumptive lifestyles, we offer a panoramic picture of contemporary Britain's foodscape in order to identify how such mediatised life-quests uphold earlier culinary/consumptive motifs while mobilising a distinctive 'austerity aesthetic' that coincides and colludes with the state's neoliberal austerity narrative.

In part one, 'The British State of Home-Economics', we examine this austerity aesthetic as it came to the fore during the 'Great British Summer' of 2012, tracking the tensions evident in spectacles of citizenly consumption and competition-orientated inclusion that characterised the Queen's Diamond Jubilee, the London's Olympic Games and surrounding televisual events. We consider how these events functioned – individually and collectively – as home-economic festivities that served to reinforce state self-assertion at a time of obvious uncertainty, typically through faux-ironic nostalgia and feigned inclusivity. In part two, 'Localism, Veg Patch Capitalism and Austerity', we unpack the fundamental contradictions found in the modesty claims of gentrified culinary activities and pastoralised localist discourses – stretching from the late 1990s – positioning these as building towards, becoming part of and bolstering the state's austerity narrative. Lastly, in part three, 'Temporal Deficit and Culinary Work-for-Labour', we analyse the foodscape's investment in temporal presumptions, metaphors, promises and paradoxes in order to expose how the structure of deficit that shapes the way capitalism's 'economy of time' is maintained through culinary 'work-for-labour', which has become more obvious since the 2007-8 financial crisis, especially when considered in relation to domestic spaces. Throughout, we use the term 'foodscape' to 'map food geographies' onto cultural activities and socio-economic patterns.[14] Like Josée Johnston and Kate Cairns,[15] we follow Arjun Appadurai by using the suffix 'scape' to mark 'cultural flows' of influence and 'the fluid, irregular shapes of [...] landscapes that characterise international capital'.[16] However, where Appadurai contends that the 'global cultural economy' has upheld 'fundamental disjunctures between economy, culture, politics',[17] we investigate the continuities between the culinary economy of British food culture and the political economy of neoliberal austerity, reading this apparent lack of 'disjuncture' as part of the ideological foreclosure upon which the state, and capitalism more broadly, depend.

THE BRITISH STATE OF HOME ECONOMICS

At the start of 2012 David Cameron argued that a newly 'responsible' capitalism, based on a market that is 'fair as well as free', would emerge, phoenix-like, from the current crisis to bring forth a 'moral' economic recovery.[18] This claim for a 'genuinely popular capitalism' stood hand-in-hand with his longstanding, and explicitly neoliberal, assertion that his coalition would move Britain away from 'Big Government' towards a 'Big Society' by enabling 'the biggest, most dramatic redistribution of power from Whitehall to people on the street'.[19] The celebratory summer of 2012 offered the Con-Lib government a platform for their claim to reconcile these ideals of inclusive participation and responsible entrepreneurship. Yet the surge in street parties, industrious home-economic creativity, and British union iconography (with flags, bunting, clothing, party accessories and more besides) only highlighted the state's co-option of citizens as consumer-spectators subject to compensatory extravagance branded as moral civic endeavour. Across state and private message-media, the government's austerity narrative was taken up and used to advance collective stoicism as a stereotypically British response to necessity, recasting the Jubilee and Olympic festivities as healing the home 'nation' (and its constituent nations) by insisting on the 'non-death' of neoliberalism.[20] A home-economics of thrift and survival had been growing since 2008, but 2012 brought the triumphant glorification of such an outlook. While recession loomed large, Britain's constitutional uncertainty (particularly in the face of potential Scottish independence) helped reveal how such unionising statist activities – and the neoliberal British state itself – consistently depend upon privatising enclosure, consumptive silence, and an amnesia-inducing pastiche of imperial mythology and wartime nostalgia.

The 'Thames Jubilee Pageant' and Danny Boyle's 'Isles of Wonder' Olympic Opening Ceremony brought to mind both Frederic Jameson's description of the 'insensible colonisation of the present by the nostalgia mode',[21] and the ongoing pertinence of Tom Nairn's reading of 'parody-Britain' as the 'ceaseless puppet show of sere age, ever-unfolding legitimacy, and constant evocation of 1940'.[22] Recalling Britain's post-WWII euphoria and London's Olympic 'Austerity Games' of 1948, the 2012 celebrations employed this parodic nostalgia to inculcate celebratory consumption as patriotic self-restraint and to reawaken the 1940s wartime ideal of consensual socio-political perseverance during 'national' crisis. Pushing together Cameron's Big Society bluster with Blair's fashionably-bold Britannia and Thatcher's domestic management, the foodscape aided British self-projection as self-protection in 2012 through a culinary aesthetic that functioned in three primary ways. First, as an austerity-bound development of former Prime Minister Gordon Brown's 2008 invocation of Britain's WWII blitz 'spirit',[23] redirecting 'make-do' wartime resilience towards Cameron's 'can-do' Big Society.[24] Second, as a mutation of earlier British food iconography and celebrity culture to fit with the state's austerity narrative and its Britishness claims. Third, as a choreographed mode of conviviality which, from 'public' street parties to 'private' garden picnics, animated neoliberal tensions between claims of popular participation and multiple forms of exclusion and enclosure. Through these dominant functions, the British foodscape revealed the state's ongoing insistence on capital's right to structure the union and shape domestic life on the 'home front'.

Although numerous celebrity chefs bridge New Labour and Con-Lib phases, the public personae and career trajectory of Jamie Oliver make clear post-1997 continuities and the rhetorical and aesthetic mutations that have occurred under austerity. From the inception of *The Naked Chef* (1998), 'Jamie' the 'mockney charmer' stood for the state-endorsed entrepreneurial adventure of London's 'Brit-Pop' food culture, and the popular rise of soft lad-ism on primetime British TV.[25] While Oliver's Thatcherite/Blairite upward mobility appeared to contradict his reputation as a 'modern day Robin Hood',[26] his marketised social conscience exposed what Gerry Hassan calls 'social democracy's ... collusion with neoliberalism'.[27] Oliver's socially-aware programming and food-health campaigns between 2002 and 2008 underlined the state's longstanding failure to educate, nourish and provide for its working/would-be-working classes,[28] but also highlighted his proximity to the hypocrisies of New Labour's 'Third Way' welfare and its reliance on privatising adjustments. In the mid-to-late-2000s, Oliver's increasing awareness of Britishness also coincided with Gordon Brown's promotion of Britain's 'multi-cultural, multinational' uniqueness.[29] Praising Britain's 'patchwork' food culture, *Jamie's Great Britain* (2011) worked imperially nostalgic recipes (e.g. 'Empire Roast Chicken') and retro-royalist dishes (e.g. 'ER's Diamond Jubilee Chicken') into a unionist narrative that endorsed the 'magpie nation' and its imperial-derived ability to absorb all it encounters – an ability captured visually during the Olympic Closing Ceremony.[30] Oliver's latest ventures into 'brand Britain' via his *Union Jacks* restaurants and *Jamie* magazine reveal the persistence of this imperial-unionist outlook. As Owen Hatherley rightly observes, brand Oliver has also tapped into the retrogressive statism characterising recession Britain with his *Ministry of Food* TV programme and post-2008 public-engagement efforts, which overlapped with the 'austere consumerism' that enabled the 'Keep Calm and Carry On' poster campaign to gain ground within 'austerity nostalgia'.[31] Indeed, Oliver's Jubilympic[32] offerings were notably aligned with the state's austerity programme. The cover of his Olympic magazine issue pictured the eponymous culinary hero championing the union flag, and the Jubilee issue captured 2012's 'retro-chic' reimagining of Britishness with the strap-line 'Food Fit for the Queen' emblazoned on its cover alongside an image of a 'royally blinged-up' cupcake.[33]

The cupcake was the definitive food item of 2012. Indeed, the Jubilympic austerity aesthetic managed to mobilise the cupcake's longstanding association with Manhattan's 1950s-inspired Magnolia Bakery (as eroticised in HBO's Sex and the City) and to re-orient and extend its flirtatious, feminine, metro-fashionista appeal by amalgamating references to postwar US prosperity and trendy 1950s diners with Britain's postwar rationing, Women's Institute baking and English village fetes.[34] This mix-and-match pastiche was supplemented by a particularly bourgeois air of self-deprecation and quasi-ironic thriftiness alongside media coverage of the popularity of the miniature cakes among celebrities and Britain's political elites. With images of David and Samantha Cameron tucking in to seemingly homemade and patriotically-iced cupcakes, British newspapers suggested that public celebrations of laboured domesticity were united with the state's investment in retro-nostalgic collectivity and sexualised/infantilised pleasure, as sugar-coated escape.[35] Dan Hancox has similarly analysed the 'post-colonial melancholia' of cupcake-overload as captured by 'Keep Calm and Eat Cupcakes' posters, and rightly identified the purposefulness of Jeremy Gilbert's examination of 'Keep Calm and Carry On' memorabilia as evidence of austerity Britain's reliance on 'nostalgic kitsch'.[36] For Gilbert, this fetishised campaign 'condenses … the whole affective regime through which emotional responses to the crisis of neoliberalism are being organised'.[37] The iconic phrase works not to reclaim a 'stiff upper lip', nor to refute nostalgic attachments to the past, but rather to convey the painful, potentially paralysing, rupture that results from being caught between the impossibility of calmness in late capitalism's disaster-melee and the desire to maintain sanity in the face of all-consuming chaos.[38] Hatherley's earlier examination brought out the poster campaign's coupling of faux-ironic humour with neoliberal terror – conflating 1936 invasion paranoia (when the poster was first designed but not deployed), wartime survival (with which it is mistakenly associated) and the 2000s 'boom' (when it was first sold). Significantly, he also highlights the 'hauntology' of a benevolent, protective/repressive and all-seeing state that is offered through the campaign's 'legislated nostalgia' – a term coined by Douglas Coupland to explain how a population can be commanded to remember that which never existed.[39]

As Hancox observes, union-adorned street party images set a 'counterfactual' historical tone during the Jubilympics,[40] drawing from the 1919 'Peace Teas', Victory in Europe or 'VE Day' celebrations, the 1951 'Festival of Britain' exhibition, and numerous royal coronations and weddings. Despite contemporary anti-austerity resistance, the 2011 London riots, and the difficult realities of 'home-front' struggle, this counterfactual nostalgia allowed Britain's (but specifically England's) streets to appear as wholesomely supportive of the state and its dignitaries. Further, although repeatedly described as all-inclusive celebrations, the parties consistently revealed the ways in which British 'public' space is always-already enclosed, state-managed and defined by ownership and access patterns. With at least 9,500 Jubilee road closure requests in England and Wales, street party enclosures were widely reported as evidence of communal integration, 'public' participation and recession rallying.[41] Cameron even 'hosted' his own weather-affected 'Big Society occasion', inviting an assortment of guests, including organisers of the Eden Project's 'Big Jubilee Lunch'[42] to a closed/private Downing Street party.[43] With advertisements rearticulating the Con-Lib rationale of contributive participation, asking celebrities and 'ordinary' Britons 'what will you bring to the table?', the Eden Project's neighbourly efforts built a nostalgic ensemble of imagined equality and inclusivity that reportedly attracted some 8.5 million picnickers during summer 2012.[44] Notably, this Big Society-inflected campaign relied upon a public-private amalgamation of support, revealing how state, private business and 'third sector' organisations collectively endorsed consumptive camaraderie.[45] Unsurprisingly, British supermarkets led 2012's ideological push for food-based participation with advertising centred on 'retro' street parties, garden summers and domestic provisions. Tesco's black-and-white, mock-BBC infomercial portrayed a 1950s housewifely baking enthusiast offering jubilee discounts and employing faux-ironic humour to account for the suggestion that feminine re-domestication might cure economic instability. Despite Tesco's leading marketing position (and long-running 'Every Little Helps' TV ad campaign), Morrisons had perhaps the most telling advert, depicting former England cricketing star Andrew Flintoff at the centre of an in-store 'street' party just as staff claimed to 'feed the street' with an impressive spread of flag-adorned British party food. This was a scene of enclosure, of private capital reworking popular 'patriotic' participation into aisle-based insularity and excessive 'bargain' purchases, which rearticulated the state's attempts to co-opt 'the public' into consensus-led purchasing as a form of consumptive 'responsibility', even state-capital teamwork, and resonated with the Con-Lib's neoliberal rhetoric of participation as market-determined, all-inclusive competition.

Markedly similar motifs were deployed by McDonalds in its Olympic 'We All Make the Games' TV ad campaign. Here, supposedly 'voluntary' participation was enacted through a series of 'user-generated' corporate ads making inclusive participatory claims whereby even the young or disinterested were still Olympic contributors. With a background piano version of the 1985 Tears for Fears hit 'Everybody Wants to Rule the World', McDonald's presumes to 'welcome [you] to your life' as they, together with the wider 'Food Vision' for 'London 2012', replicate the neoliberal buzz vocabulary used by multinational corporations and neoliberal states to call on 'people' to join their 'vision' for the world.[46] While McDonalds' status as Olympic world sponsor has already been much critiqued,[47] corporate capital's capacity to embody the official rhetoric of public-private relations was crystallised in 2012 through the temporary creation of the 'Biggest McDonald's on the planet' inside the Olympic Park, with four additional branches – 'two open to the public, one for the athletes and officials in the Olympic Village and one at the press centre'.[48] The separation of paying populations as well as the organisation of once-public space into corporate realms of urgent excess conformed to the larger pattern of collective- or common-cost and private benefit that characterised the Olympics. Yet the construction and redevelopment of the 'Queen Elizabeth Olympic Park' in the London Borough of Hackney in East London also draws from longer patterns of urban regeneration and gentrification of London's marginal or outlying neighbourhoods.[49]

The state's dominant role in the gentrification of Britain's foodscape has been played out in recent years through the food-based interests of the BBC – the broadcaster subsidised by compulsory license payments from every UK TV viewer. Backed by commercial subsidiary BBC Worldwide, the BBC heads up a raft of food programming that consistently relies upon consumptive 'participation' as a sign of 'good' and 'active' citizenship, as evidenced by BBC2's 'Great British' programming.[50] *The Great British Menu* (2006-2012), *The Great British Bake-Off* (2010 onwards) and *The Great British Food Revival* (2011-2012) consistently expose the fallacies of their own participatory idiom by insisting upon internally-judged competition and elite modes of consumption while claiming unity with and among an imagined 'great British public'. Repeatedly, the domesticated world of culinary normativity these programmes create serves to distract from their exclusionary norms. *The Great British Menu* fetishises gastronomic meritocracy but brings its Michelin-starred cookery and regional competition to 'the public' via its own distancing televisual spectacle. Each series culminates in an extravagant banquet finale seeking to capture and exploit the cultural/culinary zeitgeist of the time. In 2012, the show's 'Olympic Banquet' conflated the marketised language of time-pressured culinary risk with wartime perseverance and sportsmanlike glory in a display of culinary-sporting exclusivity that series judge Matthew Fort portrayed as ripe for popular domestication in one online BBC blog post.[51] A comparable predicament arises from the 'amateur' competition offered up by *The Great British Bake Off*. Pivotal to 2012's culinary aesthetic, this show's cake-baking nostalgia, ironic self-deprecation and quaintly competitive spirit brought the BBC record viewing figures alongside gushing media reports of viewers being 'galvanized' into Women's Institute-related baking – despite the BBC offering no direct route for viewer participation.[52] Significantly, the 'Bake Off' capitalises upon an imperially-rooted presentation of Britain's saleable version of pastoral Englishness, offering pseudo-colonial fair-play claims alongside cricketing countryside visuals and re-uniting the nostalgic 'charms' of British bunting with English village tea-parties and countrified kitchen aesthetics. The *Great British Food Revival* similarly uses ruralised farmhouse visuals alongside a peculiarly military 'call to action' to support celebrity chefs' claims to 'rediscover' the 'heritage' foods of a non-identified culinary golden age.[53] Rallying viewers to consume, cook or grow prized artisan ingredients themselves, participation is again reduced to consumer purchasing power and/or individual domestic work offered up as moral 'foodie' endeavor. In each programme 'Great British' consumers are encouraged collectively to buy in to the seemingly wholesome lifestyle and imagined culinary authenticity embedded within specific localities, food products and cookery techniques.[54] Reconnecting the home-economics of England's suburban middle class with the state's worldly ambitions/ Britishness claims, the BBC's culinary invocations of archaic, rural and 'local' aesthetics markedly overlap with and re-enforce state politics in a manner that becomes increasingly evident in relation to the Con-Lib's growing localist agenda.

LOCALISM, VEG PATCH CAPITALISM AND AUSTERITY

The contemporary British foodscape has experienced a burgeoning of culinary localism that has been successful across 'boom' and 'bust' largely because its sale of local self-sufficiency as moral, ecological and economic 'good' upholds the neoliberal incongruities consistently disseminated by the state. By instigating local governance strategies to advance environmental and socio-economic wellbeing in support of their community engagement and responsibility drive, the Con-Lib coalition – like their New Labour predecessors – have endorsed an 'eco-sustainability' ethos that follows Britain's signing up to the United Nation's 'Agenda 21' (LA21) in 1992.[55] Unsurprisingly, where Blair's neighbourly 'new localism' relied upon the 'managerial marketisation'[56] and centralising control mechanisms that characterised New Labour governmentality,[57] Cameron has repeatedly insisted that his coalition will bring 'emancipation' into being by allowing people to act for themselves within their local communities. This message took legislative form with the 2011 'Localism Act', which proclaimed ambitions to devolve unprecedented 'power to the people', to cultivate local 'enterprise zones', and to minimise bureaucratic intervention in favour of communal/voluntary assistance within the Big Society.[58] For all his 'new approach' insistence, Cameron's localism-as-change programme entails a transparent continuation of earlier state efforts to manage 'the public' and the economy through 'the local'. His austerity-led localism is, if anything, an extension of Thatcherite 'small state' domestic self-management rhetoric coupled with a Blairite insistence on equal 'opportunity for all' rather than actual socio-economic equality.[59] Akin to the rhetoric surrounding new 'free' schools and especially 'farm' schools, Con-Lib localism is clearly a way of articulating conserving and reactionary ambitions with 'liberatory' self-determination and 'liberal' socio-green motifs. As Harvey has argued, 'there is more than a hint of authoritarianism, surveillance, and confinement in [...] enforced localism'.[60] Furthermore, the coalition's state-managed local 'emancipation' narrative not only upholds centralised power, but redeploys neoliberalism's 'lure of localism' to offer gestural compensation for the very destruction of 'public' or, better still, common spaces at the behest of the private interests determining its recovery agenda.[61] Following Harvey, we can therefore read the government's localist agenda as evidence of the neoliberal state's ability to create and enable 'an extensive oppositional culture' that nonetheless accepts the 'basic principles of neoliberalism' thereby foreclosing potential for significant radical opposition.[62]

Reclaiming social responsibility alongside domesticated entrepreneurship, the expansion of what we call 'veg patch capitalism' helps maintain the state's austerity-localism narrative despite and even by means of its own oppositional self-projection. Gentrified food crusades and urban agricultural projects commonly work to re-articulate neoliberal empowerment tropes and to bind participants to the state's interest in small-scale compensatory gestures. The Capital Growth scheme's 'Big Idea' to create 2,012 new community gardens as part of 2012's 'leafy Olympic legacy' epitomised Con-Lib efforts to recuperate self-reliant communal participation through consensus-building public-private partnerships and cooperative 'green' endorsements.[63] Moreover, despite using the language of 'alternatives', the wholesome face of culinary localism means its own well-intentioned ideals repeatedly ignore, conceal or simply miss the superficiality of its gestural opposition.[64] Prevailing discourses insist that localised foodways and domestic caution offer viable alternatives to globalised exploitation by working towards socio-economic liberation and against waste creation, mass consumerism, corporate retail, and agri-business corruption. Although worthy and useful imperatives, this vague anti-capitalist positioning regularly overlooks a series of incongruities and contradictions within its own practices. In Britain this is often accompanied by a wholly romanticised image of the rural past as a quasi-feudal golden age. Such a fantasy serves to erase or obscure the connections between contemporary localism and the uneven global expansion of capitalism and its asymmetric labour relations. Thus, locally-branded produce frequently depends upon extensive 'food miles' and global labour exploitation;[65] middle-class 'foodies' often drive to farmers' markets, despite individual claims to environmental responsibility, in order to seek out fresh 'bargains' even as farmers face supermarket price-pressures;[66] and, celebrity-endorsed frugality campaigns invariably reify aestheticised gastronomic excess and property ownership while portraying lifestyles to which most cannot aspire.

In line with Con-Lib efforts to 'manage' economic recovery through oxymoronic calls to conserve and consume, culinary localism seeks to showcase consumptive privilege and yet conceal class-based unevenness. This is achieved by holding on to an aspirational 'Cool Britannic' mindset while simultaneously returning to the self-conscious modesty of traditional English domesticity. The growth of urban farmers' markets is particularly indicative of how the aspirational culture of Blair's Britain has been reworked to combine notions of thrifty pastoralism with accumulated affluence, organic wellbeing and consumptive enjoyment.[67] Since the 1997 opening of Bath Farmers' Market (BFM), the local food 'enterprise' has proliferated into an assortment of business opportunities: farm shops and on-site eating venues; 'pick your own' activities and home delivery schemes; and temporary food vans and 'pop-up' restaurants. Such ventures often benefit from state endorsements, offering promotional literatures that repeat compensatory neoliberal claims to the environmental 'good' provided by local 'economic development strateg[ies]'.[68] Having arisen in direct response to LA21,[69] BFM positions itself as taking a 'leading role' in the eco-sustainable 'development' cause and, like the coalition government, promotes farmers' markets as bypassing the 'middleman' to provide mutually beneficial 'exchange'.[70] Culinary localism hereby epitomises Con-Lib endorsements of local consumer-collectives selling 'directly' to 'known' consumer-allies by extending opportunities for consuming rurality among a wealthy urban-suburban clientele. In this vein, Borough Market (an early Jamie Oliver haunt) sells itself as a local 'open public amenity' despite its profit-seeking reliance upon the consumptive investments and cosmopolitan ambitions of the international and urban gastro-tourists arriving daily at London's South Bank.[71]

Gastronomic localism has prompted mimicry and mutation within a variety of commercial settings seeking to capitalise on the quasi-farming appeal of this ever-expanding 'market'. One online venture called 'The Virtual Farmers' Market' domesticates and reformulates localism's directness claims so as to disconnect those it claims to digitally unite.[72] Meanwhile, British supermarkets increasingly exploit localist aesthetics by partitioning stores into market-like grocery, bakery and 'deli' sections. Morrisons uses their new 'Fresh Market' to display 'locally-sourced' produce alongside 'exotic vegetables', cultivating an urban-pastoral cosmopolitanism that emulates high-end, transnational urban food markets like Borough.

While such cosmo-chic food venues proliferate in London's gentrified areas, Morrisons sells their trendy status to those lower down the class-food-chain. As private price-competitive spaces, these commercial markets and local eateries all forcefully qualify Amanda Wise's generally positive reading of the spatial contexts in which 'low-level cosmopolitanism' might facilitate 'commensal practices'.[73] Instead, the explosion and evolution of farmers' markets has palpably underscored the mapping of exclusion that connects culinary gentrification, poverty-exploiting price disparities, the erosion of small town market spaces, and the failure of recession-hit retail to foster local 'spirit'. Supporting Local Government MP Eric Pickles' ambitions to reinvigorate British high streets, the state-commissioned 'Portas Review' (2011) championed by TV retail guru Mary Portas called for further deregulation and recommended a British-localist 'National Market Day', positing that 'once we invest in and create social capital in the heart of our communities, the economic capital will follow'.[74] In this version of reality, our hearts and our social worlds are only about preparing the way for capital and cultivating growth whereby all markets ultimately lead to the 'free' and 'fair' market of Cameron's neoliberal fantasy.[75]

The popularity of farmers' markets speaks to their insistence upon gastronomic pleasure and vegetable abundance in conjunction with ethical, frugal and wholesome lifestyles. This aesthetic is crucial to veg patch capitalism and the ways in which localist vocabulary has merged seamlessly into the discourse of contemporary foodism. With the fashionable resurgence of allotments, communal gardens and domestic self-sufficiency campaigns, the affectionate abbreviation 'veg patch' ('vegetable patch') circulates on television programmes and in culinary texts.[76] Yet kitchen gardens have been deeply embedded within British (though predominantly English) self-understanding, at least since the Small Holdings and Allotment Act of 1908. Rebecca Bramall foregrounds the 'function of historicity' in renewed, austerity-linked calls to 'Dig for Victory' as a central feature of the affective mythologies accompanying contemporary anti-consumerist discourses.[77] Expanding on Bramall's point, it is clear that vegetable patches have evolved to fulfill period-specific requirements and now draw upon an assortment of historicised ideals – from Victorian kitchen gardens and wartime 'home-front' nourishment, through 1970s 'green' aspiration and new-age holistic retreats, to the rooftop gardens popular among today's urban-trendies.[78] Typically, the nostalgic idealisation of allotments as collections of publicly-available, domestic growing spaces nevertheless fails to register their historic ties to the English enclosures, the destruction of the

commons, and capitalism's growth via land acquisition.[79] The food-writing
'home chef' Nigel Slater captures this in his 2009 book *Tender*, volume 1, by
equating his vegetable patch with a 'feeling of enclosure and protection',
of individual 'sanctuary' from the urban frenzy 'outside' his garden walls.[80]
The veg patch aesthetic here works to claim pastoral retreat as possible in
the city, to carve out privileged, private and privatising green spaces that
exclude the undesirable aspects of city life while remaining within and
relying upon its globally-networked, wealth-producing potential. This
urban-pastoral dialectic marks out veg patch capitalism's interaction with
state efforts to build 'brand' Britain as a sustainable urban metropolis by
maintaining an imperially-derived and elastic vision of English ruralism
trapped within (the) British 'capital'.

With escalating commands to 'eat local' inevitably overlapping with 'buy
British' campaigns, Britain's 'localised' foodscape increasingly combines
patriotic iconography with romantic ruralism in its appeals to collective
harmony. Indeed, food marketing repeatedly deploys statist insignia
and pastoral connotations simultaneously. With its twee aesthetics and
monarchist connections, the Prince of Wales' 'Royal Duchy' brand is a
telling case; yet the union flag also adorns an array of 'heritage' foods and
earth-clad 'local' produce. Lacking geographical specificity, such 'local'
food promotions repeatedly rely upon vague nostalgic appeals to a typically
English reserve and to the hazy bucolic bounty and 'organic community'
of 'the countryside'. In this manner, adverts for supermarket Sainsbury's
2010 'Taste the Difference' campaign used Jamie Oliver's celebrity
credentials and rambling monologue during a countryside romp to sell the
supermarket's 'locally-sourced' but '100% British' pork sausages.[81] Similarly,
a recent Morrisons ad saw celebrity TV hosts 'Ant and Dec' learning about
the store's 'local-sourcing' policy through chatty in-store repartee and
source-site visits.[82] While the reified 'local' producers remain either absent
or spatially-bound in these adverts, the easy countryside access displayed
by both sets of celebrity-consumers compellingly reinforces Raymond
Williams' sense that Britain's privileged classes connect the urban and
rural through their capacity to shape, inhabit and consume both spaces.[83]

Seemingly fleeing London to find domestic-pastoral bliss, TV chefs
Hugh Fearnley-Whittingstall and Jamie Oliver encapsulate middle-class
urban-rural mobility. Fearnley-Whittingstall's *Escape to River Cottage* (1999)
was a paradigmatic case of localism's insistence on pastoral escape as self-
protective, self-indulgent, 'downsizing' retreat. Following his self-sufficiency
'dream', the successful London chef apparently chose to relinquish urban

privilege in order to embark upon a 'pioneering' homestead adventure and become a 'Dorset downsizer' in his charmingly dilapidated rural 'cottage' only later to upsize into a fully-fledged farm at 'River Cottage HQ'.[84] Financed by private capital accumulated in the metro-financial centre, this series packaged the home-economic risk of Hugh's food-autonomy quest into fulfilling self-reliance and the satisfaction of domestic growth. Throughout, the chef-presenter relied on a familiar self-mocking tone to claim knowing ironic distance from his consumptive privilege, and this stylised whimsicality continues to defend and secure his ever-expanding River Cottage empire and online product overflow.[85] A similar pattern characterises Oliver's *Jamie at Home* series (2007-2008), in which the celebrity chef narrates his newfound gardening pleasure by showcasing the culinary potential of the seasonal, organic and heritage foods cultivated in his sizeable veg patch.[86] The accompanying book, subtitled '*Cook your way to the Good Life*', referenced the BBC's 1970s suburban self-sufficiency sitcom *The Good Life* (1975-8) to reclaim the aspirational logic of domestic modesty, while deploying Oliver's roots 'in a village in Essex' to reinforce ideas of both quasi-rural 'return' and aspiration-based self-improvement.[87] 'Jamie' consistently portrays this accessible-inaccessible domesticity and class-based self-referentiality to advertise his own entrepreneurial path as part of the sales pitch for his expanding culinary empire. With both Jamie Oliver and Hugh Fearnley-Whittingstall, the celebrity performance of growing home produce, displaying domestic perseverance, and showcasing semi-ruralised entrepreneurial success has since been translated into the austerity rhetoric of culinary self-sufficiency and home economic restraint during recession.

In the context of socio-economic upheaval, the self-deprecating tone of localist discourse is loaded with the moral and nostalgic implications of home economy. Citing Delia Smith's return to 'make do' wartime frugality in her re-released *Frugal Food* (1970-2008), John Burridge rightly observes that, under austerity, food-based 'incitements to economy sit alongside incitements to extravagance'.[88] While Fearnley-Whittingstall's trend-setting 'back-to-nature' enterprise indicated how celebrity chefs have long led the 'modest' lifestyle campaign, the media personae and culinary offerings of Nigel Slater are especially useful in this context. Slater's autobiographical *Kitchen Diaries* series notably tracks the mutation of New Labour's cosmopolitan self-indulgence into the frugality-morality discourse underpinning Con-Lib austerity-localism. Where *Kitchen Diaries* (2005) foregrounded his fondness for North London's elite gastronomic hideouts, its 2012 sequel created an imagined anti-commercial domesticity that privileged frugal living. Slater increasingly performs the domestication of hard times through his narration of individualising home retreat and repetition of the mantra of frugality entrancing today's self-declared 'foodies'.[89] The cook's delight in the 'homely smell[s]' of thrifty grain-based meals sits alongside his appetite for 'humble pleasures' based on carefully selected specialist ingredients.[90] This insistence on frugality as culinary choice reinforces localism's emphasis on the bourgeois ideology of thrift,[91] reminding us of Bourdieu's 'self-imposed austerity' which, for most, is no austerity at all.[92] Characteristic of post-crash governmentality, Slater's rhetoric of austere choice and domestic resourcefulness becomes a means of (re)claiming privacy, time and space – a therapeutic compensation always-already set within excessive consumptive comfort. Numerous recipes and anecdotes predicated upon 'leftovers' provide telling evidence of purchase and culinary preparation beyond the point of consumptive need. Slater even considers 'leftovers as treasure, morsels of frugal goodness', delighting in the 'gorgeous, frugal little snacks' made from leftover 'cold-cuts'.[93] Here, 'using up' items is seemingly optional, to be encouraged, but never make-or-break – a far cry from the living realities of shopping budgets, income prioritisation, and the daily 'burden' of economising faced by Britain's growing number of low-income and/or indebted families.[94]

With his Boxing Day 'Celebration of Frugality',[95] Slater's innovative use of leftovers vividly highlights the self-contradictory logic of recycling as a form of home economic prudence predicated upon previous excess, present satisfaction, and a secure future. This gesture of thrift as compensation for over-consumption invites direct comparison with government spending cutbacks. Such measures are consistently justified by the coalition as future-oriented self-protection, as compensating for past excess or excessive practices, and as a supposedly resourceful way of repaying fiscal/moral debt. In May 2012, Cameron rebranded austerity as an 'efficient' way of compensating for capitalist profligacy – a competent management of resources and labour-time that supposedly 'saves' wasteful expenditure and allows the 'streamlining' of labour fundamental to the accumulation of capital.[96] The 'recycling' here is simply a move back around the 'boom-bust' mentality that enables the capitalist cycle to continue ad infinitum. Where overworked, underpaid or simply unpaid labour represents successful state-led corporate 'efficiency', localism's veg patch rhetoric frames anti-waste as pro-ecology and pro-sustainability, and simultaneously pro-health and pro-pleasure. Yet, from the unwanted surfeit typical of organic 'veg boxes' to the energy costs accompanying small-scale production,[97] 'eco'-foodie initiatives are repeatedly tied to capitalist excess, to consumptive privilege, and to the gestures of disavowal enabled by the state's quasi-Thatcherite 'waste not want not' attitude that nonetheless demands consumptive indulgence.

TEMPORAL DEFICIT AND CULINARY WORK-FOR-LABOUR

In the *Grundrisse* (1857-8), Marx states that 'all economy' is reducible to the 'economy of time' because capital's insatiable need for evermore surplus-value is largely dependent upon the prolongation and extraction of evermore surplus-labour time.[98] As explained in *Capital* (1867), this involves a combination of 'absolute surplus-value', achieved by compressing all non-work activities and lengthening overall work hours, and 'relative surplus-value', achieved by compressing necessary-labour into ever-smaller portions of time.[99] In late capitalism, the multiple ways in which time–labour relations are manipulated to facilitate the elongation, compression, and exploitation of wage-labour have become easy to observe. So too the demand for speed in relation to the unending openness of time-for-labour through the normalisation of variable work hours, multiple/multiplying tasks, work-time domestication, and mobile technological access. Such pressure-and-expansion patterns relate to the 'time–space compression' with which Harvey characterises postmodernity and the neoliberal 'efficiencies' of globalised financialisation.[100] In contemporary Britain, the language of 'time-saving' as 'cost-saving' efficiency has been brought into sharp relief as it is deployed against labour in all its forms. Unpaid labour came to the fore as UK unemployment figures began to rise substantially in the late 2000s and, as Guy Standing makes explicit, 'work-for-labour' – any task outside of wage-labour that is oriented towards capital accumulation – is prospering in flexible labour markets.[101] Under neoliberal austerity, working hard to gain wage-labourer status (e.g. job applications, interviews, re-skilling and CV updating) or to enhance wage-labourer security/prestige (e.g. working during 'leisure' time or enhancing work-skill efficiency) is increasingly demanded and glorified as part of a self-flagellating response to precarity. In the UK this has become an essential part of the move from welfare to 'workfare' that began under New Labour and has made a headline assault on benefit claimants, the disabled, and the young and out-of-work under the Con-Libs.[102]

The neoliberal rhetoric of workfare and working-for-labour has been readily absorbed, reified and refashioned by the British foodscape through its promotion of culinary work-for-labour. Time has always been of the essence when it comes to food production, distribution, preparation and consumption, with each phase revealing the manipulation of time and time–labour relations for surplus-value creation. Within the professional domain, long working hours, restaurant kitchen efficiency, just-in-time (JIT) delivery logistics and best-before/use-by dates are all obviously geared towards maximising profit. Meanwhile, the time-pushed work-force is typically maintained via quick, easy access to cheap, fast calories – often via instant, frozen or ready-made meals, in-house restaurant provisions, and the exploitation of domestic, typically gendered, work-for-labour.[103] Distinct from food-based wage-labour, we define 'culinary work-for-labour' as any task involved in food purchasing, preparation and consumption that is outside of paid work but serves the accumulation of capital by reproducing labour-power (e.g. practicing culinary skills and acquiring dietetic knowledge in order to create quick, nutritionally-balanced meals after work); by facilitating surplus-labour exploitation (e.g. consuming foods and supplements in order to prolong productive activity, pre-preparing and eating office-based lunches, or food-shopping in 24-hour supermarkets); and, by catering for extended wage labour-time by offering fast solutions for food consumption (e.g. buying fast food or snacks 'on-the-go', mastering speedy cooking techniques, or purchasing kitchen efficiency aids). The language of time is also deeply embedded in culinary literature, from precise recipe timings and meal planners to evocative time-based descriptions of consuming seasonal produce. Yet, significantly, the temporal vocabulary of culinary texts increasingly connects consumption with the desire to compensate for the speedy and productive lifestyles that disrupt, even destroy, ideas of domestic routine or consumptive regularity. As food consumption takes on evermore uncertain forms, with increasingly limited, non-existent or individualised meal times, culinary discourse point to the ways in which we respond to time-pressure by managing our domestic time–spaces and daily rhythms through techniques of culinary self-mastery. In different but overlapping works, Dale Southerton (2009), Mark Fisher (2009) and Peter Fleming and Carl Cederström (2012) have all analysed the explosion of a lifestyle management industry geared toward curing the psychosomatic consequences of neoliberalism's vast apparatus of time-based exploitation. We argue that Britain's austerity foodscape plays a crucial role in what Southerton describes as the 'contemporary malady' of time-pressure.[104] We posit that a 'temporal deficit' – or, the sense of a loss or lack of time, of an excess of temporal obligation, of perpetual time-task arrears – is pivotal to the foodscape's compensatory culture, feeding into the reification of culinary work-for-labour and consumptive self-management as 'remedies' that nonetheless support capital's self-serving temporal logic. Such culinary 'solutions' are propagated most forcefully through televisual spectacles, advertising campaigns and celebrity-endorsed products connecting consumptive pleasure with aspirational organisation. Promoting culinary competence as home-economic prudence, these food-media commodities notably support the Con-Lib's austerity-efficiency plan wherein to 'save' or avoid 'wasting' time is to become a 'good' citizen of economic recovery. Britain's time-obsessed food culture then glorifies and strengthens a neoliberal understanding of individual agency and domestic efficiency as social 'goods' that can free-up 'spare' time for both additional consumptive leisure and additional work-for-labour activities.[105]

Today's foodscape insists upon dual compensatory motifs of time-saving acceleration and calming deceleration, reminding us of the ways in which fast and slow temporalities exist in dialectical tension. Food discourses repeatedly equate daily nourishment with temporal burden, and propagate the need to 'save' time via culinary efficiency but also to 'savour' time via culinary pleasure and escape. Carlo Petrini's 1986 description of Slow Food's opposition to 'Fast Food' hegemony even demonstrates how the gastro-ethical 'slow' claim is bound to and by 'fast' as its imagined nemesis but also its raison d'être.[106] This slow-fast dialectic is integral to the culinary 'economy of time', the promotion of temporal deficit, and the boom/bust mythology embedded in the state's austerity narrative. For the dialectical bind between 'fast' and 'slow' vividly maps onto the mutual co-dependence of economic 'boom' and 'bust'. Where the latest 'boom' accumulated rapidly accelerating debt and long-term repayment chaos, the 'bust' has brought short-term repayment together with drawn-out phases of low-interest and structural unemployment. The boom-narrative of the wealth-producing 'fast' life and associated 'fast' pleasures also promises the 'slow' pace of pleasure-pausing or temporal escape via holiday homes and rural retreats. Meanwhile, the bust-narrative of 'slow' recovery after a lightning-fast market collapse has yielded 'efficiency' claims and the persistent frenzy of work-for-labour tasks. In these interweaving narratives, the fast-slow dialectic connects with the ways in which time and consumption are manipulated so as to enable consumers to 'buy out' of capitalist frenzy by 'buying in' to temporal deficit.

Daniel Miller observes that one of the 'most curious aspects of the relationship between time and consumption is the circumstances under which we are able, in some sense or other, to 'buy time'.[107] Indeed, the temporal deficit is consistently deployed to sell products indicating that we can 'buy time' by purchasing time-saving, task-saving culinary commodities. Contemporary food retail is replete with products enabling domestic consumers to 'save' kitchen time – or to minimise the time-costs of culinary work-for-labour – in order to 'buy time' for other activities. This market appears to have widened under austerity despite specifically catering to Britain's flourishing food culture. Luxury time-related food products include: an expanding range of gastro-friendly pre-packaged options (e.g. nutritionally-tested 'food-on-the-go' ranges and celebrity-endorsed ready-meals); a proliferation of cooking aids and high-tech domestic equipment (e.g. multi-tasking food processors and convection microwave-oven hybrids); and a plethora of pre-prepared ingredients (e.g. pre-washed salad bags and pre-chopped vegetables). Many of these products speak to capital's slow-fast dialectic by marketing speedy solutions that maintain the idea or aesthetic of slowness by offering culinary shortcuts for traditionally slow-cooked or leisure-linked foods. Stews, soups and curries are ostensibly made quicker and easier by using stock cubes, ready-pulverised garlic or pre-mixed spice blends, just as part-baked bread or pre-mixed cake batters enable consumers to capture the feeling of leisurely baking without the temporal cost or affective culinary risk. Mimicking professional expertise and enabling celebrity-endorsed accomplishment, such time-saving high-demand commodities highlight the coercive nature of the temporal deficit within which we are consistently told that we can 'buy time' but only if we also 'buy in' to fetishising excess and celebrity culture. Meanwhile, the culinary market offers temporal compensation through acts of purchasing that not only contribute to surplus-value in production, but help to 'free up' more surplus labour-time for its creation. The temporal deficit thus results in a double-bind: to 'buy time' is repeatedly sold as a way to 'buy into' an alternate temporal rhythm so as to 'buy out' of today's profit-driven rush; yet this 'buy out' is always-already defined by the necessity both to buy and 'buy in' to capitalism and the myth that we have 'no time' for ourselves.

Food discourses commonly promote culinary work-for-labour as a leisurely activity that compensates for temporal deficit through the temporal wealth of unhurried consumptive pleasure and sensory escape. Taking time over shared meals, losing oneself in moments of sensual enjoyment, and savouring episodes of culinary creation or product selection are all exoticised and eroticised even as they are packaged as domestic bliss, culinary care and holistic self-fulfillment. TV chefs have capitalised on the popular uptake of Slow Food's gastronomic localism to depict their own pastoral meanderings into culinary work-for-labour as forms of protection or flight from the urban rush. Tellingly, River Cottage programmes open with an audible 'slow-down' by moving from traffic sounds to bluegrass jazz, and *Jamie at Home* uses Tim Kay's (2008) song 'My World' to frame countryside cookery as 'making up for losing so much time'. Both make clear that the attractive 'slow' life always relies upon, just as it seeks to escape, a lifestyle built upon professional city-speed and personal wealth. Recuperative 'slowness' and domestic harmony have also been the bedrock of Nigella Lawson's urbanite claims for 'work-life balance' as described in her TV programming and accompanying cookbooks. In 2000, the 'domestic goddess' imagined a split between the professional 'working week' and her domesticated 'weekend alter-ego',[108] and in *Nigella Express* (2007) Lawson similarly claimed that, although dedicating 'the odd weekend' to the 'general pursuit of unhurried cooking', she usually exists in a 'state of obligation-overload' where 'food has to be fitted in'.[109] Here, temporal deficit and compensatory weekends premised on abundance allow culinary work-for-labour to function as an exercise in the time-management needed to balance family and professional commitments. Sainsbury's current 'Live Well For Less' TV ad campaign moves this culinary management into the time/cost-saving mindset of austerity-efficiency while maintaining the week-to-weekend split of earlier industrial work patterns. One advert encourages consumers to use Sunday roast 'leftovers' to create speedy and thrifty follow-up weekday meals. With idealised family mealtimes and a musical appeal to 'slow down' on Sundays, the advert romanticises the consumptive leisure of lavish weekend dining as well as the efficient acceleration and economic efficiency of extending one meal into several.

Combining the slow-oriented implications of gastronomic 'goodness' with the speed-oriented demands of flexible labour, 'Good Food Fast' has become the culinary slogan of middle-class foodism. *Jamie's 30 Minute Meals* (2010) capitalised on this temporal mantra by deploying the consumptive aspiration accompanying the domestication of professionalised efficiency. 'Jamie' even boasts that 'this is an energetic workhorse of a book' as his own culinary labour is fetishised as a fast-paced, competitive, masculine endeavour.[110] The book's quick exposure shots and photographic 'busyness' celebrate rapid culinary activity, and the televisual counterpart uses dramatic music and a visual countdown to impart an exhilarating sense of labour-driven urgency. In line with Con-Lib 'crisis' discourse, speed is sold as a compensatory risk-based response to temporal deficit just as the series visibly reinforces Cameron's work-fare-inspired 'connection' between labour, risk and rewards.[111] This neoliberal matrix of domesticated efficiency and faux-competitive risk-taking is then incorporated into the book's illustration and Oliver's televised creation of fresh, vibrant food, as well as the imagined sociable leisure-time set aside for its consumption. Oliver's latest book release *Jamie's 15 Minute Meals* (2012) repeats these gestures, with an introduction explaining that to enter the 'world of *15 Minute Meals*' readers must first purchase the 'kitchen gadgets' needed to 'get the meals done in time'.[112] As the fake clock-time, challenging time-scale, and display of expertise all make clear, the aspirational spectacle of Jamie's 15 minute 'world' is defined by the consumptive access and professional skill-set that cogently distances 'the public' with whom Oliver claims empathy and to whom he dedicates the book. Such distancing was reinforced by a recent advert for Freeview TV which depicted a young couple, dinners in hand, repeatedly rushing to watch *Jamie's 15 Minute Meals* on TV. The advert ingeniously juxtaposes Oliver's time-pressured proficiency with the sale of a product designed to record, delay, pause and rewind; that is, to manipulate time in accordance with the demands of neoliberalism's time-efficiency, flexible labour, and meal-rush realities.

The fast-slow dialectic of culinary media consistently relays aspirational spectacle through highly gendered, sexualised or fetishistic depictions of work-for-labour and food consumption. Although programming such as Oliver's or BBC2's *Masterchef* fetishise hyper-active culinary masculinity, food is most commonly associated with the female body as a provider of both nurturing domesticity and carnal satisfaction. No British celebrity is more famous in this regard than Nigella Lawson, whose televisual performances consistently exploit her maternal and feminised curves to emphasise the already eroticised temporalities of food consumption. *Nigella Express* carries a particularly sexualised slow/fast temporal dynamic with a 'Quick quick slow' chapter offering up '[p]repare ahead' recipes designed to delay and heighten satisfaction.[113] Similarly, the *Nigella Bites* (1999-2001) TV show saw 'Nigella' storing away her culinary creations then returning at night to indulge in secretive acts of gustatory self-pleasure. With an erotic marketing history dating back to Cadburys' infamous Flake adverts of the 1960s-1980s, the British foodscape's investment in chocolate provides overt examples of this sexualised 'guilty pleasures' narrative. Mars' 2011 'I know what I fancy' campaign for Galaxy chocolate granted allusions to female self-pleasuring as a way of unwinding after a busy working day, using slow-seduction to suggest an absent moment of climatic satisfaction. Likewise, in the early 2000s, Marks & Spencer (Britain's middle-class staple-retailer) launched its famous 'This is not just …' TV ad campaign, which similarly used sensual jazz sounds, elongated breathy descriptions and drawn-out 'gastro-porn' visuals to create temporal-aesthetic tension. The explicitly sexualised consumptive slowness worked to flaunt 'M&S' excellence as the exclusivity of temporal opulence while offering up ready-made gastronomic pleasure without work-for-labour time-investment. Although repositioning slightly post-crash, M&S has upheld its play with culinary temporality in their 'Terribly Clever' (2011) and 'Simply M&S' (2012) ready-meal advertisements, using audible tempo shifts to move from meticulous culinary instructions to the task-saving time-provision claim of pre-prepared gastronomy. A further play on temporal expansion compensating for temporal contraction is offered in the brand's 2010 'Fuller for Longer' range, offering to delay hunger by providing high-protein options to help weight loss. Clearly, M&S continues to appeal to a 'guilt' consumption paradigm, selling exclusivity to middle-class consumers while moving from elongated gustatory pleasure to dietary purpose via protracted satiety. Aspirational rationale here becomes entwined with the neoliberal achievement of self-regulatory weight-loss achieved by managing consumptive timings. Self-managed bodily normativity then becomes compensation for protracted labour-time and an economic market wherein one must have less, to last longer, and work harder, in order to be more.

In 2012, a triad of cookbooks – *Cook Yourself Thin Faster*, *Jamie's 15 Minute Meals*, and *Laura Santini's Flash Cookery* – all used the triple rationalisation of time, price and caloric/nutritional breakdown to gesture towards the accumulating guilt-based pressures weighing down today's consumers. These diet-culinary hybrids indicate the ways in which dietary techniques and culinary work-for-labour are increasingly positioned as fruitful, even necessary, methods of self-improvement. With its reflexive title, the expanding *Cook Yourself Thin* brand markedly rearticulates neoliberalism's entrepreneurial self-management as the aspirational self-moderation achieved by acquiring a new skills-set. Indeed, their culinary philosophy speaks to the Con-Lib's 'Welfare to Work' insistence on attaining 'independence' (from benefits) via apparently admirable, yet necessarily unpaid, work-for-labour activities that enhance 'employment prospects'.[114] *Cook Yourself Thin Faster* (2012) even promotes culinary re-skilling in order to break the boom/bust dietary 'cycle of self-deprivation and cheating' in language explicitly akin to the neoliberal mantra of re-skilling for renewed wage-labour opportunities. Such compensatory promises underpin all 'new start' resolutions, as captured by the 'wipe the slate clean' and 'get back on track' ethos of Activia's 2011 New Year's TV ad campaign. While both brands claim respite from the dietary pendulum, they nonetheless hold to the vocabulary of guilt, denial and regret that simply re-affirms the cyclical dietary-temporal economy of debt and credit – the logic of restricting, purging, exercising or delaying hunger in order to repay the 'debt' of past indulgence and to purchase dietary 'credit' for speculative future consumption. These well-known dietary techniques echo, in dietetic form, austerity-based claims for a new beginning, positioned as compensating for previous debt-based excess by inaugurating a new cycle of growth. Moreover, just as an ever-expanding diet-food industry continues to profit from consumers' attempts to manage a controlled, consumptive life, this almost bulimic-based hope for ongoing 'boom-and-bust' looks set to continue and to do so as demanded by a system of cyclical, if accelerating, surplus-value creation.[115]

CONCLUDING NOTE

This discussion has been concerned with the culinary austerity aesthetic of 2012, its ties to earlier and ongoing localist discourses and motifs, and the imagined temporal deficit and dominating fast-slow dialectic that structures experiences of food and food's televisual presentation in the contemporary British foodscape. We have shown how food and food culture have performed a central role in connecting wartime/postwar thriftiness with home-front jubilation; promoting 'veg patch' self-provision as a form of green capital; and cultivating self-managed domestic routines that aid capital accumulation and rearticulate the coalition government's 'Get Britain Working' campaign.[116] These culinary tropes have thrown into sharp relief the ways in which the state's governing austerity narrative enables consumptive excess but demands consumptive modesty and positions individual and competitive moral 'goodness' as the basis for economic self-maintenance. Advancing such neoliberal 'freedoms', the Con-Lib government has helped spawn and foster an austerity-defined culture of 'disavowal' within which ironic and knowing distance might be claimed by those able to engage in state-defined yet culturally reified acts of 'gestural anti-capitalism'.[117] This has become a central feature of Britain's austerity food culture wherein claims for 'modest' or 'responsible' consumption and 'all in it together' quips are deployed as compensation for unacceptable living standards, a lack of democratic freedoms, and the absence of an oppositional politics of substance. In 2013, the 'Horsemeat Scandal' that continues to rock Europe and the UK has crystallized this superficial non-opposition by instigating' moral panic over – and widespread disavowal of – a widely discredited food/financial system. Yet here, as elsewhere, the claimed 'solutions' to the 'crisis' only serve to bolster structural asymmetry by justifying privileged forms of 'alternative' consumption and prioritising expensive home-made, local, slow(er) food.

Britain's contemporary foodscape consistently fuels and reveals the self-contradictory yet self-perpetuating logic of capital as manifest in the neoliberal enterprise of state-led austerity as the latest self-serving response to capitalism's ongoing/permanent crisis. Fundamentally, the relationship between capitalism, its crises, and state intervention has been at the core of leftist critiques of the mode of production at least since Marx, and more recently Noam Chomsky, David Harvey, Naomi Klein, Slavoj Žižek[118] and others have explored the self-induced nature of capitalist crises and the means by which crises are capitalised upon, as Milton Friedman famously declared, to 'produce real change'.[119] Citing Friedman, Stuart Hall situates the Con-Lib's policy 'avalanche' within Britain's longer neoliberal trajectory to reveal how 'change' has been the rhetorical calling card of new governments despite their acceptance of pre-established neoliberal patterns.[120] Harvey has similarly enumerated the brazen contradictions of neoliberal states which typically advocate individual and market freedoms while imposing 'good' business conditions and 'favour[ing] the integrity of the financial system [...] over the well-being of the population'.[121] In dealing with their 'credit-crunch' inheritance the Con-Lib government has made these impulses more obvious than they were under both New Labour and Thatcherism. Consequently, with a 'master narrative' advancing 'Reform' and 'Choice',[122] the government of austerity offers neoliberal pronouncements, faintly recalling bourgeois liberalism, insisting that the individual remains free to choose and to consume, but only if s/he chooses to be an exploited labourer and a fetishised as well as fetishising consumer, caught in a marketplace described as open and equal but predicated upon asymmetry, inequality and exclusion.

Throughout 2012, British food culture and food-based asymmetries became integral features of the flagrant contradictions between state-enforced austerity and state-sponsored mega-events. By December, a flurry of news stories documenting the rapid rise in food banks ran alongside festive supermarket adverts advocating domestic entrenchment via familial meal times.[123] In Westminster, David Cameron maintained that food bank volunteers should be praised as part of his Big Society and responded to food poverty questions with promises of inflation avoidance, tax improvements, benefits management and business developments.[124] Unsurprisingly, the prime minister ended the year as he began, advocating the neoliberal fallacies of economic moralism, political voluntarism and asymmetric growth as holding the key to recovery-survival. Operating within the discursive mode of 'capitalist realism', the Con-Lib coalition thus bespeaks the neoliberal language of ready-made 'solutions' to an ongoing economic downturn that has come to stand for capitalism's end even as it is used to perpetuate capitalism and reinforce the myth of its pre-eminence.[125] In 2009, Cameron mobilised a markedly Platonic metaphor to characterise his government as '[s]teering our country through this storm'.[126] At the start of 2013, he reworked this image of directional leadership to describe his resolution to 'stick to the course' in order to steer clear of 'the abyss'.[127] Resuscitating the rhetoric of pre-determined capitalist-paralysis to explain austerity's persistence, Cameron admitted his government 'are making tough choices about our future' yet repeated the Thatcherite mantra that 'there is no alternative'.[128] In so doing, Britain's PM revealed the neoliberal state's guiding principle: that the choices made by governments can offer no alternative realities for those they govern.[129]

NOTES

1. See David Cameron, 'The Age of Austerity Speech', 26 April 2009. Full recording available from: http://www.conservatives.com/Video/Webcameron.aspx?id=b3b3d2c1-353a-4d53-bef2-c5ab79fbae5d.
2. 'Cool Britannia' was the name given to a supposed upsurge of commercial and popular cultural vitality in the UK under the auspices of the early New Labour government 1997-2001.
3. Anthony Giddens, *Modernity and Self-Identity: Self and Society in the Late Modern Age*, Cambridge, Polity Press, 1991, p5.
4. Alan Warde, *Consumption, Food & Taste: Culinary Antinomies and Commodity Culture*, London, Sage, 1997, p3.
5. See, for example, *Cultural Studies*, Special Issue 'Cultural Studies and Anti-Consumerism: A Critical Encounter', 22, 5, (2008).
6. See Roopali Murkerjee and Sarah Banet-Weiser (eds), *Commodity Activism; Cultural Resistance in Neoliberal Times*, New York, New York University Press, 2012; Josée Johnston, 'Counter-hegemony or Bourgeois Piggery?: Food Politics and the Case of Foodshare' in Wynne Wright and Gerad Middendorf (eds), *The Fight Over Food: Producers, Consumers, and Activists Challenge the Global Food System*, Pennsylvania,

Pennsylvania State University Press, 2008, pp93-121; Wendy Parkins and Geoffrey Craig, *Slow Living*, Oxford and New York, Berg, 2006.

7. See, for example, 'Food and Foodways; Explorations in the History and Culture of Human Nourishment', Special Issue Food Globality and Foodways, *Localities* 19, 1-2, (2011); Tim Lang, 'Conclusion: Big Choices about the Food System' in Geoffrey Lawrence, Kristen Lyons & Tabatha Wallington (eds), *Food Security, Nutrition and Sustainability*, London, Earthscan, 2010, pp271-288; and Tim Lang, Sue Dibb, and Shivani Reddy, *Looking Back Looking Forward: Sustainability and UK Food Policy 2000-2011*, London, Sustainable Development Commission, 2011.

8. See Ben Highmore, 'Introduction: "Out of the strong came forth sweetness" – sugar on the move', *New Formations*, 74, (2011): 5-17, http://doi.org/fxndd6.

9. Ibid., p9.

10. Tracey Jenson, 'Tough Love in Tough Times', *Studies in the Maternal*, 4, 2, (2012): 1-26, available at www.mamsie.bbk.ac.uk.

11. See, Martin Caraher, Tim Lang and Paul Dixon, 'The influence of TV and celebrity chefs on public attitudes and behaviour among the English public', *Journal of the Association for the Study of Food and Society*, 4, 1, (2000): 27-46; Heather Nunn, 'Investing in the "Forever Home": from Property Programming to "Retreat TV"' in Helen Wood and Beverley Skeggs (eds), *Reality Television and Class*, Basingstoke, Palgrave Macmillan, 2011, pp169-183.

12. Lyn Thomas, 'Alternative realities: downshifting narratives in contemporary lifestyle television', *Culture Studies*, 22, 5, (2008): 558-572.

13. See, *'The Royal Charter for the Continuance of the British Broadcasting Corporation'*, available online, http://www.bbc.co.uk/bbctrust/assets/files/pdf/about/how_we_govern/charter.pdf; and, Channel 4's self-defining corporate statement, http://www.channel4.com/info/corporate/about.

14. Bent Egbery Mikkelsen, 'Images of Foodscapes: Introduction to foodscape studies and their application in the study of healthy eating out of home environments', *Perspectives in Public Health*, 131, 5, (2011): 209-216.

15. See Josée Johnston and Kate Cairns, 'Eating for Change', in Roopali Mukherjeen and Sarah Banet-Weiser (eds), *Commodity Activism: Cultural Resistance in Neoliberal Times*, New York, New York University Press, 2012, pp219-237.

16. Arjun Appadurai, *Modernity at Large: Cultural Dimensions of Globalization*, Minneapolis, University of Minnesota Press, 1996, p33.

17. Ibid., pp32-33.

18. David Cameron, 'Moral Capitalism' Speech, 19.01.2012. Full transcript available from: http://www.newstatesman.com/uk-politics/2012/01/economy-capitalism-market.

19. David Cameron, 'Big Society' Speech, 19 July 2010. Full transcript available from: http://www.number10.gov.uk/news/big-society-speech/.

20. See Colin Crouch, *The Strange Non-Death of Neoliberalism*, Cambridge, Polity Press, 2011.

21. Frederic Jameson, 'Postmodernism: Or the Cultural Logic of Late Capitalism', *New Left Review* I/146, July-August (1984): 59-92.

22. Tom Nairn, *Pariah: Misfortunes of the British Kingdom*, London, Verso, 2002, pp16-17. This point is also made by Michael Gardiner in 'London and the Right to

Govern', *Bella Caledonia*, 14 January 2013, available from:
http://bellacaledonia.org.uk/2013/01/14/london-and-the-right-to-govern.

23. Gordon Brown maintained that the 'calm, determined British spirit' will 'lead the way' through and beyond global financial crisis in 'Stake could not be higher, this is the moment of truth', *Sunday Mirror*, 11 October 2008, available from: http://www.mirror.co.uk/news/uk-news/stakes-could-not-be-higher-this-is-moment-346891.

24. David Cameron, 'Leadership for a Better Britain' Speech, 5.10.2011. Full transcript available from: http://www.conservatives.com/News/Speeches/2011/10/David_Cameron_Leadership_for_a_better_Britain.aspx.

25. Rachel Moseley, '"Real lads do cook ... but some things are still hard to talk about": the gendering of 8-9', in Charlotte Brunsdon, Catherine Johnson, Rachel Moseley, and Helen Wheatley, 'Factual Entertainment on British Television: The Midlands TV Research Group's 8-9 Project', *European Journal of Cultural Studies*, 4, 1, (2001): 29-62.

26. Gilly Smith, *The Jamie Oliver Effect*, André Deutsch, London 2006, p181.

27. Gerry Hassan, 'Don't Mess with the Missionary Man: Brown, Moral Compasses and the Road to Britishness' in Andrew Wright and Tony Gamble (eds), *Britishness: Perspectives on the British Question, The Political Quarterly Special Issues*, 2009, pp86-100.

28. Notable TV examples include Channel 4's *Jamie's Kitchen* (Nov-Dec 2002), *Jamie's School Dinners* (Feb-March 2005) and *Jamie's Ministry of Food* (Sept-Oct 2008).

29. Gerry Hassan, op. cit., p89.

30. Jamie Oliver, *Jamie's Great Britain*, London, Penguin, 2011, pp12, 138, 146.

31. See Owen Hatherley, op. cit., p3.

32. 'Jubilympic' was a 2012 UK media coinage referring to the convergence of the Queen's diamond jubilee and the London Olympic Games during the summer of that year.

33. 'Jamie: making you a better cook', *Jamie Magazine*, Issue 29, A. Harris (ed), London, 2012, p13.

34. See Xanthe Clay, 'Cupcakes, Sex and the City style', *Telegraph*, 23 May 2008, available from: http://www.telegraph.co.uk/foodanddrink/recipes/3343601/Recipes-cupcakes-Sex-and-the-City-style.html.

35. See, for example, images by David Hartley, *Daily Mail*, 4.06.2012, available from: http://www.dailymail.co.uk/news/article-2154478/Dave-SamCam-enjoy-jubilee-party-near-Oxfordshire-home-sun-comes-day-celebrations.

36. Dan Hancox, 'Let Them Eat Cupcakes', *Open Democracy*, 4.01.2013, available from: http://www.opendemocracy.net/dan-hancox/let-them-eat-cupcakes.

37. Jeremy Gilbert, 'Sharing the Pain: The Emotional Politics of Austerity', *Open Democracy*, 28.01.2011, available from: http://www.opendemocracy.net/ourkingdom/jeremy-gilbert/sharing-pain-emotional-politics-of-austerity.

38. Ibid.

39. Owen Hatherley, op. cit., p2.

40. Hancox, op. cit.

41. BBC News (quoting the LGA) reported that the 'appetite for a street party ha[d] "ratcheted up" since the wedding' because, 'with the economic climate and red tape being relaxed, people [we]re keen to be distracted' while, as one party

attendant said, 'you need your neighbours when times are hard'. See Caroline Gall, 'Diamond Jubilee: Almost 10,000 Street Parties Planned', 26.05.2012, available from: http://www.bbc.co.uk/news/uk-england-18210417.

42. An extension of the 'Big Lunch' project to encourage neighbourly street-parties (effectively the equivalent of neighbourhood barbecues in the US, but a far rarer occurrence in the UK, traditionally only associated with major royal occasions or very major, non-repeating national holidays).

43. See The Guardian Press Association Release, 3.06.2012, available from: http://www.guardian.co.uk/politics/2012/jun/03/downing-street-jubilee-party.

44. See http://www.thebiglunch.com.

45. This included sponsorship from the Department for Communities and Local Government, 'The Big Lottery Fund', MasterCard, breadmaker Kingsmill, and supermarket chain Asda. See http://www.thebiglunch.com/partners/index.php.

46. This 'Food Vision' claimed to celebrate 'British regional food', promote 'sustainable change' and support 'the growing public agenda on healthy living'. Full document available from: http://www.london2012.com/documents/locog-publications/food-vision.pdf.

47. See, for example, John Amis and T. Bettina Cornwell (eds), *Global Sport Sponsorship*, Oxford, Berg, 2005.

48. See Louise Eccles, 'McDonald's Supersized', Mail Online, 25.06.2012, available from http://www.dailymail.co.uk/news/article-2164517/Worlds-biggest-McDonalds-First-pictures-inside-Olympic-Stadium-fast-food-restaurant.

49. See Anna Minton's *Ground Control: Fear and Happiness in the Twenty-First Century City*, 2nd edition, Penguin, London 2012; and, Michael Hall's 'Urban entrepreneurship, corporate interests and sports mega-events: the thin policies of competitiveness within the hard outcomes of neoliberalism', *The Sociological Review*, 54, (2006): 59-70.

50. *The Great British Menu* involves regional chefs from across the UK competing for the prize and prestige of catering the annual celebration banquet; *The Great British Bake-Off* sees amateur cooks bake in competition with another in order to be named 'Bake Off' winner and earn a place in the accompanying cookbook; and *The Great British Food Revival* has celebrity chefs and food personalities state their case for the revival and protection of heritage ingredients or outmoded culinary techniques.

51. Matthew Fort, 'Let the GastrOlympics Begin', BBC Food Blog, 13.04.2012, available from: http://www.bbc.co.uk/blogs/food/2012/04/let-the-gastrolympics-begin.shtml.

52. See, for instance, Clemmie Moodie, 'The Great British Bake Off inspires 50,000 to join the Women's Institute', which reports a peak audience of 7.2 million for the grand final. In the *Mirror*, 18.10.2012, available from: http://www.mirror.co.uk/tv/tv-news/the-great-british-bake-off-inspires-50000-1384738.

53. See the BBC website http://www.bbc.co.uk/programmes/b00zf9vd.

54. The show has spawned several BBC-endorsed cookbooks, for example, *Great British Food Revival; The Revolution Continues*, London, Orion Publishing, 2011.

55. For a qualitative examination of LA21's impact in Britain, see Karen Lucas, Andrew Ross and Sara Fuller, *What's in a name? Local Agenda 21, community planning and neighbourhood renewal*, Joseph Roundtree Foundation, York 2003.

56. Stuart Hall, 'The Neo-Liberal Revolution', *Cultural Studies* 25, 6, (2011): 705-728.

57. See Nick Ellison and Sarah Ellison, 'Creating "Opportunity for all"?: New Labour, new localism and the opportunity society', *Social policy and society*, 5, 3, (2006): 337-348.

58. For full documentation of the Local Government Information Unit's (LGIU's) updated guide to the Localism Act, see online: http://www.lgiu.org.uk/wp-content/uploads/2012/10/The-Localism-Act-an-LGiU-Guide-updated-September-2012.pdf.

59. Tony Blair mobilised this phrase repeatedly during his premiership, including at the Labour Party Conference in Brighton (September 2004) in anticipation of his third-term in government. Full transcript available from BBC News online: http://news.bbc.co.uk/1/hi/uk_politics/3697434.stm. For a useful examination of New Labour's claim to equal opportunity without economic equity see, Nick Ellison and Ellison, above, particularly pp343-5.

60. David Harvey, *Justice, Nature and the Geography of Difference*, Oxford, Blackwell, 1996, p202.

61. Hall, op. cit., p720.

62. David Harvey, *A Brief History of Neoliberalism*, Oxford, OUP, 2005, pp70-71.

63. The 'Big Idea' was established in November 2008 with an amalgamation of financial support from London Food Link, the Mayor of London, and the Big Lottery's Local Food Fund. Available from: http://www.capitalgrowth.org/big_idea/.

64. For a discussion of attempts at 'alternative consumption' and their pre-emptive co-option, see Jo Littler, *Radical Consumption: Shopping for Change in Contemporary Society*, Maidenhead, Open University Press, 2009.

65. Highmore explains the 'bizarre trips some foods make' according to the 'assymetrical divisions of global labour' and in the interests of profit. For instance, Scottish langoustines are flown to Bangkok to be hand-shelled by cheap labourers, then travel back to the UK to be sold as scampi in 'local' British pubs. See Highmore, op. cit., p5.

66. For an analysis of farmers' market car-reliance, see Cathy Banwell et al., 'Fast and Slow Food in the Fast Lane: Automobility and the Australian Diet' in Richard Wilk (ed), *Fast food/Slow food: The Cultural Economy of the Global Food System*, AltaMira Press, Plymouth 2006, pp219-240.

67. For a comparative reading of the rise of the Farmers' Market in Union Park Square, New York, and the associated discourses of authenticity and process of gentrification see Sharon Zukin, 'Consuming Authenticity', *Cultural Studies*, 22, 5, (2008): 724-748.

68. See Lewis Holloway and Moya Kneafsey, 'Reading the Space of the Farmers' Market: A Preliminary Investigation from the UK', *Sociologica Ruralis*, 40, 3, (July 2000): 285-299.

69. BFM's current website explains that it was 'the first Farmers' Market in the UK', 'established in September 1997 in response to Local Agenda 21', available from: http://www.bathfarmersmarket.co.uk/about.

70. The socio-economic benefits of farmers' market are promoted by the 'Department of Environment, Food and Rural Affairs' homepage, see online: https://www.gov.uk/farm-shops-and-farmers-markets.

71. See http://www.boroughmarket.org.uk/about-us.

72. See http://www.vfmuk.com/about-the-virtual-farmers-market.html.

73. Amanda Wise, 'Moving Food: Gustatory Commensality and Disjuncture in Everyday Multiculturalism', *New Formations*, 74, (2011): 82-107, http://doi.org/fxwxfx.

74. This supposed investigation into 'the future of our high streets' was led by Mary Portas, fashion-consumer-advice expert of BBC fame. Full report is available online: https://www.gov.uk/government/uploads/system/uploads/attachment_data/file/31797/11-1434-portas-review-future-of-high-streets.pdf.

75. See Nick Ellison and Sarah Ellison, above, for a delineation of the uneven distribution of 'social capital' as 'social closure', p342.

76. Examples include Jimmy Doherty's *Grow Your Own Christmas Dinner* (aired on Channel 4, 12.12.2012), Hugh Fearnley-Whittingstall's *Veg Patch: River Cottage Handbook 4*, Bloomsbury Publishing, London 2009, and the Royal Horticultural Society's *Step-by-Step Veg Patch*, London, DK Ltd, 2012.

77. Rebecca Bramal, 'Dig for Victory!: Anti-consumerism, austerity, and new historical subjectivities', *Subjectivity*, 4, 1, (2011): 68-86.

78. The latest veg patch craze is captured in recent publications, including Alys Fowler's *The Edible Garden; How to Have Your Garden and Eat It*, BBC Books, London 2010, and Alex Mitchell's *The Edible Balcony; Growing Fresh Produce in the Heart of the City*, London, Kyle Cathie, 2011.

79. Greg Sharzer outlines localism's aesthetic and ideological 'return' to the enclosures as part of its investment in the falsities of neo-classical economics and bourgeois liberalism in his *No Local; Why Small-Scale Alternatives Won't Change the World*, Winchester, John Hunt, 2012, see particularly pp52-55.

80. Nigel Slater, *Tender: Volume One, A cook and his vegetable patch*, London, Fourth Estate, 2009, p9.

81. Oliver's promotion of Sainsbury's 'Taste British sausages' first aired on 24 April 2010, during the *Britain's Got Talent* advertising break – as noted by one televisual campaign-tracking website, available from: http://www.campaignlive.co.uk/news/999022/.

82. Adverts coincide with the supermarket's 2012 'Market Street' revamp where in-store Butchers, Fishmongers and Greengrocers offer consumers the 'pick of the street'.

83. See Raymond Williams, *The Country and the City*, London, Chatto & Windus, 1973.

84. Hugh Fearnley-Whittingstall, 'Episode 1', *Escape to River Cottage*. First aired on Channel 4, 18.03.1999 – 22.04.1999.

85. This point was also made by Lyn Thomas in her analysis of lifestyle TV's 'downshifting' narratives. See Thomas op. cit., p690.

86. *Jamie at Home*. First aired on Channel 4, 7 August 2007 – 8.02.2008.

87. Oliver, 'A nice little chat', *Jamie at Home*, London, Penguin, 2007, p6.

88. Joseph Burridge, 'Introduction: Frugality and Food in Contemporary Historical Perspective', *Food and Foodways*, 20, 1, (2012): 1-7.

89. For a comparable analysis in the context America's 'gourmet foodscape', see Josée Johnston and Shyon Baumann, *Foodies: Democracy and Distinction in the Gourmet Foodscape*, New York, Routledge, 2010.

90. Nigel Slater, *Kitchen Diaries Two*, London, Fourth Estate, 2012, pp58, 89.

91. Sharzer explains how the petit bourgeoisie's 'ethical system thrives on thrift and self-discipline', which 'creates a part of localist ideology', op. cit., p92. Also useful in this context is Alan Warde's understanding of the 'structural antinomies of taste', including the culinary dialectic of 'economy and extravagance'. See his *Consumption, Food & Taste* (1997).

92. Pierre Bourdieu, *Distinction: A Social Critique of the Judgment of Taste*, London, Routledge & Kegan Paul, 1984, p173.

93. Slater, 2012, op. cit., pp19, 120.

94. For a qualitative study of low income and indebted food consumption patterns, see Jackie Goode, 'Feeding the Family When the Wolf's at the Door: The Impact of Over-Indebtedness on Contemporary Foodways in Low-Income Families in the UK', *Food and Foodways*, 20, 1, (2012): 8-30.

95. Slater, 2012, op. cit., p510.

96. Speaking at a tractor factory in Essex, Cameron rebranded 'austerity' as 'efficiency'. See Kiran Stacey, 'Cameron defends efficiency drive', *Financial Times*, 8.05.2012, available from: http://www.ft.com/cms/s/0/8b5333ce-9939-11e1-948a-00144feabdc0.html.

97. Sharzer argues that the environmentalist claims of small-scale producers are often limited by their inability to utilize the expensive eco-efficiency techniques of large-scale industry, op. cit., p25.

98. Karl Marx, *Grundrisse*, Martin Nicolaus (trans), 1973, London, Penguin, 1993, p173.

99. Karl Marx, *Capital*, David McLellan (ed), Oxford, Oxford University Press, 1999, pp300-301.

100. See Harvey, 2005, op. cit., p4, 161; and Andrew Gamble, *The Spectre at the Feast: Capitalist Crisis and the Politics of Recession*, Basingstoke, Palgrave, 2009, pp178-179.

101. Guy Standing, *The Precariat: The New Dangerous Class*, London, Bloomsbury, 2011, p120, http://doi.org/fxwcdg.

102. See Julie MacLeavy, 'A 'new politics' of austerity, workfare and gender?: The UK coalition government's welfare reform proposals', *Cambridge Journal of Regions, Economy and Society*, 4, (2011): 355–367.

103. See, Anne Murcott, 'Women's place: cookbooks' images of technique and technology in the British kitchen', *Women's Studies International Forum*, 6, 1, (1983): 33–39; and, in another context, Meg Luxton, *More Than A Labour of Love: Three Generations of Women's Work In The Home*, Toronto, Women's Press of Canada, 1980.

104. Dale Southerton, 'Re-ordering temporal rhythms: coordinating daily practices in the UK in 1937 and 2000' in Elizabeth Shove, Frank Trentmann and Richard Wilk (eds), *Time, Consumption and Everyday Life: Practice, Materiality and Culture*, Oxford, Berg, 2009, pp49-63.

105. Here we are drawing on Standing, op. cit., p118.

106. Carlo Petrini, *Slow Food: The Case for Taste*, New York, Columbia University Press, 2001, pxxii.

107. Daniel Miller, 'Buying Time' in Elizabeth Shove, Frank Trentmann and Richard Wilk (eds), op. cit., pp157-170.

108. Nigella Lawson, *How to be a Domestic Goddess: Baking and the Art of Comfort Cooking*, London, Chatto & Windus, 2000, pvii.

109. Nigella Lawson, *Nigella Express*, London, Chatto & Windus, 2007, pvi.

110. Jamie Oliver, *Jamie's 30 Minute Meals*, London, Penguin, 2010, p14.

111. David Cameron, 'Moral Capitalism' Speech, 19.01.2012. Full transcript available from: http://www.newstatesman.com/uk-politics/2012/01/economy-capitalism-market.

112. Jamie Oliver, *Jamie's 15 Minute Meals*, London, Penguin, 2012, p15.

113. Lawson, 2007, op. cit.

114. See Department of Work & Pensions '*Get Britain Working*', available from: http://www.dwp.gov.uk/policy/welfare-reform/get-britain-working.

115. This phenomenon was revealed by a recent Channel 4 documentary exposing the restrictive bind of Weight Watchers' 'points system'. See *Weight Watchers: How They Make Their Money*, first aired on Channel 4 on 28.01.2013.

116. See online: http://www.conservatives.com/getbritainworking/.

117. Mark Fisher, *Capitalist Realism: Is There No Alternative?*, London, Zero Books, 2009, pp12-13.

118. See Noam Chomsky, *Profit Over People: Neoliberalism and the Global Order*, New York, Seven Stories Press, 1998; David Harvey, *A Brief History of Neoliberalism*, Oxford, OUP, 2005; Naomi Klein, *The Shock Doctrine: The Rise of Disaster Capitalism*, London, Allen Lane, 2007; and Slavoj Žižek, *Living in End Times*, London, Verso, 2010.

119. Milton Friedman, *Capitalism and Freedom*, Chicago, University of Chicago Press, 1962, pxiv.

120. Hall, op. cit., p707.

121. Harvey, 2005, op. cit., pp70-71.

122. Hall, op. cit., p719.

123. Tesco recommended all family members 'Get It On' with Christmas cracker hats; Sainsbury's showed children 'Being Good for Santa' by clearing dinner plates; Asda suggested that 'Behind Every Great Christmas There's Mum'; and Morrisons had a harried Mum wrestling a turkey.

124. PMQs 19.12.2012. Full recording and transcript available from: http://www.parliament.uk/business/news/2012/december/prime-ministers-questions-19-december-2012.

125. See Mark Fisher, op. cit., particularly pp16-20.

126. David Cameron, 'The Age of Austerity Speech', op. cit.

127. David Cameron, 'Speech on the Economy', 7.03.2013. Full transcript available from: http://www.politics.co.uk/comment-analysis/2013/03/07/david-cameron-s-economy-speech-in-full

128. Ibid.

129. Ibid.

'HIT YOUR EDUCABLE PUBLIC RIGHT IN THE SUPERMARKET WHERE THEY LIVE': RISK AND FAILURE IN THE WORK OF WILLIAM GADDIS

Nicky Marsh

Risk is a risky business: a calculated balancing of failure against success which necessarily leaves open the possibility of both. It was superficially surprising, then, that the language of failure was employed with such careful ambivalence in the aftermath of the financial crisis of 2008. The failure of neoliberal assumptions about the self-regulating market was a self-evident fact, but also the basis for a careful defence of the status quo, in the months immediately following the crisis. When asked by the House Committee of Government Oversight and Reform whether his 'view of the world', his 'ideology was not right?' Alan Greenspan, for example, was notoriously blunt, 'absolutely, precisely'. Yet his candour could be taken to suggest neither accountability nor the need for greater oversight, it was a 'once in a century credit tsunami' and 'whatever regulatory changes' are subsequently made will only ever 'pale in comparison to the change already evident in today's markets ... This crisis will pass, and America will re-emerge with a far sounder financial system'.[1] The perverse logic that accepts failure but denies its consequences found its fullest form in the ubiquitous language of 'too big to fail': the banks' bloated asset sheets were the cause of the failure whilst also necessitating their unquestioned rescue. This failure of failure, these riskless risks, revealed, as Žižek commented at the time, that the 'self-propelling circulation of Capital thus remains more than ever the ultimate Real of our lives, a beast that by definition can't be controlled, since it itself controls our activity, blinding us to even the most obvious dangers'.[2]

   This absence of failure's critical purchase at a moment of crisis offers one kind of explanation for the ironical fact that it is those on the left that have begun to identify themselves with the term in the years following the financial crisis. Richard Dienst, for example, concluded the 2011 *The Bonds of Debt* by gesturing to a Marxist tradition of failure. Dienst cites Walter Benjamin, Bertolt Brecht, Perry Anderson and Fredric Jameson in order to suggest that 'as opposed to the more coolly conceptual notions of dominance and hegemony, the notions of defeat and failure never lose their unsettling sting, which is why they, rather than some idea of ultimate success, mark the place of the Real in revolutionary discourse'.[3] One must be 'able to go through defeat *without saving anything*, and to go through failure *without losing everything*' Dienst counsels, and although it is 'a terribly risky political strategy' that excluding 'such words from our vocabulary would leave us nothing to do but jostle for a better place in that triumphal procession already underway'.[4] Joshua Cohen's editing of a special 'Failure Issue' of *The Review of Contemporary Fiction* in the same year also gestured to the importance of failure as a resistant critical concept. The collection focused on a literary notion of failure, the necessity of experimentation, that recalls the tradition most evocatively summarised by Samuel Beckett's 'Ever tried. Ever failed. No matter. Try again. Fail again. Fail better'. For the eclectic writers gathered together by Cohen failure is a painful form of freedom, an 'ongoingness' in Wayne Kostenbaum's echo of Beckett, that allows for works which 'pay exclusive attention to their own unfolding' outside of the demands of the market'.[5]

A copy of the novelist William Gaddis' tightly typed and deceptively slight 'English 241: Literature of Failure' is included amongst the excoriating confessions and impassioned accounts of marginalised writers that constitute the journal issue.[6] The 'Literature of Failure' is a course that Gaddis taught at Bard in 1979 and it suggests connections between Dienst's concept of failure as a Marxist critique, a pushing back 'against the dead weight of history', and Cohen's advocacy of the formal and social freedoms that failure allows.[7] Gaddis' course ranges from Weber's *The Protestant Ethic and the Spirit of Capitalism* to Edward Bellamy's *Looking Backward*, Upton Sinclair's *The Jungle*, Dale Carnegie's *How to Win Friends and Influence People* and A. Alvarez's *The Savage God*. The reading list provides a condensed account of the American dialectic, the contradiction between a utopian promise of radical freedom and the diminishing returns of the market-led model it assumes can deliver it. One of the more eclectic choices on the list is Sue Kauffman's 1967 *Diary of a Mad Housewife*. The book is notable not because it recounts the frustrations of middle class American women in the late sixties, familiar from Plath's *The Bell Jar*, but because it contrasts this directly with the rise of financial speculation. The female protagonist terms her writing her 'Accounts', rejecting 'journal or diary' as the latter makes her 'think of those girls at camp, always fat and damp little girls' and the former 'Gide or Woolf or Gorky or Baudelaire, though I must admit that something like Baudelaire's "I have felt the wing of madness pass over me" comes pretty close to what I have in mind'.[8] On one side of these Accounts is the housewife's 'failure', the depression that leads to the dereliction of her domestic duties. On the other side are her husband's 'successes', the wealth he accrues through a sideline in financial speculation. In the novel's denouement the positions are reversed: the wife retreats from a dangerously liberating affair just as the husband's investments prove disastrous. The wife now takes charge 'in a Girl Scout voice that revolted even me' as the husband acknowledges that it is actually he who needs therapy, he who needs 'a complete character change, a rehabilitation'.[9] Failure is actually success when the expanding social horizons of America are contrasted against the narrowing of financial speculation.

Gaddis' suggestive pedagogy critiques a society that readily accepts failure only in order to deny its implications. His essay 'The Rush for Second Place: Missed Victories in America' (originally entitled 'Failure' when first submitted for publication) functions as an introduction to the Bard 'Literature of Failure' course. In it Gaddis condemns America for accepting failure, 'even impotence is briefly chic; the movie screen offers the dreary sentimental humanisms of Woody Allen achieved at the expense of cast and audience alike and, for the beer crowd, *Rocky*' whilst also emptying out the possibility that failure correspond to the 'final assertion of accountability' and produces instead only '"successful survivors"'.[10]

Gaddis was also interested in failure as an aesthetic freedom from the demands of a commercial literary marketplace. Formally uncompromising and Joycean in its allusiveness, his work provides no easy or passive read. In one recent version of 'The Great American Novel' debate, for example, he is cast as a modernist 'Mr Difficult' in comparison to the 'pleasure and connection' that a postmodernist Jonathan Franzen provides.[11] Indeed, Gaddis' erudition goes way beyond that suggested by his 'Literature of Failure' reading list, as Steven Moore's exhaustive compendium of his references suggests.[12] The formal and intertextual 'difficulty' of Gaddis' writing marked his career in ways that critics interested in failure have not been slow to note: Dan Visel, for example, put Gaddis alongside Stein and Melville as a writer consistently thwarted by commercialism: '*The Recognitions* is the work of an author who hadn't published a book. *JR* is the work of an author who had ... *The Recognitions* depicts a world of artists, good and bad, which is periodically disturbed by the forces of commerce. *JR* might be an inversion of this: it depicts a world of commerce through which artists struggle to make their way'.[13]

The specific 'sourcebook' for Gaddis' 1975 novel *JR* was Norbert Wiener's 1950 *The Human Use of Human Beings: Cybernetics and Society*. I want to develop the significance of Gaddis' use of Wiener in order to elucidate what it suggests about the necessity of failure as a site of both political and aesthetic resistance. In Wiener Gaddis found a thinker who had his roots in the postwar economic empiricism that Gaddis loathed so much, the 'analytic revolution of the 1950s [that ...] enthroned mathematical reasoning', but who resisted its triumphalist conclusions, preferring instead to focus upon the inevitability of entropy.[14] Wiener is thus an appropriately ambivalent and notoriously difficult figure in American intellectual history. He drew cybernetics, the conflation of man and machine that is at the heart of so much postmodern thinking, from his war-time research whilst explicitly condemning the militarisation of knowledge in the immediate postwar period.[15] He developed the mathematical formulae that made the 'quant revolution' in finance possible whilst writing caustically about the social implications of American fantasies of financial escape.[16] Wiener represents, then, an alternative trajectory in post-war American intellectual life, one that clearly contributed to the neoliberal, militarised logic of 'risk management' described by writers such as Randy Martin and Phillip Mirowski, whilst also critiquing it in vociferous ways.

Understanding Gaddis' adaptation of Wiener's critiques, and their relevance for neoliberalism, rests on two relatively discrete arguments. Firstly, I want to contextualise the work of Wiener within this postwar intellectual history, specifically the history of neoliberalism. I do this by making evident both the close parallels and important divergences between Wiener and his erstwhile war-time colleague, Milton Friedman. This reading contextualises Wiener's writing about risk and failure in terms of the wider meanings these concepts were gaining in postwar America and contrasts Wiener against Friedman as the latter has come to embody the most truculent, and crudely simplified, version of a neoliberal empiricism that denied the possibility of its own failure. The second section focuses on Gaddis' *JR*, drawing out the ways in which the novelist used Wiener in order to make evident what he was suggesting about the critical importance of failure as a site of critique. In this section I highlight how the 'difficult' formal properties of the novel offer their own parodic critique of an empirical methodology: as they force us to question what it is that we know we know in an entirely different way.

Wiener and Friedman were both part of a generation of intellectuals that participated in the rapid technological developments that took place during the war and shaped the 'information society' that emerged in its aftermath. Both were members of the University of Columbia's Statistical Research Grouping in the early forties, Wiener as a consultant and Friedman as a core member, and developed statistical research methods to improve the performance of antiaircraft ordnance. Philip Mirowski's history of neoliberalism, *Machine Dreams; Economic Becomes a Cyborg Science*, notes that the group had been carefully chosen and the intellectual principles that underpinned its coherence were made clear when it formed the basis 'of what later became known as the "Chicago School"'.[17] Mirowksi argues that the move from statistical war-research to neoliberal economics that the SRG embodied was actually characteristic of the development of much postwar American economic thinking, also evident in the RAND corporation in Santa Monica 'which had a profound influence on the evolution of the Cowles Commission' and the Rad Lab at MIT which was to shape the institutions' postwar economics department.[18] Mirowski's contentions regarding the centrality of military preoccupations to postwar economics, especially to the languages of risk, have been more recently echoed by Randy Martin. Martin cites Wiener in particular when describing the 'mechanical models of thought and perception, operations research and systems analysis' that saw the military's mantra of 'command, control and communication' transferred to the domestic in the post-war period.[19] For Martin, the war economy moved into the information economy and rendered 'machines as smart as people and people as reliable as machines, on the assumption that the machinic and humanistic ideals can be applied in practice to places where people work with technology. As such, the utopias are as much about labour that doesn't resist being told what to do as they are about frictionless machines'.[20]

Friedman and Wiener were both expansive about the importance of their research in realising this new science-led utopia. The shared assumption regarding the generalised applicability of statistical research to everyday life led them both to be accused of a scientific imperialism. Wiener's cybernetics, as Kathryn Hayles has noted, presented itself as a 'science of information that would remap existing intellectual terrains. Branching out in disciplines as different as biology, psychology and electrical engineering, it claimed to be a universal solvent that would dissolve traditional disciplinary boundaries'.[21] Friedman's 'rational choice theory' made similar claims, as its assumptions about the consistency and reliability of risk analysis – of rational decision making – was extended into all areas of human life. Friedman, as recent historical accounts of neoliberalism have made clear, was pivotal in both simplifying and popularising the core messages that had formed around the Mont Pelerin society and his cruder vision of rational decision making was quickly extended to education and training, to government and states, to the familial and domestic spheres.[22] Indeed, a recent interview with Gary Becker begins by noting that the term 'economic imperialism' has entirely lost its initial negative connotations and that 'American economists nowadays have grown to use [it] with almost complete self-confidence'.[23]

The originator of cybernetics, Wiener had a close but ambivalent relationship to the intersections between military, scientific and economic thinking in postwar America. He worked alongside key figures of the nascent 'Chicago School' during the Second World War and afterwards he shared the grandiose assumption that their predicative accounts of risk were capable of changing the world. Yet Wiener was also fiercely critical of the language of militarised success that characterised what was to become a neoliberal theory of risk, and his emphasis upon entropy, upon the inevitably of failure, made him appear a maverick for much of his career. Wiener's influence, although less epoch-defining, is also substantial: the cybernetic thinking that has informed much of what we know and experience of the digital age has its roots in Wiener's insights and his work on mathematical probability is recognised by no less a figure than Robert C Merton as a key component of the financial quant revolutions of the 1990s.[24] Yet, as I want to explore, Wiener's influence is much less easy to wholly recuperate into these narratives and it is his, perhaps uncharacteristic, diffidence that provided Gaddis with an alternative interpretation of recent intellectual history.

The brash confidence that allowed both Friedman and Wiener to extend their disciplinary expertise over such a wide area was grounded in their wartime research: in a shared commitment to the centrality of the rational subject who is formed through a continuous dialogue with the evidence provided by their own experiential knowledge. Both published seminal work in the early fifties establishing this as a methodological principle, but extrapolated from it a set of very different implications.

The relationship between the machine and the subject that is at the centre of Wiener's 1950 *The Human Use of Human Beings: Cybernetics and*

Society maintains that 'the individuality of a mind lies in the retention of its earlier tapings and memory, and in its continued development along lines already laid out'.[25] Wiener was interested in the parallels between the feedback mechanisms of early computers and the mind of the 'living individual' and his thesis is that 'in both of them, their *performed* action on the outer world, and not merely their *intended* action, is reported back to the central regulatory apparatus'. For Wiener, language is a performative act that inaugurates a continuous and self-reflexive loop of exchange and development: to be 'alive in the figurative sense to what is happening in the world, means to participate in a continual development of knowledge and its unhampered exchange' (*Human Use*, p135). He compares people to mechanical devices because both are 'taping' machines that record and respond to external stimuli in ways that stress the rational decision making at the core of the subject: 'the physical identity of an individual does not consist in the matter of which it is made … the biological individuality of an organism seems to lie in a certain continuity of process, and in the memory by the organism of the effects of its past development' (*Human Use*, p108).

Friedman's description of his own methodology in the early fifties also presents a subject defined by a rational calculation of empirical evidence, although the desire to maintain this response above all others led to his controversial and counter-intuitive rejection of that he calls 'realism'. It was, as Daniel T. Rogers has recently noted, a 'heroic analytical simplification' that Friedman was always happy to defend.[26] His aim, he clearly stated in his methodological essay of 1953 'Utility analysis of choices involving risk', was 'to provide a system of generalisation that can be used to make correct predictions about the consequence of any change in circumstances. Its performance is to be judged by the precision, scope and conformity with experience of the predictions it yields'. Friedman's narrow focus on the ability of the hypothesis to accurately predict a set of empirically proved results effectively served to filter out any of the extraneous and contingent complications of lived experience as something that is 'clearly unobtainable and the question whether a theory is realistic "enough" can be settled only by seeing whether it yields predictions that are good enough for the purpose in hand or are better than predictions from alternative theories'.[27]

Yet Wiener and Friedman treated the implications of this mechanised rationality in very different ways. Friedman assumed it to be a stable and endlessly repeatable process, so much so that Mirowski suggested that his logic remained crudely rooted in the wartime thinking of 'Operations

Research' (OR): 'the Chicago school of economics, with its rough and ready pragmatism, about the nature of the underlying objective functions, *was little more than Blackett's OR imported back into economics* ... assume repeated operations tend to a maximum of the function. Marvel at the extent to which large bodies of men and equipment behave in "an astonishingly regular manner". Treat the set of designated causes as comprising a closed system, invoking ceteris paribus if necessary to avoid the fact that the list cannot be exhaustive'.[28] Wiener's model of cybernetic feedback assumed the opposite: it was inherently entropic, founded upon the process of degradation suggested by the 'second law of thermodynamics, which asserts that a system may lose order and regularity spontaneously, but that it practically never gains it' (*Human Use*, p7). Wiener may apply a rational mechanistic language to the subject, viewing the 'human being as a terminal machine' possessing a 'communication network' but this language produces failure rather than success: 'we can show by general considerations that phonetic language contains less over-all information when compared with the input ... and that both semantic and behaviour language contain less still. This fact is again a form of the second law of thermodynamic' (*Human Use*, p91).

The differences between the two positions became overtly political as Wiener brought them to bear on the narratives of progression that were informing public debate in the postwar period, noting that 'most of us are too involved in this world of progress to take cognisance of the fact that this belief in progress belongs only to a small part of recorded history' (*Human Use*, p26). Wiener's account of the rhetoric of Manifest Destiny is particularly scathing as he explicitly connects it to the self-creative fantasies of finance capital that are predicated upon denying the sources of their own wealth. He contradicts American pioneering fantasies of origin, suggesting that 'New England' was actually a 'community of merchant adventurers' who quickly became 'a community of rentiers, of absentee landlords' bolstered by the 'new gospel' of 'Christian Science' and notes that the 'owner of gilt-edged bonds is prone to deny any contact with the source of his income, and any responsibility for the means by which it is obtained. In this rentier heaven, the prospect of floating through eternity on a continual magic carpet of other people's inventions seems no more remote than any reality of life. Responsibility has been banished with death and sickness' (*Human Use*, pp29-30). Alongside this 'comfortable passive aspect of the belief in progress', that underpins American nationalism, Wiener further notes, 'there is another one which seems to have a more masculine, vigorous connotation. To the average American, progress means the winning of the West. It means the economic anarchy of the frontier' (*Human Use*, p30). Wiener concludes his acerbic account of the exploitations that underlay the apparently sanguine twinning of finance capital with American nationalism by castigating 'our national hero [who] has been the exploiter who has done the most to turn this endowment into ready cash. In our theories of free enterprise, we have exalted him as if he had been the creator of the riches which he has stolen and squandered ... thus in depending on the future of invention to extricate us from the situations into which our squandering of our natural resources has brought us we are manifesting our national love for gambling and our national worship of the gambler, but in circumstances in which no intelligent gambler would care to make a bet' (*Human Use*, pp37-40).

Wiener's account of the 'cheap optimism in vogue among the more conservative sort of economists' might well have been a prescient description not only of Friedman but also of the languages of his supporters who were keen to realise America as a 'rentier heaven' once more in the postwar period (*Human Use*, p53). Indeed, it was precisely the desire to rationalise the action of the gambler behaving in what are ostensibly irrational ways that underpinned Friedman's exclusion of the varied complexities of lived experience, of the 'real', in favour of the predicative capabilities of his theories. Friedman found, as Abraham Hirsch and Neil De Marchi have explained, 'that he could explain gambling only on the basis of a utility function which would not generally be considered plausible (i.e. did not look "right")' hence Friedman was 'faced with maintaining the traditional view that gambling could not be explained by economic theory or rejecting the traditional methodological prejudice which required that assumptions be plausible. He chose the latter course. One element in his procedure was an argument that it is not essential that individuals are *aware* that they actually prefer risk but rather that their observed behaviour is "as if" they do in some instances'.[29]

Friedman's justification of the rationality of the gamble was to feed a view in which the risk-taker was central to a masculinised fantasy of entitlement and reward that characterised the financialised cultures of the very early seventies. Early supporters of financial deregulation, such as Leo Melamed (Chair of the Chicago Mercantile Exchange), repeatedly called upon the language of the frontier in celebrating financialisation. When the first International Monetary Market opened in the Chicago Merc in the early seventies Melamed was triumphant in precisely the terms that Wiener mocks: 'futures trading today represents one of the last frontiers of the business world. A frontier where the courageous trader must rely solely on his own ingenuity and common sense ... where the challenges demand intelligence, fortitude, character and adventuresome spirit and where the reward justifies the risks'.[30] This nationalist language of the pioneering spirit required a somewhat awkward reconciliation with financial technologies that posed themselves resolutely against national financial sovereignty. 'With the demise of Bretton Woods', Melamed acknowledged, 'we believed a new era was dawning, not only with respect to flexible exchange rates, but in the very essence of American psychology' as Americans would have to renegotiate its isolationism and recognise that 'the United States was no longer alone' and that the 'value of the dollar was not absolute, but relative to the value of other currencies. Indeed, we foresaw a rude awakening for many Americans'.[31]

Friedman's optimism and Wiener's pessimism diverged around their different views of the capacity of 'science' to meaningfully gauge risk. The rigid empiricism of Friedman's reliance on the apparent accuracy of prediction led him to claim that his positive economics, including its rather counter-intuitive approach to economic decision making, was an 'objective science, in precisely the same way as any of the physical sciences'.[32] This claiming the status of a physical science for conservative economics was essential to its strategic positioning and allowed its economics to be 'portrayed as self-sufficient, abstract methods, independent of any examination of what physicists actually did or how they did it'.[33] Wiener, conversely, was fiercely critical of such crude empiricism and of the unchallenged ascendancy of science in a 'Two Cultures' dichotomy and noted that the 'present age is anomalous' in the lowly status that it accorded 'intellectuals or men of letters' in comparison to that of the 'scientists'. Wiener deplores the lowering of standards in a system of mass education where a challenging education 'came to have the significance of a special privilege for the brilliant' and rejects 'the curious idea' that democracy 'involves an education which is not beyond the capacity of the dullest' (*Human Use*, p153 and p157). Wiener considers that it is the industrialisation of the arts, the financial demands and constraints of mass media forms such as cinema, magazines, radio, that are to blame for the 'sterility' of art and literature. The 'arts', he laments, 'are in the hands of entrepreneurs who cannot afford to take a risk' who cannot afford, in other words, to face the possibility of failure (*Human Use*, p47).

Wiener's *The Human Use of Human Beings* lies barely beneath the surface of William Gaddis' 1975 novel *JR*, as it models failure as a critical response to a still-emerging neoliberalism, especially as it was shaping the discourses of high finance. Gaddis' novel draws out the militarised implications of the languages of financial risk, their origins in, and inextricability from, fantasies of American imperialism, whilst also making evident that a critique of this language must primarily be a *formal* one: it is neoliberalism's ability to define the terms of its own debate that Gaddis' novel proves so adept at parodying. For Gaddis, failure was the necessary cost of both experimentation and social change, and literature offered the space for talking back to the assumptions gripping the social sciences.

JR is constructed, almost in its entirety, by unattributed dialogue. The novel gives us sounds, and refers us to seeing, but primarily uses direct discourse rather than the mimesis of most prose fiction. This is, as its own protagonist ruefully notes, a 'hard' novel and the reader is required to work to construct any meaning at all from it. One way to read its difficulty is as an echo of Wiener and Friedman's methodological emphasis on the primacy of experiential knowledge: the lack of narrative continuity, context or sign-posting requires the reader to evaluate what it is that they know and how they know it from the writing at every point in the novel. The conclusions that Gaddis encourages the reader to reach regarding this process are, unsurprisingly, much closer to the frustrations of Wiener's entropy than to Friedman's positivism. Yet failure begins, rather than ends, Gaddis' critical resistance to Friedman's logic.

The novel's use of unassigned speech, for example, requires the reader to identify protagonists primarily through their speech patterns, vocabularies and personal concerns. It is one of the novel's major ironies that these speeches are rendered recognisable more by their reliance on pre-existing discourses than by the individual speech markers of the characters. As Joseph Tabbi, one of Gaddis' closest readers, has argued, Gaddis lets the 'language of systems – office talk, depositions, press releases, legal judgements and such – act as a medium through which his own work, as fiction, achieves its form … composing largely with found language, the language of headlines, talk, box carton labels, advertisements, and innumerable social others, *JR* realises an order and form of its own'.[34] Tabbi reads Gaddis through Niklas Luhmann's systems theory to suggest that Gaddis and Luhmann share an 'understanding of the self-exemplifying nature of any imposed order', the 'autopoetic circularity' of the discourses of law and economics that function through tautology. Formally, then, the novel echoes the auto-poetic assumptions of Friedman which were dependent on precisely this kind of circularity, a theoretical sleight of hand by which the 'real' is replaced by the narrowly defined predicative capacities of any theoretical position and the messy complexities of political life are excluded from consideration. Such self-confirming self-referentiality is, as Tabbi explicitly points out, also at the core of the speculative cultures of contemporary finance, that facilitate 'a shift from first-order credit to a second-order system of derivatives that make "speculation" itself the primary object ... and has shifted its bases of security from property and reliable debtors (such as states and large corporations) to speculation itself'.[35]

Entropy is used by Gaddis to explicitly unsettle and challenge the closed logic of the autopoetic circuit and he specifically focuses on law and finance. The novel's opening conversation quickly descends into farce as the two speakers, the elderly Aunts of Edward Bast, the novel's unsteady anti-hero, respond to decorously obfuscating legalese – a lawyer's attempt to ascertain their nephew's paternity – with either unending and unfinished interruptions or an apparently equally obscure and irrelevant set of family anecdotes. Yet the nonsense produced by this apparent vortex of mutual incomprehension is tightly controlled and becomes a defence against the invasive rationalisations of the lawyer. It is only when the exchange is near its increasingly fraught end that it becomes apparent that the women's dogged failure not to mishear the lawyer (the written fictiousness of which is ironically driven home by Gaddis as they are represented as addressing him with the homonym 'Cohen' despite being repeatedly told that his name is 'Coen') is revealed as capable of inverting the assumed basis of the conversation.

> – To protect his interests as well as your own re, recalling Egnaczyk versus Rowland where the infant sought to recover his car and disaffirm the repair contract the infant lost out in this case ladies, the defense of infancy in this case ladies, in this case the court refused to permit it, using infancy as a sword instead of a shield ... there! I hear something. Don't I hear him now? Your nephew coming downstairs at last?
> – Edward?
> – Hammering, Julia.
> – Yes, it couldn't be Edward. He left long ago, didn't he Anne?
> – I think I heard him leave when I was sewing that button on. He has class today you know, Mister Cohen. At the Jewish temple, rehearsing Wagner.[36]

The women's apparent failure to comprehend is revealed to be a site of effective resistance to an authority whose auto-poetic circularity makes it literally impossible to engage with. That this failure involves their ability to use their own innocence as a 'sword instead of a shield' – the very thing that Coen's example of precedent suggests he is facing – further reinforces the irony of a dialectical negation which rapidly becomes one of the novel's key formal characteristics.

The two aunts are at pains to successfully defend their nephew from an embarrassing inquisition into his own paternity, and the nature of his claim upon his uncle's (or possibly father's) Grand Roll Piano company is deferred. The choice is a deeply symbolic one in the novel as Edward Bast's two potential fathers can be read against what Wiener presented as the Manichean dangers of a cybernetic culture. He may have been the son of Thomas, the President of the General Roll Company, 'whose business is to reduce music to the separate points or "holes" of a piano role' (a technology in demand for its potential to the development of the computer) or the son of James, an internationally celebrated composer. The 'legacy' from the former, as Steven Weisenburger has pointed out, is 'one of technology, the rational separation of the musical flux into bits' whereas the latter represents 'a devotion to art and an alienation from monetary culture'.[37] The opposition between the composer and engineer could well have come straight from Wiener, as he illuminates the destruction of the arts by pointing to the fact that in 'music we have seen the dwindling of a race of composers. Performers we have in plenty, but it must be confessed that it is the composers, not the performers, who keep the flame of music burning'(*Human Use*, p145).

Bast's two absent fathers are substituted in the novel by two failing mentors. The first is the eponymous JR, the grubby avaricious school boy who spins a fraudulent empire from a series of speculative deals made from the telephone booths installed in the school lobby. The connections between JR's deals and the American military are represented as foundational to both. JR immerses himself in the trading opportunities offered by the 'Defense Surplus Sales Office' on a school trip to buy a single share of the Diamond Cable Corporation (*JR*, p79). The director of the company is introduced to the children as a frontiersman who 'opened America's industrial frontiers, her natural resources that make us the wealthiest country in the world' (*JR*, p91). The novel's account of the trip is interspersed with a dialogue between JR and a peer as they jointly canvas the trade press.

No but wait I got more. Look ... Department of Defense, Sealed Bid
Sale offering tab cards, tires, crane engines ...
What else.
Look. General Services Administration, Region Seven, sales of civilian
agency surplus property, see? Automotive, Medical, clothing, hand tools
and wait hey look, Spot Bid Sale, Defense Logistics Center, pipe fittings,
valves, hardware, generator sets, test sets and stands, electrical.......
Is that all? (*JR*, p79).

The absurdity of the borrowed language is highlighted by the appeals
to vision – look, see – as the interlocutor attempts to make tangible the
nonsensical phrases that he is reciting. The latent violence of this absurdity
is realised in JR's very first deal, in which he buys nine thousand wooden
picnic forks from the Navy and sells them to the Army. The trade is a
microcosm of an endless circuit of leveraged profits and superfluous goods
and its profound redundancy is clearly satirised in the image of the child
profiting from selling the sailor's wooden picnic fork to the soldier.

Bast's other mentor in the novel is Jack Gibbs (a figure whose name
links him directly to Josiah Willard Gibbs, the originator of the second law
of thermodynamics concerning the entropic principle). Gibbs is a stand-in
for a failed version of Gaddis himself and his recurring attempts to simply
announce the very thing that the novel is attempting to *enact* makes this
clear. At one point, for example, Gibbs begins to recite from Gaddis' own
unpublished novel *Agape Agape*, which he claims is his own, to a bemused
Bast (who notes that this writing is 'hard'). The speech is a passionate but
confused critique of the industrialisation of the arts:

> born of the beast of two backs called arts and sciences whose
> rambunctious coupling came crashing the jealous enclosures of class,
> taste, and talent, to open the arts to Americans for democratic action
> and leave history to bunk. Now Godd damn it Bast anything hard about
> that? ... A remarkable characteristics of the Americans is the manner in
> which they have applied the science to modern life Wilde marvelled on,
> struck by the noisiest country that ever existed. One is waked up in the
> morning, not by the singing of the nightingale, but by the steam whistle
> ... All art depends upon exquisite and delicate sensibility, and such
> constant turmoil must be ultimately destructive of the musical faculty
> and thus, though the flute is not an instrument which is expressive of
> moral ... what's the matter (*JR*, p289).

Gibbs is unable to realise the significance of his critique of a culture debased by science, or make sense of his references to Shakespeare, Wilde and Keats. Instead, he and Bast blunder helplessly around a room dominated by the detritus of JR's erratic business decisions. The failure of Gibbs as an authorial double confirms the necessity of *JR*'s form. Gibbs' tirade fails because it is simply that: he names the problem with a pompous literalism, hoping that 'every reader will, from this history, take warning and stamp improvement on the wings of time' whilst being simultaneously hopeless about a strategy for realising this ambition, knowing that 'most God dammed writing's written for readers perfectly happy who they are rather be at the movies' (*JR*, p289). In a parallel manner Bast's failure as a reader – appealed to by an impatient Gibbs 'anything hard about that', 'what's the matter' – confirms the necessity of our own reading practice: the reader is given their own pedagogical double in Bast and implored to accept the complexity that he cannot.

The possibilities of the text's self-reflexive account of failure can be found not, then, in this blunt reiteration of the problem but in the richly allusive and suggestive texture of the writing that it offers as an alternative. The passages that offer the reader the most textual difficulty are not Gibbs' furious recitations but the fragments of conversation that emanate from Typhon International. It is in these conversations that the financial economy's aggrandising rhetoric and promises of radical new freedoms are most viciously parodied. Typhon International's appetite for investment is insatiable and its interests range from politics, foreign affairs, defence, health and education to telecommunications, sport, and literature. The rapid and constant change in subjects and speakers allows Gaddis to parodically enact the reductive conflation of the political, social and the aesthetic to the economic that Gibbs is more vainly striving to speak to.

The privatisation of a highly technologised and alienating system of education, for example (itself one of the primary ambitions of Rose and Milton Friedman's political campaigning), is at the centre of much of the novel's financial machinations. 'Dug out the name of this educator Thomas Dewey for the PW announcement of this children's encyclopaedia', a member of Typhon International casually announces at one point, 'turned it into a crash project, team of salesmen out blanketing the city with samples of volume four pull in enough orders for the set we can go through with the other nine paying half a cent a word all that ad space bypass … hit your educable public right in the supermarket where they live' (*JR*, pp518-9). Beyond the critique of the familiar movement of capital – that turns knowledge into a commodity and then the commodity into a speculative device – is a suggestive critique of the importance of both historical nuance and complexity.

The name 'Thomas Dewey' rings false here: it seems to be a mistake. Dewey was not an educator at all, but rather a lawyer and a relatively liberal Republican Presidential nominee in the 1940s. The political histories and worldviews of the two educators who *were* named Dewey, who seem to be the more likely reference points for a children's encyclopaedia in this context, open the text to a suggestive alternative reading of this apparent mis-appropriation of the Dewey name. The most widely known educator named Dewey is, of course, the Dewey who originated the nineteenth century Dewey decimal classification system widely used to organise public libraries. This Melvil Dewey (originally Melville, but shortened as a commitment to simplifying American spelling) epitomises the idea that knowledge, specifically a 'mid-nineteenth century male white Western (and largely Christian) view of' it, can be universally ordered for a universal good. This is the very idea that Gaddis' Gibbs lectures the children explicitly against believing, and Dewey's recent biographer doesn't shy away from the prejudicial fault-lines of Dewey's work and life.[38] Yet Dewey's work also reminds us of the lost possibilities of even such personally compromised progressive ideals. His passionate commitment to liberal social reform, and especially to the role of education and the mass accessibility of the public library as a means for achieving it, aren't too far removed from the liberal principles of figures like Wiener and Gaddis.

The other potential Dewey in this context reinforces the ironical possibilities of a liberal education even further. It is, of course, John Dewey, the pragmatic philosopher and educational revolutionary. This Dewey was an important figure for Gaddis: a reference to him is included in the encyclopaedic 'player piano chronology' that is appended to the end of *Agape Agape and other writings* where Gaddis notes that in 1904, the same year that 'Thorndike published the first handbook on measurement in the social sciences and that 260,000 pianolas were built' (as opposed to only 7,000 grand pianos), that 'John Dewey comes to join philosophy department at Columbia: revolutionizes education reflecting industrial revolution and development of democracy'.[39] Dewey also appears in the citations that we are given from Gibbs' novel. Gibbs condemns the impoverishment of contemporary democracy by a technologised bureaucracy, 'roused by the steam whistle, democracy claimed technology's promise to banish failure', and wrestles with how literature itself will be 'catalogued' in this context (the frequent repetition of the word reinforcing the uncertainty as to which Dewey is being discussed). In this context, however, John Dewey is named and his 'groping for the close and intimate acquaintance got with nature at first wait' is cited as part of a tradition of writing by social activists and organisations, which includes Jack London, Stephen Crane and Chicago's Hull House. Again, Dewey speaks to the profound ambivalence of Gaddis' political identifications. On the one hand he is part of a movement that allies education with democracy and thus is complicit with the downgrading of its intent that both Gaddis and Wiener despair of. And yet, on the other, as Michael Slazy has pointed out, Dewey's aesthetic defence of the New Deal, his insistence on 'the difference between quotidian and artistic labor' and assertion that the latter offers nothing less than the 'last holdout against industrialization and the alienation of human labor' comes close to Gaddis' own position.[40] Dewey's defence echoes not only Gaddis' critique of industrialised art but the words of John Maynard Keynes, to whom he has been explicitly compared. As a citation from Dewey used by Slazy to suggest the connections with Keynes makes clear, the 'psychology and morale of business are based on trading in insecurity. They are criticised by serious moralists as if the animating spirit were that of acquisition. The accusations do not reach the mark ... It is the excitement of the game that counts ...We hunt the dollar. But hunting is hunting, not dollars'.[41]

The apparently accidental misuse of the name Dewey thus allows Gaddis to cryptically suggest a broad intellectual genealogy that resists neoliberal certainty and simplifications. As a point of resistance it is also, necessarily, dialectical, characterised by failing. It is this, after all, that Thomas Dewey has become an historical reference for: he is the only American to have failed to be elected President twice and yet his failures were, arguably, America's successes: they allowed first Roosevelt and then Truman to become President. Hence, the numbers of failures quickly mount up into something positive – the failure of Thomas and the success of the New Deal, the failures of both Melvil and John to realise their very ordered social visions which suggest both the dangerously entropic nature of order and the importance of resistance, of experimentation, itself.

The notion of failure as an aesthetic counterpart to the winner-takes-all, riskless risks of high finance, is central to the novel's conclusion. One of the ventures that fail in the novel's end is 'Frigicom', a collaboration between the Department of Defense and the JR Family of Companies. The project involves freezing sound shards in order to safely remove them from the urban environment and thus eliminate noise pollution. Frigicom reverses the implications of Walter Pater's dictum – that all art aspires to the condition of music and that the experience of beauty is akin to 'frozen music' – by presenting the aural as a contaminant that can be frozen and reworked into a weapon. The failure of Frigicom allows Gaddis to explicitly valorise the energy of the aesthetic that cannot be commodified or contained. The novel ends with a hearing of a Senate subcommittee which describes how the 'shards comprising Beethoven's Fifth symphony proved more difficult to handle than had been anticipated … Appearing before the committee with his left hand in a cast and his face partially hidden by bandages, the colourful research director stated that the injuries sustained … occurred with the entire first movement thawed in an unscheduled four seconds' (*JR*, p673). Yet, inevitably, the violent resistance of the aesthetic is too powerful to be abandoned and the hearing concludes by acknowledging that the project 'has attracted the interest of the recording industry due to the complete absence of friction associated with conventional transcription' (*JR*, p673). Gaddis' sense of irony never quite closes: the attempt to turn music into a weapon fails because the aesthetic is too powerful and yet the experiment itself produces a process able to nullify the entropy of information, to produce the 'frictionless machine' of Randy Martin's information economy.

Gaddis poses failure as a formal and thematic alternative to the tautological success story that neoliberalism has promulgated for so long. He represents its triumphalism in two ways. Firstly, the sheer difficulty of *JR*, the struggle to understand 'what matter who's speaking?', embodies Wiener's view of entropy, a recognition of the contingency that makes some kind of failure nearly inevitable. Wiener's recognition of this failure, I have attempted to argue, offers a refutation of the 'eager and terrible simplification' of Friedman's positive economics, a model that assumed it could simply filter-out contingency as extraneous to its predicative capacities.[42] *JR* suggests that the only way to resist this tautological definition of success is to establish its auto-poetic circularity as the centre of the critique: to resist engaging in its internal logic. Yet *JR*'s critique of the triumphalism of neoliberalism goes beyond these formal assumptions; it also recognises that they became powerful because they were elaborated by the powerful. He makes apparent, as had Wiener before him, that this notion of risk as success, as masculine self-realisation, spoke to the intimate connections between the war economy and the speculative economy, a set of connections that we now understand as a reframing of American imperialism in the postwar period.[43] It is hardly surprising, then, that the crude positivism of Friedman's thinking, the 'rough and ready' pragmatism of military Operations Research as Mirowski has it, came to influence the cultures of speculation that were also already indebted to a militarised language of success. There is 'no alternative' to neoliberalism, as its first British Premier so confidently claimed, not because there is no alternative but because it is so predicated on its own concept of success that it is impossible for it to be imagined.

NOTES

1. Alan Greenspan spoke to a Congressional hearing on the 'The Financial Crisis and the Role of Federal Regulators' on Thursday, 23.10.2008. His words were widely reported, see, for example, http://www.nytimes.com/2008/10/24.
2. Slavoj Žižek, *First as Tragedy, Then as Farce*, London, Verso, 2009, p37.
3. Richard Dienst, *The Bonds of Debt*, London, Verso, 2011, p168.
4. Ibid., p168.
5. Wayne Koestenbaum, 'Thomas Bernhard's Virtues', *Review of Contemporary Fiction: The Failure Issue*, Josh Cohen (ed), Spring 2011, vol xxxi, pp53-54.
6. William Gaddis, 'Syllabus, English 241, Literature of Failure', *The Review of Contemporary Fiction: The Failure Issue*, op. cit., pp116-7.
7. Dienst, *The Bonds of Debt*, op. cit., p170.
8. Sue Kaufman, *Diary of a Mad Housewife*, London, Serpents Tail, 2002, p3.
9. Ibid., p299.
10. William Gaddis, *The Rush for Second Place: Essays and Occasional Writings*, London, Penguin Books, 2002, p157.
11. J.M. Tyree, 'Is It Ok to Be a Philistine?: Franzen, Gaddis, and the Politics of Difficult Literature', *Radical Society*, December (2002).
12. http://www.williamgaddis.org/.
13. Dan Visel, 'The Failing of Americans', *The Review of Contemporary Fiction: The Failure Issue*, op. cit., p93
14. Daniel T Rogers, *The Age of Fracture*, Cambridge, Harvard University Press, 2011, p45.
15. See Flo Conway and Jim Siegelman, *Dark Hero of the Information Age: In Search of Norbert Wiener, the Father of Cybernetics*, New York, Perseus Books, 2005 and Peter Galison, 'The Ontology of the Enemy: Norbert Wiener and the Cybernetic Vision', *Critical Inquiry*, 21, 1, (1994): 228-66.
16. Robert C. Merton, 'On the Role of the Wiener Process in Finance Theory and Practice: The Case of Replicating Portfolios', *Proceedings of Symposia in Pure Mathematics*, 60. The legacy of Norbert Wiener: a centennial symposium in honour of the 100th Anniversary of Norbert Wiener's Birth (1997).
17. Philip Mirowski, *Machine Dreams: Economics Becomes a Cyborg Science*, Cambridge, Cambridge University Press, 2001, p203, http://doi.org/c9v288.
18. Ibid., p203.

19. Randy Martin, *American War and the Financial Logic of Risk Management*, New York, Duke University Press, 2007, p71.

20. Ibid., p73.

21. Katherine N. Hayles, *How We Became Posthuman: Virtual Bodies in Cybernetics, Literature, and Informatics*, Chicago, University of Chicago Press, 1999, p85, http://doi.org/n5g.

22. See Daniel Stedman Jones, *Masters of the Universe: Hayek, Friedman and the Birth of Neoliberal Politics*, Princeton, Princeton University Press, 2012, Angus Burgin, *The Great Persuasion: Reinventing Free Market Since the Depression*, Cambridge, Mass., Harvard University Press, 2012.

23. Karen Ilse Horn, 'Gary S Becker', *Roads to Wisdom, Conversations with Ten Nobel Laureates in Economics*, Karen Ilse Horn (ed), Cheltenham, Edward Elgar Publishing, 2009, p134.

24. Merton, 'On the Role of the Wiener Process', op. cit.

25. Norbert Wiener, *The Human Use of Human Beings: Cybernetics and Society*, London, Eyre and Spottiswoode, 1950, p108, hereafter in the text as *Human Use*.

26. Rogers, *The Age of Fracture*, op. cit., p51.

27. Milton Friedman, *Essays in Positive Economics*, Chicago, Chicago University Press, 1953, p41.

28. Mirowski, *Machine Dreams*, op. cit., p204.

29. Abraham Hirsch and Neil De Marchi, *Milton Friedman: Economics in Theory and Practice*, London, Harvester Wheatsheaf, 1990.

30. Leo Melamed, *Leo Melamed on the Market: Twenty Years of Financial History as Seen by the Man Who Revolutionized the Markets*, New York, John Wiley & Sons, 1993, p7.

31. Leo Melamed, 'The Sleazy Speculator' speech to the University of Chicago Law School, 27.11.1974.

32. Friedman, *Essays in Positive Economics*, op. cit.

33. Philip Mirowski, 'Shall I Compare Thee to a Monkowski – Ricardo – Leontief – Metzler Matrix of the Mosak-Hicks Type', in Arjo Klamer, Donald N. McCloskey and Robert M. Solow (eds), *The Consequences of Economic Rhetoric*, Cambridge, Cambridge University Press, 1988.

34. Joseph Tabbi, 'William Gaddis and the Autopoesis of American Literature', in Joseph Tabbi and Rone Shavers (eds), *Paper Empire: William Gaddis and the World System*, Tuscaloosa, University of Alabama Press, 2007, pp106-7.

35. Tabbi, 'William Gaddis and the Autopoesis of American Literature', op. cit., p15.

36. William Gaddis, *JR*, London, Atlantic Books, 2005, p16.

37. Steven Weisenburger, 'Paper Currencies: Reading William Gaddis' in John Kuehl and Steven Moore (eds), *In Recognition of William Gaddis*, Syracuse, Syracuse University Press, 1984, p151.

38. Wayne Wiegand, *Irrepressible Reformer: A Biography of Melvil Dewey*, American Library Association, 1986, p33.

39. William Gaddis, *Agape Agape and Other Writings*, London, Atlantic Books, 2002, p258.

40. Michael Szalay, *New Deal Modernism: American Literature and the Invention of the Welfare State*, Durham, NC, Duke University Press, 2000, p66.

41. Ibid., p56.

42. Rogers, *The Age of Fracture*, op. cit., p51.

43. See, for example, Leo, Panitch and Sam Gindin, 'Global Capitalism and American Empire', in *The New Imperial Challenge: The Socialist Register*, 2004, and Christian Marazzi, *Capital and Language: From the New Economy to the War Economy*, Gregory Conti (trans), Los Angeles, *Semiotext(e)*, 2008.

ATMS, TELEPROMPTERS AND PHOTOBOOTHS: A SHORT HISTORY OF NEOLIBERAL OPTICS

Mark Hayward

INTRODUCTION

The term 'neoliberal optics' refers to the uses of light that contribute to forms of sociality and subjectivity that constitute neoliberal culture. In the discussion of neoliberal optics that follows, two tendencies in neoliberal culture are focused on: the distribution and extension of elements of the self and body by technological means and the appropriation of forms of direct, personal address in order to maintain and exploit affective engagement on the part of individuals towards institutions. This essay examines the role that optical technologies play in the above-mentioned components of neoliberal subjectivity and embodiment by means of an historical analysis of three technologies and their associated practices: the popular photographic self-portrait made possible via the photo booth, the teleprompter and the automated teller machine (ATM). These technologies are popular sites where the intersecting, and at times contradictory, tendencies of fragmentation and engagement common in neoliberal culture are enacted.

The essay is divided into two parts. In the first section, the discussions of the teleprompter and the self-portrait provide a general overview of some key characteristics of neoliberal optics, situating them within a broader cultural context. The discussion of the ATM in the second part of the paper contributes to the preceding discussion of neoliberal optics in a different manner, complicating and extending the claims made in the first part. Rather than simply providing more evidence of those aspects of neoliberal optics discussed in regard to the teleprompter and the self-portrait, the historical development of the ATM draws attention to the ways that, while neoliberal optics continue to be of considerable importance in neoliberal culture, these logics do not wholly define contemporary experience of visual phenomena. However, as much as the implementation of the ATM differed from the structures of neoliberal optics discussed in the first part of the paper, the dynamics of neoliberal optics have been repeatedly invoked throughout the ATM's development as a way of overcoming anxieties surrounding the technology with regard to personal security and engagement.

While invented and introduced before neoliberalism became hegemonic, the technologies discussed here speak directly to the optical aspects of the present conjuncture. For this reason, before exploring these devices further, it is worth pausing to consider the nature of the 'neoliberal' in neoliberal optics. Several scholars have identified neoliberalism with the consolidation of a set of concepts and assumptions in economic theory and public policy in the 1960s and 1970s in various parts of the world with origins going back to the 1930s.[1] At the heart of this tradition of neoliberalism are claims regarding the perfect efficiency of market structures and the superiority of competition between individuals rather than other forms of social interaction. The technologies discussed here are not direct products of such beliefs. Yet recognition of this independence from the 'market fundamentalism' of neoliberalism should not be taken as an argument for the autonomous development of neoliberal culture. Rather, it is recognition that neoliberalism is a complex social formation that involves many different elements; it is more than simply a body of conceptual and theoretical arguments about the economy which has subsequently been implemented within various contexts, a process by which 'neoliberalism proper' fans out across society.[2] The technologies discussed here, and their analysis in light of neoliberal optics, draw our attention to the way that a number of pre-existing technologies and cultural practices have been enlisted in the service of the process of neoliberalization. And, by focusing the ways in which they contributed to forms of technologically-augmented subjectivity as well as the maintenance of affective engagement, they draw attention to the 'regime of individuation' that determine modes of existence and ways of living that define neoliberalism.[3]

In the discussion that follows, the popular self-photography and the optical teleprompter are used as examples because both inventions separate the subject as the source of intentional perception from the site of presence. The teleprompter calls into question the idea of the public figure as a unified, intentional subject and positions them as puppet or actor in their public remarks at the same time as it produces forms of direct, albeit mediated, forms of address through screen. Along related lines, and following numerous historians of the self-portrait, the optical relations of self-photography (particularly in the popular version to which the photobooth would contribute) fundamentally transform the relationship between the object and subject of photography. The gaze of the television presenter is only 'natural' when looking through the glass of the teleprompter; and you are only yourself on film when looking through the mirrored aperture of the photobooth. By looking at the role of Luther George Simjian in the development of these inventions, this essay will explore the institutional, cultural and technological formations that would come to determine some key characteristics of the distributed self and body that constitute the individual in neoliberalism, from neoclassical economics to contemporary art practices.[4]

In this way, developing the concept of neoliberal optics by means of an historical analysis of these technologies compliments, rather than contradicts, both research analyzing subjectivity in age of distributed, or networked, technology as well as the ways in which various technologies have been used to produce forms of intimacy necessary for the exploitation of affective and immaterial labour that are central to neoliberal capitalism. The focus on the *optical* serves as a necessary compliment to the study of *representations* that serve to create, constrain and manage forms of subjectivity conducive to neoliberal governance, on the one hand, and *technologies* of subjective affective engagement and subjective extension fragmentation such as those found in discussions of mobile technologies. (It is worth noting here, although only in passing, that Simjian also made significant contributions to the development of the flight simulator, certainly a privileged site of the distributed militarised body, as founder of the Reflectone corporation that continues to build commercial and military simulators as CAE Incorporated.)

LUTHER GEORGE SIMJIAN AND NEOLIBERAL OPTICS

Luther George Simjian's self-published *Portions of an Autobiography* offers a suggestive, if unintentional, entry point into material configurations that constitute neoliberal optics.[5] An Armenian born in Turkey, Simjian emigrated to the United States in 1920 where he found employment as a technician and later administrator in the photography labs of the medical school of Yale University. Bored with medical photography after a few years, Simjian recounts how he turned his attention towards other projects, eventually becoming a professional inventor and entrepreneur. The owner of dozens of patents, three of these inventions in particular stand out in relation to the subsequent role of the optical within neoliberal culture: the optical teleprompter, a camera designed for photographing oneself (marketed as the PhotoReflex), and an early version of automated teller machines.[6] Simjian's significance to the analysis of neoliberal culture is not as the inventor of the photographic self-portrait, just as he was not the sole inventor of the teleprompter. Rather, Simjian's contributions involve the development of optical innovations which extended and transformed already existing socio-technical assemblages. The biographical link that binds them together often goes unremarked, and does not, on its own, constitute the field of neoliberal optics. However, Simjian's role in the invention and development of these technologies draws attention to their shared relationship to the uses of light in the second half of the twentieth century.

The purpose of presenting the origins of these three optical devices is two-fold: first, to make an argument that Simjian's career as an inventor highlights the extent to which the optical retains significance in the contemporary era; second, to demonstrate that they are sites which contribute to the form that the individual takes under neoliberal hegemony. Jonathan Crary's seminal work on the place of optical sciences within nineteenth century culture is helpful for contextualising these inventions in relation to broader shifts in the practices and technologies of neoliberal culture. In *Techniques of the Observer*, Crary describes the ways in which optical science, as well as photographic and proto-filmic media, mirror and complicate theories of the subject emerging in medical sciences and psychoanalysis. He writes,

> From the beginning of the nineteenth century a science of vision will tend to mean increasingly an interrogation of the makeup of the human subject, rather than of the mechanics of light and optical transmission. It is a moment when the visible escapes from the timeless incorporeal order of the camera obscura and becomes lodged in another apparatus, within the unstable physiology and temporality of the human body.[7]

For Crary, this shift is part of what he calls, borrowing a phrase from Foucault, 'the threshold of our modernity.' Yet, in turning to the field of optics as traced in Simjian's autobiography, one notes a different thematic from that which Crary draws from his study of optics in the nineteenth century. The function of the optical is no longer the embedding of vision within the unstable human body, but the fragmentation and distribution of the perceiving subject, even in relation to one's 'own' body, by means of technology. Yet the distribution of the self is not an experience of attenuation of experience or alienation. Rather, it serves to produce greater intimacy and engagement.

In histories of the teleprompter, the claim for the invention of an automatic cueing device is often credited to Hubert Schlafly, an engineer working with the CBS television network, and Fred Barton, an actor, in the 1950s.[8] However, the mechanical cueing device developed by Schlafly and Barton was quickly improved upon and replaced by the optical teleprompter proposed almost simultaneously by Simjian and Jess Oppenheimer, best known as the creator and producer of the classic American sitcom, *I Love Lucy*. The advantage of the optical teleprompter proposed by Simjian and Oppenheimer was its ability to break down the division between the viewer and person on camera by allowing for direct eye contact on the part of the presenter with the camera aperture (see figure 1). In his patent application, Simjian explains the improvements the optical system made to existing technologies, writing that the older methods of prompting have proved insufficient for a variety of reasons because

> The speaker may look at the placards so intensely for help that the use of such prompting becomes very obvious due to the aversion of the speaker's eyes from the aperture of the camera ... Furthermore, if the speaker focuses his eyes on a screen located in a place materially beyond the camera, the personal 'touch' between the speaker and the viewing audience is lost.[9]

Oppenheimer, in his patent application for a similar optical prompting system, notes that the advantage of this system is not simply improving the ability of actors and news presenters to 'look' their audiences in the eye, but also has 'psychological value ... since even accomplished speakers and actors are given a feeling of confidence by the availability of script material'.[10]

Given his extensive examination of the relationship between writing and presence, it is not surprising that Jacques Derrida turns to the teleprompter on several occasions when reflecting on the forms that subjectivity and agency take under televisual hegemony. For Derrida, the teleprompter is central to the production of artifactuality, that set of material and representational relations in which what is 'actual' is 'not given but actively produced, sifted, invested, performatively interpreted by numerous apparatuses which are factitious or artificial, hierarchizing and selective, always in the service of forces and interests to which 'subjects' and agents (producers and consumers of actuality – sometimes they are "philosophers" and always interpreters, too) are never sensitive enough'.[11] His primary example of the infrastructure of artifactuality or actufactuality is 'when a journalist or politician seems to be speaking to us, in our homes, while looking us straight in the eye, he (or she) is in the process of reading, on screen, at the dictation of a 'prompter,' a text composed somewhere else, at some other time, sometimes by others, or even a whole network of anonymous authors'.[12] For Derrida, the introduction of such technologies is cause for suspicion regarding the structure of scopic relations between the televisual subject and the audience (as is evident in Derrida's neologism 'artifactuality'). Echoes of this position can be heard in popular anxieties about the teleprompter and its status as one of the focal points for interrogating the nature of mediated authenticity in public life (with Barack Obama's use of the technology serving as a consistent talking point for critics and satirists alike.)

However, such an approach runs the risk of overstating the pre-televisual as outside of these relations of reality production. This is a point that Paddy Scannell has recently addressed, noting that the question is not the extent to which television distorted 'reality' (and produces forms of 'actufactuality'), but the ways in which devices like the teleprompter were 'contributive to the overall communicative ethos of television as talk-as-conversation and its implicit normative underpinnings'.[13] The broader significance of the teleprompter, then, is the production of a form of public intersubjectivity

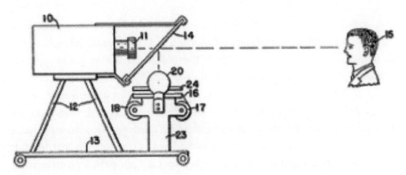

Figure 1, Simjian's prompting device, showing the line of sight towards both the camera's aperture and the script (US Patent #2,796,801 – 'Prompting Device').

which is personalised rather than distant, formal and institutional in its modes of address. As Scannell explains, building on his analysis of the teleprompter, 'Radio and television did not invent conversation, but they have made it the dominant, preferred style of talk in public since they entered into general social life'.[14]

In this way, Simjian's contribution must be interpreted as more than simply a contribution to the technological infrastructure of television, but a material shift in those techniques which structure norms about how to present oneself while on screen as natural and comfortable before physically absent audiences. There are a variety of venues in which the modes of address made possible by the teleprompter have been operationalised including, as will be discussed below, the ATM. Common across all of these areas, and already referred to in the discussions of the optical teleprompter's uses presented by Simjian and Oppenheimer, is the relationship that the modes of address have to engagement, trust as well as the more ephemeral forms of affective connection connoted by the idea of the 'personal touch.' In this way, the contribution that the teleprompter made to the production of televisual intimacy starting in the 1950s must be situated as an enabling support for the increasingly important role that affect plays, whether as part of a process for identity formation or as productive labour itself, within the reconfiguration of the division between personal and public life and the distinction between cognitive and physical activity that defines the regime of exploitation of expropriation under neoliberalism.

Turning to Simjian's account of the development of the PhotoReflex – an apparatus for seeing oneself while taking one's own picture – one finds a similar blending of the personal and the public in the transformation the device effected in the practice of taking photographic self-portraits. The invention of the PhotoReflex was, according to Simjian, the pivotal experience that transformed him from technician to inventor. His inspiration for the device, he recounts in his autobiography, was his unhappiness with the repetitive nature of portraits in Yale's student yearbook. In his telling of the story:

> I noticed that every student in the book looked alike in his or her expression. I couldn't believe that they had all gone through four years of learning and come out with the same expression on their faces. There was something funny about this ... I went one afternoon [to the studio]. And I noticed that he [the photographer] told every student, 'Pose this way, look this way, smile this way', and he directed

them in exactly what they should do ... Well, I said, this is where the problem is. These people are made to pose according to this man's direction. They go for four years of education, and in the end they're all made to look alike.[15]

The purpose of the 'pose-reflecting system for photographic apparatus' he designed was a democratisation of self-representation in photography. Simjian sums up this break with the traditional portrait declaring: 'These people have to be their own photographers, so they can pose themselves as they would like to be'.[16]

In Simjian's telling, this democratisation of photographic self-representation – 'posing themselves as they would like to be' – is one that cannot be separated from the institutions of the upper middle class of the eastern United States (as evident in the repeated invocations of 'four years of education'). Yet its eventual use in photobooths link it to the practices of popular personal photography that were foundational to the expansion of photographic self-portraiture (see figure 2). Richard Hornsey observes the importance of this mode of self-expression that followed the introduction of the *Photomaton* in Britain:

What they saw in the reflection of their face (and later reproduced on the strip of printed photographs) was the visualisation of their own free sovereignty and ontological security as a unique individual. The photobooth, therefore, offered the mass urban populace a new process of individuation, not just by expanding the number of people who sat for their portrait, but by implicating them, pictorially and architecturally, within a specific articulation of their own personal sovereignty.[17]

Hornsey's discussion of the photobooth draws particular attention to its architectural form, at once a 'degraded evocation' of the camera obscura and intimate private space within the flow of urban traffic. However, at the centre of the social and spatial relations that resulted from its use, the practice of photobooth photography entailed a popular form of self-representation. Echoing Simjian's statement about posing 'as they would like to be', Hornsey writes that 'The booth became an enclosure in which one could playfully try out multiple presentations of self as fleeting and inconsequential as the apparatus and its output, and a rehearsal space for a diverse set of performances in an increasingly mediated city'.[18] In the photobooth, in which the reflective image of the subject is incorporated into photographic practice (in other words, the PhotoReflex), appears the reflexive production of images of the self in real time.

While such forms of reflexivity in representations were not new in the twentieth century, their transformation into a mass practice should be seen, as Hornsey argues, as a visual complement to the shifting horizon of the modern subject. The idea of personal sovereignty found in photobooth photography is echoed in Simjian's descriptions of the PhotoReflex from the 1920s, where it is described as a way of letting the photographic subject appear as their true selves, freed from the constraints of being laid out on display before the camera by the photographer or feelings of being 'self-conscious'. 'It is claimed', a profile in the Yale College newspaper describing the invention from 1929 explains, 'that all self consciousness will be taken out of the art of photography by the invention of a camera in which the subject is his own photographer'.[19]

The idea of the photobooth as potential resource for self-realisation and transformation, which resonates with the notion of commodities as tools for both consumption and cultural resistance, is much closer to the

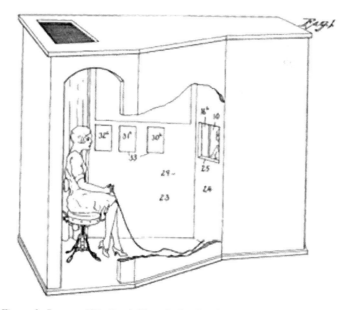

Figure 2, Image of Simjian's PhotoReflex Booth with mirrors for multiple perspectives from the patent application (US Patent #1,830,770 – 'Pose-Reflecting System for Photographic Apparatus').

practices and critical discourses that precede the hegemony of neoliberal logics (a moment capably and extensively analysed by cultural studies in the 1960s and 1970s.) Yet, by underestimating the extent to which these photos, self-posed or not, continued to serve a number of institutional purposes – such as on a variety of forms of official identification – such approaches to popular portraiture are insufficient for analysing their status within neoliberal culture. The narrative of the PhotoReflex's invention dramatises the break between mass portraiture and the tradition of bureaucratic portraits. This older tradition of bureaucratic portraiture was, in the words of John Tagg, a process involving the accumulation of 'a vast and repetitive archive of images ... in which the smallest deviations may be noted, classified and filed'.[20] The contribution of the PhotoReflex to the formation of the neoliberal individual is the naturalisation and internalisation of the technique and technologies of visual surveillance. In the present moment, the circulation of the photographic self-portrait is increasingly managed and monitored as part of flexible structures of data. A precursor to the proliferation of 'selfies' and their centrality to the mode of generalised surveillance that structure social media, this device spans the personal and official uses of portrait photography.

In tracing the invention of the teleprompter and the PhotoReflex and its eventual integration into neoliberal modes of individuation, it cannot escape notice that the emergence of neoliberal optics covers similar territory to that found in the discussions about the transformation of modes and models of visualisation that have resulted from the rise of digital media. The effects of the emergent digital ontology of images is a transformation noted by Crary as well, arguing that this has lead to the eclipse of the observer as figured in discourses of the visual in the late nineteenth and early twentieth centuries. He explains:

> Most of the historically important functions of the human eye are being supplanted by practices in which visual images no longer have any reference to the position of an observer in a 'real', optically perceived world. If these images can be said to refer to anything, it is to millions of bits of electronic mathematical data.[21]

Mark Hansen, who quotes the above passage in *New Philosophy for New Media*, takes up the theme of the digitalisation of the visual to argue that, although the nineteenth century subject may no longer ground visual experience, vision remains an embodied, 'haptic' means of sensing the world. According to Hansen, the body does not disappear into a stream of digital information. On the contrary, new forms of representation draw on practices of viewing deeper into forms of affective, embodied experience of space or, as Hansen writes, 'a modality of spacing that has been wholly detached from vision, that has become affective'.[22]

Crary and Hansen offer two different understandings of visuality in the age of digital media (or, as Hansen calls it, post-photography), yet both are in agreement regarding the reconfiguration of the optical's relationship to experience and the formation of subjectivity. For both, the homology between the optical and the visual experience is that which is disrupted by contemporary digital technologies. Simjian's contributions remind us that the optical register remains an important site for understanding the structures of visuality in the contemporary moment, particularly as a way in which structural shifts in the ontology of information relate to the lived realities of daily life. This is not to suggest that the optical is the determinant factor in the contemporary period, and that consequently it holds the key to understanding the visual structures of contemporary culture. Rather, it is to argue that the significance of the optical has not wholly been subsumed by the logic of digital networks.

Simjian's autobiography is useful because it traces the outlines of neoliberal optics, even though much of it unfolds separately from (if not prior to) the adoption of computational systems for the handling of information. Laying out neoliberal optics as a heuristic for highlighting the ways in which a series of problems and resolutions were put forward that, while linked to elements of visualisation in the digital age, are not entirely coherent or consistent with its elements. The optical register of materiality remains a space in which certain problems within the organisation of the visualisation of space, the disposition of bodies and attention are worked upon. Echoing (but also extending) Hansen's discussions of agency and action in the age of ubiquitous computing, the inventions developed by Simjian similarly speak to the separation of presence from intention. For this reason, neoliberal optics should be understood as an important contributing factor in the transformation of media technologies and visual culture that has taken place over the past fifty years, the period that witnessed the development and triumph of neoliberalism as a cultural, economic and political logic.

THE ATM

In order to make sense of the ATM's relationship to neoliberal optics, it is necessary to situate its development within the longer history of attempts to introduce remote banking to the public. In the context of this history, it is necessary to analyse the development of the ATM's interface rather than position it as a mere support for the automation and digitalisation of the banking industry in the 1960s and 1970s.[23] Such a perspective on the ATM draws attention to the extent to which the important aspects of the ATM's development emerge directly from the forms of subjectivity and material configurations that were characterised as neoliberal optics above. However, the ATM's history is instructive not simply because it provides another example of the tendencies already discussed. Rather, it requires attention because of the way it breaks with and negotiates its place within the technologies and practices of neoliberal optics.

By expanding the history of the ATM to include a broader analysis of the interface in the development of remote banking, we return to the work of Luther Simjian. While Simjian's role in the invention of the ATM is contested, he is recognised as the inventor of a photo-mechanical automated banking terminal patented in 1961 as a 'depository machine', but popularly known as the *Bankograph*.[24] In Simjian's telling, it was a response to changing payroll laws in New York State that required certain workers to be paid in cash at the end of the week in order to prevent companies from defaulting on their payroll obligations. An alternative mode of depositing was necessary because this left thousands of people carrying around their entire weekly salaries in cash, often after the end of banking hours. Unlike the modern ATM, Simjian's *Bankograph* did not update accounts or give access to cash. As he explains, 'I decided I would use microfilm and take films of whatever cash or checks were deposited ... The machine would take a microfilm of the money and the deposit slip, and give a copy to the customer as a receipt. It also took a picture of the person depositing the money as they deposited it'.[25]

Simjian's ATM was ultimately a failure because very few patrons felt comfortable depositing money into a 'hole-in-the-wall' bank. Given the other inventions he worked on, and their grounding in an understanding of the relationship between vision, identity and intersubjectivity, we might speculate that the depository machine developed by Simjian failed precisely because of its evasion of established norms of visuality associated with banking at the time. (Although this absence was exploited by those individuals whose professions preferred to avoid the bureaucratic gaze of institutions, such as the street hoods and prostitutes mentioned by Simjian in his retelling of the depository machine's introduction.) Such conjecture seems more likely given that the development of the ATM, as part of the history of remote banking, was initially situated clearly within the visual and mechanical structures of neoliberal optics outlined in the previous section.

There is a history of experiments that sought to bring the private space of the bank into public spaces beginning in the middle of the twentieth century. While a longer history of these devices and their relationship to media culture is yet to be written, they are essential context for the development of the ATM as public interface with private information. Of particular interest here are the ways in which the interaction between the teller and the client was transformed in order to allow for greater distance between the two parties. If early forms of 'convenience' banking, such as the 'drive-through' and 'walk-up' teller, maintained the face-to-face aspect of the interactions of commercial banking, other experiments relied on various optical technologies in order to extend the distance covered by this relationship. In 1950, the Mosler Safe Company of Ohio introduced the 'periscope' bank which allowed customers to interact and engage with bank staff situated in nearby underground bunkers that were 'built like a fortress' by means of a series of mirrors and telephones.[26] In the mid-fifties, Diebold, another safe company from Ohio (now better known for their voting terminals), introduced 'television banking', which allowed for bank tellers to communicate with clients by means of a closed-circuit television system.[27] These units were rolled out for the next two decades, part of a broader program to find industrial uses for the new medium.[28]

The advantages of these models, over fully 'automatic' models like the one proposed by Simjian, was that they offered a smooth transition from the modes of interaction with tellers to which clients were accustomed. However, these experimental models, while offering advances in security and efficiency, created a problem of ensuring or producing the effect of face-to-face interactions with clients at a distance. When the International City Bank opened an 'all Television' branch in New Orleans in 1970, the managers found it necessary to train tellers who were not 'good on TV'.[29] While no information is available regarding the training provided to these tellers, the use of the phrase being 'good on TV' suggests an interest in producing a certain kind of natural self-presentation via the technology.

However, this was not exclusively a problem for the tellers themselves. It was, according to manufacturers, built into the technology itself.

Diebold, in the promotional material for their first television terminal the Auto Teller DCV (with 'auto' signifying both automation and access via automobile), noted that the 'camera was arranged for normal viewing'. The promotional pamphlet goes on, noting that:

> As in the teller unit, the camera and monitor in customer units are placed in the most 'normal' locations to duplicate personal transactions. Size, height of camera, and monitor location have been 'human engineered' to best accommodate a person seated in an automobile.[30]

The promotional materials for the subsequent model, the Auto Teller II from the early 1960s, similarly proclaim that 'We've got Angle', noting that the angle of screen and camera is one that replicates the placement of the home television – slightly below eye level – because 'it is familiar to customers and therefore minimises any feeling of unfamiliarity on the part of the customer'. Furthermore, the organisation of the camera and the screen for the teller replicated closely the organisation of the teleprompter, ensuring that the personal 'touch' of individual banking was not lost.

The desire to develop a fully automatic bank kiosk that integrated advances in computerisation taking place simultaneously in the banking industry meant that these visual interfaces would prove to be a transitional technology. Communicating with users by means of coloured lights and routinised patterns of interaction, the ATMs introduced to the public in the late 1960s (by Barclays Bank in the UK and Chemical Bank in the United States) radically refigured established forms of personal presentation in the banking industry by dispensing with the face-to-face aspects of banking transactions entirely. The success of the fully automated ATM in which the screen was exclusively used to transmit data rather than the human likeness did away with some aspects of the problem of managing the relationship between clients and banks, at least with regard to eye contact and other modes of non-verbal address. As most other forms of remote banking (aside from drive-in banking in parts of the United States) disappeared, the figure of the face-to-face nature of the encounter with the bank remained in name only. In Spokane, Washington, for example, we find this ironically coded into the branding of the kiosks as 'the homely teller', a name and advertising campaign that invoked the gendered history of clerical labour in banks.

Yet, if the transformation of the ATM's cathode ray tube from television screens to data display marks a break with important aspects of neoliberal optics, the new material configuration of the ATM brought into focus through their absence the significance of optical technologies in linking the distributed self of neoliberal culture with practices which involved personal affective engagement with institutions. The initial removal of transactions from the enclosure of the bank to the 'hole-in-the-wall' kiosk entailed a re-conceptualisation of the relationship between the visible and the invisible within the banking industry that were articulated as problems of security and safety for the technology and the users alike. Rather than fortress-like spaces that allowed for private exchange between clients and staff, new forms of remote banking required improved visibility. In the case of remote banking, this was explicitly written into the Banking Protection Act, adopted in 1968 in the United States. The act specifies that 'drive-in tellers' stations or windows should be located in such a manner as to reproduce identifiable images of persons in a position to transact business at each such station or window and areas of such station or window that are vulnerable to robbery or larceny'.

These concerns would expand with the widespread introduction of wholly computerised terminals, with the 1980s witnessing an explosion of ATM-related crime. Over time, the desire to ensure that remote banking transactions were visible was extended to include attempts to visually identify and authenticate the user. While few of the other elements of Simjian's Bankograph were adopted, it is worth recalling that a part of its mechanism for ensuring the identity and security of the transaction was taking a photograph of the user. It was perhaps this line of thought that would lead to Simjian filing a patent in 1968 for a verification system that would involve a rudimentary form of facial recognition using photography.[31] This, however, should not be surprising since, as Kelly Gates notes in her history of facial recognition, 'Banks became early adopters of biometric technologies, testing systems for controlling employee access and also envisioning how these technologies might be extended for automatically verifying the identity of banking customers'.[32]

The transformation of banks and ATMs to conform with structures and technologies of optical surveillance was not, however, the only transformation taking place. While the making visible of remote banking to systems of surveillance helped to secure ATMs and users, such visibility conflicted with the private nature of banking information itself. Even if the machines were fully secure and reliable (which they weren't), there was no guarantee that the privacy of the user would be protected. It is not surprising, then, that the primary issues related to the design of the interface involved the production of spaces and zones of partial privacy. A number of patents and systems were introduced during the 1980s and 1990s that sought to limit the visibility of the screen or of the input pad.[33] Most of these, of which 3M's micro-louver system is the most widely used, involved the framing of the screen behind technologies that structured the diffusion of light from the ATM screen so that it would only be visible to the user directly in front of the interface. Another option proposed at the time used metal grates as blinder to restrict the line of sight for those standing at any angle other than roughly 45 degrees.[34] While significant attention has been given to the way that the ATM has been integrated into surveillance networks, less attention has been paid to the way that the interfaces simultaneously produced spaces of visual privacy through the use of light-control films that shaped and directed the visibility of the screen.

Of course, the development of the ATM's interface did not take place in isolation. Rather, it was part of a radical shift in the place of the bank within communities. It is difficult for the modern banking customer to understand how much more personal banking in the early twentieth century was in comparison to its contemporary organisation. Grant Bollmer's discussion of Frank Capra's *It's a Wonderful Life* (1946) is useful for making the relationship between the personal and the financial in mid-century America explicit. Bollmer writes:

> It is rarely acknowledged that the role of banking and the circulation of capital is central to *It's a Wonderful Life*'s representation of community. Throughout the film, George Bailey's life is continuously shown not only in the context of his relation to those around him, but in the context of his relation to money ... But more than simply the constant references back to money, *It's a Wonderful Life* locates banking and mortgages as the central agent in determining the character of a community.[35]

Bollmer convincingly situates the discourse connecting the moral and market economies together within contemporary popular culture in the United States in order to understand the financial crisis of 2008. However, I would like to situate his reading more as a snapshot of a banking industry that was soon to disappear in the wake of automation, expansion and the rapid concentration of banking that took place between 1950 and 1970.

The transition away from the face-to-face aspects of banking marked a clear break from the aspects of neoliberal optics outlined in the previous section. However, it is important to note that this break was not complete. Rather, the promise of direct visual contact via ATM continues to haunt proposals for improving existing forms of ATM and anxieties about the technology. If the intersection between the surveillance camera and the privacy screen created a sufficient amount of trust in the ATM apparatus to ensure its widespread use in many parts of the globe, concerns about the depersonalisation of banking should serve as a reminder of the discontinuity between the ATM and other forms of optical space that characterise the present moment.

The film *ATM*, which tells the story of three work colleagues trapped and tortured in a fully automated bank branch located in a desolate shopping-mall parking lot by a stranger in a parka, provides an explicit working out of these anxieties.[36] The automated branch, consisting of two ATMs in a glass enclosure, highlights the disconnect between being visible and being seen. Taking these anxieties to absurd ends – at one point the ATM enclosure is filled with water – the film nonetheless performs the insecurity of a surveillance culture in which nobody is monitoring the video feed of the CCTV. Such representations of anxiety about the visual aspects of depersonalisation find their counterpoint in promises to modernise the ATM in ways that might return it to the fold of tropes that characterise neoliberal optics, namely a more personalised mode of address. In 2013, one of the oldest ATM manufacturers, NCR, invested heavily in the production of video ATMs that allow users to connect face-to-face with remote bank employees. A number of articles in the popular press heralded this as giving ATMs a human face, and a way to return a feeling of personal connection to banking.[37]

While these innovations will involve a number of institutional, technological and legal changes that are beyond the scope of this paper to discuss, the relationship between client and bank teller as mediated by optical technologies provides insight into the complexities of visual experience in neoliberal culture. In its continuities with, and disconnections from, other technologies and visual practices of subsequent decades, tracing the history of the ATM as a site of optical subjectivity contributes to the ways in which we are able to study the material and representational modes that sustain neoliberal culture. It remains to be seen whether the human face will return to ATM screens in the near future. However, the reappearance of fears and desires associated with the now institutionalised form of depersonalisation symbolised by the ATM helps us to position the anecdote about the failure of Simjian's Bankograph as well as the development and eventual disappearance of alternate forms of remote banking as part of the visual complex which regulates the relationship between private information and public life that shapes the experience of the individual in neoliberal culture.[38]

***

In *The Victorian Eye: A Political History of Light and Vision in Britain, 1800-1910,* Chris Otter traces the place of optics and the rise of illumination at the intersection of political liberalism and the use of large scale technological infrastructure as a mode of governance. According to Otter, 'freedom, whether conceived by J.S. Mill or by sanitarians and engineers, was routinely conceived to be at least partially securable through technology'. Otter's detailed discussion of the construction of a material infrastructure that aides particular kinds of visibility (whether through electric light or more open architecture) is a more thorough analysis of a socio-technical assemblage that is quite similar in scope and purpose to what has been discussed here as 'neoliberal optics'. For this reason, it is helpful to conclude by considering the ways in which Otter's analysis differs from the account of technologies and relations sketched out in this article.

Similar to the preceding discussion, at the centre of Otter's analysis of Victorian optics is the emergence of a particular kind of individual: intentional, objective and mobile. The Victorian individual maintained a distance from what was observed, and a variety of technologies were put in place to ensure that this vantage point was preserved and secured. Given the preceding discussion, there are two primary distinctions that separate the liberal from the neoliberal modes of visualisation. First, there is the changing relationship to technology. If during the nineteenth century, the age of classic liberalism, technology was constructed and described as a tool, exterior to the body, the neoliberalisation of technology entails its integration into the body. While neoliberal ideology is often cited as entailing the apotheosis of the individual, this overlooks the extent to which a variety of media and communication technologies have enacted an undoing of the personal sovereignty that defined the liberal individual. As a number of contemporary authors have noted – for example, through the revival of the idea of the 'general intellect' by the Italian autonomists – the integration of technologically mediated forms of collectivity is central to contemporary forms of capitalist exploitation. At the same time, such writers point to the growing centrality of affective engagement as a means for maintaining engagement as well as a source of value which can be expropriated. Less a part of the discourse which surrounded the liberal individual, modes of address which solicit affective address have proliferated across public life.

In the preceding discussion, both of these elements have been considered as part of the structures and relational dynamics which constitute neoliberal optics. Neoliberal optics is fundamentally transactional in nature, having impacted on both what it means to see and be seen as an individual, and the modes of collectivity that are possible and how they are made visual. The importance of neoliberal optics to the future study of neoliberal culture is that it highlights the extent to which, beyond the limits and failings of neoliberal market ideology, an entire mode of being and experience has been implemented as part of the neoliberal project. In the present moment, as market crises become endemic rather than occasional, it is not unlikely that these 'other' aspects of neoliberal culture will remain even as appeals to the free market and the entrepreneurial individual fade. Their power comes not only from their efficacy as tools for governance, control and exploitation but also from the ways in which they have been made to seem natural and intimate to our everyday lives and personal experiences.

NOTES

1. David Harvey, *A Brief History of Neoliberalism,* London, Oxford University Press, 2005.
2. Nick Couldry, *Voice Matters: Culture and Politics after Neoliberalism,* London, Sage Publications, 2010, p5.
3. Individuation is most associated with the work of Gilbert Simondon. See Muriel Combes, *Gilbert Simondon and the Philosophy of the Transindividual,* London, The MIT Press, 2013.
4. Discussions of these aspects of neoliberal culture include Jack Amariglio and David Ruccio, 'Modern Economics: The Case of the Disappearing Body?', *Cambridge Journal of Economics,* 26, 1, (2002): 81-103; Erin Manning, *Politics of Touch: Sense, Movement, Sovereignty,* Minneapolis, University of Minnesota Press, 2006; and Lisa Blackman, *Immaterial Bodies: Affect, Embodiment, Mediation,* London, Sage Publications, 2013.
5. Luther George Simjian, *Portions of an Autobiography,* 1997.
6. Ibid., pp283-298.
7. Jonathan Crary, *Techniques of the Observer: On Vision and Modernity in the Nineteenth Century,* Cambridge, MIT Press, 1990, p70.
8. Fred Barton and Hubert J. Schlafly, 'TelePrompter – New Production Tool',

Journal of the Society of Motion Picture and Television Engineers 58, 6, (1952): 515-521. Also see Schlafly's obituaries, especially Dennis Hevesi, 'Hubert Schlafly, Who Helped Build Teleprompter, is Dead at 91', *New York Times,* 27.04.2011.

9. US Patent # 2,711,667 – 'Prompting Device'
10. US Patent #2,883,902 – 'Prompting Apparatus'
11. Jacques Derrida and Bernard Stiegler, *Echographies of Television: Filmed Interviews,* Cambridge, Polity Press, 2002, p3.
12. Ibid., p4.
13. Paddy Scannell, 'Television and History: Questioning the Archive', *The Communication Review,* 13: 49.
14. Ibid.
15. Simjian, *Portions of an Autobiography,* op. cit., p162.
16. Ibid., p163.
17. Richard Hornsey, 'Francis Bacon and the Photobooth: Facing the Homosexual in Post-war Britain', *Visual Culture in Britain,* 8: 86.
18. Ibid., p87.
19. 'Yale Scientist Discovers Remarkable New Camera', *Yale Daily News,* 42, (12 November 1929).
20. John Tagg, *The Burden of Representation,* Amherst, University of Massachusetts Press, 1988, p64.
21. Crary, *Techniques of the Observer,* op. cit., p2, cited in Mark B.N. Hansen, *New Philosophy for New Media,* Cambridge, MA, MIT Press, 2004
22. Hansen, *New Philosophy for New Media,* op. cit., p230.
23. The common periodisation found in histories of the ATM's development involve the transition from off-line automated cash deposit and dispensing units to networked on-line kiosks that offered a variety of financial services in real time. Both of these periods are presented as mere precursors to truly cashless economies mediated by point-of-sale terminals, personal computers and mobile devices that has yet to be fully realised. For a consideration of this approach to the ATM, see Richard Coopey, 'A Passing Technology: The Automated Teller Machine' in Peter Lyth and Helmuth Trischler (eds), *Wiring Prometheus: Globalisation, History and Technology,* Aarhus, Aarhus University Press, 2004.
24. US Patent # 3,358,992 – 'Depository Machine'; Simjian, *Portions of an Autobiography,* op. cit., pp258-260; Stacy Jones, 'Robot Bank Teller is invented to give Photograph as Receipt', *New York Times,* 2.04.1960, p29.
25. Simjian, *Portions of an Autobiography,* op. cit., p259.
26. 'Remote Banking Comes to Focus', *New York Times,* 8.08.1956, p46.
27. Diebold Incorporated, *Catalogue: Undercounter Products, Drive-Up/Walk-Up & Remote Banking,* Canton, Ohio, Diebold, 1960.
28. H.F. Schneider, 'How Can Industry Use Television?', *Industrial Electronics,* 1956, pp23-31; J.E.H. Brace, 'Industrial Television: A Survey of History, Requirements and Applications', *Journal of British Industrial Relations,* June 1960.
29. Milton O'Neal, 'All-TV banking Catches On', *Banking,* 65, (September 1972): 39.
30. Diebold Incorporated, *Catalogue,* op. cit.
31. US Patent #3,569,619 – 'Verification System Using Coded Identifying and Storage Means'.

32. Kelly Gates, *Our Biometric Future: Facial Recognition Technology and the Culture of Surveillance,* New York, New York University Press, 2011.

33. US Patent #5,528,319 – 'Privacy Filter for Display Device'; US Patent #5,528,319 – 'Polarizing Privacy System for Use with a Visual Display Terminal'.

34. US Patent #4,812,709 – 'Privacy Screen for a Color Cathode Ray Display Tube'.

35. Grant Bollmer, 'Community as a Financial Network: Mortgages, Citizenship and Connectivity', *Democratic Communiqué,* 24, (2011): 39.

36. David Brooks (director), *ATM,* Buffalo Gal Productions, 2012.

37. Martha White, 'ATMs with a Human Touch: How New ATMs May Replace Bank Tellers' *Time,* 17.05.2012; and Hadley Malcolm, 'Video ATMs let customers interact remotely', *USA Today,* 4.12.2012.

38. For more on 'visual complexes' see Nicholas Mirzeoff, *The Right to Look: A Counterhistory of Visuality,* Durham, NC., Duke University Press, 2011.

Notes on Contributors

Neal Curtis is Associate Professor in the Department of Film, Television and Media Studies at the University of Auckland. He is the author of *Against Autonomy* (Ashgate, 2001), *War and Social Theory* (Palgrave, 2006), and *Idiotism* (Pluto, 2013), *Sovereignty and Superheroes* (Manchester University Press, 2016).

Jodi Dean is the Donald R. Harter '39 Professor of the Humanities and Social Sciences at Hobart and William Smith Colleges in Geneva, NY.

Mark Fisher has written widely on music, politics and theory. He teaches in the Department of Visual Cultures, Goldsmiths, London. He is the author of *Capitalist Realism: Is There No Alternative* (Zero 2009).

Jeremy Gilbert is the Editor of *New Formations*. He is Professor of Cultural and Political Theory at the University of East London.

Paul Gilroy teaches at Kings College, London.

Mark Hayward is Associate Professor in the Department of Communication Studies at York University, Canada. He researches and writes about television and the philosophy of technology.

Jo Littler is Reader in Cultural Industries at City University London. She is the author of *Radical Consumption* (Open University Press, 2009) and is writing a book on meritocracy.

Stephen Maddison is Professor of Cultural Studies & Creative Industries in the School of Arts and Digital Industries at the University of East London.

Nicky Marsh works in the Department of English at the University of Southampton. She is the author of *Money, Speculation and Finance in Contemporary British Fiction* (2007) and *Democracy in Contemporary US Women's*

Poetry (2007) and editor of *Literature and Globalization* (with Liam Connell, 2010) and *Teaching Modernist Poetry* (with Peter Middleton, 2010).

Scott McCracken is Professor of Twentieth-Century Literature at Queen Mary, University of London. He is currently writing a book, *Thinking Through Defeat: Literary Responses to Political Failure from the Paris Commune to the Berlin Wall.*

Angela McRobbie is Professor of Communications Goldsmiths University of London. She is author of *The Aftermath of Feminism* (2009) and *Be Creative? Making a Living in the New Culture Industries* (2014).

Paul Patton is Scientia Professor of Philosophy at The University of New South Wales in Sydney, Australia. He is the author of *Deleuze and the Political* (Routledge, 2000) and *Deleuzian Concepts: Philosophy, Colonization, Politics* (Stanford, 2010).

Lucy Potter completed her MA in Culture and Thought After 1945, at York University in 2012 and is now a doctoral candidate in the department of English and Related Literature, at York, working on world literature and the politics of food.

Claire Westall is Lecturer in Contemporary Literature in the Department of English and Related Literature at York University. She is co-editor of *Cross-Gendered Literary Voices: Appropriating, Resisting, Embracing* (Palgrave Macmillan, 2012) and *Literature of an Independent England* (Palgrave Macmillan, 2013).